WORLD FACTS

AN ESSENTIAL A–Z GUIDE

This is a Starfire Book
First published in 2001

02 04 05 03

1 3 5 7 9 10 8 6 4 2

Starfire is part of
The Foundry Creative Media Company Limited
Crabtree Hall, Crabtree Lane, Fulham, London, SW6 6TY

Visit the Foundry website: www.foundry.co.uk

ISBN 1 903817 19 6

A copy of the CIP data for this book is available from the British Library

Printed in China

SPECIAL THANKS TO EVERYONE INVOLVED WITH THIS PROJECT:
Anna Amari, Frances Banfield, Lucy Bradbury, Roger Buckley, Helen Courtney, Claire Dashwood, Giskin Day, Karen Fitzpatrick, Vicky Garrard, Phil Hempell, George Keyes, Lesley Malkin, Geoffrey Meadon, Sonya Newland, Colin Rudderham, Mel Shaw, Andrea Simmonds, Graham Stride, Helen Tovey, Helen Wall, Sharon Weiss, Nick Wells.

WORLD FACTS

AN ESSENTIAL A–Z GUIDE

Camilla de la Bédoyère, Guy de la Bédoyère , Kirsten Bradbury,
Alan Drummond, Nigel Gross, James Mackay, Helen Tovey

GENERAL EDITOR: DR JAMES MACKAY

STAR FIRE

CONTENTS

THEMES

Each A–Z entry is tagged by themes which can be followed as threads throughout the book

Arts
Culture, Belief & Faith
Geography
History
Natural World
Science, Technology & Industry
Society
War & Politics

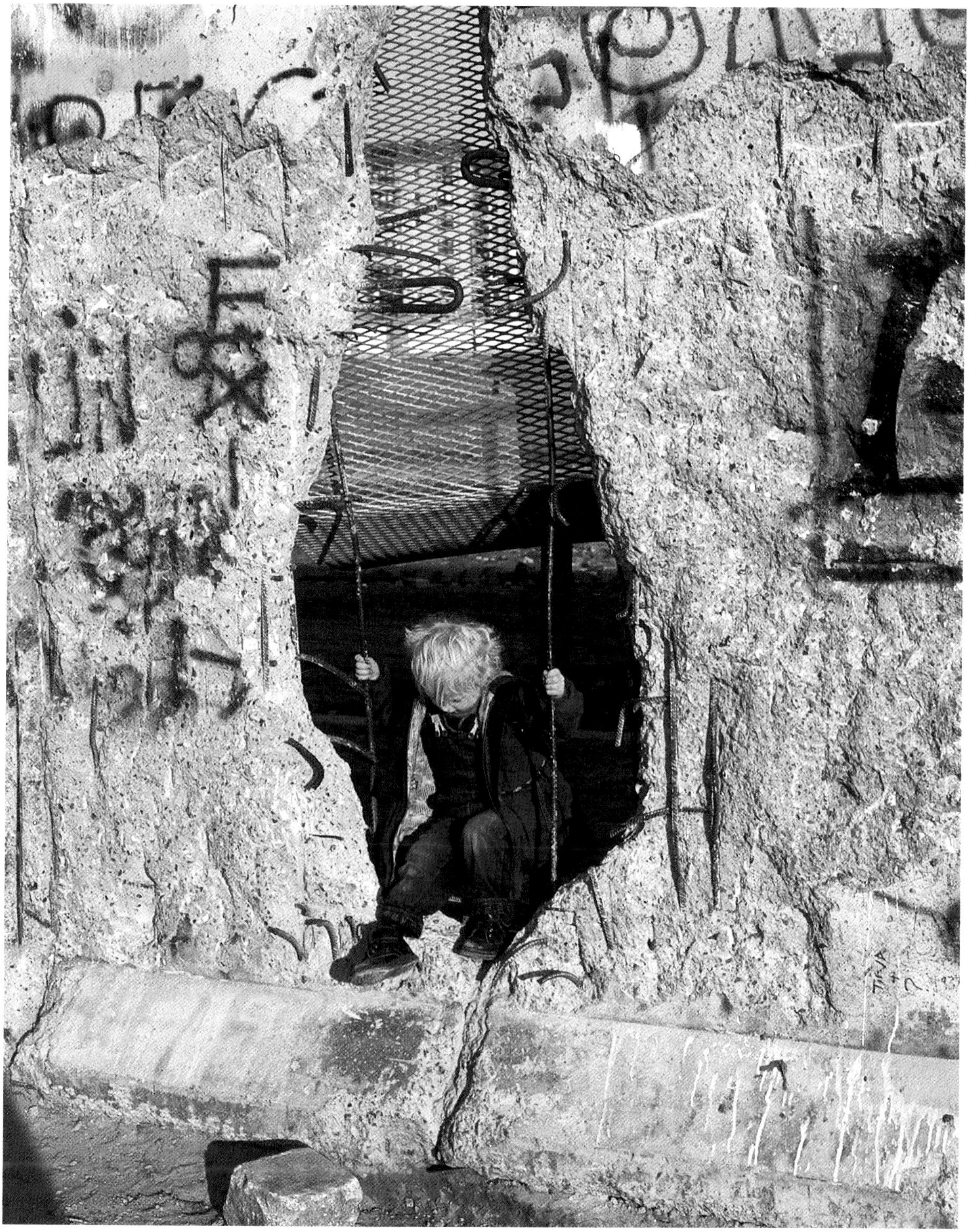

INTRODUCTION

WHAT HAVE serendipity and Sri Lanka got in common? The Sanskrit (ancient Indian) name for this Indian Ocean island was Simhalanam Dvipah (Island of the Sinhalese). The Arab traders who sailed the ocean in their dhows corrupted this to Sarandib. From this came the title of a Persian fairy tale about the three Princes of Serendip who set out on an important quest and kept finding all manner of things by chance along the way.

Dipping into this book is rather like that. You might look up the entry on Fred Astaire, for example, and find your eye straying to the entries on Assyria and Asteroids. This might stimulate your mind to search for other articles on ancient civilisations or astronomy, and so it goes on, with neighbouring entries attracting your passing attention.

This is essentially a book for browsing through, rather than the last word on every subject. That would be quite impossible, even in a whole series of volumes many times the size of this book. We hope that this approach provides the incentive for further enquiry and that we have whetted your appetite to seek out further information from encyclopedias and other reference material. Increasingly, people are 'surfing the Net' for data, but the problem is often knowing where to begin. Treat this book as a search engine if you like, a collection of signposts that point the way to other aspects. Of course, the biggest problem in compiling a reference work of this nature is deciding what to include and what to leave out. The second biggest problem is how much space to allocate to each topic. In many cases a brief definition is provided, designed to spark your interest, while other entries have fuller explanations.

'Give us the facts' was the catchphrase of Sergeant Joe Friday in the popular 1950s television drama series *Dragnet*, and this is what we have set out to do. Almost 1200 entries are presented here in alphabetical order, ranging from Aboriginal People to Zürich. Every aspect of the human and natural world is covered, from the dawn of mankind and the mists of prehistory right up to the present time. This is a veritable treasury of Trivial Pursuit material, a fantastic sourcebook for pub and family quizzes, game shows and general knowledge contests. It is also an extremely useful educational aide, the facts being presented in an easy-to-assimilate form. We have set out to entertain as well as edify and educate.

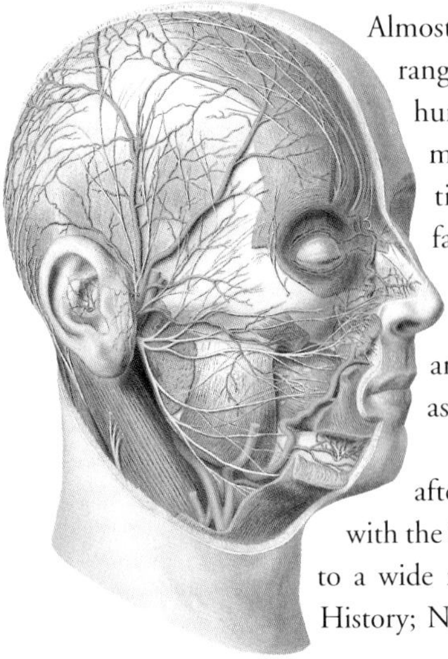

The entries in this volume have been very carefully selected after long and serious consideration. They have been chosen with the intention of providing as comprehensive a coverage as possible to a wide range of themes: Arts; Culture, Belief & Faith; Geography; History; Natural World; Science, Technology & Industry; Society and

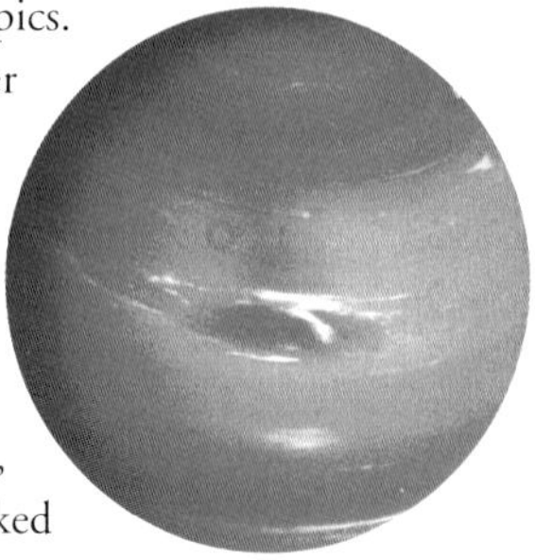

War & Politics. Where possible, there are cross-references to related topics. Finally, there is a comprehensive bibliography suggesting other recommended reading material.

Working on this project has been an eye-opener for me personally. Our team of experts can always be relied upon to deliver an amazing amount of entirely new material; but even the entries on well-known subjects have been given a fresh slant, incorporating new interpretations that reflect the most up-to-date research. The text is lively and accessible, but always authoritative. Each statement or date has been carefully checked to ensure accuracy. Inevitably there will still be facts on which the experts are bitterly divided and issues which are matters of burning controversy, but we have striven for balance and objectivity.

Of one fact I am certain: this is not the last word on any subject. Rather it is a book to be opened at random. Then let your mind and imagination take over, as something you read triggers off a mental chain reaction and sets you off on the by-ways of knowledge, just like those three Princes of Serendip all those centuries ago. And may your discoveries be just as happy and fortunate.

DR JAMES MACKAY

Biographer, broadcaster and historian

AALTO, ALVAR (1898–1976)

Finnish architect of great repute. Aalto believed that architecture could be a mediator between humankind and the natural world. He did not follow fashions within architecture but developed his own ingenious approach; he explored the use of natural materials, especially wood. Among his finest designs are the Finlandia Concert Hall in Helsinki (1970–75).

Architecture, Frank Lloyd Wright

ABORIGINAL PEOPLE

Indigenous people of Australia. Aboriginals were hunter-gatherers with a land-centred culture: Ayers Rock (Uluru) was sacred and their creation myth, The Dreaming, held that humankind came from the earth. Europeans annexed Aboriginal territory from 1788. The 1970s saw campaigns for Aboriginal rights and by 1988 10% of Australia was restored to them.

Maori, Native American Peoples

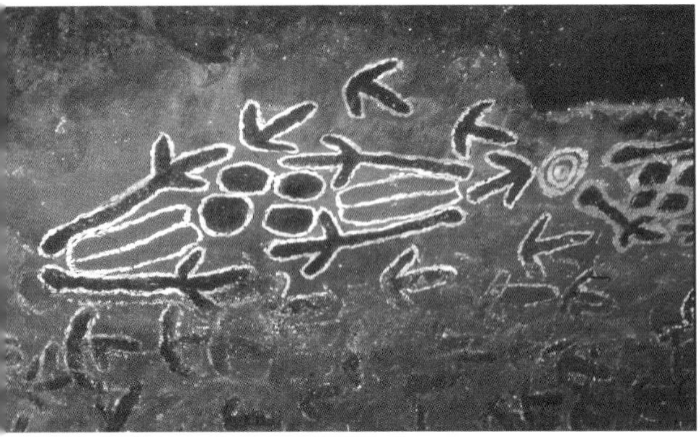

ABSTRACT ART (20TH CENTURY)

Encompassing term relating to the art that arose during the early twentieth century. Derived in part from the work of the Cubists, among its pioneers were Wassily Kandinsky and Piet Mondrian. Abstract art rejected representation in art, instead placing greater import on shapes and colours in an attempt to affect the viewer in a direct, less logical way.

Cubism, Wassily Kandinsky, Piet Mondrian

ABOVE: Aboriginal Art from The Emu Cave in Yuendumu.

ABOVE RIGHT: Left to right: Marcia Gay Harden, Julia Roberts and Russell Crowe at the 72nd annual Academy Awards.

FAR RIGHT: Africa is home to approximately 10% of the world population.

ACADEMY AWARDS (1927)

Presented annually by the American Academy of Motion Picture Arts since 1927. Nicknamed the Oscars since 1931, they recognize excellence in the world of cinema.

BAFTAs, Films

AFGHANISTAN

Land-locked Asian country between the Middle East and India. **Capital:** Kabul. **Other principal cities:** Kandahar, Herat, Mazar-I-Sharif, Jalalabad. **Climate:** dry and windy with hot summers and cold winters. **Geographical features:** mountainous, land-locked. **Main languages:** Pushtu, Kirgiz, Dari, Turkoman, Uzbek. **Main religion:** Islam. Rule: administered through 30 provinces, power lies with religious-based political parties. **Currency:** afgháni. **Primary industry:** little apart from skin- and hide-based products. **Agriculture:** nomadic pastoral and settled arable. **Economy:** primarily agricultural. **Exports:** natural gas, carpets, hides, lambskins, pottery, jewellery and fruit.

AFRICA

World's second largest continent, containing approximately 10% of the world's population. Africa straddles the equator; it is 8,000 km (5,000 miles) from north to south, and 7,360 km (4,600 miles) from east to west. Africa is entirely surrounded by water, with the Atlantic Ocean to the west, the Indian Ocean to the south and east and the Mediterranean Sea to the north. It joins Asia at its north-east tip in Sinai, now separated by the Suez Canal.

Climate and latitude split Africa into separate regions. The equatorial zone is primarily rain forest, but on either side this gives way to grasslands and then desert. The Sahara Desert dominates the north, and the Kalahari the south. However, the northern and southern coastal zones are temperate and fertile. These zones primarily reflect the amount of rainfall received. Rainfall is extremely heavy through the central region and some of the west coast, but tails off to north and south where the deserts are, returning once more in the temperate northern and southern coastal zones.

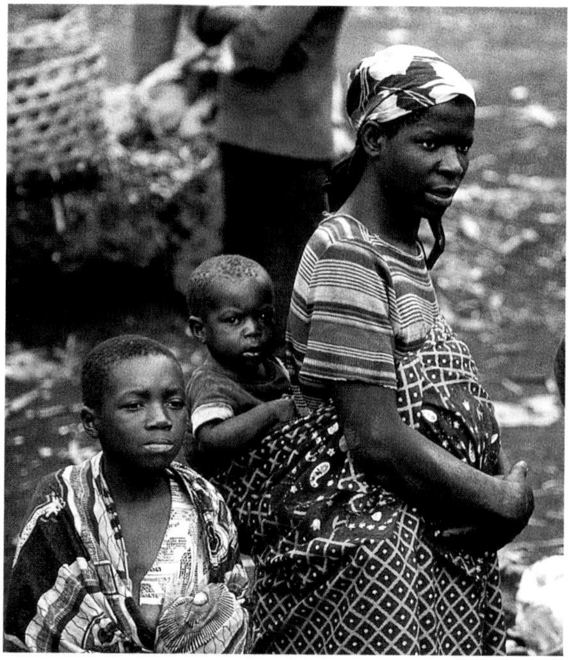

East Africa is higher than the west, with the Ethiopian Highlands and the Drakensberg Range, but mountainous regions also appear in the west – such as the Atlas Mountains which lie across the extreme north-west of the continent. West Africa also features large depressions such as the Niger and Chad basins.

The landscape is criss-crossed by vast rivers and faults. The Rift Valley system runs through East Africa, and is characterized by troughs and lakes, the largest of which is Lake Victoria. Some of the world's longest rivers flow through Africa. The River Nile, the world's longest, runs for 6,680 km (4,150 miles) north to the Nile Delta in Egypt. Other rivers include the Niger, Zambezi and Zaire (Congo).

Africa's animal life is among the world's most varied. Predators such as lions and hyenas prey on the many grass-eating animals which roam the plains (elephant, zebra, giraffe and antelope), while the rainforests are home to exceptional communities of primates such as mountain gorillas. The warm and wet areas also foster species harmful to human life such as malaria and yellow-fever-carrying mosquitoes, while plagues of locusts and termites can also destroy settlements.

The variable wealth and stability of Africa's nations reflect the range of landscapes and climates, as well as European colonization, political and tribal strife. Africa is increasingly playing a part in world events, but is continually troubled by man-made and natural disasters.

AGAMEMNON

Legendary Greek king. Hero of Homer's *Iliad* and the conqueror of Troy. Agamemnon is based on the ruler of Achaea, whose tomb at Mycenae became a place of pilgrimage.

➤ ***Ancient Greece, Greek Gods and Mythology, Homer***

AGRICULTURE

General term to describe all types of farming, both the growing of crops and the raising of livestock. The earliest known examples come from the Middle East and are at least 10,000 years old, and it is no coincidence that this coincides with the first examples of permanent settlements and 'civilization' in general.

Just as there was an Industrial Revolution, so there was an Agricultural Revolution. This took place in the UK between 1750 and 1850, during which time there were sweeping changes to accommodate the vast increase in demand caused by the new cities. These included the introduction of machinery and carefully selected breeding to improve livestock.

Today agriculture is a true industry in its own right, and has the ability to produce more food at lower prices than ever before. However, there is growing concern over the way animals are treated, the amount of chemicals used and the growing use of genetically modified crops.

➤ ***Farming, Industrial Revolution***

AID ORGANIZATIONS

Organizations established to facilitate the flow of aid to countries in need. These can be state run, such as the UK's Overseas Development Administration, internationally run, such as the various United Nations bodies, or charitable organisations like Oxfam and Medicine sans Frontières. The usual recipients will be less developed countries, or nations who have had a disaster that has temporarily overwhelmed their own resources.

➤ ***Charities***

AIDS

Acquired Immune Deficiency Syndrome. A suite of symptoms caused by infection with the HIV (Human Immuno-defficiency Virus). The infection can lie dormant for many years before becoming full-blown AIDS. First noticed in the early 1980s, the disease is now global. It is spread by body fluids, notably during sexual intercourse.

AIR

Mixture of gases that constitutes the Earth's atmosphere. The predominant gases are nitrogen (78%) and oxygen (21%). The remaining 1% is made up of gases such as argon, carbon dioxide, ozone, helium and water vapour. However, the composition of air varies according to environmental factors; volcanic eruptions may result in a local increase in sulphur dioxide while the combustion of fossil fuels gives rise to widespread pollutants in the air. The ability of the air to cleanse itself of pollutants has been reduced by increased atmospheric methane. This is partly the result of a growth in livestock farming.

➧ ***Atmosphere***

AIR FORCES

Military organizations. The military use of aircraft emerged just before World War I. In less than 90 years air forces have become a crucial part of the military forces in most countries.

➧ ***Armies***

AIRCRAFT

Any vehicle designed to move through the Earth's atmosphere. The vehicle can be lighter than air, in which case it stays aloft by a buoyancy effect, or heavier than air, when it is kept up by the action of air moving over its surfaces. The first successful flight was made by the Wright Brothers in 1903; today aircraft such as Concorde can fly faster than the speed of sound.

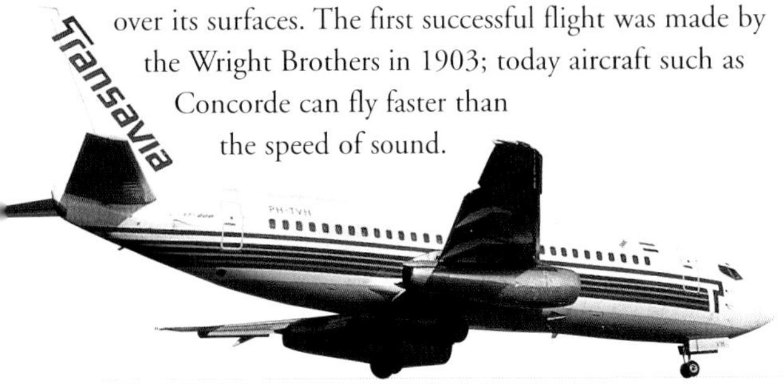

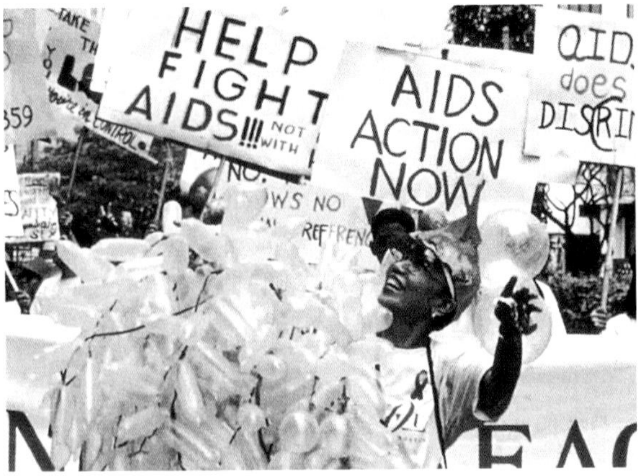

AIRPORTS

Facilities for civil aircraft carrying passengers and cargo to take off and land. They usually have good road and rail links and customs and immigration facilities. The largest airport in the world is the King Khalid International Airport in Saudi Arabia, which opened in 1993 and covers 55,000 acres.

AIRSHIPS

Powered aircraft which are lighter than air. Airships have a large streamlined compartment containing the light gas helium and are usually powered by a propeller turbine engine. Airships are slow compared with heavier-than-air craft, but are economical on fuel and can carry very large loads. The most famous airship was the *Hindenburg,* which caught fire and crashed in 1937.

ALBANIA

Southern European country on the Adriatic coast. Continent: Europe. **Capital:** Tirana. **Other principal cities:** Elbasan, Korçë, Shkodër, Vlorë. **Climate:** Mediterranean but fiercely cold winters on high ground. **Geographical features:** Adriatic Sea coastline, inland mountains, valleys, rivers and lakes. **Main languages:** Albanian, Greek. Main religions: Muslim, Greek Orthodox, Roman Catholic. Rule: democracy. **Currency:** lek. **Primary industry:** mainly by-products of farming and forestry. **Agriculture:** pastoral (sheep, goats, cattle) and arable (cereals, tobacco, cotton). **Economy:** mainly agricultural. **Exports:** oil and coal, minerals (iron, chrome, nickel), tobacco, agricultural produce.

LEFT: An AIDS day (1 December) demonstrator marches through the streets of Manila carrying condoms.
RIGHT: Muhammad Ali in the film The Greatest, *which was about himself.*

ALBUMS

Collection of songs and/or music brought together as a package. The term was first applied to analogue records invented by the company Decca in the late 1940s, and latterly to both cassette tapes and compact discs.

Singles

ALCOHOL

Ethyl Alcohol (C_2H_5OH) is the intoxicating chemical present in all alcoholic drinks. It is produced by the action of microscopic organisms called yeast, which break down sugars by a process known as fermentation. Alcoholic drinks produced in this way are relatively weak as the alcohol is poisonous to the yeast. Stronger drinks are produced by distilling the alcohol produced by fermentation. The social use of alcohol dates back to prehistory, but appears to have become a problem when the production of cheap spirits on an industrial scale started in the mid-eighteenth century. It is said by many that if alcoholic drinks had been invented today they would be immediately banned.

Drugs

ALEXANDER THE GREAT (356–323 BC)

Ruler of Macedon who united the Greek states against Persia, which he conquered. Alexander liberated Egypt and founded Alexandria (331 BC), then invaded India (327 BC). He died at Babylon after a drunken orgy. He created an empire which spread Greek civilization to the east.

Ancient Greece, Persia

ALGERIA

North African coastal country. **Capital:** Algiers. **Other principal cities:** Qacentina. **Climate:** dry and hot. **Geographical features:** temperate coastal zone, Atlas mountains, the Sahara desert which covers two-thirds of the country. **Main languages:** Arabic, Berber, French. **Main religion:** Islam. Rule: military. **Currency:** Algerian dinar. **Primary industry:** oil and natural gas. **Agriculture:** cereal, tobacco, fruit, grapes. **Economy:** mainly agricultural, and oil and petroleum gas extraction. **Exports:** oil and gas, minerals (iron, zinc, lead), wine.

Africa

ALI, MOHAMMED (b. 1942)

Born Cassius Marcellus Clay; nicknamed The Greatest. Three times world heavyweight boxing champion. Ali retired in 1981 and was selected to light the Olympic Torch in Atlanta 1996.

Boxing, Olympic Games

ALLEN, WOODY (b. 1935)

American independent film director, writer and star of many of his films. Allen's work is filled with persistent themes of religion, relationships and society – Allen's society being confined largely to a cultural 'high society' in New York. Among his 30 plus films are *Annie Hall* (1977), *Hannah and her Sisters* (1986) and *Bullets Over Broadway* (1994).

ALPS

Best-known European mountain range, stretching about 1,000 km (620 miles) in a band from eastern France through Switzerland and northern Italy to Slovenia. Caused by continental movements around 65 million years ago as Africa pushed northwards into Europe, the Alps feature high peaks and slopes beloved by skiers, and dramatic glaciers, lakes and valleys.

Austria, France, Italy, Switzerland

ALTERNATIVE MEDICINE

Forms of medical treatment which aim to treat the patient as a whole, and emphasize dealing with the underlying cause of health problems rather than their symptoms. The most widely used forms of alternative medicine include homeopathy, which involves the administration of extremely dilute doses of natural substances; herbalism, which uses plants and materials derived from them; and acupuncture, in which long thin needles are inserted into specified parts of the body to relieve pain and promote healing. Treatments are available from some orthodox medical practitioners, but specialists in some fields of alternative medicine do not necessarily have orthodox medical training.

AMAZON RIVER

South American river. The Amazon rises from streams flowing down from the Andes in Peru, creating a 6,437-km (4,000-mile) long river. It crosses Brazil to meet the Atlantic on the east coast in a 270-km (167-mile) wide estuary. The volume contained is the greatest of any river in the world.

➠ ***Brazil***

AMERICAN FOOTBALL

Contact ball game popular mainly in the USA. It is similar to rugby football, but its players are heavily armoured and are allowed to throw the ball forwards. The sport is widely played both at amateur and professional levels and has two governing bodies: the National Football Conference (NFC) and the American Football Conference (AFC). The champions of these two leagues meet annually to contest the Superbowl trophy. The game is played over 60 minutes divided into four 15-minute quarters. Teams can consist of up to 40 players, but only 11 are allowed on the pitch at any one time. There are no limits on substitutions.

➠ ***Rugby***

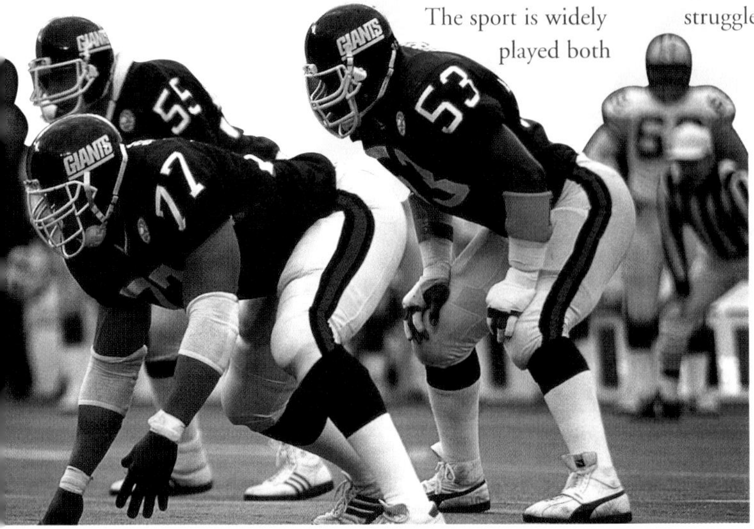

AMERICAN REVOLUTION (1775–83)

Conflict between the American colonies and Britain. The war demonstrated the hopeless impossibility of controlling remote colonies from Europe and led to the founding of the United States.

By the late eighteenth century, the American colonies of the eastern seaboard had grown wealthy. Britain sought to exploit this resource to help pay for control of her empire through new taxes. This offended anti-monarchist sentiment among colonists who enjoyed relative autonomy. Resistance grew into armed conflict when British soldiers were sent to confiscate illegal armaments near Boston.

A series of battles followed, with inconclusive results, but in July 1776 the colonies produced a declaration of independence. Reinforcements soon arrived from Britain, but the campaign rapidly foundered in the face of widespread hostility from the general population and the struggle to supply troops.

By contrast, the American forces were motivated, knew the ground, and had a patriotic leader in George Washington. Defeat of the British army at Saratoga Springs in 1777 set the pace in the north. Support for the Americans came from Spain and Holland, while the French navy helped force the surrender of Lord Cornwallis at Yorktown, Virginia, in 1781. Thereafter, British attempts to fight faded away and culminated in the Treaty of Paris in 1783.

➠ ***United States of America***

*FAR RIGHT: Northern Kid salamander (*Pseudotriton suber suber*), a member of the vertebrate class* Amphibia.
RIGHT: An anarchic demonstrator in West Germany, 1987.

AMERICAN STATES

The United States is made up of 50 states, 48 of which are joined (the 'contiguous states') across North America from the Atlantic to the Pacific Oceans. To these are added Alaska (the most northerly), and the islands of Hawaii (the most southerly). Together they make an area of 9.37 million sq km (3.62 million sq miles). Hawaii and Alaska represent the greatest extremes, as well as being the most recently added. Hawaii is a group of volcanic tropical islands, Alaska is an arctic zone.

The eastern seaboard states range from temperate Maine to low-lying and sub-tropical Florida which lies between the Gulf of Mexico and the Atlantic. Moving west the landscape crosses the farmland of the south and Appalachian Mountain regions, gradually rising to the grasslands of the Mid-West in states such as Oklahoma and Kansas, which form part of the vast grain belt stretching across central North America up into Canada. The Great Lakes dominate the central northern belt.

Beyond the Mid-West the land rises further towards the Rocky Mountains across increasingly barren and thinly populated states which feature increasingly dramatic landscapes in Arizona (the Grand Canyon) and Nevada (desert).

The Pacific coastal states run from the temperate and wet Washington state in the north-east down to California. California features the broadest range of conditions, with snow-covered mountains to the north-east, the desert of the Joshua Tree National Monument in the south, to the Mediterranean-type climate and sun of the coastal region from Los Angeles to San Diego.

The American states feature a huge variety in climate, ranging from long periods of snowfall in the north to the tropical thunderstorms, hurricanes and tornadoes in the south. Vast rivers drain the continent, such as the Hudson, Mississippi, Rio Grande, Colorado and Ohio.

➧ ***Grand Canyon, Rocky Mountains, United States of America***

AMPHIBIANS

Members of the vertebrate class, *Amphibia*. The class includes frogs, toads, newts, salamanders and caecilians. Believed to have left the oceans nearly 400 million years ago, amphibians were the first back-boned animals to live on land and are probably the immediate ancestor of reptiles. Amphibians characteristically have a moist, smooth skin that is constantly renewed. They rely on external heat to maintain their own body temperature, necessitating hibernation in colder climates. Amphibians, unlike reptiles, lay their eggs in water and many species metamorphose; their bodies change as they mature into adulthood. The number of amphibians is dwindling, owing in part to the destruction of their habitat by humans.

➧ ***Reptiles, Vertebrates***

ANARCHY

Derived from the Greek for 'No Leader'. An occasionally popular minority political view, first seen in the late-nineteenth century. Anarchists believe that 'government', as a concept, should not exist.

ANGELICO, FRA (*c.* 1395–1455)

Italian artist who trained as a painter before becoming a Dominican monk. Highly esteemed and much emulated, especially in Florence, an example of his finest work is *The Deposition* (*c.* 1440–45).

ANATOMY

Structure of the human or animal body and its constituents. Anatomy is distinguished from physiology, which studies the functions of the body. Anatomists specialize in the structure of different constituents of the body, for example the bones, the muscles or skin. Branches of anatomy include radiographic anatomy using X-rays, and comparative anatomy, examining similar organs in different species.

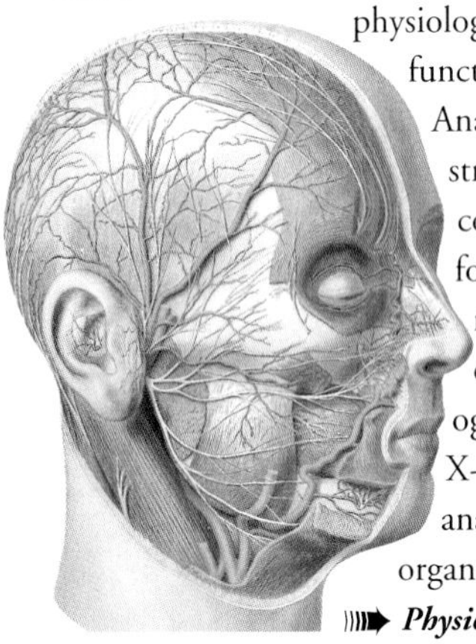

➧ ***Physiology***

ANGLO-DUTCH WARS (1652–54, 1665–67, 1670–74, 1780–84)

Four wars between England and the Dutch Republic in the seventeenth and eighteenth centuries, caused by the commercial rivalry of Europe's two premier naval powers.

The first Anglo-Dutch war broke out in 1652 after England's 1651 Navigation Act closed England's sea trade. The war ended with a Dutch defeat, settled by the Treaty of Westminster in 1654.

In 1664, England captured New Amsterdam (New York) and with commercial tension unabated, war was declared in 1665. The Dutch had the upper hand throughout, climaxing in June 1667 with their daring attack on the English fleet moored off Chatham. Settlement followed in July.

The third war occurred when Louis XIV of France made an alliance with England in 1670, before his Spanish Netherlands campaign (1672–78). The Dutch Republic's naval resistance caused England to withdraw in 1674.

The fourth Anglo-Dutch War formed part of the American Revolution, when the Dutch supplied the colonists. English naval power was such that she was able to seize Dutch possessions in the Far East, despite a minor Dutch victory in the North Sea in 1781.

➧ ***American Revolution***

ANGOLA

Atlantic coastal country of southern Africa. **Capital:** Luanda. **Other principal cities:** Lobito, Huambo, Benguela. **Climate:** cool on the coast, hot and damp inland. **Geographical features:** grassy plains and forested river valleys. **Main languages:** Portuguese, Bantu. Main religions: Roman Catholic, Protestant. Rule: democracy. **Currency:** kwanza. Primary industries: cotton textiles, diamond mining, fishing, oil and timber. **Agriculture:** limited by the landscape. **Exports:** coffee, diamonds, fish, hardwoods, maize, oil, palm oil, sisal.

➧ ***Africa***

ANIMAL RIGHTS

Campaign to prevent cruelty to animals. The concern for animal rights came to prominence in the 1980s with the rise in 'Green Politics'. It was spurred by the ever-increasing industrialisation of farming and the use of animals for experimentation. There was wide support for groups such as Greenpeace, but small minorities such as the Animal Liberation Front in UK are now resorting to terrorism.

➧ ***Greenpeace, Worldwide Fund for Nature***

ANIMATION

Method of producing moving pictures using a series of still images. These can be hand drawn, photographs of models or – increasingly – computer images. The earliest known example of the art dates from 1906, although it was with the rise of Walt Disney in the 1930s that the art form really took off.

➧ ***Walt Disney***

TOP RIGHT: Queen Maud Land, Antarctica. These tourists are completely dwarfed by the gigantic iceberg on Princess Martha's Coast.
RIGHT: Sociocultural anthropology studies the customs, cultures and evolution of human races. The physical diversity of mankind can be seen in these runners.

ANTARCTICA

Continent occupying the extreme south of the globe and containing the South Pole. At 13.9 million sq km (5.4 million sq miles), Antarctica contains 10% of the world's land surface, but 98% is covered with ice which extends out into the sea to create the Ross Ice Shelf. The extreme weather conditions restrict its flora and fauna to a bare minimum.

ANTHROPOLOGY

Study of the origin of human beings and their social and cultural development. Two main areas are recognized: physical anthropology examines the biological development and evolutionary adaptation of the species, while sociocultural anthropology explores the ways that language, customs and culture have developed. Anthropology began in ancient times as travellers and writers studied and recorded the new cultures they encountered. The development of archeology in the nineteenth century saw the beginnings of research into the evolution of modern human beings and their ancestors. Modern sociocultural anthropology is an increasingly applied science in which teams of specialists examine all aspects of communities, often working on behalf of governments.

➡ ***Archeology, Cro-Magnon Man, Human Evolution***

ANTIBIOTICS

Drugs which kill or prevent the growth of bacteria or fungi. They are derived from living organisms, but may be chemically changed to make them more effective. They have no effect on viruses. The earliest antibiotics were the penicillins, developed in the 1940s and still widely used.

➡ ***Bacteria, Fungi, Penicillin***

ANTIQUES

Objects of some age which have cultural, historical or financial worth. It seems that the collecting of antiques is as old as the antiques themselves. As early as the sixteenth century, countries were already assembling national collections, and there are now many fine museums dedicated to their display throughout the world. Collecting antiques is a popular hobby in many countries, with shops, magazines and TV shows all dedicated to them.

APARTHEID (1948–94)

Method of government in the Republic of South Africa from 1948 to its abolition in 1994. Civil and political rights were decided by the citizen's race. All people were divided into the classifications: White, Coloured (mixed race), Indian and Black.

The term 'Apartheid' was first used in the 1930s and was made law by the Afrikaaner government of South Africa in 1948. At its core was the concept of 'separate development' that would keep the various cultures of South Africa apart from each other. This was understandably far from popular with many South Africans and received international condemnation. South Africa was expelled from the Commonwealth in 1961 and by the 1980s was an international pariah.

Internal opposition also grew, and was met with ruthless repression by the state, most notably with the imprisonment of Nelson Mandela, leader of the African National Congress (ANC). President F. W. De Klerk finally released Mandela in 1991 and started the liberalisation process that culminated in the full and free elections of 1994.

➠ ***Commonwealth, Nelson Mandela***

ARCHEOLOGY

Excavation and study of artefacts, dwellings and other remains of past human life and activities as an adjunct to the industry, culture and history of different civilizations, from the primitive to the most advanced. It has developed into an exact science, involving other disciplines, from soil analysis to the use of metal detectors. It is concerned with the conservation, restoration and reconstruction of relics and the interpretation of material objects, encompassing all periods from the Stone Age to recent times, from cave paintings to the pill-boxes of World War II and from flint arrowheads to factory machinery.

➠ ***Anthropology***

ARCHERY

Shooting a given target using arrows fired from a bow. Historically an accomplished hunting skill, archery is now an Olympic sport.

ARCHITECTURE

Term originally used to describe the artistic design of a building, but now used to denote the design of buildings, of surroundings (e.g. plazas) and landscapes (e.g. gardens).

As with all arts, architecture is bound by societal rules and fashions; it is influenced by religion and politics. It develops through historical changes and events (such as the upsurge of Neoclassicism following the French Revolution). It equally develops through technical progression, for instance the introduction of prefabricated buildings in the Industrial Age or the dominance of skyscrapers in modern cities.

The first evidence we have of an architectural theory comes from the ancient Greek scholar Vitruvius. His text *De architectura* was consulted in medieval times and was increasingly referred to by architects during the Renaissance, when the ancient Greek style was greatly admired and emulated. Ancient architecture, such as the Egyptian pyramids, holds an enduring fascination and the study of such buildings provides us with valuable information on ancient cultures.

➠ ***Ancient Egypt, Ancient Greece, Neoclassicism, Renaissance***

ARCTIC

Region around the North Pole as far south as 66° 32' N. The 36 million sq km (14 million sq mile) region is made up of the northern parts of America and Asia, Greenland and scattered islands of the Arctic Ocean. Almost all the land is ice-covered, with the extent of sea pack-ice varying according to season.

LEFT: A feline/human head found by archaeologists in the Moche Valley, Peru.
RIGHT: The Town Hall in Georgetown, Guyana. Styles of architecture vary according to local customs, traditions and building materials, as well as the climate and the level of expertise of the designers and builders.

ARGENTINA

Atlantic coastal country of South America. **Capital:** Buenos Aires (to be replaced by Viedma). **Other principal cities:** Rosario, Córdoba, La Plata, Bahía Blanca. **Climate:** tropical in the north giving way to a temperate south, but dry west. **Geographical features:** mountains in west, northern forests and savanna give way to treeless plains in the south. **Main language**: Spanish. **Main religion:** Roman Catholic. Rule: democratic federal republic. **Currency:** peso. **Primary industries**: petroleum, steel, chemicals, paper, rubber, tobacco. **Agriculture:** cereals, sugar, tobacco, fruit and cattle. **Exports:** meat, cereals, beans, vegetable oils, petroleum.

ARMIES

Military organizations. Humanity has resorted to the use of arms to settle arguments since prehistory. The first organized armies originated in the Middle East around 500 BC with the Assyrian, Persian and Macedonian Empires. The present-day Chinese army is the largest in the world and that of the USA is the most technologically advanced.

ART DECO (1925)

Name taken from a 1925 Paris exhibition and applied to a movement in design, art and architecture that followed Art Nouveau. Art Deco was prominent during the 1920s and 30s and, like its predecessor, was principally focused upon design. It merged Cubist form with the colours of the Fauvists and placed emphasis on the use of opulent materials like marble, bronze and walnut. The style was sleekly elegant with a stress on linearity.

Art Deco was particularly influential in architecture and is evident in the striking buildings of the era, such as the Chrysler Building (New York). Through the coinciding rise of mass-production techniques Art Deco became common in interior design.

Art Nouveau, Cubism

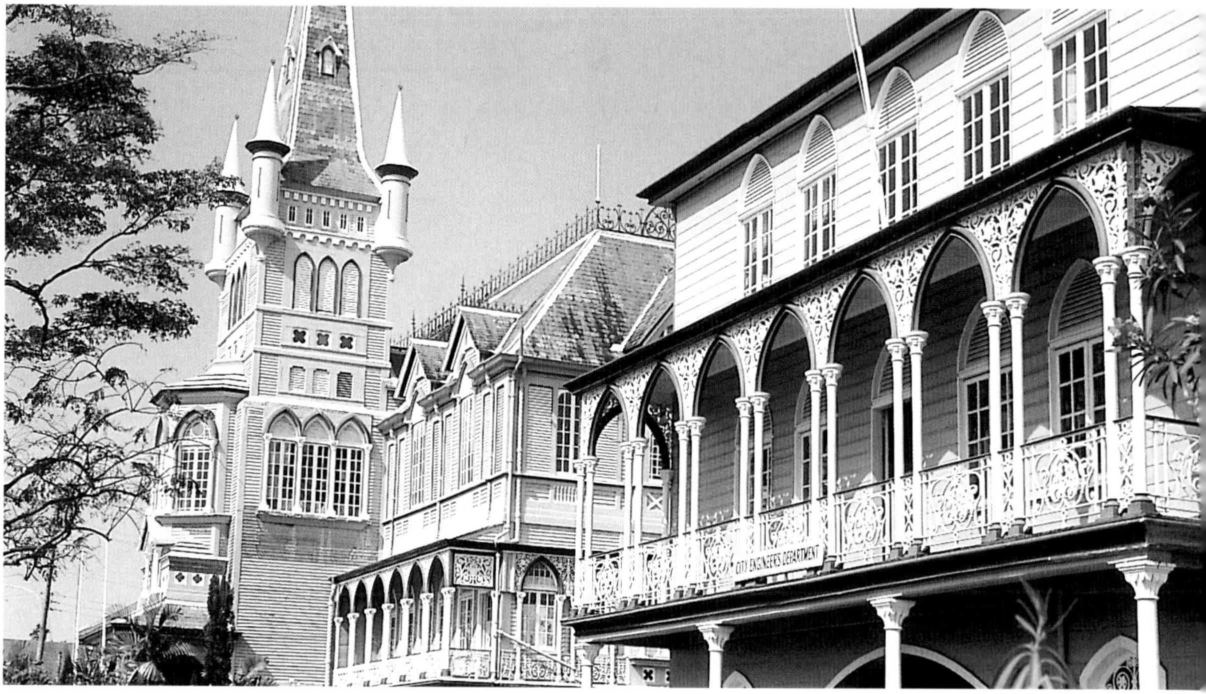

ARISTOTLE (384–322 BC)

Last of the celebrated Greek philosophers. Aristotle challenged the theories of Plato to concentrate upon the natural world, becoming essentially the first eminent biologist. Through his extensive studies and writings (producing over 170 works, although only 47 survived), Aristotle created the scientific classification systems that are still in use today.

Ancient Greece, Philosophy

ART GALLERIES

Buildings for viewing works of art. Larger galleries, such as the Louvre in Paris, offer the public education and entertainment. Smaller galleries (whose numbers have increased dramatically with the decline of individual art patronage) provide artists with the opportunity to display their works in efforts to gain financial support. Aside from their educational and promotional purposes, galleries are equally important to the development of art. Galleries, through their choice of displays, contribute to the prosperity or decline of certain art or artistic styles. Galleries' specific exhibitions similarly impact upon art: in 1910 an exhibition of art was given the title Post-Impressionism, a term which has now entered art history.

Louvre, Post-Impressionism

ABOVE: A tourist admires the impressive Canalettos in London's National Gallery.

RIGHT: The legend of King Arthur dates from the twelfth century.

ART NOUVEAU (19TH CENTURY)

Initially a French art movement (meaning 'new art'), Art Nouveau spread through Europe and America during the final 20 years of the nineteenth century and the first decade of the twentieth century. Art Nouveau was mainly influential in design, both interior and architectural. The style of design was sensuous and dramatic, moving away from a purely realistic representation while still focusing upon shapes taken from nature, particularly plants. There was also an attention to flowing movement and to distinctive colour schemes. Among the proponents of Art Nouveau were Aubrey Beardsley (1872–98) and Gustav Klimt (1862–1918). Among the most famous architects is Charles Rennie Mackintosh.

Architecture, Charles Rennie Mackintosh

ARTHUR, KING

Legendary British king. Although controversy surrounds King Arthur's existence, the legend is an enduring one. In 1136 Geoffrey of Monmouth included Arthur in his *History of British Kings*. The fictional stories of Arthur were turned into romantic, chivalrous tales by twelfth-century French writer Chrétien de Troyes. In the fifteenth century Thomas Malory skilfully combined the many tales of Arthurian legend.

Medieval

ARTIFICIAL INTELLIGENCE

Use of computer technology to reproduce actions which are like those of an intelligent human being, such as interpreting human speech.

Computers

ARTS AND CRAFTS MOVEMENT (1882)

Deriving its name from an English exhibition society begun in 1882, although originally British Arts and Crafts Movements' impact was felt in America and Europe. The movement was concerned with reviving craftsmanship in design – moving away from the depersonalisation of mass production dominant in the late-nineteenth century. Greatly shaped by the work of William Morris and his colleagues, the movement cultivated many socialist views, although the designs themselves were, on the whole, restricted to the wealthy. Like the movements that followed it (and were inspired by it, particularly Art Nouveau), Arts and Crafts was mainly influential in design and architecture.

➧ ***Art Nouveau, William Morris***

ASIA

Largest continent in the world. Asia reaches from the Pacific to the Near East, and from the Arctic to the Indian Ocean and across the Far East to Indonesia. It is separated from Africa now only by the Suez Canal. The land mass is 44.6 million sq km (6.7 million sq miles).

Asia includes the world's highest peak (Mount Everest) and lowest point (the shores of the Dead Sea). The landscape varies from virtually unpopulated desert regions to the tropical rainforests of Borneo. Around 60% of the world's population live in Asia, but almost all of them are clustered along Asia's southern regions, many in a band including the cities of the Indian sub-continent to those of China and Japan.

Northern Asia is a land of plains and forests, where economic development has been restrained by the frozen rivers in winter, and ice-locked ports. The economy here is mainly agriculture and forestry.

Central Asia is a band of mountain ranges, desert and plateaux which stretches from China to Turkey. The effect has been to restrict contact and movement north and south across Asia.

Southern and Eastern Asia provide its vast population with river valleys and low-lying swampy coastal regions in which to live. The great rivers of Asia, such as the Indus, Ganges and Mekong flow out to the south. Vast river deltas favour rice-growing, while other exotic goods such as tea and spices, attracted European settlers and traders. Some of these regions are highly prone to disastrous flooding.

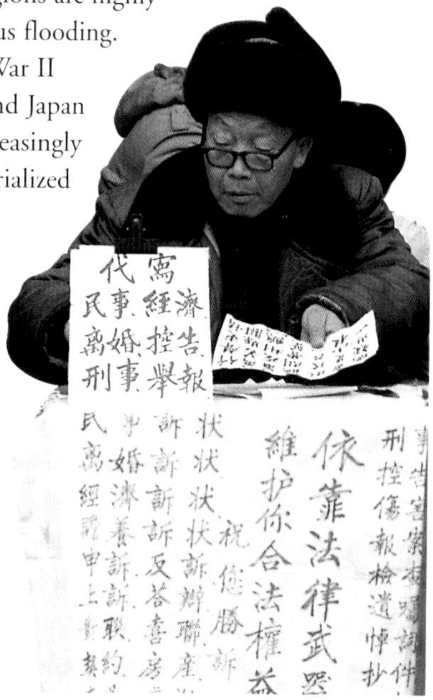

Since World War II south-east Asia and Japan have become increasingly important industrialized regions where vast quantities of electronic goods, cars and motorcycles are manufactured for the world's markets. This has caused a movement of people away from villages into cities like Hong Kong and Tokyo. Currently the population is expanding fast as modern medicine allows traditionally large families a better chance of survival.

➧ ***Mount Everest***

ASSYRIA

Ancient empire of the Middle East, lasting from *c.* 2500 BC to 612 BC, covering modern Iraq. At its greatest extent it included the Near East, Egypt, and the Tigris and Euphrates valleys to the Persian Gulf. Assyria was ruled from Ashur, and then Nineveh, destroyed in 612 BC. Thereafter, Assyria became part of the Persian Empire.

➧ ***Iraq, Persia***

ASTAIRE, FRED (1899–1987)

US film star. Born in Nebraska, USA, Astaire found fame as a film actor/dancer. Together with dance partner Ginger Rogers, he was prominent in the emerging genre of musical films during the 1930s and 40s.

➧ ***Ginger Rogers***

ABOVE: A calligrapher proudly displays examples of this ancient Chinese craft.

ASTEROIDS

Tens of thousands of small rocky bodies in orbit around the Sun, most of which move in the region between the orbits of Mars and Jupiter. The largest, Ceres, has less than a third of the diameter of Earth's Moon. Most are very much smaller and some cross Earth's orbit.

➜ ***Moon, Planets, Sun***

ASTHMA

Difficulty in breathing due to the air passages going into spasm. Asthma attacks may have a variety of causes, including allergic reactions and stress.

ASTROLOGY

Study of the positions of the Sun, Moon and planets in a band of the sky called the Zodiac in which they appear to move, in the belief that they can influence human events on Earth. The Zodiac is given 12 equal divisions, called signs, starting from the First Point of Aries. The apparent positions of these bodies at the time and place of a person's birth is supposed to determine character. Astrology in the western world stems from ancient Babylon; different forms of astrology occur in other regions such as India and China.

➜ ***Moon, Planets, Sun***

ASTRONOMY

Study of all celestial bodies, which include planets, stars and galaxies. Unlike many other sciences, knowledge in astronomy has to be gained by observation, not experiment. Until the invention of the telescope, observations were limited to the positions and apparent motions of the naked-eye bodies. Now, observations are nearly all made by telescope, although professional astronomers never look through an eyepiece – electronic detectors are used. Observations can now be made in wavelengths other than those of light, as in radio astronomy. Some can only be made from above the atmosphere, by satellites such as the Hubble Space Telescope.

➜ ***Edwin Hubble, Planets, Space Exploration, Stars***

ASWAN DAM (1970)

Dam on the River Nile in Egypt, near the town of Aswan. Completed in 1970, the dam is designed to control the flow of the Nile to avoid the effects of annual flooding. Two ancient temples at Abu Simbel were removed before the valley was flooded.

➜ ***Egypt, River Nile***

ATHLETICS

Form of sporting endeavour, originating in Bronze Age Greece. The basic disciplines (running, high jump, long jump, discus, javelin and shot put) have remained largely unchanged since this time. Originally a male-only sport carried out naked, athletics is now a global activity with an audience of millions.

➜ ***Ancient Greece, Olympic Games***

ATLANTIS

Mythical island west of the Straits of Gibraltar. According to the Egyptians it was larger than Libya and Asia Minor combined, but was believed to have been inundated by the ocean. Greek writers maintained that it flourished around 10,000 BC. Similar legends concern the lost Isles of the Blest, Lyonesse (off Cornwall) and Brazil. The quest for its fabled riches inspired many voyages of discovery in the fourteenth and fifteenth centuries.

ATMOSPHERE

Mixture of gases surrounding a celestial body, especially Earth. A gravitational field is necessary to stop the gases escaping into space. The Earth's current atmosphere is predominantly a mixture of nitrogen and

LEFT: A sky chart showing the signs of the zodiac and celestial features.
ABOVE RIGHT: An illustration of a bathing cove on the mythological island of Atlantis by Sir Gerald Hargreaves in his book Atlanta, A Story of Atlantis.
FAR RIGHT: Attila and his Huns invaded Western Europe via Germany, killing, pillaging and raping as they went.

oxygen but there is little doubt that when the atmosphere first formed it was very different. The primary source of Earth's atmosphere is generally believed to be the release of gases from the planet's interior due to internal heat and chemical activity. This atmosphere was modified as life forms developed that could photosynthesize, emitting oxygen as a by-product. The production of oxygen contributed to the development of our modern atmosphere.

➡ ***Air, Earth, Photosynthesis***

ATOMIC BOMB

Bombs in which atoms of either uranium or plutonium are bombarded with neutrons, causing an explosive release of energy as atoms split apart. The current type of bomb is the much more powerful hydrogen bomb. An atom bomb is used to make hydrogen atoms merge in a fusion reaction.

➡ ***Hiroshima***

ATTILA THE HUN (c. 406–53)

King of the Huns from AD 434. Attila was known as the Scourge of God and briefly created an empire that stretched from Germany to the Black Sea and the frontiers of China.

➡ ***Huns***

AURELIUS, MARCUS (AD 121–80)

Adopted son of Emperor Antoninus Pius, whose daughter Faustina he married. Marcus Aurelius became Consul (AD 140) and succeeded Antoninus as Roman emperor in AD 161. Noted for his wise and beneficent rule, he was idealized by later generations of Romans as the model emperor.

➡ ***Ancient Rome***

AUSTEN, JANE (1775–1817)

Prestigious nineteeth-century English novelist. Austen was an astute recorder of her restrictive (particularly for women) middle class society. Her fiction focuses upon male-female relationships and upon social interaction on the whole. Full of precise, witty dialogue and a discerning narrative tone, Austen's work continues in popularity today.

AUSTRALASIA

Collective term for Australia, New Zealand, New Guinea and their associated islands. Australasia translates as 'south of Asia', and was coined to refer to the continent that was believed before the eighteenth century to exist there. The name was retained once Australia and New Zealand had been discovered, but today the term Oceania is used, and adds islands across the central and south Pacific Ocean.

➠ ***Australia, New Zealand, Oceania***

AUSTRALIA

Continental island of Oceania between the Indian Ocean and South Pacific. **Capital:** Canberra. **Other principal cities:** Sydney, Melbourne, Brisbane, Adelaide, Perth. **Climate:** largely hot and dry, but some coastal areas are wetter. **Geographical features:** central Australia is largely arid grass plains, becoming desert towards the west, but the land rises to the forested Highlands in the east. Main language: English. Main religions: Protestant, Roman Catholic. Rule: federal parliament. **Currency:** Australian dollar. Primary industries: farming, food, engineering, mining, forestry, textiles. **Agriculture:** mainly livestock (cattle and sheep). **Economy:** becoming increasingly industrial. **Exports:** metals, minerals, food, machinery.

Australia's harsh landscape has dictated the distribution of settlement in the south-east, mainly as a result of European immigration, principally from Britain, adding to the small and very widely dispersed Aboriginal population. Refugees from south-east Asia are now altering the balance. Australia's geographical features are not exceptional, apart from the Great Barrier Reef, the world's longest coral reef.

➠ ***Aboriginal People***

AUSTRIA

Land-locked mountainous central European country, dominated by the Alps. **Capital:** Vienna. **Other principal cities:** Graz, Innsbruck, Linz, Salzburg. **Climate:** cold with snow in the higher areas, milder with warm summers in the valleys. Main language: German. Main religions: Roman Catholic, Protestant. Rule: democratic federal republic. **Currency:** schilling. Primary industries: steel, machinery, cement, fertilizer, timber and paper products, dairy products, sugar. **Agriculture:** mainly cereals and dairy produce. **Exports:** agricultural produce, chemicals, steel and machinery, timber products.

Austria's share of the Alps makes much of the land inaccessible, apart from the series of central valleys where most of the population, industry and agriculture exist. However, it is the mountains, with their forests and lakes, which attract much of the tourism.

➠ ***Alps, Europe***

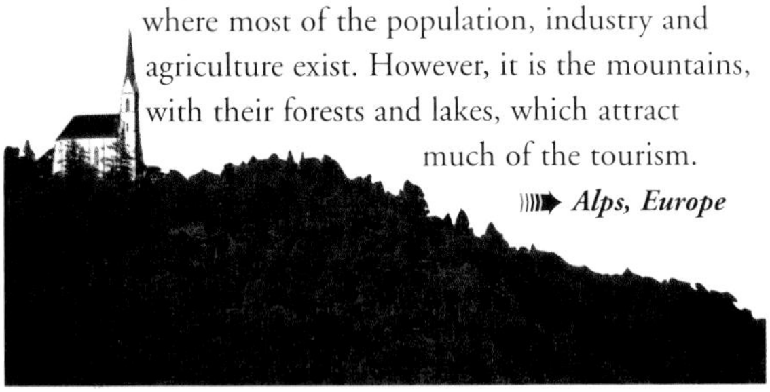

AUSTRIAN SUCCESSION, WAR OF THE (1740–48)

War between Austria and Prussia, and their allies, resulting from the disputed succession of Maria Theresia, daughter of the emperor Charles VI, forming part of a general European conflict.

Charles VI hoped that Maria Theresia could succeed as Empress of Austria on his death. However, the succession was promptly disputed in 1740. Spain, Bavaria and Saxony all made claims to the Habsburg possessions, which France supported as a sworn enemy of Austria. France also supported Frederick the Great of Prussia's seizure of Silesia from Austria in 1740.

Frederick's success confirmed the weakness of the Habsburg-controlled Holy Roman Empire, and Britain's fears of French power. In 1743 France suffered setbacks

LEFT: Ayres Rock in Australia's Northern territories.

ABOVE: Austria's Tyrol mountains.

RIGHT: Tula, Toltec columns in Mexico. Such impressive relics testify to the skill and ability of Aztec craftsmen.

when Britain, Hanover and Hesse joined Austria, defeating France at Dettingen. France's fortunes improved with a victory at Fontenoy in 1746 and conquest of the Austrian Netherlands, but the Jacobite Rebellion distracted Britain and sheer cost led to peace at Aix-la-Chapelle in 1748. Maria Theresia's succession was confirmed but Prussia retained Silesia.

➨ ***Holy Roman Empire***

AZTECS

Mexican native Americans emerging in the twelfth century. Key ruler was empire-building Montezuma I. The capital, Tenochtitlán (present-day Mexico City), was built on rafts and the site of daily human sacrifice. Their main god was Huitzilopochtli ('Humming-bird wizard') and they offered blood to feed Tonatiuh (the Sun god). Self-laceration with cactus thorns and the mass slaughter of some players at the end of a primitive football match were also practised. The Aztecs were particularly skilled in architecture, textiles and jewellery and their writing was a hybrid of hieroglyph and pictograph. In 1519 Hernán Cortés arrived bringing Christianity, horses, gunnery and disease: the Aztec empire now disintegrated.

BABYLON (c. 1792 BC)

Empire that became significant in Mesopotamia *c.* 1792 BC under Hammurabi. Babylon is renowned for its decadence, but also its advanced technology. Most famously Nebuchadnezzar II captured Jerusalem in 586 BC and exiled the Jews to Babylon for 70 years to work on the hydraulically irrigated Hanging Gardens. Astronomical and mathematical developments included the establishment of an hour of 60 minutes and 360 degrees in a circle. In 539 BC Babylon itself fell to Cyrus the Great of Persia. From then on the civilization was in decline, but from the palace at Mari, which had 12-m (40-ft) thick walls, clay tablets survive with extensive information.

➜ ***Mesopotamia***

BACH, JOHANN SEBASTIAN (1685–1750)

German composer. Born in Eisenach, Germany, Bach was the son of an organist and it was to church and organ music that he dedicated much of his career. He worked as musical director in churches around Germany, principally in Leipzig. During his lifetime, although Bach had a successful musical career as an organist, his compositions did not bring him the popularity that his work has since found. A prolific composer, Bach's great volume of orchestral, chamber and keyboard music took influences and themes both from earlier periods and from his contemporaries, elaborating and developing them. His ornamental style has earned him the description of Baroque.

➜ ***Baroque***

BACON, FRANCIS (1561–1626)

British philosopher and producer of scientific methodology. Bacon wrote the influential *Novum Organon* (1620) and is perhaps best remembered for his pronouncement that 'knowledge is power'.

➜ ***Philosophy***

BELOW: The archetypal tropical paradise, Harbour Island, Bahamas.
RIGHT: Perhaps Edgar Degas' (1834–1917) most famous painting, The Star. *Scenes of ballet rehearsals and dancers were among Degas preferred subject matter.*

BADMINTON

Game similar in principle to tennis. The most obvious difference is the use of a shuttlecock instead of a ball: a half sphere of cork with a plastic or feather skirt.

➜ ***Tennis***

BACTERIA

Single-celled living organisms of microscopic size. The cell of a bacterium does not have a nucleus, and its DNA is contained in a single loop, rather than in separate chromosomes. Bacteria reproduce by binary fission, in which a cell splits into two. This process can happen every 20 minutes, so bacteria can multiply rapidly. While some types of bacteria are disease-causing, most are harmless or beneficial, such as those which are used in food production.

BAFTAS

British Academy of Film and Television Arts awards. The BAFTAs are held annually in a ceremony that focuses upon successes within all areas of British film and television, including acting and direction.

➜ ***Academy Awards***

BAHAMAS

Island nation in the Atlantic, north of the Caribbean and east of Florida. **Capital:** Nassau. **Climate:** semi-tropical. **Geographical features:** about 700 (29 inhabited) tropical islands. **Main languages:** English and Creole. **Main religion:** Christian denominations. **Rule:** constitutional monarchy. **Currency:** Bahamian dollar. **Primary industry:** tourism. **Agriculture:** minimal, with most food imported. **Exports:** cement, pharmaceuticals, rum, crawfish, petroleum products.

BAHRAIN

Island state in the Persian Gulf. **Capital:** Manama. **Climate:** hot and dry. **Geographical features:** Bahrain consists of about 35 islands, mostly uninhabited, with most of the population on Bahrain Island and Muharraq. **Main language:** Arabic. **Main religion:** Islam. **Rule:** monarchy. **Currency:** Bahraini dinar. **Primary industries:** oil-refining, docking, banking, tourism. **Exports:** petroleum products, aluminium.

BALLET

Mix of theatre, music and dance originating in Renaissance Italy, most characterized by the grace and athleticism of its dancers. Many of the steps are carried out on tiptoe and require special shoes with a block in the toe to help support the dancer's weight. Famous ballet dancers include Segei Diaghilev (1872–1929), Margot Fonteyn (1919–91) and Rudolf Nureyev (1938–93).

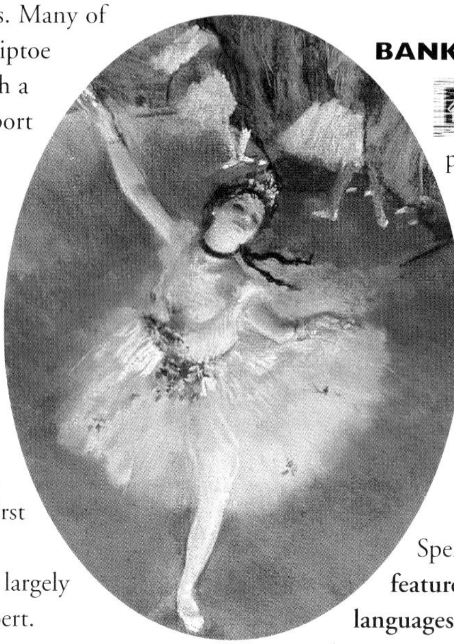

BALMORAL (1853)

Home of the British monarchy, situated on the River Dee in Scotland. First used extensively by Queen Victoria. Built of granite and largely rebuilt in 1853 by Prince Albert.

➧ ***Queens of England***

BANCROFT, ANNE (b. 1931)

American actress. Bancroft is perhaps best known for her celebrated role as the deviously seductive Mrs Robinson in the film *The Graduate* (1967), for which she received one of many Oscar nominations.

➧ ***Academy Awards, Dustin Hoffman***

BANGLADESH

Flood-plain coastal state on India's eastern border. **Capital:** Dhaka. **Other principal cities:** Chittagong, Khulna. **Climate:** semi-tropical with monsoons, floods and droughts. **Geographical features:** the flood plain of the Ganges and Brahmaputra is the world's largest. **Main languages:** Bengali, English. **Main religions:** Islam and Hinduism. **Rule:** democratic republic. **Currency:** taka. **Primary industry:** agriculture, producing rice and jute. **Exports:** jute, tea, fish, hides, skins, newsprint.

Created as part of Pakistan at Indian independence in 1947 to divide Hindu and Muslim communities, Bangladesh fought a civil war in 1971 for independence. Political instability has followed, and the country is also beset by constant natural disasters.

➧ ***India***

BANKING

The first banks were founded around the fifteenth century in Italy and Spain, primarily to allow merchants to pay for goods without carrying large amounts of money around with them. By 1900 half of all the banks in the world were British-owned. By 1950 the USA had become the world's dominant banker, before losing this position to the Japanese by the late 1980s.

BARBADOS

Island in the Caribbean. **Capital:** Bridgetown. **Other towns:** Speightstown. **Climate:** tropical. **Geographical features:** flat coral island with a central ridge. **Main languages:** English and Bajan. **Main religion:** Christian denominations. **Rule:** constitutional monarchy. **Currency:** Barbados dollar. **Primary industries:** tourism and sugar. **Agriculture:** sugarcane. **Exports:** sugar, molasses, clothing, food and drink (rum), chemicals, electrical goods.

BARBIZON (1830s)

School of painting named after a village in the Forest of Fontainebleau, near Paris. The pristine countryside attracted several artists who produced naturalistic landscapes with an accent upon the traditional peasant lifestyle. Chief among Barbizon artists was Jean-François Millet. Emerging in the 1830s, Barbizon declined in popularity after Millet's death in 1875.

BARDOT, BRIGITTE (b. 1934)

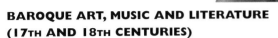

French model-turned-actress. Bardot was made an international sex symbol in the 1956 film by Roger Vadim (her first husband) *And God Created Woman.*

➧ ***Films***

BAROQUE ART, MUSIC AND LITERATURE (17TH AND 18TH CENTURIES)

The Baroque movement was widespread in western Europe during the seventeenth and early eighteenth centuries, influencing art, architecture, literature and music. The term Baroque was applied posthumously to a style that had moved away from the domineering popularity of Classicism and embraced the dramatic; Baroque style was theatrical and elaborate.

Baroque art made much use of movement within the paintings and the colours were vivid, such as can be seen in the works of Michelangelo Caravaggio. Baroque architecture was ornate, incorporating many embellishments and flourishes. The music followed suit, with composers such as Johann Sebastian Bach and George Frideric Handel creating complex pieces with a striking use of contrast.

➧ ***Johann Sebastian Bach, Michelangelo Caravaggio, Classical, George Frideric Handel***

BASEBALL (1839)

Popular game in the USA played with a bat and ball, invented in 1839 by Abner Doubleday. There are nine players in a team and the pitch is called a 'diamond'.

BASKETBALL (1892)

Ball game invented by James Naismith in 1892. The object was to throw a ball through a hoop placed 3.05 m (10 ft) above the ground, with one at either end of the playing area. There are general similarities with the game of netball. Teams consist of five players on each side and games are divided into four quarters of 12 minutes each.

ABOVE: International model and star of the big screen, Brigitte Bardot.

RIGHT: Perhaps one of the most well-known images of The Beatles, the famous foursome on the cover of their hit album, Abbey Road.

FAR RIGHT: A child plays in a gap of the Berlin Wall in 1990. Only one year previously a scene such as this would have been unimaginable.

BEARS

Large carnivorous mammals characterized by short tails, short rounded ears and plantigrade feet (both heel and sole touch the ground) with five clawed toes.

BEATLES, THE (1956)

Engish pop band. Paul McCartney (bass guitar), John Lennon (rhythm guitar), Ringo Starr (drums) and George Harrison (guitar) formed The Beatles in Liverpool (*c.* 1956). With the formidable song-writing team of Lennon and McCartney, the Beatles were arguably the most influential band of the twentieth century. Their phenomenally successful music was guitar orientated, with an emphasis on vocal harmonies.

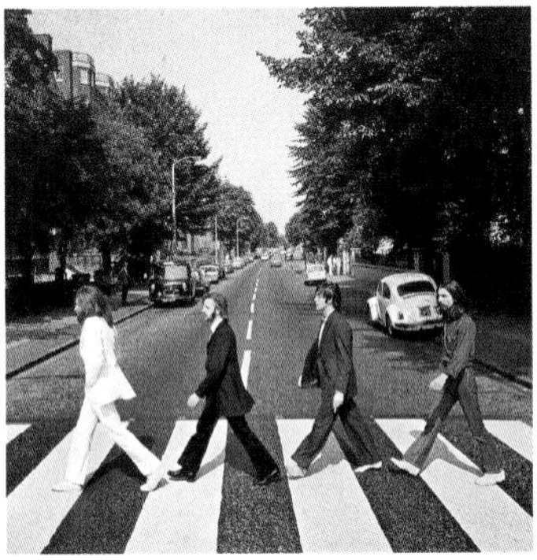

Among their work, their 'concept album' *Sergeant Pepper's Lonely Hearts Club Band* (1967) was particularly influential. The band also made several films, including *Help!* (1965). The group disbanded in 1970.

➧ ***John Lennon, Paul McCartney***

BEER

Alcoholic drink made from water and malted grain, often flavoured with hops. Beer is an ancient drink that is globally popular. Its alcohol content generally varies between 1% and 6% (occasionally higher). There are thousands of varieties, including: bitter, mild, stout and lager. Individual recipes are often closely guarded secrets.

➧ ***Alcohol***

BEETHOVEN, LUDWIG VAN (1770–1827)

German composer. Beethoven began his career primarily as a keyboard player and his many piano compositions reflect this. From around 1800 Beethoven began to lose his hearing and so concentrated more upon composing orchestral works (he was completely deaf by

1824). Beethoven worked in a variety of musical genres such as opera, symphony and sonatas. Unusually, Beethoven achieved wide recognition and acclaim as an undisputed musical genius during his lifetime. Although working primarily in a classical manner, Beethoven's later works show a greater emotional expression that link him to Romanticism.

Romantic

BELGIUM

Northern European coastal country. **Capital:** Brussels. **Other principal cities:** Ghent, Liège, Charleroi, Bruges, Maastricht. **Climate:** cool and temperate. **Geographical features:** flat fertile coastal plain becoming hillier and forested to the south. **Main languages:** German, Dutch, French. **Main religion:** Roman Catholicism. Rule: federal constitutional monarchy. **Currency:** Belgian franc. Primary industries: steel, glass, chemicals, beer, textiles, plastics. Agriculture (mainly self-sufficient): cereals and livestock. **Exports:** food, livestock, machinery, petroleum products, chemicals.

BELL, ALEXANDER GRAHAM (1847–1922)

British inventor and scientist, best known for his invention of the telephone (1876). Bell moved to Boston in the USA in 1871 and became professor of vocal physiology there. Experiments on conversion of sound to other vibrations led to his invention, which he patented, and he formed the Bell Telephone Company in 1877.

BERGMAN, INGRID (1915–82)

Swedish born actress, whose roles were often intense and emotional. Bergman's work includes classic films such as *Casablanca* (1943) and *For Whom the Bell Tolls* (1943).

Humphrey Bogart, Films

BERLIN WALL (1961)

Physical division between East and West Germany in the post-war era. Built by the then East Germany to prevent the exodus of its citizens to the western sectors of Berlin, it became one of the most enduring symbols of the Cold War. Along with Checkpoint Charlie (one of the few gates in the wall) it was used as the scene of a thousand fictional spy stories. The Berlin Wall was pulled down in 1989 by the jubilant Berliners when the Cold War finally thawed.

Cold War, Germany, World War II

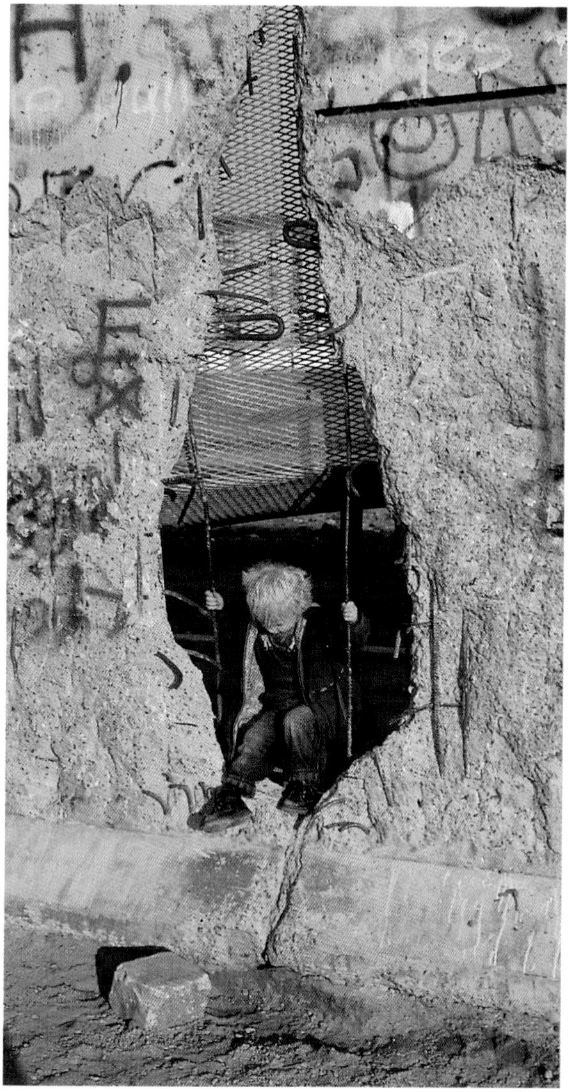

BERNHARDT, SARAH (1844–1923)

French actress and darling of the stage. Bernhardt specialized in melodramatic starring roles. She also gained much praise for her work in early cinema with the 1912 film *Queen Elizabeth.*

Films, Theatre

BHUTAN

Land-locked country on India's north-east border. **Capital:** Thimphu. **Other principal cities:** Paro, Punakha. **Climate:** sub-tropical in south, temperate centre, cold north. **Geographical features:** forested Himalayan valleys. **Main language:** Dzongkha. **Main religion:** Buddhism. **Rule:** absolute monarchy. **Currency:** ngultrum. **Industry:** virtually nil, the economy is reliant on import of manufactured goods. **Agriculture:** self-sufficient. **Exports:** timber, fruit, vegetables, distilled spirits, cement.

➤ ***India***

BIBLE

Christian holy book. The Bible consists of the Old Testament, inherited from Christianity's Jewish roots, and still used in Judaism in the original Hebrew; and the New Testament, originally written in Greek and collated since Jesus's death. Of the New Testament, the four key books are the Gospels (Matthew, Mark, Luke and John), which relate the life of Jesus and the values of Christianity, encapsulated in the idea 'love your neighbour as yourself'.

➤ ***Christianity, Judaism, Torah***

BICYCLES (1870)

Two-wheeled vehicles, driven by pedals linked to the rear wheel. A metal or carbon-fibre frame, fitted with a saddle and handlebars, is mounted on two spoked wheels. The first bicycle was a French design, but it was popularized in 1870 by James Sarley's Penny Farthing. The bicycle is an energy efficient and almost non-polluting form of transport and the most common type of vehicle in the world.

BIG BANG THEORY

Theory that the Universe began at a moment in the past in an extremely dense, extremely hot state and has been expanding and cooling ever since. Evidence for the theory include the existence of the microwave background radiation – radio waves coming in all directions from space.

➤ ***Astronomy, Universe***

BIOLOGY

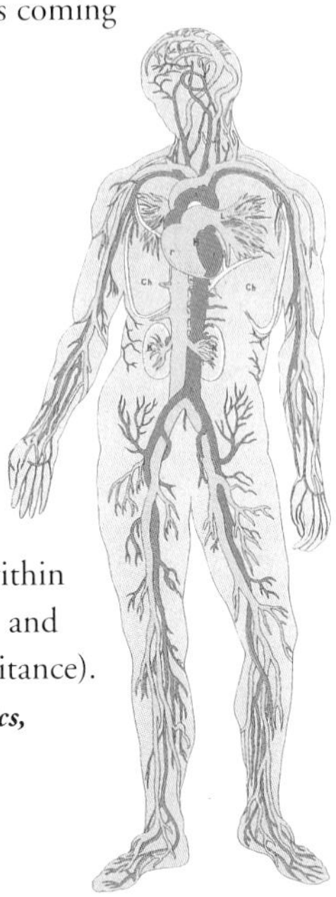

Collective name for all the sciences involving the study of life. Among the sciences included in biology are botany (the study of plants), zoology (the study of animals), ecology (the study of living organisms within their natural environment), and genetics (the study of inheritance).

➤ ***Botany, Ecology, Genetics, Zoology***

BIRDS

Name given to any feathered vertebrate. Birds have many characteristics that make them unique in the animal kingdom, enabling them to exhibit huge diversity and occupy many varied habitats.

Fossil remains suggest that birds descended from dinosaurs separately from reptiles and mammals. While some modern birds cannot fly it is believed that all birds are descended from ancestors that could. To achieve flight birds' bodies have a number of modifications; bones are formed in thin sheets and tubes containing air sacs; there are no heavy teeth or jaws and respiratory and metabolic systems are high-performance. This combination of features gives to birds the advantage of low weight and high power.

Birds' brains are small but complex, enabling them to develop elaborate social structures and behaviours. The diversity and sheer numbers in this group of animals demonstrates its success; the world's bird population is estimated to be 100 billion.

➤ ***Ornithology***

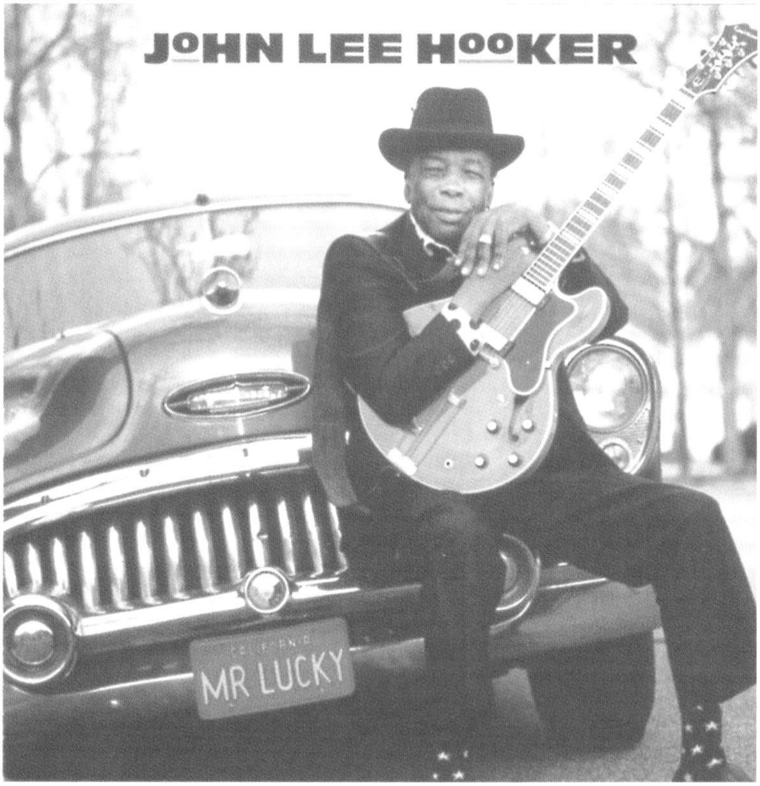

BLUES

Originating from African-American spirituals and work songs, the Blues gained popularity around the 1900s, primarily in America. It has influenced many spheres of popular music, such as Soul and Rhythm and Blues. Blues are slow in tempo, vocally led and are so-called because of the predominance of 'blue notes' which gives the music a melancholic feel.

➧ ***Soul Music***

BOER WAR (1899–1902)

War between the South African Boer republics of Transvaal and Orange Free State and Great Britain. South Africa's gold was vital to British interests but the Boers resisted increased British power in South Africa. The Boer republics launched a two-pronged assault on the British. Initial successes in battle and the sieges of Ladysmith and Mafeking were reversed when British reinforcements arrived. At their peak, British troops numbered nearly half a million, around five times the Boer forces.

By 1900, Britain's advances were compromised by Boer guerrilla tactics. The British, under Lord Kitchener, began a ruthless campaign of destroying farmland and imprisoning Boers, including women and children. In 1902 the Boers capitulated at the Peace of Vereeniging.

➧ ***British Empire, South Africa***

BLENHEIM PALACE (1705–24)

One of the UK's great stately homes. Presented to John Churchill, 1st Duke of Marlborough, by the state after his victory over the French at Blenheim (Germany) in 1704 during the War of the Austrian Succession and landscaped by Capability Brown.

➧ ***War of the Austrian Succession, Capability Brown***

BLOODY SUNDAY (1972)

Name given to the day when civilians were killed and injured by the British army in Ulster, Northern Ireland. On Sunday 30 January 1972 the Northern Ireland Civil Rights Movement organized a protest march against internment. Internment began in August 1971 as a device to control terrorism, but most internees were Catholic Republicans, with only a few Protestant Loyalists. Some marchers confronted British soldiers and a riot broke out. The First Battalion Parachute Regiment killed 13 protesters and injured at least the same number.

➧ ***Ireland***

BOGARDE, SIR DIRK (1921–99)

English actor. Bogarde became a household name playing a doctor in a series of 1950s films and later won critical acclaim for his skilful portrayal of evil in *The Servant* (1963).

➧ ***Films***

FAR LEFT: The cover of the Echternach Bible, dating back to the tenth century.
CENTRE LEFT: Biology is the study of life. The understanding of how the human body functions is just a very small part of this wide ranging subject.
ABOVE: John Lee Hooker is one of the greatest living exponents of the Blues.

BOGART, HUMPHREY (1899–1957)

US actor. An icon of film, Bogart starred in many enduring 1940 and 50s films, including *Casablanca* (1943) and *The African Queen* (1951), starring in the latter with his fourth wife, Lauren Bacall.

➡ ***Ingrid Bergman, Films***

BOLIVÁR, SIMON (1783–1830)

Latin American revolutionary soldier and leader. Bolivár's campaigns wrested independence from Spanish control of South America, but factionalism frustrated hopes for a federation of states.

BOLIVIA

Land-locked South American country. **Capitals:** La Paz and Sucre. **Other principal cities:** Santa Cruz, Cochabamba. **Climate:** tropical in lowlands, cool at altitude. **Geographical features:** west dominated by an Andean high plateau. **Main language:** Spanish. **Main religion:** Roman Catholicism. **Rule:** democratic republic. **Currency:** boliviano. **Primary industries:** mining, natural gas and illegal drugs. A richly resourced nation but under-developed economy. **Exports:** metals, natural gas, soya beans, timber, illegal drugs.

BONAPARTE, NAPOLEON (1769–1821)

Emperor of France (1804–15). Establishing his reputation as a soldier in the Revolutionary Wars, Bonaparte exploited France's post-Revolution political chaos to seize power as dictator in 1799, becoming emperor in 1804. Domestic reform was compromised by the Napoleonic Wars, which pitted Europe against him. Defeat at Waterloo led to exile.

➡ ***Napoleonic Wars***

BOTANY

Scientific study of plants. Also includes the study of fungi, algae and bacteria. Palaeobotany is the study of fossilized plants. Botanists examine the structure and function of plant tissues, classification of plant species, their distribution and ecological importance. Horticulture, agriculture and forestry are economically important branches of botany.

➡ ***Agriculture, Bacteria, Ecology***

BOVINE SPONGIFORM ENCEPHALOPATHY (BSE)

Disease found mainly in cattle (hence its popular name 'Mad Cow Disease'). BSE destroys the brains of the affected animals. It is believed to cause Creutzfeld Jacob Disease (CJD) in humans, with similar symptoms. Presently incurable.

BOWLS

Ball game reminiscent of marbles played in the UK since the thirteenth century. There are two distinct codes: lawn bowls played on a flat surface, and crown bowls played on a slightly curved surface.

BOXING

Fist fighting as a sport with recognized rules dates from the eighteenth century. Initially these were contested with bare knuckles and had a limitless number of rounds. The use of gloves was codified under the Queensberry Rules of 1867, whose principles still apply to the sport today. There is growing pressure to ban the sport on medical grounds.

➡ ***Mohammed Ali***

RIGHT: Bandsmen playing tuba's in London's St James' Park.

FAR RIGHT: The magnificent bridge that spans Sydney's harbour, Australia.

BRANDO, MARLON (b. 1924)

US actor. Regard for Brando, like his career, is erratic. He is best known for his early role in *On the Waterfront* (1954) and latterly as Don Corleone in the *Godfather* (1972).

➧ ***Films***

BRASS INSTRUMENTS

Musical instruments made from metal, using a cup- or funnel-shaped mouthpiece. The term includes trumpets, trombones, tubas and horns but excludes saxophones (as they have a reed mouthpiece). Their sound is created by the vibration of the players' lips against the mouthpiece. The tone of the note the instrument produces is affected by the bell at the end of the tube and by the mouthpiece: a long funnel gives a smoother sound while a cup gives a sharper sound. Brass instruments are fundamental to certain types of music, such as jazz, orchestral and brass bands.

➧ ***Jazz, Orchestra***

BRAZIL

Largest country in South America. **Capital:** Brasilia. **Other principal cities:** Sao Paulo, Belo Horizonte, Belém, Rio de Janeiro, Manaus, Fortaleza. **Climate:** semi-tropical to tropical. **Geographical features:** densely forested Amazon basin. **Main language:** Portuguese. **Main religion:** Roman Catholicism. **Rule:** democratic federal republic. **Currency:** real. **Primary industries:** chemicals, mining (ores and diamonds), steel, engineering, food, textiles, cement, timber. **Agriculture:** coffee, cocoa, tobacco, sugar, soya beans, maize, rice, oranges, beef, poultry. **Exports:** metals, steel, ores, transport products, orange juice, sugar, tobacco, soya beans, leather goods, textiles, beef.

Brazil is the fifth-largest country in the world, the largest and most populous nation in South America. It has an extremely diverse population made up of indigenous peoples, descendants of Portuguese immigrants and black slaves, and other immigrants from Europe and Japan. Indigenous tribes now constitute about 1% of the population. Economic development really began in the mid-nineteenth century, attracting European settlers.

Brazil's size and landscape make it dependent on air transport and use of rivers as waterways. Brazil has vast natural resources. The Amazon basin contains the world's largest rainforest, covering about half the country. It is increasingly being cleared for timber, and for farmland, creating an environmental issue for the nation and the world. The Amazon valley is also particularly important for its wide variety of flora and fauna, with around 30,000 species of butterflies alone.

The southern plateau is dominated by commercial farming and most of the country's major cities where industry, the largest concentration in South America, and most of the population are located. Mineral resources, such as iron in the north and east, and manganese in the lower reaches of the Amazon, add to the nation's wealth. But exploitation of these and most of the other resources is very inequitably distributed among Brazilians. This has led to calls for land reform and a national issue over foreign debt.

➧ ***Amazon River, Rainforests***

BRIDGES

Structures designed to provide a means of passage over waterways, valleys, roads or railway tracks, There are four main types of bridge. Beam bridges have supports at either end bearing the weight; arch bridges and cantilever bridges are variations of the beam bridge; and suspension bridges use cables to support the main structure.

➧ ***Engineering***

BRITISH EMPIRE

Countries and territories under the control of Great Britain (UK) from around 1600. At its height in the 1920s it contained roughly 25% of the world's area and population. Now almost totally dismantled, the bulk of countries that once made it up have formed the Commonwealth. The first colony to be established in the Empire was Jamestown in Virginia, present-day USA (1607). The USA is one of only two countries to have left the Empire by armed rebellion, Ireland being the other. By the 1930s many countries were agitating for independence, and by the late 1940s the wholesale granting of independence had started, notably that of India in 1947. Today there are only small remnants remaining, notably the Falkland Islands, Gibraltar and Bermuda.

➧ ***American Revolution, Commonwealth***

BRONTË SISTERS

Three English sisters who wrote under the pseudonyms of Currer, Ellis and Acton Bell. Charlotte (1816–55), Emily (1818–48) and Anne (1820–49) are chiefly remembered for their successful novels. Charlotte wrote the enduring classic *Jane Eyre* (1847). Anne wrote *Agnes Grey* in 1847. Perhaps most significant was Emily's exemplary novel *Wuthering Heights* (1847) which employed an innovative narrative structure.

BRONZE AGE

Period of prehistory when bronze, an alloy of copper and tin, was first used extensively for tools and weapons. Although there are overlaps, the period is generally considered to be later than the Stone Age and preceded the Iron Age. Copper was originally used on its own, until the discovery that tin made it much harder. The technology for making bronze spread slowly – so the dates given to the Bronze Age vary according to location. For the Middle East, dates of 5000 BC to 1000 BC are used, but in Europe the period 2000 BC to 500 BC is more appropriate.

➧ ***Iron Age, Stone Ages***

RIGHT: Pupils receive lessons from a Buddhist monk in the Wat Sutat monastery in Bangkok, Thailand.

BROWN, LANCELOT 'CAPABILITY' (1716–83)

English landscape gardener. Beginning his career as a gardener, Capability Brown became the foremost landscape architect in England. His work can still be seen today in the gardens of Blenheim Palace, Warwick Castle and Croome Court, Worcestershire.

➧ ***Architecture***

BROWNING, ELIZABETH BARRATT (1806–61) AND ROBERT (1812–89)

Victorian poets, married in 1846, eloping to escape Elizabeth's tyrannical father. A gifted child, (first published at just 14), Elizabeth wrote poetry that looked at social problems such as the question of women and child labour. Her most famous work, *Aurora Leigh* (1857), is a combination of poetry, autobiography and social debate. Robert's poetry explored long narratives and deeper character development in his attempt to compete with the novels' popularity. He has influenced many poets, including T. S. Elliot.

BRUNEL, ISAMBARD KINGDOM (1806–59)

British inventor and engineer, whose achievements include the Clifton Suspension Bridge at Bristol and iron ships such as the screw propeller-driven *Great Britain*.

➧ ***Engineering, Railways***

BUCHAREST

Capital city of Romania, with a population of about 2.1 million. Founded in the fourteenth century as a defensive citadel, it lies on the Dambovita, a tributary of the Danube. A communications hub, Bucharest is also an industrial centre. Most buildings belong to the nineteenth century or later, but earthquakes and the 1989 revolution have led to much rebuilding.

➧ ***Romania***

BUCKINGHAM PALACE

London residence of the British monarch. Originally built for the Duke of Buckingham in 1762. Major renovations were carried out in 1821–36 and 1913.

➧ ***Kings of England, Queens of England***

BUDDHISM

Eastern religion. Buddhism was established in the Ganges Valley, India, by Siddhartha Gautama (the Buddha, *c.* 563–483 BC), a warrior-prince who became an ascetic. He studied the Hindu *Upanishads*, out of which Buddhism and its practice of yoga emerged. Buddhism upholds 'karma', the doctrine that deeds are rewarded or avenged, either in that lifetime or through reincarnation. Buddhist monks spread Buddhism and it remained important in India, with Buddha himself being worshipped, until the coming of Islam. After the end

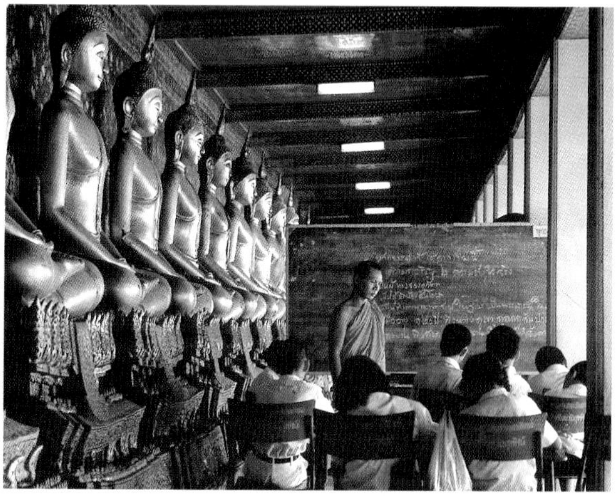

of the Han dynasty, despite persecution, Buddhism gained a foothold in China and in thirteenth- and fourteenth-century Japan Zen Buddhism developed.

Chinese Dynasties, Hinduism, Islam

BUFFALO

Large members of the bovine family native to Asia and Africa. Like domestic cattle they chew cud and have cloven hooves. American bison are sometimes referred to as buffalo.

BULGARIA

East European country on the Black Sea. **Capital:** Sofia. **Other principal cities:** Plovdiv, Rusa. **Climate:** temperate. **Geographical features:** mainly mountainous with plains in the north and south-east. **Main languages:** Bulgarian, Turkish. **Main religions:** Eastern Orthodox Christian, Islam. **Rule:** democratic republic. **Currency:** lev. **Primary industries:** textiles, tobacco, electric motors, footwear. **Agriculture:** livestock and grain. **Exports:** machinery, agricultural produce, cigarettes, metals, ores, chemicals.

Bulgaria is gradually changing from a rural into an industrial nation, with government policy seeking to develop a market economy after the Soviet era. A privatisation programme was begun in 1993. However, inflation caused economic hardship during the 1990s, leading to further political turmoil.

Europe

BURTON, RICHARD (1925–1984)

Welsh-born actor. Burton achieved fame equally for his reputation and relationship with Elizabeth Taylor as he did for impressive acting in films such as *Who's Afraid of Virginia Woolf?* (1966).

Elizabeth Taylor, films

BUSES

Vehicles which carry fare-paying passengers, usually over a fixed route, making frequent stops to allow the passengers to get on or off. The original buses were horse-drawn, but were replaced by motor-driven vehicles in the early twentieth century. They are mainly used in urban areas.

BYRON, LORD (1788–1824)

Romantic English poet. Byron was made famous when *Childe Harold* was published in 1812. Beginning as a chivalrous tale the poem descends into autobiography of Byron's European travels during 1809–11. His (then) shockingly sexual poem *Don Juan*, combined with his death while intending to fight for Greek Independence, endowed Byron with the image as a dangerously alluring but heroic nobleman.

Poetry, Romantic

BYZANTIUM (675 BC)

Greek city on the Bosporus, founded in 675 BC. It was the nucleus of the later city of Constantinople (AD 330) but gave its name to the Byzantine Empire which survived the collapse of the western Roman Empire (AD 476) and continued until 1453 when it was overrun by the Osmanli Turks.

CACTI

Plant family native to the continent of America. Can survive in conditions of low or infrequent supplies of water. Most are succulents and possess spines.

CAESAR, JULIUS (c. 101–44 BC)

Roman emperor. Born into one of Rome's oldest and most aristocratic families, Caesar's marriage to Cornelia incurred the enmity of Sulla, until whose death in 78 BC he served in the army in Asia. Elected Pontifex (73 BC) and Quaestor (68 BC), he gradually moved up through the ranks of Roman government and became Consul and virtual head of state in 59 BC. He spent most of the next 15 years campaigning abroad, invading Britain in 55–54 BC. In 45 BC he was appointed Dictator for life but was assassinated in March 44 BC. Regarded as the father of his country, the month of July was named after him.

➡ ***Ancient Rome***

CAGNEY, JAMES (1899–1986)

US actor. Born in New York, Cagney achieved great acclaim with his roles as a troubled gangster in classic films such as *Public Enemy* (1931) and *Angels with Dirty Faces* (1938).

➡ ***Films***

CAINE, MICHAEL (b. 1933)

English actor. Caine established himself in the 1960s playing working-class characters such as the infamous *Alfie* (1966). Recently Caine has earned praise with films such as *Little Voice* (1998).

➡ ***Films***

CALENDARS

System to keep track of passing time by dividing it up into days, weeks, months and years. Although the motions of the Sun, Moon and the passing seasons provide the basis for all calendars there are still many variations. The Gregorian calendar used in the western world dates from 1752 and was derived from the Julian calendar introduced by Julius Caesar in 46 BC.

CALLIGRAPHY

Art of creating writing that is a work of art in its own right. Many fine examples appear in medieval religious manuscripts, notably the *Book of Days*. Development of the art form continues to this day, although with the aid of modern technology it is very much easier. There are many purists, however, who still insist on using ink, pen and brush – notably the Japanese.

➡ ***Graphic Art***

CALVIN, JOHN (1509–1564)

Pre-eminent figure in the sixteenth-century Protestant Reformation. Calvin studied in Geneva (a hot-bed of Protestant extremism), supported the Huguenots and sowed seeds for Presbyterianism.

➡ ***Protestantism***

CAMEL

Large humped ruminant native to desert regions of Asia and North Africa. The bactrian camel has two humps and the dromedary has one hump.

CAMEROON

Central African Atlantic coastal country. **Capital:** Yaoundé. **Other principal cities:** Garoua, Maroua, Bamenda. **Climate:** hot and humid. **Geographical features:** northern marsh and savanna, central plateaux, southern coastal plains and rainforests. **Main languages:** French, English. **Main religions:** Roman Catholic, animist, Islam. **Rule:** democratic republic. **Currency:** franc. **Primary industry:** agriculture. **Exports:** aluminium, bananas, cocoa, coffee, cotton, gold, groundnuts, oil, rubber.

»» ***Africa***

CAMUS, ALBERT (1913–60)

French writer, originally a philosophy student. Camus' work looks at the paradox of life and death. *L'Étranger* (1942) and *La Chute* (1956) are among his best-known books.

»» ***Philosophy***

CANADA

North American country. **Capital:** Ottawa. **Other principal cities:** Toronto, Montreal, Vancouver, Edmonton, Calgary, Winnipeg. **Climate:** moderate summers, cold and harsh winters. **Geographical features:** western mountains give way to central plains and eastern hills. **Main languages:** French, English. **Main religions:** Roman Catholicism, Protestant denominations. **Rule:** federal constitutional monarchy. **Currency:** Canadian dollar. **Primary industries:** transport and machinery, food, paper and wood-based industries, chemicals. **Agriculture:** cereals and livestock (cattle and pigs). **Exports:** vehicles, timber and paper products, petroleum products, aluminium.

Almost half of Canada is covered in forest and its landscape ranges from the frozen Arctic tundra wastes of its northern islands to the temperate grasslands of the south on its border with the USA. Colonization began with Asian peoples, followed briefly by Vikings around the year 1000. French and English wars over Canada were concluded in 1763 when the Treaty of Paris granted Canada to Britain. Considerable effort was expended on finding a north-west passage past Canada to Asia.

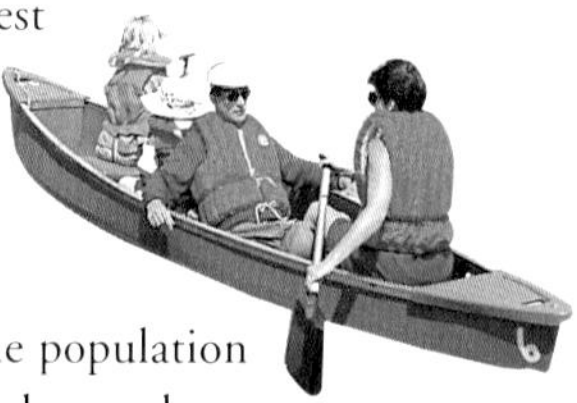

Canada's vast resources have made it extremely prosperous, and its industries are very well-developed. However, most of the population and industry is concentrated in the south-east and extreme south-west, allowing much influence from the USA. The French identity has remained extremely strong and the nation has a powerful separatist lobby.

»» ***Rocky Mountains***

ABOVE LEFT: Cacti in Arizona, USA, grow to several metres high.

LEFT: Using traditional brushes and inks a contestant participates in a calligraphy competition in Tokyo, Japan.

ABOVE: The Rocky Mountains seen from the Emerald Lake in Yoho National Park, Canada.

CANALS

Artificial waterways used for two main purposes: for irrigation and navigation. Irrigation canals take water from rivers, lakes or reservoirs to farmland. They are constructed with a slight gradient to provide a slow movement of water. Irrigation canals have been used in Egypt for millennia, collecting water from the Nile. Navigation canals provide a route for water craft where no suitable river exists or link two separate waterways. The world's major canals for shipping are the Panama Canal, linking the Pacific and Atlantic Oceans, completed in 1914, and the Suez Canal between the Mediterranean and the Arabian Gulf, completed in 1869. These canals are very heavily used. Navigation canals often link places of different heights, and therefore require a system of locks, with gates at each end to regulate the flow of water and allow vessels to ascend or descend.

»» ***Suez Canal***

CANNABIS

Narcotic drug obtained from the Indian Hemp plant (*Cannabis sativa*). Still illegal in most countries, there is growing public pressure to de-criminalize its use.

»» ***Drugs***

CANNES FILM FESTIVAL (1946)

Cannes Film Festival (so named because it is held annually in Cannes, France) is considered one of the most esteemed awards ceremonies in the film industry. It was first held in 1946.

»» ***Academy Awards, BAFTAs, Films***

CANOEING

Sport involving a shallow, lightweight boat propelled with paddles. There are two types of boat, the kayak and the Canadian canoe. Both types feature in the Olympic Games.

Olympic Games

CANTERBURY TALES

Unfinished collection of narrative poetry by Geoffrey Chaucer. The stories are told by 30 pilgrims travelling to Canterbury. The *Tales* humorously illustrate fourteenth-century life in England.

Geoffrey Chaucer

CAPES

Headland or promontory. May be result of erosion of surrounding rocks by wind or water. This leaves bands (or strata) of more resistant rock to form the cape.

CARAVAGGIO, MICHELANGELO MERISI DA (c. 1571–1610)

Italian artist. Named after his home town, Caravaggio has been championed by some as the early hero of naturalism in art. From the beginning of his career, Caravaggio rejected the idealized beauty of Renaissance art, instead attempting social realism both through his choice of subject (such as *The Fortune Teller*) and through his choice of model. In his later work Caravaggio employed an intense contrast of light and dark, a technique that has become known as tenebrism.

Baroque, Renaissance

CARBON

Non-metallic element with atomic number 6 and chemical symbol C. Carbon forms a huge variety of complex compounds owing to its unique ability to bond with other carbon atoms in a ring structure. Many of these exist in living organisms and thus the study of carbon is called 'organic chemistry'.

Chemical Elements, Coal, Diamond

CARICATURE

Term used for portraits that over-emphasize a feature of a person to produce an exaggerated, humorous representation. The technique is most ferquently employed in cartoons.

Comics, Graphic Art

CARS

Small four-wheeled vehicles mainly for private transport, and usually powered by water-cooled petrol or diesel engines. The modern car stems from the petrol-engined motor cars of 1884 of Gottlieb Daimler and Karl Benz. Cars typically have a monocoque construction in which the body panels provide much of the vehicle's strength. The engine is usually in the front, driving either front or rear wheels via a gearbox and transmission system. Some 300 million motor vehicles are produced annually, most of them cars. Motor vehicles are inefficient users of fossil fuels but at present have no rivals.

FAR LEFT: The Lute Player by Caravaggio.
LEFT: A 1935 four-door saloon Bugatti. Vintage cars in mint condition can fetch almost as much money today as modern vehicles straight off the production line.
RIGHT: Cuban Communist leader, Fidel Castro.

CARTOGRAPHY

Art of making maps from geographical information. Maps are usually drawn or printed on paper, although a map can be in other forms, for example on a computer screen. Only a restricted amount of information can be represented on any map, and special-purpose maps showing just one type of information such as physical contours are common.

CASTLES

Fortified structures designed to act as strongholds when attacked and as a means of controlling areas of land, particularly river crossings, mountain passes and other critical areas.

The history of castle building is a long one. The ancient Britons were building wood and earth hill forts before the Roman invasion. However it was in the medieval period that castle building reached its heyday. Originally of simple wooden construction, the classic early medieval type was the motte-and-bailey design. In this a square wooden keep was surrounded by a larger area enclosed with a simple wooden palisade: the bailey. This developed into a stone-built structure over time.

Crusaders brought back a lot of ideas from the Middle East in the twelfth and thirteenth centuries, the most important being the creation of round, rather than square castles, which proved to be far stronger.

The discovery of gunpowder marked the decline of castles, and by the seventeenth century they were obsolete, although the numerous surviving examples are testament to the quality of their construction.

Feudalism, Sieges

CASTRO, FIDEL (b. 1927)

Prime minister of Cuba (1959–76) and president from 1976. Castro overthrew the US-backed right-wing government of Batista in 1959, establishing a Communist regime dependent on USSR support and leading to the Cuban Missile Crisis of 1962 and the US trade embargo. The end of USSR support in 1990 has led to more economic openness.

Cuba

CATHEDRALS

Place of Christian worship, a cathedral is the principal church building in a diocese. From Latin *cathedra,* meaning 'throne': the bishop's, or archbishop's, throne is set on the south side of the choir. In England, before the Dissolution of the Monasteries, cathedrals could be secular or monastic; afterwards they became Cathedrals of the New Foundation. The Middle Ages saw the architectural apogee of cathedrals with technological advances resulting in Gothic delicacy: lancet arches, spires, fan vaulting and flying buttresses. Particularly beautiful examples were built in France and England.

➜ ***Christianity, Churches***

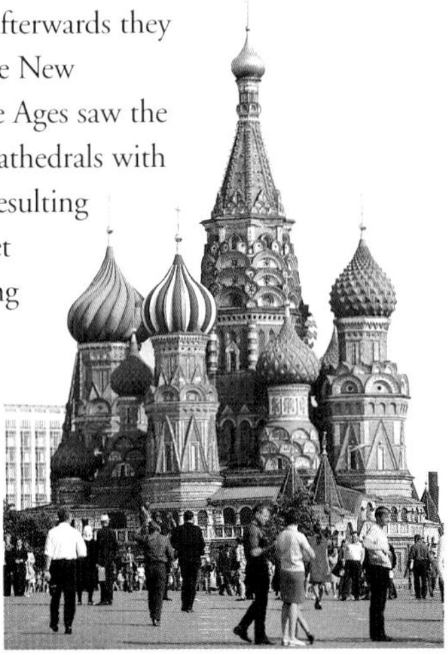

CATHOLICISM

Roman Catholicism is, and always has been, the largest branch of Christianity worldwide; membership: 585 million. Jesus's disciple Peter is said to have travelled to Rome, consequently the Roman Catholic headquarters (St Peter's Basilica and the Vatican) since the third century. The central organisation of the pope enabled Catholic domination of Europe until the sixteenth-century Protestant Reformation. The Counter-Reformation retaliated and missionaries (principally the Jesuits) took Catholicism to Asia and South America. Catholicism is Marian (venerates the Virgin Mary) and one of its central tenets is transubstantiation (that the bread and wine actually become Jesus's body and blood at the Mass).

➜ ***Christianity, Protestantism***

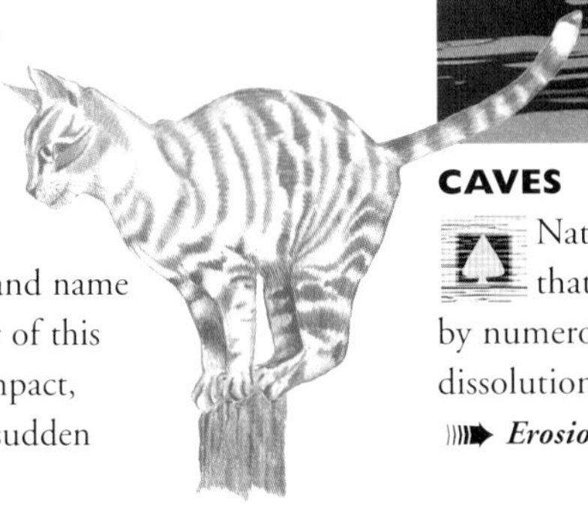

CATS

Common name for family of carnivorous, vertebrate mammals, *Felidae,* and name given to the domestic member of this family. Characterized by a compact, muscular body well-suited to sudden leaping movements, excellent senses of hearing and sight, large brain and complex social behaviour. Cats have long and well-developed canine teeth. Wild species are native to all continents except Australasia although many are under threat owing to hunting and loss of habitat. Wild species include the lion, leopard, cheetah (Africa), tiger (Asia), ocelot, puma and jaguar (America). The domestic cat, now widespread, is probably derived from wild cats bred by the ancient Egyptians.

➜ ***Lion, Tiger***

CAVALRY

Horse-mounted soldiers. Used from antiquity, cavalry could provide swift and decisive attacks in battle. Susceptible to intense barrage, cavalry were made obsolete by artillery and the machine-gun.

➜ ***Infantry***

CAVES

Natural openings in rock, also known as caverns, that are large enough for humans to enter. Formed by numerous processes, such as erosion and the dissolution of limestone by water.

➜ ***Erosion***

CELTS

Ancient race of central and western Europe occupying the Danube valley. The Celts migrated westwards north of the Alps as far as the British Isles, where their distinctive culture and languages have survived longest. The Brythons crossed the Channel from Gaul and settled in England and Wales, while the Goidels moved from the Loire to Ireland and thence to Scotland. Today, the Brythons (from whom the names Brittany and Britain derive) are represented by Cumbrians, Welsh, Cornish and Bretons, while the Gaelic-speaking Irish, Scots and Manx are descended from the Goidels.

➧ ***Druids***

CERVANTES, MIGUEL DE (1547–1616)

Spanish writer of *Don Quixote de la Mancha* (1605–15), a burlesque romantic adventure following the idealistic Don Quixote and his servant, the shrewder Sancho Panza.

CÉZANNE, PAUL (1839–1906)

French painter. Cézanne is considered by many art critics to be the 'father of modern art'. He trained in Paris and together with Pissarro (who Cézanne recognized as his mentor), Cézanne exhibited in the first Impressionist exhibition in 1874. However Cézanne's own critical success came later, once he had rejected Impressionism. Though still representational, Cézanne now moved toward a more abstract art, with his use of colour and shape reflecting the internal reactions he felt about the images he was depicting, rather than attempting a realistic portrayal. This stylistic development led to the Cubists of the early twentieth century.

➧ ***Abstract Art, Cubism, Impressionism***

CHAGALL, MARC (1887–1985)

Russian artist. Originally Cubist in style, Chagall developed a unique style that defies categorization. His highly personal paintings are filled with dream and fantasy images.

➧ ***Abstract Art, Cubism***

FAR LEFT: St Basil's Cathedral, Moscow.

LEFT: A familiar sight in the environs of London's Buckingham Palace: the queen's Household Cavalry descend Pall Mall.

CHANNEL TUNNEL (1987)

Tunnel under the English Channel, linking Folkestone, Kent with Sangatte, near Calais in France. Opened in 1997, it is a rail-only tunnel, road vehicles being carried on special transporters.

➧ ***Railways, Trains***

CHAPLIN, CHARLIE (1889–1977)

US comic actor. Chaplin explored the medium of mime in film (first speaking on film in 1936). Chaplin also wrote, directed and produced most of his later films.

➧ ***Films***

CHARITIES

Originally a purely Christian term related to the giving of alms, the term has come to encompass a far more widespread meaning. Charities are now often big businesses in their own right and a strict set of rules to govern them as been codified in the UK. Prominent UK charities include: Oxfam, Comic Relief and Scope.

CHARLEMAGNE (AD 742–814)

Frankish king (AD 771–814). The son of Pepin the Short, Charlemagne became King of the Franksin AD 771 and Emperor of the West (AD 800), defeating Saxons, Lombards and the Moors of Spain. His court was the envy of Europe at the time.

CHAUCER, GEOFFREY (c. 1343–1400)

Fourteenth-century English poet, known mainly for his *Canterbury Tales.* Poetry was merely Chaucer's hobby but his bawdy, accessible writing style has ensured his works' longevity.

➧ **Canterbury Tales**

CHEMISTRY

Science of the composition, structure and properties of matter and the changes which the structure can undergo. All matter is made of atoms, extremely small elementary particles, of which there are about 100 types. The chemical elements, each of which consists of only one type of atom, can form chemical bonds to make compounds, containing more than one type of atom. The nature of these bonds and how they can be changed is central to chemistry.

Chemical Elements

CHERNOBYL (1986)

Town in the northern Ukraine and site of the world's worst nuclear disaster to date. Two huge explosions literally blew apart the nuclear reactor there. Although only 31 people died at the time, the World Health Organisation estimate that 600,000 people are still at risk from the resultant radiation pollution.

Nuclear Power

CHESS

Board game played with equal forces representing a stylized form of warfare. At least 500 years old, it is a game of pure skill with a global following.

CHILD LABOUR

The use of school-age children as a source of labour still makes a considerable contribution to the world's economy. Although frowned on in many countries the statistics speak for themselves. In 1996, 20 million children worked in India, two million of them in dangerous occupations. Estimates say that around 22% of children in Africa also go out to work. Present EU legislation prohibits children in member states working more than 12 hours a week, but it is still estimated that two million children have some part time work in the UK.

CHILE

South American Pacific coastal country. **Capital:** Santiago. **Other principal cities:** Concepción, Viña del Mar, Talcahuano. **Climate:** mild. **Geographical features:** defined by extremely long west coast, the Andes to the east and the northern desert. **Main language:** Spanish. **Main religion:** Roman Catholicism. **Rule:** democratic republic. **Currency:** peso. **Primary industries:** metals, chemicals, food, petroleum refining, paper products, vehicles and tyres, beer, glass. **Agriculture:** wheat, maize, sugar, potatoes, fruit and vegetables, livestock. **Exports:** copper, food, fruit, timber.

Chile's resources are inequitably distributed among the population, but the country enjoys the diverse benefits of the mineral resources in its northern zone, the central farming area, and the forests, grazing and oil of the extreme south.

CHINA

Largest country in South-east Asia. **Capital:** Beijing. **Other principal cities:** Chongqing, Shenyang, Wuhan, Guangzhou, Tianjin, Nanjing, Shanghai. **Climate:** hot, humid summers, cold and dry winters. **Geographical features:** mountainous and arid land occupies two-thirds of China, with fertile lowlands and deltas in the east. **Main languages:** Mandarin, Cantonese. **Main religions:** Taoism, Confucianism, Buddhism, Islam, Roman Catholicism. **Rule:** Communist republic. **Currency:** yuan. **Primary industries:** bicycles, cement, cotton and textiles (including wool and silk), chemicals, electrical goods, aluminium and steel, tourism. **Agriculture:** cereals, cotton, jute, soya beans, rice, sugar, tobacco. **Exports:** food (including fish and tea), cotton and silk, machinery, crude petroleum.

China has the world's largest population, most of whom live in the south-east, somewhere in excess of

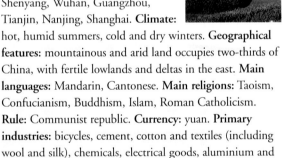

BOTTOM LEFT: This American postcard c. 1905 depicts young boys picking slate out of mined coal in an American mine.
LEFT: The impressive and imposing Tien An Men gate in Beijing, China.
RIGHT: Caravaggio's Deposition of Christ *from the Vatican.*

1.1 billion and equal to about one-quarter of the world's total. The majority of the population are Han Chinese, the balance being made up from various minority groups, including Zhuang, Manchu and Tibetan peoples.

China is contained within the natural barriers of deserts and mountains around the north, west and south, with the Tibetan plateau at 4,000 m (13,000 ft), the highest area. It also contains Mount Everest, the highest point in the world. The flora and fauna include unique varieties and species, such as the giant panda, and goat antelope.

The country's modern development began in 1949 when the People's Republic began post-World War II reconstruction. Agriculture remains the most important activity with all available land being utilized, by constructing hill terraces, to produce rice and wheat. Industrial growth has continued apace, with domestic tastes becoming gradually more westernized. China has vast natural resources, most of which remain to be exploited. Transport is heavily reliant on railways. The Changjiang (Yangtse) river cuts east-west across much of the country, providing a vital commercial artery. China remains dependent on importing manufactured goods, mainly from Japan.

➧ ***Mount Everest, Panda***

CHINESE DYNASTIES

Dynasties evolved slowly: China's magnitude and emphasis on tradition handicapped change. The emperors continued to be worshipped and peasant revolts suppressed, until the arrival of Communism.

The earliest recorded dynasty is the Shang (*c.* 1500–1066 BC), followed by the Zhou (1050–221 BC). The Qin (*c.* 221–206 BC) is renowned for beginning building the Great Wall. The Han (206 BC–AD 220) united almost all of modern China. China was divided by internal fighting and Tatar invasions and the next major dynasty was the Tan (AD 618–907) whose cosmopolitan capital, Ch'ang-an, was at the end of the Silk Road. The Song (AD 960–1279) was an era of idyllic landscape painters that ended with Ghengis Khan's arrival in 1213. The Ming's (1368–1644) blue and white porcelain is its enduring legacy. The last dynasty, the Manchu or Qing (1644–1912) came to power at a cost of 25 million lives and ended with the overthrow of the emperor.

➧ ***Buddhism, Communism, Confucianism, Ghengis Khan***

CHIPPENDALE, THOMAS (1718–79)

English furniture-maker. Born in Yorkshire, Chippendale was an inspired and gifted furniture-maker, whose name is now synonymous with fine antiques. He also wrote books that greatly furthered cabinet making as an art.

CHLOROPHYLL

Group of pigments that gives green colour to most plants. Chlorophyll absorbs light energy which is converted, by the process of photosynthesis, into organic chemicals.

➧ ***Photosynthesis***

CHRISTIANITY

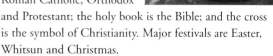

Established in the first third of the first century AD by Jesus Christ. His 12 disciples began the spread of His word and there are now one billion Christians worldwide. The main branches are Roman Catholic, Orthodox and Protestant; the holy book is the Bible; and the cross is the symbol of Christianity. Major festivals are Easter, Whitsun and Christmas.

Jesus was God incarnate, born of the Virgin Mary. He was crucified to remove the sins of the people, as remembered by Communion services, then resurrected to eternal life. Christians believe in God's omnipotence. The Christian message has led to educational and charitable foundations, such as the monastic orders of the Franciscans and Jesuits, and it has also been used to justify political ends, for example, the Crusades.

➧ ***Bible, Catholicism, Christmas, Easter, Eastern Orthodox Church, Protestantism***

CHRISTMAS

The most important celebration in the Christian calendar; said to be the birthday of Christ. Now a largely secular celebration it is believed to be based on much older, pagan celebrations to mark mid-winter. The celebration is marked by the exchange of gifts, festive meals and decorations.

Christianity

CHURCHES

Buildings for Christian worship and services led by a priest. Although differing architecturally due to era and geography, the key elements are constant. Externally a church often has a spire or bell tower, for visibility and to call the faithful. Placed centrally is the altar, a table for symbolic sacrifice, on which the communion bread and wine are prepared. The lectern, a stand for the Bible, and the pulpit, a platform for preaching, are also prominent to aid the spreading of the word of God.

Bible, Cathedrals, Catholicism, Christianity, Protestantism

CHURCHILL, WINSTON (1874–1965)

English politician, soldier, writer and painter. Churchill fought in the Sudan (1898) and served as a war correspondent in the Boer War before entering parliament in 1900. During World War I he planned the disastrous campaign at Gallipoli and resigned as first lord of the admiralty. He returned to office in 1917, holding a variety of posts before becoming chancellor of the Exchequer in 1924. During the 1930s Churchill opposed appeasement of Germany and condemned Chamberlain. In 1940 Churchill was made prime minister of the wartime coalition government. He excelled as leader but lost the election of 1945, returning as prime minister 1951–55.

World War I, World War II

ABOVE: Celebrating a traditional Christmas in Finland are Jack Frost and Father Christmas.

RIGHT: Horses, clowns and acrobats are popular circus attractions the world over.

FAR RIGHT: Dusk falls over America's famous New York cityscape.

CINEMATOGRAPHY

Art and techniques of film photography. Cinematography includes the setting of a scene, the lighting of the set, the location, etc. Cinematography also refers to the shots used, such as close-up, and to the technical equipment employed (e.g. camera filters). A cinematographer (or director of photography) is usually employed to create the director's desired effects.

Films

CIRCUS

Traditional form of entertainment, often featuring animals. Other acts include acrobats and clowns. The circus is fading in popularity in many countries due to concerns over the welfare of the animals used.

Animal Rights

CITIES

A large or important town, usually with a significant national or regional administrative role. In the UK, a town needs to have a cathedral (the seat of a bishop) to be classified as a city. In the USA, the term is applied much more loosely.

Cities developed in the ancient world, sometimes as states in their own right, such as Athens and Mexico City. Cities have gradually developed in importance as modern transportation and communications have made it possible to accumulate larger populations over more sprawling areas.

The largest cities in the world are Tokyo (Japan) at about 27 million inhabitants, Bombay (India) with 18 mllion, Saõ Paulo (Brazil) with 17.8 million, Shanghai (China) with 17.2 million, and New York City (USA) with 16.6 million. Cities use around three-quarters of the world's supplies of food, energy and resources, reflecting the fact that most of the world's population now live in them.

CIVIL WAR

War between the peoples of the same nation. Civil wars prove socially and economically devastating for the country concerned. The American Civil War cost more lives than all America's other wars put together until the Vietnam War. Its emotional scars proved astonishingly durable. More recently, the Yugoslavian disintegration into nationalist states has left terrible destruction and resentment.

➠ ***American Civil War, English Civil War, Spanish Civil War***

CIVIL WAR, AMERICAN (1861–65)

'War between the States' between the Southern (Confederate) and the Northern (Union) states. Bloody and costly, the war ended in total defeat for the South, the end of slavery, and the assassination of Abraham Lincoln, a unionist.

In 1861, South Carolina seceded from the Union, rapidly followed by the other southern states. The origin lay in the balance of free (northern) and slave-owning (southern) states in the US Congress. While slavery was an increasing moral issue, the war was based on holding the Union together.

The sides were not equally balanced. The North had far more men and more resources but poor military leadership compromised these advantages until the tide was turned at Gettysburg in Pennsylvania, and Vicksburg, Missouri, in July 1863, the year in which Lincoln announced slave emancipation to be a war aim. The South finally surrendered at Appomattox in 1865, leaving many of its cities razed and its plantations destroyed. Reconstruction was bitter and protracted.

CIVIL WAR, ENGLISH (1642–49)

War between the Charles I and parliament, leading to defeat for Charles and his execution.

The English Civil War grew out of the increasingly arbitrary rule of the first two Stuart monarchs of England, James I and Charles I. A series of unconstitutional acts created a conflict over the powers wielded by the Crown and parliament. The war broke out when Charles raised his standard in 1642. Regional support was unbalanced, the Royalists enjoying support mainly in the poorer areas of the north and west, while parliament always retained London.

Initial Royalist successes soon dwindled when the Scots joined parliament in 1643, and parliament won the Battle of Marston Moor in 1644. A final defeat followed at Naseby in June 1645. Charles surrendered in 1646 but escaped to start the Second Civil War in 1648, this time with Scottish support. He was captured in December, tried and executed in January 1649.

➠ ***Kings of England, Oliver Cromwell***

CIVIL WAR, SPANISH (1936–39)

War following a failed military coup against the Republican government developing into a conflict between conservative interests and socialism, anticipating World War II.

The election of a left-wing government in February 1936 was followed by a military-led Nationalist uprising in July, gaining strongholds in the north, island possessions, Morocco and some cities. Both sides imposed ruthless control on their regions through murder and execution. The Nationalists, led by General Francisco Franco, received support from the Fascist states of Germany and Italy. The Republicans, led by Francisco Largo Caballero, then Juan Negrín from 1937, were helped by the Soviet Union and individual foreign volunteers. Nationalist victory followed vicious fighting, a drive through Republican territory and Communist factional divisions. They took Madrid on 28 March 1939.

➧ ***Francisco Franco***

CLASSICAL ART, MUSIC AND LITERATURE

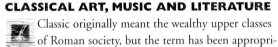

Classic originally meant the wealthy upper classes of Roman society, but the term has been appropriated to mean any works of art, architecture or design from the ancient Greek and Roman societies. Art during the Classical era became a significant contributor to the culture of the Graeco-Roman societies, as the success of their civilizations meant more money and time was available to be spent on purely aesthetic pursuits, such as the creation and patronage of the arts. The Classical style was gracefully balanced and harmonious; it sought a perfection in idealized beauty. The Classical era further inspired the Renaissance and later Neoclassicism.

➧ ***Ancient Greece, Neoclassicism, Renaissance, Ancient Rome***

CLASSIFICATION OF LIVING ORGANISMS

Organization of all living organisms using a system invented by the Swedish scientist Carolus Linnaeus (1707–78) and subsequently adopted by all scientists. This system, also known as taxonomy, is carried out according to the selection of important, shared characteristics. Animals with jointed bodies and six legs, for example, are placed in the class *Insecta.* Individual species are further identified by two names (binomial nomenclature) and are recognized by biologists throughout the world. The names are often based on Latin words e.g. *Homo* (man) *sapiens* (wise) is the name given to humans. Modern taxonomy also aims to reflect evolutionary paths and relationships.

➧ ***Taxonomy***

CLEOPATRA (69–30 BC)

Egyptian queen. The last of the Ptolemaic dynasty to rule Egypt, Cleopatra exerted her charm over Julius Caesar and Marc Antony by both of whom she had several children. She committed suicide by snake-bite.

➧ ***Julius Caesar, Ancient Egypt***

LEFT: Decorating the walls of this taverna in Pompeii is a beautifully preserved example of Classical Art.
ABOVE: Helen Mirren stars as Cleopatra alongside Alan Rickman's Anthony in London's Olivier Theatre's adaptation of Shakespeare's play in 1998.

CLIMATE

Long-term prevailing weather conditions of a geographical area. Determined by latitude and altitude as well as by variables such as solar activity, wind and ocean currents, atmospheric conditions and rain. Climates vary hugely around the globe but also vary through time. Meteorologists record prevailing weather conditions over a period of time to monitor changes to the climate. These records have helped identify various climatic regions e.g. tropical, equatorial and polar regions and long-term changes to them.

Weather

CLOUDS

Masses of water or ice particles visibly suspended in the sky. Cool air causes water vapour to condense into tiny droplets, forming clouds. The temperature at which condensation occurs and prevailing winds affect the formation of the cloud. Clouds represent an important part of the water cycle as water returns to the Earth's surface as rain.

Rain

COAL

Black rock, formed from compressed vegetation, which is used as a fuel. The most important coal beds were formed during the Carboniferous period, 345 to 280 million years ago. Coal is a widespread energy source, but the extent to which the by-product of burning coal – carbon dioxide – has caused global warming is yet to be determined.

Carbon

COCA COLA

Brand of carbonated soft drink originating in the US. Originally a health tonic it is now perhaps the best-known brand name in the world.

COCAINE

Narcotic, stimulant drug extracted from coca leaves. It is addictive in its raw state but can also be processed into the extremely addictive 'crack cocaine'.

Drugs

COCKTAILS

A (usually) alcoholic drink mixed from a variety of ingredients. Cocktails date from the early nineteenth century in the US and had spread to the UK by the 1850s, but they only became really fashionable in the 1920s. The most popular cocktail worldwide is the martini.

COFFEE

Drink made from the ground and roasted beans of the *Coffea* shrub. This plant, originally a native of Ethiopia, is now cultivated through the tropical regions of the globe. First drunk by the Arabs in the fourteenth century, coffee took a further 300 years to reach Europe, where it was first sold in Vienna, Austria. Coffee contains the drug caffeine, a mild stimulant, which can have a detrimental effect on health if consumed in great quantities.

COINS

Pieces of metal of a known weight and fineness, bearing some mark of origin as a guarantee, developed in Asia Minor in the eighth century BC and independently in China about the same time. They are among the most important documentary material for the art and history of all civilizations.

COLD WAR (1945–90)

Name given to the constant economic, ideological and political sparring between the Soviet Union and its satellites, and the US and western Europe after World War II.

From the Russian Revolution of 1917 the forces of capitalism in the West distrusted the growth of Communism. Germany's defeat in 1945 led to a division of the spoils between West and East, and a pathological suspicion by each side that the other represented an economic and military threat. In 1949 the West organized itself into NATO (North Atlantic Treaty Organisation), and the Soviet bloc created a counter military alliance in the Warsaw Pact (1955). The conflict was sustained by espionage, competition over military hardware, and words, but ended with the break-up of the Soviet Union in 1990.

➧ ***NATO, Warsaw Pact***

COLOMBIA

North-west South American country. **Capital:** Bogotá. **Other principal cities:** Medellín, Cali. **Climate:** tropical coastal, temperate highlands. **Geographical features:** eastern plains give way to central highlands and flat coastal land. **Main language:** Spanish. **Main religion:** Roman Catholicism. **Rule:** democratic republic. **Currency:** peso. **Primary industries:** mining, agriculture, and illegal drugs. **Exports:** emeralds, coffee, cocaine, meat, hides and skins, sugar, tobacco, petroleum.

Although Colombia has considerable natural resources, its most valuable export is cocaine. Despite attempts to clamp down, Colombia's proximity to the US markets, and its remote regions, have made cocaine impossible to control.

➧ ***Cocaine***

COLONIALISM

Political policy by which one country subjugates another to is own rule, with the aim of creating an empire. This can be by economic, religious or military means.

By the end of the nineteenth century most of the less-developed world was under the rule of a European power, Britain, France, Belgium and the Netherlands all having extensive overseas possessions. Much debate continues around the ethical aspects of this subjugation. There is no doubt that exploitation occurred; however many countries received significant benefits in return. Some people view the spread of American culture across the globe as simply colonialism made politically acceptable.

➧ ***British Empire***

COLOUR

Sensation seen in the eye when light of particular wavelengths enters it. White light contains all visible wavelengths; colours are seen when some wavelengths are missing.

COLUMBUS, CHRISTOPHER (1451–1506)

Portuguese explorer. Born in Genoa, Columbus went to sea at the age of 14 and travelled widely between Iceland and Madeira, gaining invaluable experience of the Atlantic. His ambition of leading an expedition westward in search of India to prove that the world was round was realized in 1492 when he discovered America.

COMETS

Small bodies in the Solar System containing a mixture of rocky and icy materials. When a comet is close to the Sun some ice evaporates to form a region of gas and dust called the coma. Particles from the Sun can expel some of this material to form a tail.

➧ ***Solar System***

COMICS

Series of narrative drawings bound into a magazine or book. Comics stem from the comic strips of popular newspapers. The first colour comic strip was in *The New York Times* in 1896, a character called Yellow Kid. During the 1930s comics grew in popularity, following the adventures of such characters as Superman and Buck Rogers.

➜ ***Caricature, Graphic Art***

COMMONWEALTH

Trading and cultural alliance of countries, mostly drawn from ex-colonies of the British Empire. There are 53 member states, along with a further 19 dependent territories, that meet every two years. There is no official charter or constitution.

➜ ***British Empire, Colonialism***

COMMUNISM

Political ideology of revolutionary socialism. Communism became a defining feature of twentieth-century history but only a few countries, like China and Cuba, have retained it.

Communism was developed by Friedrich Engels and Karl Marx, and published in the *Communist Manifesto* of 1848. They believed in common ownership of resources, divided according to needs, and work allocated according to ability. To achieve this, capitalist interests (where control and ownership of resources is restricted) should be toppled through working-class (proletariat) revolution. This was seen as part of the natural progression of development.

The 1917 Russian Revolution established the first Communist state, and Communism became a feature of politics in many other nations. The aftermath of World War II saw it more widely established in Eastern Europe, China and Cuba. Communist states increasingly found that oppression was needed to maintain stability, while technological development lagged behind the capitalist West. The Soviet Union's inability to maintain its dominance led to the collapse of its bloc by 1990.

➜ ***Karl Marx***

LEFT: The comic strip has grown steadily in popularity since World War II. Old, well-preserved comics can fetch high prices at collectors' auctions.
RIGHT: Radiohead's number one album in the US, UK and Europe.

COMPACT DISCS

Aluminium discs with a plastic coating, used for storing digital information in the form of microscopic pits etched into the aluminium using a laser.

COMPUTERS

Electronic devices which can process data under the control of a program. Nearly all modern computers are digital, in which all information is represented using two digits, 0 and 1. The main components of a computer are the central processing unit (CPU), which carries out all the arithmetic and logic operations; the memory, which stores the program and data; and the logic arrays, which transfer information. Peripheral devices are used to input and output information. These normally include a keyboard, a screen and mass storage units such as disk drives and CD-Rom drives.

CONFUCIUS (551–479 BC)

Chinese philosopher also called Kong Zi. Born into a poor family, Confucius aimed to relieve the suffering of the poor through administrative reform: his philosophy became fundamental to Chinese government. Confucius propounded emperor and ancestor worship and sacrifices to heaven and earth. Despite the 1912 revolution the Chinese continued to base their political and social organization on Confucianism. *The Analects of Confucius* is a compilation of his teachings.

Chinese Dynasties, Philosophy

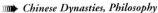

CONGO, DEMOCRATIC REPUBLIC OF (FORMERLY ZAIRE)

Central southern African country. **Capital:** Kinshasa. **Other principal cities:** Lubumbashi, Kananga, Matadi. **Climate:** equatorial, hotter and higher humidity in north and west. **Geographical features:** mountains, plateaux, rich mineral resources. **Main language:** French. **Main religion:** Christianity. **Rule:** military. **Currency:** zaïre. **Primary industries:** mining, petroleum, refining, agriculture (mainly subsistence). **Exports:** copper, diamonds, cobalt, copper, petroleum.

Africa

CONNERY, SEAN (b. 1930)

Scottish actor. Connery played James Bond six times before retiring from the role in 1971 after *Diamonds are Forever*. He received an Oscar for his role in *The Untouchables* in 1987.

Academy Awards

ABOVE: A Confucius Day Ceremony at Taipei, Taiwan.
ABOVE RIGHT: Captain Cook's landing at Botany Bay, Australia in 1770.
BELOW RIGHT: The spectacular colours in this coral and its accompanying fish, off the coast of Thailand, are illuminated by the photographers lights.

CONSERVATION

Preservation, protection and efficient management of all natural resources, including that of living organisms. The sustainable use by a country of its natural resources has long been recognized as essential for economic growth. It has become apparent in recent times that practices in farming, livestock management and urban development that ignore conservation can have a huge impact on all aspects of ecology. It is now recognized that a conflict of interests may exist between a corporate drive for profits and the need to conserve natural resources for future generations. This conflict is increasingly reflected in conservation legislation in the UK and Europe.

Ecology, Worldwide Fund for Nature

CONSERVATIVE PARTY

One of the two principal British political parties. Before 1830 the Conservatives were called Tories and traditionally represented the interests of landed society and property. In more recent years the Conservatives became associated with capitalism, being supported more widely by industry and commerce. Since World War II governments have alternated between Labour and Conservative, Conservatives until 1997 often enjoying larger majorities in parliament. Labour's alliance with the trade unions and the industrial action of the 1970s led to the Conservative control of government 1979–97, but measures like the poll tax proved catastrophically unpopular. In 1997 the party suffered a devastating defeat, reducing its parliamentary seats to the lowest number for 90 years.

British Politicians

CONSTABLE, JOHN (1776–1837)

British landscape painter. Constable was raised in the countryside of Suffolk – it was this countryside that was to both inspire him to become a painter and to dominate his work. Constable tried to realistically depict the changing beauty of nature. During his lifetime, he did not achieve the level of recognition that his work has since aroused. He became an Associate and Academician at the Royal Academy of Arts, London, but received more favourable esteem in Europe, particularly in France, where one of his most famous works, the *Hay Wain*, won a prize. The Barbizon movement and Eugene Delacroix were both inspired by Constable.

→ *Barbizon, Eugene Delacroix*

CONSTELLATIONS

Areas in the night sky containing a number of stars which form a recognizable pattern to the naked eye. In early times the constellations were named after a mythical figure, animal or object to which they were thought to bear some resemblance. There are 88 constellations now recognized, of widely varying size and shape. The stars within a constellation usually have no association with one another, but simply lie in approximately the same line of sight.

→ *Astrology, Stars*

COOK, CAPTAIN JAMES (1728–79)

English sailor and explorer. Cook's navigational skills led him to command voyages of discovery in the South Pacific. He explored New Zealand, discovered eastern Australia, Antarctica and Hawaii. His scientific approach to voyages led to his solution for avoiding scurvy in his crew. He was killed by Hawaiians in a dispute over a stolen boat.

COPERNICUS, NICOLAUS (1473–1543)

Polish astronomer who proposed that the Sun, not the Earth, lay at the centre of the Solar System. His work was not published until after his death.

CORAL REEFS

Rock-like structures that develop in shallow tropical waters. Caused by the action of tiny marine organisms. These organisms, polyps, live in large colonies and secrete a calcareous substance that, over time, builds up to form the reef. Coral reefs support a huge range of marine life and represent a unique and irreplaceable ecosystem.

CORTÉS, HERNÁN (1485–1547)

Spanish soldier. Hernán Fernando Cortés (also Cortéz) conquered the Aztec Empire of Mexico for Spain between 1519–21, at the head of an army of 600. Welcomed as a god, his true intent was uncovered and he was ejected by the emperor Montezuma. Cortés returned, strengthened with local allies, and seized the Aztec capital.

→ *Aztecs*

COSTA RICA

Central American country between Nicaragua and Panama. **Capital:** San José. **Other principal cities:** Limón, Puntarenas. **Climate:** tropical. **Geographical features:** tropical coasts enclose a high central plateau. **Main language:** Spanish. **Main religion:** Roman Catholicism. **Rule:** liberal democracy. **Currency:** colón. **Primary industries:** agriculture. **Exports:** bananas, beef, cocoa, coffee, sugar, textiles.

Costa Rica's dependence on agricultural exports has made it susceptible to the effects of variable coffee prices. Most of the population live in the central highlands, and much of the land remains forested.

COSTUMES

Cultures and regional groupings have often chosen distinctive modes of dress, often referred to as a National Costume. The importance of these have declined greatly in recent years, with the spread of western culture across the globe. However most are maintained in a ceremonial way if nothing else: notably the Scottish kilt, the red robes of the Masai and the lederhosen of the Tirol.

→ *Fashion, Scottish Clans*

COUNTRY AND WESTERN

Mixture of two musical genres: Country (rural folk based upon traditional music) and Western (narrative cowboy songs accompanied by guitar). Popularized by radio and the music halls of Nashville, US during the 1940s, the music was originally linked with white Southern Americans. Simply structured, Country and Western emphasizes a down-to-earth attitude.

COW

Common name applied to domesticated cattle that are used to supply milk, leather and by-products such as gelatine. Of great economic significance across the globe.

CRAWFORD, JOAN (1904–77)

American actress. Crawford was renowned for her fiercely strong, often embittered female leads. Crawford's reputation became bound to these harsh roles by a negative portrayal in her daughter's biography.

CRAZES

Toys or pastimes that are briefly fashionable. Seventeenth-century Europeans paid small fortunes for tulip bulbs, children in the 1970s risked life and limb with K'Nockers (two plastic balls on string that were knocked together) and now children mug each other for the latest Pokemon card. Such crazes have now become powerful selling tools and much money is spent in an attempt to produce the next big thing, children usually being the target.

➧ *Fashion*

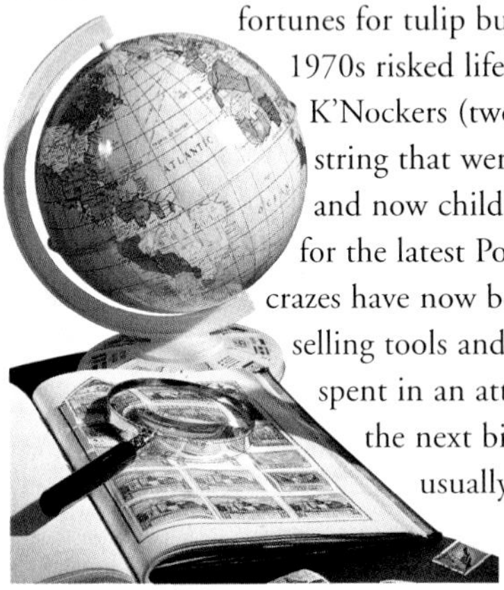

ABOVE: Crazes fade in and out of fashion. One of the most enduring crazes, with a worldwide following, is the collection of stamps.
RIGHT: Winning runs from England's Alex Stewart as Shane Warne stands by, unable to prevent Australia losing to England at a test match at Edgbaston in 1997.
FAR RIGHT: Oliver Cromwell, parliamentary leader following Charles I's execution.

CRICKET (1774)

Game played with bat and ball by two teams of 11 players each, with rules first codified in 1774. It is the national summer sport of England and is played extensively throughout Commonwealth countries. The rules of the game are impenetrable to the uninitiated, people tending to either love or loathe it. The two major international competitions are the Ashes between Australia and England, and the Wisden Cup between the West Indies and England.

CRIMEAN WAR (1853–56)

War between Russia and the allied forces of Britain, France, Turkey and later Sardinia. In 1853, Russia invaded the Balkans but was expelled by Austria, and also destroyed a Turkish naval squadron at Sinope. The French were in a religious dispute with Russia over Catholic and Orthodox interests in the Holy Land.

Suspicious of Russia's plans to increase power in southern Europe, the British and French mounted a campaign to capture the Russian port of Sevastopol in the Crimea in 1854. A year-long siege followed as well as several battles, marked by incompetent leadership and catastrophic losses from disease. In 1855, a French victory at Malakov defeated Russia. The Treaty of Paris in 1856 closed the war.

➡ ***Florence Nightingale***

CROATIA

European country on the northern Adriatic opposite Italy. **Capital:** Zagreb. **Other principal cities:** Osijek, Rijeka. **Climate:** temperate Mediterranean. **Geographical features:** a long coastline with scattered islands, and a narrow corridor leading to the inland mountainous zone. **Main language:** Serbo-Croat. **Main religion:** Roman Catholicism. **Rule:** democracy. **Currency:** kuna. **Primary industries:** agriculture, petro-chemicals, shipbuilding, tourism. **Exports:** machinery, manufactured goods, chemicals, food.

Croatia is one of the independent states created after the break-up of Yugoslavia in 1991, but it struggled for its independence in a vicious war with Serbia. The landscape is extremely variable, with Mediterranean plants like grapes and olives grown on coastal slopes. Ethnic tensions remain, with a small resident Serbian population.

➡ ***Europe***

CRO-MAGNON MAN

Early *Homo sapiens* and probable ancestors of modern Europeans. Cro-Magnons were cave-dwellers with a complex culture. Unlike Neanderthals they possessed well-defined chins and high foreheads.

➡ ***Human Evolution***

CROMWELL, OLIVER (1599–1658)

Lord Protector of the English Commonwealth from 1653. A landowner and member of parliament, Cromwell came to the fore as a soldier fighting against Charles I during the English Civil War. Frustrated by Charles I's intrigues to reverse his defeat, Cromwell brought Charles to trial and execution. Notorious for suppression of Ireland, Cromwell also moved against opposition in parliament. Made Protector in 1653, Cromwell held executive power and was a dictator in all but name. Although a sound administrator, Cromwell created nothing permanent. The Restoration swept his regime away.

➡ ***Charles I of England, English Civil War***

CROQUET

Outdoor game played with mallets and balls. The object is to negotiate a course of hoops in the least strokes. It is known to have been played in sixteenth-century France.

CRUISE, TOM (b. 1962)

American actor. Cruise's star status was secured with the 1986 film *Top Gun*. Reputed to be a committed actor, Cruise has gained much respect for roles in films such as *The Rain Man* (1988) and *Magnolia* (2000).

➡ ***Films***

CRUSTACEANS

Common name for a group of animals that includes lobsters, crabs and shrimps. Crustaceans are predominantly aquatic but there are some terrestrial species, such as the woodlouse. Crustaceans are arthropods and therefore have external skeletons and paired, jointed limbs. The first pair of limbs may be modified for use in feeding, locomotion and reproductive behaviour. Like most arthropods crustaceans are a successful group that shows a wide range of habitat and diversity of lifestyle. They range in size from the tiny shrimp-like krill, the foodstuff of many whales, to a spider crab with an impressive leg-span of 3.5 m (11.5 ft).

CRYSTAL PALACE

Designed by the English architect Sir Joseph Paxton (1803–65), the glass and iron palace housed the world's first international exhibition in 1851. The building was also the first example of prefabrication – its parts were made in a factory before being assembled in Hyde Park. Later it was dismantled and relocated to a site near Sydenham, South London. The exhibition contained eight miles of displays. It was detroyed by fire in 1936.

➤ *Architecture*

CUBA

Caribbean island nation close to Florida. **Capital:** Havana. **Other principal cities:** Santiago de Cuba, Camagüy. **Climate:** tropical. **Geographical features:** central mountains and a very long east-west coast line. **Main language:** Spanish. **Main religion:** Roman Catholicism. **Rule:** Communist republic. **Currency:** peso. **Primary industries:** sugar, tobacco and mining. **Exports:** sugar, tobacco, coffee, nickel, fish, fruit, medical supplies.

The Cuban economy relies mainly on sugar but tobacco and tourism are very important earners. Cuba has suffered from its former dependence on the Soviet Union and the government's commitment to communism. The US has maintained a trade embargo and Cuba has therefore not benefited from its proximity to Florida. Many goods remain in short supply.

➤ *Fidel Castro*

CUBISM

Style of art created by Pablo Picasso and Georges Braque, following inspiration from the posthumously displayed works of Paul Cézanne and his advice that nature should be explored through the use of 'spheres and cones'. Cubist painting, while still representational, was multi-faceted and two-dimensional, so much so that often they appear abstract.

➤ *Paul Cézanne, Pablo Picasso*

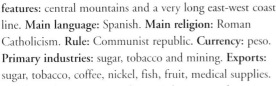

CULTURAL REVOLUTION

Subversive ideology in China that was the culmination of Mao Zedong's fears and beliefs during the last decade of his power (1966–76). Concerned by what he saw as the failure of Russian Communism and unhappy with his proposed successors, in 1966 Mao created the Red Guard from urban youths, giving them

instructions to destroy the traditional and the bourgeois. The Red Guard soon became violent and factional, fighting was widespread and the effect on China both socially and economically was devastating. Becoming disillusioned by the Red Guards' infighting, Mao involved the military. The Cultural Revolution came to a close with Mao's death in September 1976.

➡ ***Mao Zedong***

CURIE, PIERRE AND MARIE

Husband and wife, pioneers in the investigation of radioactivity. Pierre was French, Marie was born in Poland. They discovered the elements radium and polonium in 1898, and shared the Nobel Prize for Physics in 1903. After Pierre's death, Marie continued research and was awarded the Nobel Prize for Chemistry in 1911.

➡ ***Chemical Elements, Nobel Prize***

CURLING

Similar in many ways to bowls, this game is played with polished granite stones on ice. One of the national games of Scotland, the first world championships were held in 1959.

➡ ***Bowls, Winter Sports***

CURRENCIES

Tangible form of money. Each country will tend to have its own unique currency as a matter of national pride. They have taken many forms over the years, including sea shells and even stone discs weighing over a ton! Currencies that are readily exchangeable for others are referred to as Hard (US dollar, pound sterling etc.) those that are not are called Soft (Maldivian rufiya, Kenyan shilling etc.).

➡ ***Economy, Gold***

CYCLING

Sport and pastime utilizing the pedal bicycle. Races can take place on custom-made tracks, roads or cross-country. The most famous race is the annual Tour de France, which was first held in 1903.

CYCLONES

Common term used to describe weather systems involving storms that are accompanied by patterns of extremely low atmospheric pressure and wind.

➡ ***Hurricanes***

CYPRUS

Eastern Mediterranean island off Syria and Turkey, divided between the Turkish north (not internationally recognized) and Greek south. **Capital:** Nicosia. **Other principal cities:** Morphou, Limassol, Larnaca, Kyrenia, Famagusta. **Climate:** Mediterranean. **Geographical features:** barren Kyrenia mountains in the north, fertile southern plain. **Main languages:** Greek (south), Turkish (north). **Main religions:** Greek orthodox, Islam. **Rule:** democratic republic (divided). **Currency:** Cyprus pound, Turkish lira. **Primary industries:** tourism, agriculture. **Exports:** fruit, potatoes, wine, grapes, cement, textiles, footwear.

CZECH REPUBLIC

Land-locked central European country. **Capital:** Prague. **Other principal cities:** Brno, Ostrava, Olomouc. **Climate:** temperate. **Geographical features:** hills and plateaus surrounded by mountains. **Main language:** Czech. **Main religions:** Roman Catholicism and other Christian denominations. **Rule:** democracy. **Currency:** koruna. **Primary industries:** manufacturing, mining. **Exports:** machinery, transportation equipment, coal, steel, chemicals, ceramics, clothing, glass.

The Czech Republic (formerly the western part of Czechoslovakia) is primarily an industrial nation thanks to its coal and mineral resources, its relatively well-educated and professional population, and proximity to western European markets. The nation has successfully managed the change to capitalism from Communism since 1991.

➡ ***Europe, Prague***

FAR LEFT: View of the Placa de la Revolution Jose Marti in Havana, Cuba.
LEFT: Pablo Picasso's Man with a Pipe. *Picasso was one of the creators of the style of art known as Cubism.*
ABOVE: The skies darken ominously as a cyclone approaches the Pacific Island of Tuamotus.

DADAISM (1915–22)

Dada was a nonsense word describing an ostensibly anti-art movement (*c.* 1915 to 1922). The movement was a reaction against what was seen as the elitist art establishment. One of its lasting contributions to art was the ready-made object, as created by Marcel Duchamp (one of the leading Dadaists). Dadaism was greatly influential among the Surrealists.

Marcel Duchamp, Surrealism

DALAI LAMA (b. 1935)

Spiritual and temporal head of Tibet, enthroned in 1940. He temporarily fled when the Chinese invaded Tibet (1950–51) and then campaigned for Tibetan independence.

DALÍ, SALVADOR (1904–89)

Spanish artist. Dalí was one of the leading figures of the Surrealist movement. He has become one of the most publicly known artists of the twentieth century, largely through his own grandiose self-proclamations and entertaining persona. He began art training in Madrid but was expelled from the school in 1926. Greatly influenced by Sigmund Freud and ideas of the sub-conscious, Dalí was an ideal addition to the Surrealist group. Dalí described his paintings as 'hand-painted dream photographs' and many of his works, such as *The Persistence of Memory* (1931), are filled with symbolic references to himself, to sex and to death.

Sugmund Freud, Surrealism

DANCE

Fundamental form of expression using movements of the body that are both rhythmical and patterned. Dance is one of the most ancient art forms and evidence of its existence has been found in almost all cultures: ancient Egyptian Hieroglyphics show dancers, as do Greek and Roman relics. Dance has been used for ceremonial, theatrical or for purely entertainment reasons. Dance is continually evolving: from primitive and folk dances through the reserved waltzes of the eighteenth century, on to the refined culture of ballet or the sexually charged salsa dance of South America, dance remains an amazingly divergent and culturally reflective art form.

Ballet

DANCE MUSIC

Popular music designed primarily to dance to. There have been enormous variations in style over time, from nineteenth-century waltzes to house, trance and techno in the twenty-first century.

Jazz

DANES

Inhabitants of Denmark, most south-westerly of the Scandinavian countries. The Danes raided the coasts of England and Ireland in the ninth and tenth centuries. Cnut (Canute) was briefly king of England (1017–35) as well as Denmark, Norway, Iceland and Greenland.

Vikings

DARWIN, CHARLES (1809–82)

Influential British scientist and author of the innovative concept of an evolutionary process, known as 'natural selection'. Charles Darwin voyaged around the world on board HMS *Beagle* observing animal and plant life. These observations led him to believe that organisms may have undergone selective and gradual changes over a long period of time, as an adaptation to their environments. In 1859 his book, *On the Origin of Species by process of Natural Selection,* was published and sold out amidst a public furore. Although other notable scientists had contributed to Darwin's ideas, his theory rocked the foundations of society, threatening contemporary biblical and scientific beliefs about the origins of life on Earth.

➧ ***Natural Selection***

DAVIS, BETTE (1908–89)

US actress. Davis is best known for her melodramatic starring roles in films such as *Jezebel* (1938) and, most famously, alongside Joan Crawford in *What Ever Happened to Baby Jane?* (1962).

➧ ***Joan Crawford, Films***

DDT

Powerful insecticide which was formerly widely used against malaria-carrying mosquito, but due to its toxic and persistent nature is now banned in many countries.

DE NIRO, ROBERT (b. 1943)

US actor. De Niro is renowned for his use of method acting, as evinced in the 1980 film *Raging Bull.* De Niro is one of America's most accomplished film actors.

➧ ***Films***

DE STIJL

Dutch for 'the style', denoting a philosophically based art movement followed by Piet Mondrian, which proposed the confinement of art to geometrical shapes and lines, utilizing only primary colours with black, grey and white.

➧ ***Piet Mondrian***

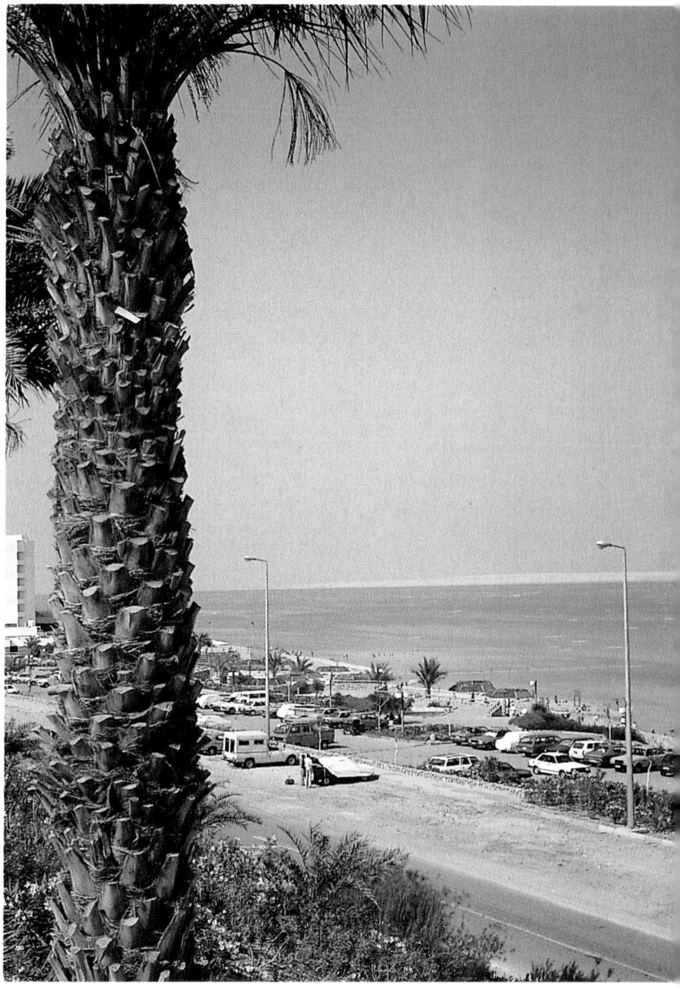

DEAD SEA

Salt lake bounded by Israel, the West Bank and Jordan. It is located 400 m (1312 ft) below sea level, giving it the lowest water surface on Earth.

DEAN, JAMES (1931–5)

US actor. A cinematic icon, Dean's early death preserved his image as an outstanding actor. Dean starred in only three films: *Rebel Without a Cause* (1955), *East of Eden* (1955) and *Giant* (1956).

➧ ***Films***

TOP LEFT: An example of work produced by the Dadaist movement by Francis Picabia (1879–1953). The movement was a rebellion against the established art world.
ABOVE: The Dead Sea as viewed from Zohar, Israel.

DEBUSSY, CLAUDE (1862–1918)

Leading French composer. Debussy studied at the Paris Conservatoire from 1872, primarily as a pianist. In 1884 he won the prestigious Prix de Rome. Debussy was influenced by the Impressionist painters and poets, with several of whom he forged friendships. During the 1890s this influence led Debussy to create a single-themed music in opposition to the more traditional variance upon themes. With music such as his celebrated *Prélude à l'aprés-midi d'un faune*, Debussy created a layering of melodies and chords that was emotionally evocative. Technically innovative, Debussy utilized the whole-tone scale and chromaticism. His work remains a great inspiration in music today.

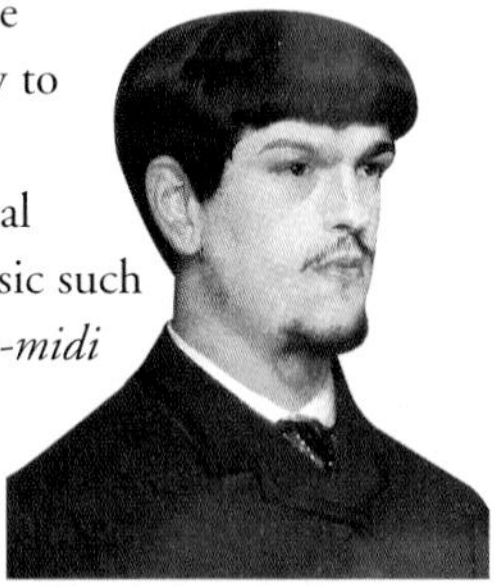

➤ ***Impressionism***

DECORATIVE ARTS

Term applied to art or craftwork that has a function, such as pottery, but is equally designed to please the eye and attract attention. Decorative art is evident in the relics of even the earliest societies and is deeply entrenched in our culture with the upsurge of interior design and the impact of groups like the Arts and Crafts movement.

➤ ***Art Deco, Arts and Crafts Movement, Art Nouveau, Interior Design***

DEGAS, EDGAR (1834–1917)

French painter. Degas began his career as a historical painter but soon moved to contemporary subjects. His work was included in most of the Impressionist Exhibitions of the late-nineteenth century, but he does not easily fit into this category. Degas' most celebrated works contain scenes of dancers or women at work or at their toilette. He was interested in the exploration of movement that these scenes offered and in attempting to capture moments from everyday life. Some of Degas' paintings proved controversial – many people were offended by the realism and modernity of his work.

➤ ***Impressionism***

DELACROIX, EUGÈNE (1798–1863)

French Romantic painter. Delacroix's work had a great and lasting impact upon art; his emphasis on colour and seemingly impulsive brushwork was influential to the Impressionists in particular. Perhaps his most famous paintings are those produced after his 1832 visit to Morocco, among them *Women of Algiers* (1934). The visit was an inspirational event in Delacroix's career and the theme of North Africa reappears often in his work from this date (depicting the exotic was common in much Romantic art). Delacroix is also known for his journals, letters and articles that offer the reader an insight into not just the author, but also the society of the day.

➤ ***Impressionism, Romantic***

DEMOCRACY

System of government for the people, by the people, normally through election. The word derives from the Greek words *demos* ('community') and *kratos* ('power'). Modern democratic principles developed in the American and French Revolutions. They repudiated the right of a single individual – the monarch – to control a community, and the rights of assemblies elected from restricted parts of the community. British democracy is based on the principle of universal adult suffrage (the right to vote), but this did not come about for men until a series of nineteenth-century acts removed the requirement for a property owning qualification. Women were not included on the same terms as men until 1928 in Britain.

➤ ***Suffrage***

DEMOCRATIC PARTY (1792)

One of the two principal US political parties. Founded in 1792, the party came to control all the southern states seceding from the Union in 1861–62. Since the Civil War, the party has remained associated with the Southern states, liberal views, and the blue-collar workers of industrial cities, but none of these loyalties has proved cast-iron.

➤ ***American Civil War***

ABOVE: A portrait of the French composer Claude Debussy in Rome in 1884.
FAR RIGHT: The El Goleta desert cliffs in the Algerian Sahara.

DENCH, JUDI (b. 1934)

English actress. Dame Judi Dench has achieved both success and acclaim with her few film roles, most notably for her portrayal of Queen Victoria in the 1997 film *Mrs Brown.*

➡ ***Films***

DENMARK

North European coastal country. **Capital:** Copenhagen. **Other principal cities:** Aarhus, Odense. **Climate:** temperate and windy. **Geographical features:** the Jutland Peninsula and surrounding islands, commanding the entrance to the Baltic Sea. **Main language:** Danish. **Main religion:** Lutheran. **Rule:** monarchic democracy. **Currency:** krone. **Primary industries:** mining, food, fishing, manufacturing of machinery, electronics and clothing, chemicals, printing. **Agriculture:** cereals, livestock (mainly pigs), dairy. **Exports:** pork and fish food products, transport equipment, chemicals. Germany is the main market but Denmark has built an economy on supplying other countries.

DEPARDIEU, GERARD (b. 1948)

French actor. Depardieu has realized a versatile and prolific career in French cinema. He also won much international acclaim with his 1989 film *Cyrano de Bergerac.*

DEPRESSION

Period in a country's economy when production is low and unemployment is high. It has a tendency to form a vicious circle, the most famous example being the great depression of the 1930s, which lasted for nearly 10 years after the Wall Street Crash in the US in 1929. It requires a great effort to lift an economy out of depression, often with enormous state intervention.

➡ ***Economics, Economy***

DESERTS

Regions of the world, usually sub-tropical, which have low rainfall, high temperatures and scarce vegetation. Typically deserts receive less than 254 mm (10 in) of rain in a year enabling the dry soil or sand to absorb solar radiation. This, in turn, produces daytime temperatures of up to 55°C that can drop to near freezing at night. Although seemingly barren, deserts can support animal and plant life. Desert organisms are often adapted to conserve water and can survive on a minimal amount.

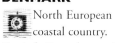

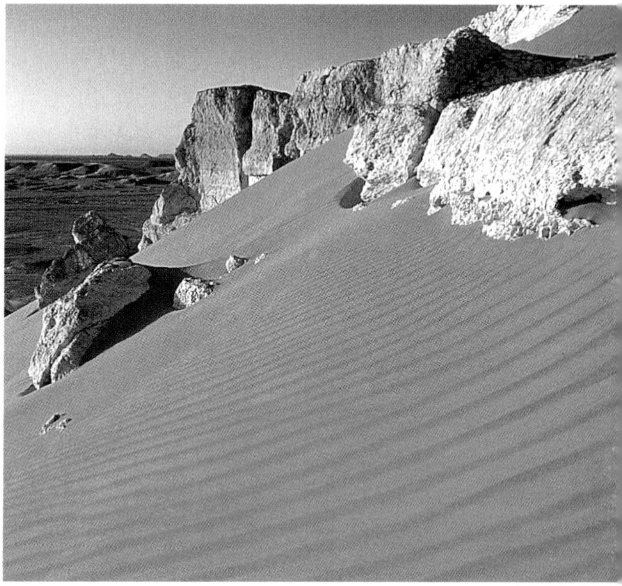

DESIGNERS

In fashion, the concept of the designer came to prominence in the 1980s, when the label on an article came to be almost more important than the item itself. Many designers became household names, including Donna Karan (DKNY), Ralph Lauren and Paul Smith. The word 'design' originates from the Italian *disegno*: 'the essence of an idea expressed as a drawing'.

➡ ***Fashion***

DIAMOND

Mineral composed entirely of crystalline carbon and the hardest known natural substance. Valued as a precious stone and used for cutting and as an abrasive.

➡ ***Carbon, Gemstones***

DICAPRIO, LEONARDO (b. 1974)

US actor. DiCaprio first came to attention for his role in *What's Eating Gilbert Grape* (1993). Since then he has starred in *Titanic* (1997) and *Romeo and Juliet* (1996).

➠ ***Films***

DICKENS, CHARLES (1812–70)

Nineteenth-century English novelist whose work has never declined in its widespread popularity. Dickens' stories are compulsive (all were initially published in serial form) and filled with comic caricatures that lighten his sometimes bleak subject matters. Much of his work focused upon social injustice and the division between rich and poor in industrialized Britain. In *Oliver Twist* (1837–38) Dickens highlighted the perils of the workhouse system for poor children. Among his lighter works, *A Christmas Carol* (1843) has become the epitome of Christmas for many. With later novels, such as *Great Expectations* (1860–61), Dickens gained a depth of vision that was to earn him the title of greatest English writer.

DICTATORSHIP

Absolute rule under one person whose powers are usually non-constitutional. Dictatorship is usually a consequence of political and economic chaos; they became common in the twentieth century after World War I and the Russian Revolution, with Adolf Hitler, Benito Mussolini and Joseph Stalin being the most notorious. In ancient Rome, dictators were voted in on six-month terms to resolve national crises.

➠ ***Ancient Rome, Adolf Hitler, Benito Mussolini, Joseph Stalin***

ABOVE: The enigmatic, sensual Marlene Dietrich.

RIGHT: The Disney empire continues to grow; from its early days producing animations for children to today's multi-million pound industry of which Eurodisney, France, is one of the more recent additions.

DIET

This has different meanings depending on the wealth of the individual. To a rich citizen of a developed country it refers to a regime of eating designed to achieve a given purpose, usually weight loss. To much of the world's population, however, it simply refers to getting enough food to stay alive.

➠ ***Famine, Food and Nutrition***

DIETRICH, MARLENE (1901–92)

German-born film actress who possessed an ethereal quality, often playing lamentably ill-fated women. Among her acclaimed films are *Witness for the Prosecution* (1957) and *Morocco* (1930).

➠ ***Films***

DINOSAURS

Group of extinct reptiles that lived 230–65 million years ago. Although a hugely diverse group the dinosaurs were unable to survive and the reason for their extinction remains a mystery.

Evidence for the existence of dinosaurs is found in fossil records. It was not until the nineteenth century that scientists who studied ancient life forms, palaeontologists, began to piece together information about dinosaurs from fossilized bones, eggs and footprints. There were at least 300 species of dinosaur and they exhibited varying degrees of complexity in body structure and behaviour. Their demise has been attributed to, among other things, a huge asteroid and the eruption of a super-volcano.

➠ ***Extinct Species, Reptiles, Palaeontology***

DISEASES

Conditions which interfere with the normal functions of a living organism. The presence of a disease is usually shown by characteristic signs, which are apparent to an examining physician, and symptoms, which are what the patient describes. The main causes of disease are infection by bacteria, fungi or viruses, and physical injury, but the causes of some diseases are unknown.

The most common disease caused by bacteria worldwide is dental caries, or tooth decay. Diseases can be present from birth; these are known as congenital diseases. Treatment of disease may involve trying to remove the cause, relief of symptoms, or both.

➧ ***Bacteria, Fungi, Viruses***

DISNEY, WALT (1901–66)

Legendary maestro of animated films. Disney began his Hollywood company in 1923 quickly gaining huge success with Mickey Mouse's exploits. He produced the first feature length animated film *Snow White* in 1937.

➧ ***Animation***

DISSOLUTION OF THE MONASTERIES (1536)

Part of Henry VIII of England's religious policy during the Protestant Reformation. Implemented by Cardinal Thomas Wolsey and then Thomas Cromwell, the policy resulted in financial gain for Henry, aquisition of property for his nobles and the displacement of about 10,000 monks and nuns. It also tempered Church corruption.

➧ ***Protestantism, Reformation***

DIVING

Underwater exploration. Popular sport made possible by the development of the aqualung in the 1940s by Frenchman Jacques Cousteau. Several professional bodies exist to provide training, notably BSAC and PADI.

DIWALI

Hindu festival of light, occurring in October or November. Lamps are lit and presents given to celebrate Lakshmi, the goddess of wealth and light.

➧ ***Hinduism***

DOGS

Common name applied to group of carnivorous mammals (*Canidae*) that includes wolves, foxes and jackals as well as the domestic dog. Members of the dog family have long canine teeth, long muzzles and claws that cannot be retracted. Typically they are territorial and often live in packs. Dogs are natural hunters and benefit from excellent senses of hearing, sight and smell.

Dogs are intelligent animals that inhabit every continent except Antarctica and survive in highly variable climates and conditions. Dogs were possibly one of the first creatures to be domesticated by humans and have enjoyed a privileged position as popular pets since ancient times.

➧ ***Fox, Pets***

DOMINICAN REPUBLIC

Caribbean island nation. **Capital:** Santo Domingo. **Other principal cities:** Santiago de los Caballeros. **Climate:** tropical. **Geographical features:** forms the eastern part of Hispaniola (Haiti occupies the west). **Main language:** Spanish. **Main religion:** Roman Catholic. **Rule:** democratic republic. **Currency:** peso. **Primary industries:** agriculture, mining and tourism. **Exports:** coffee, sugar, tobacco, gold, silver and nickel.

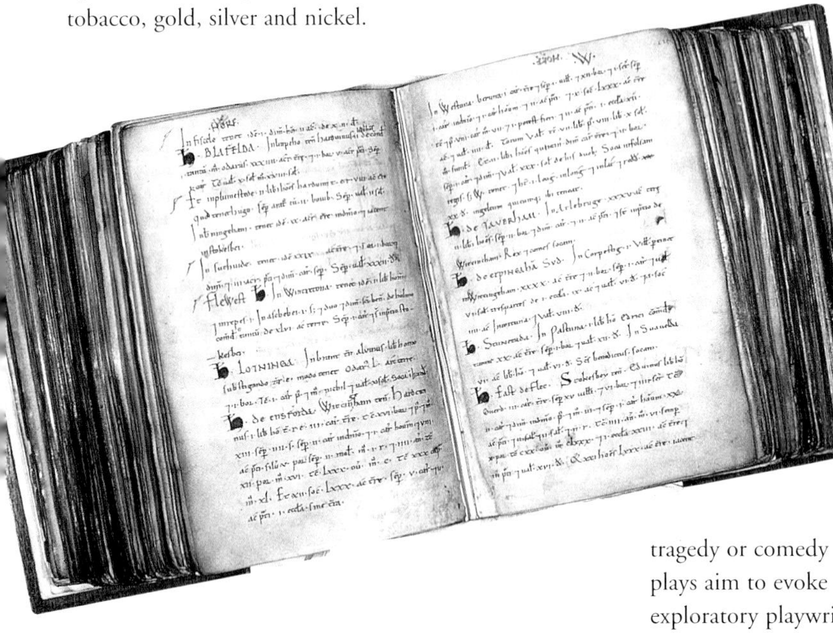

DOMESDAY BOOK (1086)

Detailed survey of England, county by county, commissioned by William the Conqueror and compiled in 1086, it forms the basis of all English local history.

➡ ***Normans***

DOSTOYEVSKY, FYODOR MIKHAILOVICH (1821–81)

Russian writer who, through novels such as *Crime and Punishment* (1866) and *The Brothers Karamazov* (1880), is viewed as a pre-eminent novelist of his generation.

ABOVE: Although fragile and fading, the Domesday Book, *commissioned by William the Conqueror in 1086, can still be admired in museums today.*

RIGHT: Druids perform at part of the first Celtic spring festival, known as Imbolo.

FAR RIGHT: The singer-songwriter Bob Dylan is an icon for the 60s generation.

DOYLE, ARTHUR CONAN (1859–1930)

British novelist. Doyle is now best remembered for his stories centring around the investigations of Sherlock Holmes. Doyle's success greatly promoted the genre of detective fiction.

➡ ***Literary Genres, Sherlock Holmes***

DRAKE, FRANCIS (c. 1540–96)

English navigator. Born in Devon, Drake went to sea at an early age and took part in the ill-fated expedition of his kinsman, Sir John Hawkins, to the Spanish Main. Throughout his career he was the implacable foe of the Spaniards, his exploits making him a national hero. In the *Golden Hind* he circumnavigated the globe (1577–80) and helped defeat the Spanish Armada (1588).

DRAMA FORMS

From its conception drama was divided into either tragedy or comedy (terms that describe the feelings the plays aim to evoke in their audience). With more exploratory playwrights of the nineteenth century, such as Henrik Ibsen, the Theatre of Ideas was born. During the twentieth century new forms of drama proliferated, such as the Theatre of the Absurd (portraying the apparent absurdity of life), with which Harold Pinter and Samuel Beckett were associated. During the 1960s The Theatre of Cruelty aimed to disturb the audience.

➡ ***Henrik Ibsen, Plays, Theatre***

DRUGS

Correctly, any chemical compound that can affect the life functions of a living organism. Commonly used to refer to (often illegal) narcotics. Despite the high profile of heroin, ecstasy, cocaine and the like, it is alcohol and tobacco that cause the most deaths. Caffeine, present in both tea and coffee is arguably the most commonly consumed drug.

➡ ***Alcohol, Coffee, Cocaine, Ecstasy, Heroin***

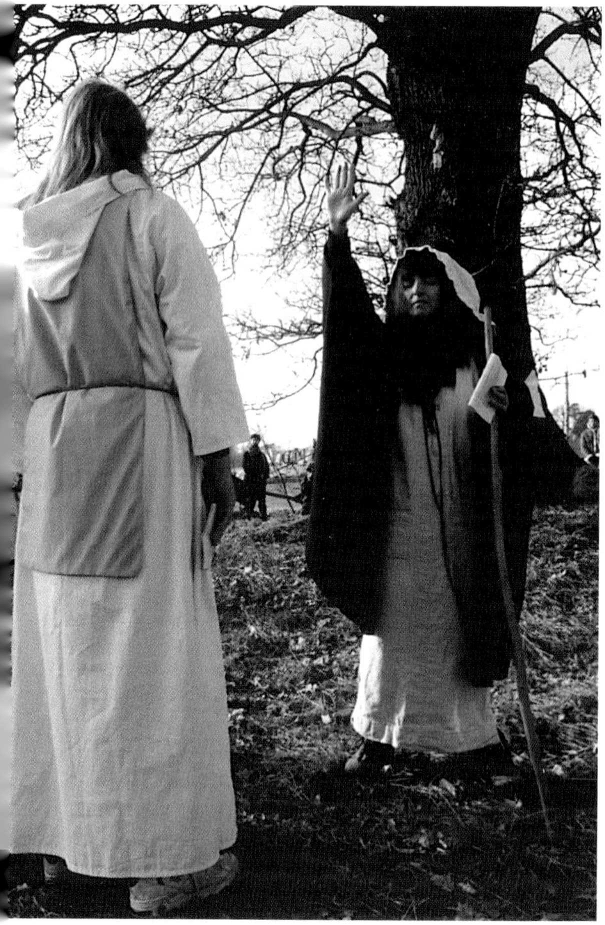

DRUIDS

Pre-Christian Celtic priests in Britain and Gaul. Druids believed in the soul's immortality and in reincarnation. The oak (drus being Greek for 'oak') was significant to them. They practised human sacrifice and were expert astronomers: possibly using Stonehenge, although it pre-dates them. The Roman Empire and later Christian missionaries ended the practice of Druidism.

➧ ***Stonehenge***

DUBUFFET, JEAN (1901–85)

French artist and creator of *Art Brut* (from his collection of art of the mentally ill and children). In his own work, often collages, Dubuffet employed various materials including bones and sand.

➧ ***Abstract Art***

DUCHAMP, MARCEL (1887–1968)

French artist. Duchamp stopped painting in the 1920s, instead exhibiting his 'ready-mades'. A prominent Dadaist, Duchamp most famously exhibited his version of the Mona Lisa, complete with moustache.

➧ ***Abstract Art, Dadaism***

DYCK, SIR ANTHONY VAN (1599–1641)

Flemish painter. At the age of just 17 van Dyck had his own studio and was later Peter Paul Rubens' assistant. Although van Dyck produced many mythological and religious paintings, it was with his aristocratic portraits whilst working at the English court that his true brilliance shone. Whilst influenced by Rubens and Titian, van Dyck's portraits reflect his own interpretation of the essence of nobility; his sitters appear aloof and superior. Van Dyck's portrait style was greatly mimicked by succeeding generations of painters.

➧ ***Baroque, Peter Paul Rubens***

DYLAN, BOB (b. 1941)

US singer/songwriter. Dylan was largely responsible for reviving the folk song genre of the 1950s and 1960s. His songs, such as *Blowin' in the Wind* (1962), were also key in the protest movement.

EARTH

Largely solid planet enveloped by a life-supporting atmosphere and the third planet from the Sun. The Earth revolves around the Sun at a velocity of approximately 106,000 kph (66,000 mph) and rotates upon its own axis approximately once every 24 hours. It has an average surface temperature of 14°C (57°F) and a total surface area of 510,100,000 sq km (316,970,000 sq m). The Earth may be around 4.65 billion years old but its true age and origin remain a matter for intense speculation.

➠ ***Solar System, Sun***

EARTHQUAKES

Series of shock waves generated by the movement of one part of the Earth's rocky crust with another. The shock waves are generated at a point called the focus and the effects felt at the epicentre. Numerous areas of the world are at risk from earthquakes, specifically where sections of the Earth's crust (plates) are colliding. Earthquakes can have disastrous consequences for the local people. Effects include the destruction of entire towns, landslides and huge waves (tsunami).

➠ ***Plate Tectonics, Richter Scale, Tsunami***

EASTER

Christian feast remembering Christ's resurrection. The Anglo-Saxon goddess, Eostre, and the Jewish Passover have links with Easter. Easter eggs are given as symbols of new life.

➠ ***Christianity***

RIGHT: A Solar eclipse at the point of totality, with the characteristic corona.
TOP RIGHT: Maintaining a balance within an ecosystem is essential for the survival of all the plant and animal life that it supports. National Parks such as this in Vancouver Island, Canada, play a vital role in conservation.
FAR RIGHT: Modern Calderon Indians in Quito, Ecuador.

EASTERN ART

Broad term encompassing arts from Eastern civilization. In China art survives from as early as 1500 BC but the first definitive artistic movement has been traced to the Han dynasty (206 BC–AD 220). The Six Principles of art (as laid out in the sixth century) guided Chinese arts development for centuries. Japanese early art, as with Chinese, was greatly influenced by Buddhism. China was also a dominant force in Japan's early art. However, Japanese art cultivated its own flavour with the emergence of the coloured painting style called *yamato-e* during the ninth to twelfth century (*Fujiwara* period).

➠ ***Pottery, Ukiyo-e***

EASTWOOD, CLINT (b. 1930)

US actor. Following success in television's *Rawhide*, Eastwood's film career took off with Sergio Leones' 'spaghetti westerns' (1960s). Eastwood has admirably tackled the dual star/director role for several films, most notably *The Unforgiven* (1989).

➠ ***Films***

ECLIPSES

Movement of one celestial body in front of another, totally or partially obscuring it. A solar eclipse occurs when the Moon passes in front of the Sun.

➠ ***Moon, Sun***

ECOLOGY

Study of relationships between all living things and their environment. Ecology is a broad discipline that encompasses many areas of science such as biology, chemistry, geology and statistics. The study of ecosystems is an intrinsic part of ecologists' work. An ecosystem is a localized habitat that is examined in its entirety; not just the living organisms it contains but also the physical environment and the flow of energy through it. Ecology has played an important role in conservation.

➧ *Conservation*

ECONOMICS

The science and study of wealth: its production, distribution and consumption. The first generally recognized work on economics was carried out by Adam Smith, who published *The Wealth of Nations* in 1776. Other milestones include the work of John Maynard Keynes and Milton Friedman. As well as the free-market view of economics there is also the view point put forward by Karl Marx, who believed in a far more planned approach to economics which is now largely discredited.

➧ *Economy, Karl Marx*

ECONOMY

Management of a country's economy is a vital function of that country's government. There are several distinct approaches to this problem, but most are a balance between 'free markets' and central planning. Free markets believe in allowing the economy to look after itself. The government simply provides the right conditions for it to flourish. Central planners believe that even minor facets should be centrally planned. A government has several powerful tools that can affect the economy; the most commonly used are interest rates, import duties, wages policies and subsidies. The management of an economy is not an exact science.

➧ *Depression, Economics*

ECSTASY

Methyenedioxymethamphetamine (MDMA). An illegal drug very popular among certain youth groups. First manufactured in 1914, it has a mild psychedelic affect.

➧ *Drugs*

ECUADOR

South American north-western coastal nation. **Capital:** Quito. **Other principal cities:** Cuenca, Guayaquil. **Climate:** tropical coast, temperate inland with cold mountains. **Geographical features:** rich Pacific coastal lands rising sharply to Andes mountains, and low-lying forest beyond, and the Galápagos Islands 966 km (600 miles) off the coast. **Main language:** Spanish. **Main religion:** Roman Catholicism. **Rule:** democratic republic.

Currency: sucre. **Primary industries:** agriculture, petroleum. **Exports:** bananas, cocoa, coffee, fish, petroleum. Ecuador's rise as an oil exporter has begun a slow process of economic development.

EDISON, THOMAS ALVA (1847–1931)

US inventor and scientist. Among a host of inventions, he produced the incandescent electric light bulb, a storage battery, the carbon microphone, and the phonograph.

EDUCATION

Process used to develop an individual's academic, social and manual skills. This begins at birth but the term is generally used to refer to the system of schooling that a child receives from around the age of five years. The earliest examples of a formal education in Europe are from Greece, where there were established schools as early as 500 BC. Further afield there are records from 165 BC of competitive examinations for the Chinese civil service. In the UK it is compulsory for all children to be educated, and this service is free – in Scotland since 1694 and England since 1870 – but this is not the case in all countries.

➡ ***Schools, Universities***

EGYPT

Country of north-east Africa. **Capital:** Cairo. **Other principal cities:** Alexandria, Port Said. **Climate:** dry and warm. **Geographical features:** almost entirely desert apart from the Nile Valley and Delta where 99% of the population is concentrated into 4% of the land. **Main language:** Arabic. **Main religions:** Islam and Coptic Christianity. **Rule:** democratic republic. **Currency:** Egyptian pound. **Primary industries:** tourism, agriculture, petroleum processing, food. **Agriculture:** wheat, rice, cotton. **Exports:** petroleum, textiles, cotton, chemicals. The country is defined by the Nile Valley.

➡ ***Africa, Ancient Egypt, Egyptian Gods and Mythology, River Nile***

EGYPT, ANCIENT

Egyptian civilization dates back more than 7,000 years and is reckoned by dynasties rather than centuries, divided into prehistoric, archaic and pyramid periods, the Middle Kingdom, the New Empire, the conquest by Alexander the Great and the Hellenistic kingdom of the Ptolemies which ended in 30 BC with the death of Cleopatra VII and Egypt's absorption into the Roman Empire. They had highly developed social structures, religion, art and architecture science and medicine, some of the earliest systems of writing and sophisticated methods of trade and commerce – evidence of this being obtained from pyramid excavation, for example.

➡ ***Pyramids, Tutankhamen***

EGYPTIAN GODS AND MYTHOLOGY

Originally totemic animal statues were worshipped; later they were turned into gods with animal heads. Osiris, god of death, was the most important god in the pantheon and had the head of a jackal. He rivalled and succeeded Re, the god of the Sun and creator of the Universe. Isis was the mother goddess of Egypt, often depicted suckling Horus, and the mythologies of ancient Greece and Rome adopted her. Nut was goddess of the sky and her arched body formed the heavens and each new day was born out of her. The Sphinx, a human-headed lion and the protector of Re, is remembered for its riddles. Immortality was valued, as evidenced by the attempt to achieve this through mummification.

➡ ***Ancient Egypt***

EIFFEL TOWER (1889)

Architect Gustave Eiffel (1832–1923) created the magnificent 300-m (1,000-ft) high Eiffel Tower in Paris for the Exposition of 1889. The dominating tower has become emblematic of Paris.

EINSTEIN, ALBERT (1879–1955)

German physicist, best known for his relativity theories, although he contributed in other fields, including quantum theory. While teaching in Zurich, he published a paper on the photoelectric effect for which he later won the Nobel Prize for Physics. He published his special theory of relativity in 1905, and the general theory in 1915. He emigrated to the US from Nazi Germany in 1933 and became professor of mathematics at Princeton.

➡ ***Nobel Prize, Quantum Mechanics, Relativity***

EL SALVADOR

Central American Pacific country. **Capital:** San Salvador. **Other principal cities:** Santa Ana, San Miguel. **Climate:** sub-tropical. **Geographical features:** southern coastal region, northern mountains. **Main language:** Spanish. **Main religions:** Roman Catholicism, Protestantism. **Rule:** democracy. **Currency:** colón. **Primary industries:** agriculture (subsistence and cash). **Economy:** disrupted by political instability and high unemployment. **Exports:** coffee, cotton, shrimp, sugar.

ELECTRICITY

Effects which are due to electric charges. As an energy source, electricity means the flow of electric charges such as the movement of electrons through a metal wire. Electricity is a versatile form of energy as it can be readily moved to where it is needed, and can be easily and efficiently converted into other forms of energy, including light, mechanical energy and heat. Electricity is mainly generated by burning fossil fuels such as oil although water (hydroelectric) power is also important.

➠ ***Oil***

ELECTRONICS

Study of effects caused by electrons through semiconductors such as silicon. Semiconductor devices include diodes, transistors and integrated circuits (microchips).

➠ ***Computers***

ELEMENTS, CHEMICAL

About 100 substances which cannot be broken down into simpler substances by chemical action. An element consists of chemically identical atoms. The elements are charted on the periodic table, invented by Dmitri Mendeleyev.

ELEPHANTS

The largest land mammals now represented by only two varieties: African and Asian. While similar in appearance, the African elephant is taller and has bigger ears than the Asian variety.

EMBARGOES

Bans on trading or dealing with nations for political, economic or ideological differences. Usually intended to force changes, e.g. the trade embargo imposed on Cuba by the US.

EMERSON, RALPH WALDO (1803–82)

American philosopher. Emerson, with Henry David Thoreau, led the New England Transcendentalism movement, which revered the ascendancy of nature instead of modern civilization and was thus linked to Romanticism.

➠ ***Romantic, Henry David Thoreau***

EMIN, TRACEY (b. 1963)

British artist. Emin uses objects and installations in her intensely personal and autobiographical work, such as *Everyone I Have Ever Slept With* (1995), which gave a history of her sex life.

EMPIRE STATE BUILDING

One of the most famous landmarks in America. Situated in New York, the building was completed in 1931. One hundred and two storeys high, it was the world's tallest building until 1954.

EMPLOYMENT

Exchange of labour in return for wages. Employment is a key feature of a developed economy. It is an effective means of ensuring that resources (the person's time and skills) and wealth (money in the form of wages) are distributed effectively. Unemployment in excess amounts is the result of recession (slowed economic growth) or depression. In most countries there is now a considerable body of legislation governing the relationship between employee and employer.

➠ ***Depression, Economics***

ENDANGERED SPECIES

Any species considered close to extinction and unlikely to survive without human intervention. An official list of endangered species is held by the International Union for the Conservation of Nature. Loss of habitat and hunting continue to be the biggest threats to the survival of many endangered species e.g. black rhino and tiger.

➠ ***Extinct Species, Worldwide Fund for Nature***

ENERGY

Ability to do mechanical work. Sources of energy available include chemical energy, as in a fuel, radiant energy from electromagnetic waves, and kinetic energy due to an object's motion. Energy can be converted from one form to another, but the conversion process usually involves some heat also being produced.

ENGINEERING

Harnessing of sources of power and materials to produce useful items. Engineering takes the discoveries and theories of science and mathematics and puts them to useful and economical use. Branches of engineering include civil engineering, industrial manufacture, mining and chemical engineering.

ENLIGHTENMENT (c. 1660–1770)

Primarily European literary and philosophical movement. The Enlightenment, sometimes referred to as the Age of Reason, emphasized the importance of humanity's experiences and reasoning as opposed to the restrictions of religion and tradition. Through its stress upon reason, upon the importance of education and its optimism for the progression of humanity, the Enlightenment led the way to the idealism of liberal democracy. Its major proponents were David Hume (Britain), Immanuel Kant (Germany) and René Descartes (France).

➧ ***David Hume, Immanuel Kant, Philosophy***

ENVIRONMENT

Term used to describe the surroundings of any organism and the factors that influence it. The environment of a beetle, for example, can be defined in terms of its climate, soil type, vegetation, predators and food resources. Through the study of ecology we have a better understanding of how all these factors interact with one another.

Environmental issues are increasingly relevant as the huge and often damaging impact humans have on the planet becomes clear. Political parties (often called the 'Greens') are committed to putting environmental issues, such as population growth, global warming and land management on the political agenda.

➧ ***Ecology, Global Warming***

EPIPHYTES

Plants, such as some mosses and orchids, which rely upon another plants purely for support, without depriving them of nutrients.

EQUATOR

Circle around the broadest part of the Earth, perpendicular to the lines between the poles, diving the world into the northern and southern hemispheres. Called 0° latitude.

➧ ***Earth, Latitude***

ERNST, MAX (1891–1976)

German painter. Originally a Dadaist, Ernst also became one of the main Surrealist painters. He combined dream images, found objects and collages in his thought provoking work.

➧ ***Abstract Art, Dadaism, Surrealism***

EROSION

Processes by which rocks are changed, broken down and transported away, thereby altering the landscape. Cheddar Gorge, for example, was formed by the chemical erosion of limestone by rain and carbon dioxide (which together form a weak acid). Physical processes of erosion include the powerful action of waves upon cliffs or rivers cutting through valleys. The Grand Canyon, 1,500 m (5,000 ft) deep, is a good example of how a river can cut through rock over time.

➧ ***Valleys***

ESKIMOS

Arctic (northern hemisphere) peoples, meaning 'eaters of raw meat', inhabiting parts of remote North America and Greenland.

They are now generally called by their own name, Inuit. Numbering around 125,000, their homeland, with rights to hunt and fish and levy royalties on mineral exploitation, is guaranteed by Canadian law since 1992.

ESQUIVEL, ADOLFO PEREZ (b. 1931)

Argentinian leader of the Servicio de Paz y Justicia (Peace and Justice Service), a Christian human rights group. A sculptor and architect by profession, he was awarded the Nobel Peace Prize in 1980.

➡ *Nobel Prize*

ESTONIA

North-east European country on the Baltic. **Capital:** Tallinn. **Other principal cities:** Tartu, Narva. **Climate:** mild. **Geographical features:** marshes, lakes and forested plain with a long coastline. **Main languages:** Estonian, Russian. **Main religions:** Lutheran, Russian Orthodox. **Rule:** democracy. **Currency:** kroon. **Primary industries:** food, manufacturing, textiles, vehicles, shale oil. **Agriculture:** livestock and dairy. **Exports:** food, oil and gas (from shale), textiles, vehicles.

➡ *Europe*

ETHIOPIA

Land-locked east African country. **Capital:** Addis Ababa. **Other principal cities:** Jimma, Dire Dawa. **Climate:** temperate plateau, hot lowlands. **Geographical features:** central plateau split by the African Rift Valley. **Main language:** Amharic. **Main religions:** Islam, Coptic Christian. **Rule:** democratic federal republic. **Currency:** birr. **Primary industries:** agriculture. **Exports:** coffee, hides, gold.

➡ *Africa*

ETRUSCANS

Among the earliest, if not the original, residents of Italy, the Etruscans migrated from Mesopotamia and their distinctive art forms betray Asiatic origins. By 700 BC they had evolved their own alphabet. At the height of their power in the fifth century BC they occupied northern Italy and defeated the Carthaginians, but they were eventually overthrown by the Romans.

FAR LEFT: Rolls Royce engine assembly at the plant in Derby, England. Industry is one of the main beneficiaries of advances in engineering.
LEFT: An Alaskan Eskimo.
TOP RIGHT: A reproduction of an Etruscan terracotta painting depicting a funeral pyre.

EUROPE

The world's second smallest continent, with 8% of all land area at 10.4 million sq km (4 million sq miles). Europe is the part of Eurasia lying west of the Ural mountains (between the Arctic and the Caspian Sea), north of the Caucasus mountains (between the Caspian and Black Seas), and north of the Sea of Marmara. Its most southerly point is at 36°N, its most northerly the Arctic Ocean. The Mediterranean Sea separates it from North Africa.

Europe's coastline is a complex series of peninsulas and bays, including Bulgaria, European Turkey, Greece, the Adriatic coastline, Italy, the Iberian Peninsula (Spain and Portugal), Denmark, and Scandinavia (Finland, Norway and Sweden). Numerous islands are dotted in European seas, of which the British Isles are the largest. Others include the Mediterranean islands of Sardinia, Corsica, Sicily, Crete and Cyprus, together with various groups including the Balearics, Malta and Gozo, Greek islands and the Azores and Canaries, off the west African coast.

Europe's weather varies from Arctic conditions in extreme northern Finland to the hot conditions of the Mediterranean. North-western Europe has cool summers and mild winters, moderated by the effects of the warm Gulf Stream across the Atlantic. Central Europe has warm summers but cold winters, and eastern Europe experiences severely cold winters. The Mediterranean area is hot and dry in summer with mild winters.

Europe is a highly-developed and industrialized part of the world though most of the industry is concentrated in the north and west, such as car manufacturing and electronics. The population is around 0.5 billion.

EUROPEAN SOVEREIGNS

The various dynasties that ruled Europe could trace their origins back to the Dark Ages. The British royal family, for example, has ancestors among the rulers of the Anglo-Saxon kingdoms, as well as the Viking Rolf or Rollo of Normandy and Kenneth Mac Alpin who united the Picts and Scots in AD 841. The Danish royal house has an unbroken line all the way back to Gorm the Old in the tenth century, while the Bourbons of France and Spain and the Habsburgs of Austria could claim similarly ancient lineage. In the German states, the Hohenzollerns of Prussia triumphed over the Guelphs and Wittelsbachs. The Jagiellonian rulers of Poland had a more chequered career, while the Romanovs of Russia had barely celebrated their tercentenary when they were overthrown by the Revolution of 1917.

The monarchical principle was applied to many of the new countries which emerged in the nineteenth century, from Belgium (1831) and Greece (1832) to Bulgaria (1878) and Romania (1866), all of which chose German princelings for their rulers. In Sweden the childless King Karl XIII chose as his successor one of Napoleon's marshals (1818) who founded the Bernadotte Dynasty. When Norway separated from Sweden in 1905 a Danish prince was elected king. Several sovereigns lost their thrones in 1918 and others in the aftermath of World War II, but Spain successfully re-introduced the monarchy in 1975 after a gap of 44 years.

➧ ***French Royalty, Kings of England, Queens of England, Russian Royalty***

EUROPEAN UNION (1993)

Current term (since 1993) for the European economic and political alliance. Formed in 1957 to create a single market, the membership has steadily grown to encompass most of western Europe with central and east countries queuing to join. The Union has continued to move towards reducing restrictions on internal movement of money and goods.

EVEREST, MOUNT

Highest mountain in the world. Mount Everest lies on the Chinese-Nepalese border and is 8,872 m (29,118 ft) high. It was first climbed by Edmund Hillary and Sherpa Tenzing Norgay in 1953.

➧ ***Edmund Hillary***

EXPLORATION

Voyages and journeys of exploration were undertaken in antiquity, leading to colonization of countries such as America and Australia thousands of years ago. It was not until the Greek and Roman worlds that accounts of journeys were recorded and gazetteers of places and locations compiled. Even so, no one people was aware of the true extent of the world and human settlement.

The first significant long-distance European explorers were the Vikings, reaching Newfoundland *c.* AD 1000. In the fifteenth century the growth in European power and trade led to searches for maritime routes to the East Indies by heading west. Christopher Columbus led the first successful expedition to the Americas in 1492, believing he had reached the Far East. In succeeding decades he and other explorers, such as Ferdinand Magellan, began to appreciate the full extent of the American continent. In 1520 Magellan found the Pacific Ocean by sailing around the southern tip of South America. He died en route but part of his flotilla continued to South Africa and made the first circumnavigation of the world. Other explorers spent centuries trying to find a north-west passage to the Pacific.

During the seventeenth and eighteenth centuries, further voyages (especially those by James Cook) and improvements in navigation equipment led to better and better maps being produced as well as discovering Australia, New Zealand, Antarctica and the Pacific Islands.

Since then, vast tracts of inland regions have steadily been explored in detail. To these should be added the satellite photography of the Earth, and space voyages of exploration since the 1960s which have taken men to the Moon, and robot craft to all the planets except Pluto.

Colonialism, Christopher Columbus, Captain James Cook, Francis Drake, Man on the Moon

TOP LEFT: A gathering of European Royalty including Queen Margarethe of Denmark (second from right, back row) ex-King Constantine (seated centre, middle row) and Queen Elizabeth I (seated right, front row).
LEFT: Mount Everest, on the Chinese-Nepalese border, is the world's highest border.
RIGHT: Skeleton remains fossilized in rock are evidence of organisms which previously inhabited our planet. Although these species are now extinct, important information can be obtained on the evolution of animals and plants that live today.

EXPRESSIONISM (20TH CENTURY)

The term Expressionism is vague in its boundaries. It is loosely used to describe the work of artists such as Edvard Munch and Kokoschka who attempted to portray their emotions, inner psyches and experiences through their art. Expressionism followed on from the work of the Impressionists and was also greatly inspired by the work of Vincent Van Gogh. Primarily German, particularly with groups such as the *Blau Reiter* ('Blue Rider'), Expressionism flourished from the start of the twentieth century until the 1930s. Expressionist art often employs a violently intense use of colour and a distortion of form: both of these elements evinced the Expressionists' rejection of the conventions of art.

Impressionism, Wassily Kandinsky, Vincent van Gogh

EXTINCT SPECIES

Any species of organism that has died out. The fossil record suggests that there have been several episodes of mass extinctions that were possibly caused by overwhelming changes in the environment e.g. ice ages. Extinction is part of the evolutionary process but many modern extinctions are the result of human activity.

Endangered Species

FALKLANDS WAR (1982)

Conflict fought in 1982 for sovereignty of the Falklands and South Georgia. Claimed by Argentina for historical and geographical reasons, as well as economic and political advantage, the Falklands were invaded in April 1982. A British task force recaptured the islands on 15 June, 12,000 Argentinian troops surrendering, and leading to the collapse of the ruling Argentinian junta.

Argentina, United Kingdom

FAMINE

Severe food shortage affecting people on a regional scale. It is estimated that over 750 million people worldwide either do not have access to enough (famine) or the right type of (malnutrition) food. There can be many reasons for famine, but all too often it is caused by wars that disrupt the normal processes of food production.

Food and Nutrition

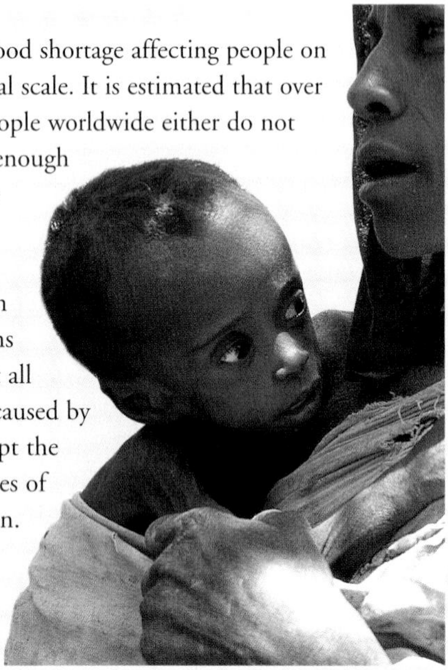

FARMING

The business of agriculture. Agricultural production began in the Middle Ages, when land began to be enclosed and landowners began to use it to grow produce and crops, although methods of farming were used in ancient civilizations. The late twentieth century saw the rise of organic farming, in which no chemicals are used to enhance crop growth.

Agriculture

FASHION

The change in demand for products based on advertising and 'herd instinct' rather than logical needs. Most notably in modes of dress, but also in music and design in general. It is a phenomenon exploited by advertisers to create demand for products.

Crazes

FBI

Abbreviation for the Federal Bureau of Investigation, an agency of the US Department of Justice, used to enforce domestic security in breaches of federal law such as spying, kidnapping, government fraud and civil rights. Founded in 1908 by J. Edgar Hoover, it originally operated beyond the law in its surveillance of people suspected of being enemies of the state.

FENCING

Sport that has its origins in duelling and warfare. There are three disciplines defined by the type of sword used, epee (lightest), foil and sabre (heaviest).

FERDINAND, FRANZ (1863–1914)

Archduke Franz Ferdinand of Austria-Hungary and heir to the throne, he was assassinated with his wife in Sarajevo by Serbian nationalists on 28 June 1914. His death was the immediate cause of World War I.

World War I

FERTILIZERS

Materials containing at least some of the chemical elements needed by plants to grow, in a form in which they can be added to the soil and taken up by the roots. Plants require nitrogen, potassium, phosphorus and smaller quantities of about 20 other elements.

Chemical Elements, Farming

FAR LEFT: Woman and child at a refugee camp at Baidoa, Somalia, which tries to accommodate the starving victims of famine, war and the hostile African climate.
LEFT: Two women attired in clothes the height of 1930s fashion.
BOTTOM LEFT: Fertilizers are used to increase crop yields but their long-term effects on the environment and food chains are still not fully understood.

FEUDALISM

Main political and social system of medieval Europe. Power spread down from the monarch through a complex stratum of nobles, each owing allegiance to those above him. At the bottom of the pile were the serfs, who were little more than slaves. The system was held together by land. Serfs worked the fields for their overlords and in return were granted small parcels of land to grow food for themselves. The system broke down with the coming of large towns and the growth in paid employment.

➧ ***Castles***

FIJI

South Pacific island group in Melanesia. **Capital:** Suva. **Other principal towns:** Lautoka, Levuka. **Climate:** tropical. **Geographical features:** about 850 islands, 100 of which are inhabited. Terrain varies from mountains to forests and plains. **Main language:** English. **Main religions:** Methodist, Hindu, Islam, Sikh. **Rule:** democratic republic. **Currency:** Fiji dollar. **Primary industries:** sugarcane, tourism. **Exports:** sugar, coconut oil, clothing, timber, fish, gold, molasses.

FILMS

From its early beginnings in the short films of the Lumière Brothers in Paris, in 1896, film has evolved to become the most dominant and powerful art form in the world. The film industry creates (and spends) billions each year and the enormous volume of work produced is likewise increasing yearly.

Films can be classified by their nationalistic style, (sometimes definitive but often superimposed), their genre or even by their studio (such as the Hollywood blockbuster or the British Ealing Comedies of the 1940s). Fundamental to film's development were the Hollywood studios that emerged at the beginning of the twentieth century and have dominated the film industry since the 1920s.

From its inception, film's development has been necessarily bound to technological progress – computerized animation and technical wizardry are now pushing the art form forward at ever-faster speeds and often supersede plot in terms of priority. The most far-reaching technological change was that of the introduction of sound in the first 'talkie', *The Jazz Singer* (1927).

➧ ***Academy Awards, BAFTAs***

FINLAND

Scandinavian country on the Baltic between Sweden and Russia. **Capital:** Helsinki. **Other principal cities:** Tampere, Espoo, Turku, Oulu. **Climate:** warm summers with long, cold winters. **Geographical features:** dominated by forest, and about 60,000 lakes, with one-third reaching into the Arctic Circle. **Main languages:** Finnish and Swedish. **Main religion:** Lutheran. **Rule:** democratic republic. **Currency:** markka. **Primary industries:** food, timber-related products, metals, ship-building, clothing. **Exports:** paper, pulp, lumber, ships, machinery, metals.

Finnish forests provide the economic foundation of trade and industry, though steel production is important. Agriculture is mainly livestock, requiring importation of feed. The nation has a highly-developed social welfare programme.

FISH

Large group of aquatic vertebrate animals that usually have long muscular bodies covered in scales, gills for breathing and limbs that are modified into fins. Approximately 23,000 species of fish have been identified so far.

The earliest known fossil of a fish dates from about 480 million years ago. Since then fish have diversified to fill almost every aquatic habitat available. Fish have been discovered at ocean depths of 7000 m (22967 ft) while the Antarctic icefish can exist at -2°C (28°F). Fish are a popular and healthy source of food for humans and are therefore of considerable economic importance throughout the world.

➧ ***Fishing, Vertebrates***

FISH FARMING

The branch of agriculture involved in the breeding and nurture of fish for commercial purposes. Both saltwater and freshwater fish can be bred in this way.

FISHING

Most popular participation sport in the UK. Various types include game, sea and coarse. The latter releases the fish (mostly) unharmed at the end of the day.

FITNESS

Keeping fit became the latest trend towards the end of the twentieth century and remains so into the twenty-first. Supporting this is a huge industry encompassing everything from clothing and food to exercise videos and gymnasia.

➡ ***Diet, Food and Nutrition, Running***

FLAGS

Standard of a country. Many flags are highly symbolic of the nation they represent. The flag of the US has 50 stars, one for each state, and 13 stripes, one for each state that originally formed the republic. In many countries it is a criminal offence to show disrespect to the national flag.

FLEMING, ALEXANDER (1881–1955)

British bacteriologist. Fleming discovered the enzyme lysozyme which is present in tears and saliva. While studying the antibacterial properties of lysozyme, he noticed that a mould growing on a neglected petri dish appeared to prevent bacterial growth, This observation led to the discovery of the antibiotic penicillin.

➡ ***Antibiotics, Bacteria, Diseases, Penicillin***

FLOODS

Overflowing of a body of water, such as a river or lake. Flash floods occur with minimal warning and tend to both rise and fall quite rapidly. Many rivers are prone to seasonal flooding owing to fluctuating tides, melting snow or excessive rainfall. Floods can damage property, endanger life and cause soil erosion.

➡ ***Aswan Dam, Erosion***

FOG

Cloud of condensed water droplets, or ice crystals, suspended in the air just above the Earth's surface thereby reducing visibility. Also known as mist.

FOOD ADDITIVES

Any of a number of materials added to processed foods which remain in the food. Additives have a number of purposes including colouring, flavouring and preserving.

FOOD AND NUTRITION

Everyone knows what food is and what it does. However the way it does it and our concern with eating the right things is a fairly recent phenomenon. Throughout most of human history people's diets have largely consisted of whatever was available. Only the privileged few could pick and choose. As general prosperity increased in the nineteenth and twentieth centuries choice arrived, and with it problems. Fat consumption increased greatly which is bad for the heart, while processed foods, with reduced fibre, are bad for the digestive system.

People in developed countries are now more aware of the impact of nutrition on their health. The present concern of genetic modification and chemical treatment of food show this clearly.

➡ ***Diet***

FOOD CHAINS

Sequence of organisms that feed off one another. Grass, for example, is eaten by cows and cows are eaten by humans. Food chains, however, are rarely that simple. Grass is eaten by other animals too, and cows are not eaten just by humans. Food chains thus interconnect, creating highly complex food webs. In general, the primary producers of a food chain, such as grass or algae, are present in a very large mass (biomass) and each subsequent level of the food chain has a lower biomass, creating a pyramid effect that also reflects how energy is dissipated through the system.

➤ ***Ecology***

FOOTBALL

Any game where a ball and the feet are used. Strictly speaking American football, rugby etc. are all forms of football, but the term is normally applied to Association Football or soccer. An enormously popular game both at amateur and professional level, it is also now a multi-billion pound industry, with top players earning over £40,000 per week in the UK.

The sport is governed by the Fédération de Football Association (FIFA) which was founded in 1904. The World Cup, the sport's most prestigious competition, was first held in 1930 and continues to be held every four years.

FAR LEFT: Fish farming produces enormous quantities of fish for human consumption. Supporters of the industry claim that it helps protect numbers of particularly vulnerable species, such as salmon.

LEFT: Sir Alexander Fleming, the British medical scientist and bacteriologist.

BELOW: Dense fog can pose a serious problem for road users.

FORBIDDEN CITY

Peking (Beijing) consisted of the Tartar City and the Chinese City. Within the former was the Imperial City, at the heart of which was the Forbidden City containing the imperial palaces and temples.

FORESTS

Large wooded areas with a thick growth of trees and plants. The type of trees that grow in a forest varies according to local factors, primarily soil and climate. Different forest types are recognized throughout the world. Deciduous (non-evergreen) forests are found in temperate countries, such as the United Kingdom. Tropical rainforests are typically located in central Africa and the Amazon watershed while the northern, exposed areas of the Tundra support forests of hardy conifers. Ancient forests are now managed to preserve their unique contribution to the environment and artificial forests are also created to ensure continued supplies of timber.

➤ ***Rainforests, Trees***

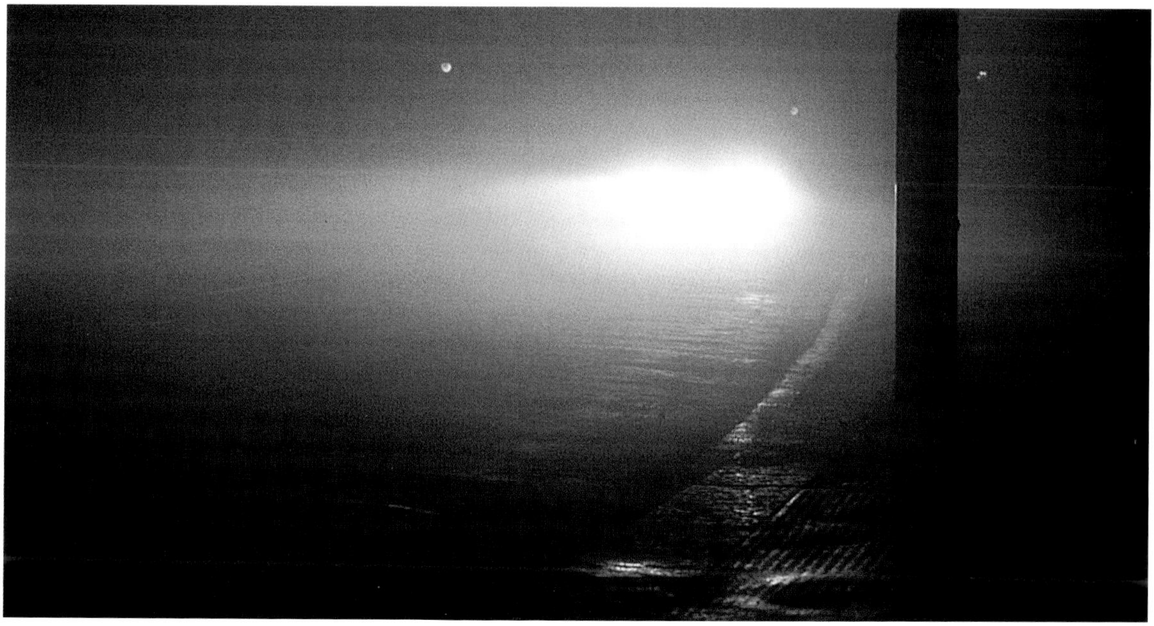

FOSSILS

Any trace of prehistoric life that has been preserved in rock. From the Latin word fossilis, meaning 'dug up'. Fossils may be – rarely – the actual remains of an ancient life form that have been preserved, e.g. insects in amber. More frequently they are the result of petrification, a chemical process which literally turns organic remains to stone. The fossil record has been of prime importance in understanding how life has evolved on Earth. Fossils are also used to date rocks.

➧ ***Dinosaurs, Geology***

FOSTER, JODIE (b. 1962)

US actress. Double Oscar winner, Foster has been acting in films since she was 10 years old. Her most accomplished roles are in *Taxi Driver* (1976), *The Accused* (1988) and *The Silence of the Lambs* (1991).

➧ ***Academy Awards, Films***

FOSTER, NORMAN (b. 1935)

English architect, sometime partner of Richard Rogers, renowned for his precise and gracious buildings, such as his 1970s design the Willis-Faber-Dumas Offices in Ipswich.

➧ ***Architecture, Richard Rogers***

FOX

Smallest member of the dog family, found throughout Europe, America and Asia. The red fox, which inhabits the United Kingdom, is the most common of 10 species of fox.

FRANCE

North-west European country. **Capital:** Paris. **Other principal cities:** Bordeaux, Lyon, Lille, Toulouse, Strasbourg. **Climate:** mild in the north, Mediterranean in the south. **Geographical features:** most of the country is low-lying, but the Pyrenees and Alps dominate the south. France enjoys Mediterranean, Atlantic and English Channel coasts. **Main language:** French. **Main religion:** Roman Catholicism. **Rule:** liberal democracy. Currency: franc. **Primary industries:** food, textiles and clothing, mining, manufacturing of transport and electrical equipment, cars and bicycles, military equipment, agriculture and tourism. **Exports:** clothing, cosmetics, food, livestock, manufactured goods such as cars, wine.

France is one of the largest European countries. Rivers have provided vital access and trade routes since prehistory. The Rhône flows south to Marseilles on the Mediterranean. The Garonne, Dordogne and Loire flow out to the Atlantic at Bordeaux and Nantes respectively, and the Seine into the Channel at Rouen. The French Alps include Europe's highest peak, Mont Blanc. The variety of scenery has contributed to France's popularity as one of the world's premier tourist destinations.

France's location allows it to capitalize on being both a Mediterranean nation and north-west European power. Today it is one of Europe's most successful agricultural and industrial communities. The population is about 58 million.

FRANCIS OF ASSISI, SAINT (1182–1226)

Founder of the Franciscan order of monks sworn to poverty and chastity, Saint Francis was renowned for his rapport with animals as well as humans. He was canonized in 1228.

FRANCO, GENERAL FRANCISCO (1892–1975)

Army general in the Spanish Civil War, who led the Nationalists to victory in 1939. Franco established a one-party state which survived to his death.

➧ ***Spanish Civil War***

FRANK, ANNE (1929–45)

German Jewish girl whose diaries record the two years she and her family spent hiding from the Nazis in occupied Amsterdam during World War II. Anne was eventually captured and died in Belsen concentration camp just before it was liberated.

➧ ***Nazism, World War II***

FRANKLIN, BENJAMIN (1706–90)

American politician and scientist. Franklin's inventions include the lightning conductor, and bifocal spectacles. He proved that lightning is a form of electricity by flying a kite during a thunderstorm. First Postmaster-General of the US.

➧ ***Electricity***

FRENCH REVOLUTION (1789–93)

Overthrow of the monarchy in France. The growth in the ideology of liberty, promoted by the American Revolution, influenced France. In 1789, the estates-general parliament was recalled after 175 years and sought to impose constitutional controls on the Crown. Attempts by Louis XVI to suppress such revolutionary acts led to the storming of the Bastille. Attempts to create a constitutional monarchy were abandoned in a wholesale attempt to build a new regime. The new First Republic foundered in faction and counter-revolution allowing extremists as the 'Committee of Public Safety' to bring in the Reign of Terror. This was replaced by the more moderate Directory, but in 1799 Napoleon seized control and proclaimed himself emperor.

➜ *American Revolution, Napoleon Bonaparte*

FRENCH ROYALTY

This monarchy traced its origins back to Clovis (AD 481–511), king of the Franks who defeated the Gallo-Romans in AD 486 and brought the whole of Gaul under his sway. The original Merovingian dynasty was gradually replaced by the mayors of the palace, Pepin the Short taking the royal title in AD 751. His son Charlemagne extended the Frankish dominions from the Elbe to the Ebro, but the empire was divided among his sons in 843, Charles the Bald getting what is now France. On the death of Louis V, Hugh Capet was elected king in AD 987 and founded the dynasty which continued till 1848 when Louis-Philippe was overthrown by Louis Napoleon Bonaparte who declared himself Emperor Napoleon III (1852–71). The disastrous Franco-German War forced him into exile and ended the monarchy.

➜ *Charlemagne*

FREUD, SIGMUND (1856–1939)

Austrian psychiatrist. Freud is the father of psychoanalysis. His theories on the workings of the mind, its desires, motives and traumas have left an indelible mark on the twentieth century. In 1899, Freud published the astonishingly influential *Interpretation of Dreams,* looking at the unconscious mind through the medium of dreams. Freud believed that many neuroses or psychological problems could be traced to sexual desires. His theories have developed psychology both through people's adherence to them and from reaction against them.

➜ *Psychology*

FROST

White deposit of ice particles that forms when the temperature drops below 0°C. Frost forms most commonly at night and can be seen as a white icy coating on objects in the morning.

FRUIT

Part of a flowering plant that contains the female organ, the ovary. The primary reason for the development of a fruit is the protection of seeds but the fruit may develop a fleshy, succulent layer which, when eaten by animals, aids distribution of the seeds. Nuts lack this fleshy layer.

FRY, ELIZABETH (1780–1845)

English Quaker active in prison reform, particularly with women (1817), and latter with men as well (1819) along with her brother Joseph Gurney.

FUJI, MOUNT

Fujiyama, near Tokyo, is a volcano, and Japan's highest peak at 3,778 m (12,400 ft). It last erupted in 1707 and has played an important part in Japanese religious and cultural identity.

➜ *Volcanoes*

FUNGI

Plural of fungus; a plant-like organism that lacks chlorophyll (the green pigment used by most plants to convert light into energy). Fungi gain nutrients by secreting a chemical directly on to food, which is then dissolved, absorbed and transported around the fungal body. Fungi, like bacteria, play an essential role in the decomposition and decay of organic matter and are found wherever other life forms exist. Approximately 100,000 species of fungi have been identified, including mushrooms, toadstools, moulds and yeast.

➜ *Moulds, Yeasts*

GABLE, CLARK (1901–60)

US actor. Star of over 60 films, Gable is best remembered as Rhett Butler in *Gone with the Wind* (1939). Died of a heart attack shortly after filming alongside Marilyn Monroe in *The Misfits*.

Gone with the Wind, *Marilyn Monroe*

GABON

West African equatorial country. **Capital:** Libreville. **Other principal cities:** Masuku, Port-Gentil. **Climate:** hot and humid. **Geographical features:** interior savanna leads to forested slopes and coastal plains. **Main language:** French. **Main religion:** Roman Catholicism. **Rule:** democracy. **Currency:** franc CFA. **Primary industries:** mining, forestry, oil production, agriculture (mainly subsistence). **Exports:** petroleum, manganese, timber, uranium.

Africa

GAINSBOROUGH, THOMAS (1727–88)

English artist. Born in Suffolk, Gainsborough moved to London to receive artistic training before making his name as a fine portrait painter in Bath. Although Gainsborough's main love was landscape painting he completed over 700 portraits. In one of his most famous works, *Mr & Mrs Andrews* (1748), Gainsborough cleverly combined these two aspects.

Together with his rival Sir Joshua Reynolds, Gainsborough was the most prodigious portrait painter of Britain. Unlike Reynolds, Gainsborough's main influences were the Dutch landscape painters and Rococo artists such as Jean-Antoine Watteau, rather than the Renaissance masters. Gainsborough had a reputation for producing a realistic likeness of his sitters, his style being refined and gracious.

Sir Joshua Reynolds, Rococo, Jean-Antoine Watteau

ABOVE: The Andromeda galaxy, the closest galaxy to our own.
TOP RIGHT: Mahatma Gandhi, the Indian nationalist and spiritual leader.
RIGHT: The Swedish actress, Greta Garbo.

GALAXIES

Extremely large groupings of stars, gas and dust, held together by gravity, with up to a million million times the mass of the Sun. Most galaxies can be described as spiral, barred spiral, or elliptical. The Milky Way, which contains our Solar System, is a spiral galaxy.

Solar System, Sun, Stars

GAMBIA

West African country. **Capital:** Banjul. **Other principal cities:** Serekunda, Bakau, Georgetown. **Climate:** sub-tropical. **Geographical features:** a narrow corridor country, dominated by the Gambia river and surrounded by Senegal. **Main language:** English. **Main religion:** Islam. **Rule:** military transitional. **Currency:** dalasi. **Primary industries:** agriculture, tourism, fishing. **Exports:** groundnut products, cotton, hides.

GAMBLING

Traditional activity that is now big business. Many countries have state-run lotteries and nearly all place taxes on winnings to ensure that the government also makes a gain. The activity can be addictive.

GANDHI, INDIRA (1917–84)

Leader of the Congress Party, prime minister of India (1966–77 and 1980–84). Gandhi involved India in Bangladesh's breakaway, by defeating Pakistan in 1971. Accused of electoral abuse in 1972 she introduced repressive measures leading to electoral defeat in 1977. Her comeback ended with assassination by her Sikh bodyguard. This followed an attack on the Sikh temple of Amritsar in reprisal for Sikh calls for an independent state.

GANDHI, MOHANDAS KARAMCHAND (1869–1948)

Pacifist Indian nationalist leader, given the name Mahatma ('great sage'). Trained as a barrister in Britain, Gandhi practised in South Africa until he led the Indian community against discrimination in 1914.

Gandhi then returned to India where he gained influence in the Congress Party and led a programme of non-cooperation in pursuit of Indian independence. His campaign was dedicated to non-violence, religious toleration and the ending of caste discrimination, but he was frequently imprisoned. Gandhi was assassinated by a Hindu fanatic in the violence which followed independence in 1947.

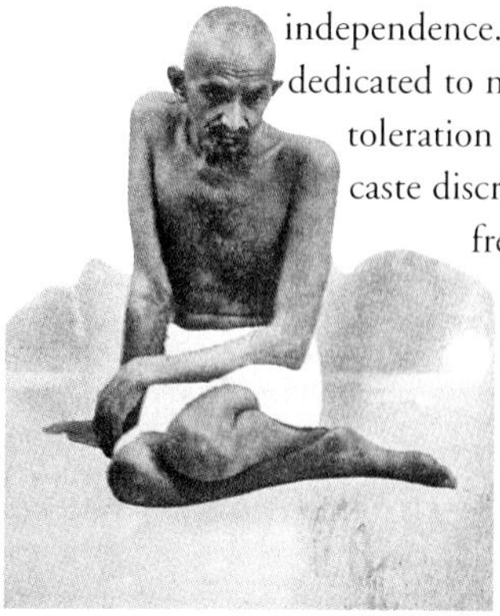

➤ *Indian Independence*

GARBO, GRETA (1905–90)

Swedish-born film actress. Garbo made 10 silent movies before her first 'talkie' in 1930 (*Anna Christie*). After 13 further films, Garbo retired at the early age of 36.

➤ *Films*

GARLAND, JUDY (1922–69)

US actress/singer, Garland was on stage at the tender age of three. She famously played Dorothy in *The Wizard of Oz* (1939) and won great acclaim in *A Star is Born* (1954).

GAS

State of matter (other than solid or liquid). Natural gas has been used as a fuel since the fifth century BC and the first known well drilled for natural gas was built in China in 211 BC. Natural gas is often found where there is crude oil, the pressure of the gas on the oil in the Earth forcing it up to the surface.

➤ *Oil*

GAUDI, ANTONI (1852–1926)

Spanish architect. Gaudi's work can be seen in his home town Barcelona. Although the impact of the current Art Nouveau movement was evident in Gaudi's work, he was clearly more affected by the Gothic, Moorish and Moroccan architectural styles. Gaudi's development of his inimitable and highly original style was aided by the extensive commissions he received from the industrialist Count Güell; Palau Güell and Park Güell are two of Gaudi's most astonishing buildings. Gaudi's style was heavily ornate, fantastical and included elements of the macabre. His work has been extensively inspirational, artists such as Salvador Dalí cite him as influence.

➤ *Architecture, Art Nouveau, Salavdor Dalí, Palau Güell*

GAULLE, CHARLES DE (1890–1970)

French general and Nationalist political leader. Leader of the Free French during World War II, he headed the provisional French government of 1944–46. In 1958 he was asked to form a new government during a national crisis. As prime minister he created a presidential system, becoming president until 1969 consistently supporting French nationalist interests.

➤ *World War II*

GEHRY, FRANK (b. 1929)

American architect, whose work includes the California Aerospace Museum, Los Angeles, and the Guggenheim Museum, Bilbao. Gehry's style is both innovative and provocative.

➤ *Architecture*

GEMSTONES

Artificially polished fragments of certain minerals that are used for decorative purposes, often in jewellery. Precious gemstones include diamonds, sapphires and emeralds. Semi-precious gemstones include topaz, garnet and zircon. The value of a gemstone is determined by its beauty, size, rarity, hardness and colour. A lapidary is a person skilled in the cutting and polishing of gemstones.

➤ *Diamond*

GENGHIS KHAN (1162–1227)

Mongol ruler and conqueror. Born in Central Asia, he expanded his father's domains through many campaigns. By 1227 his dominions extended from Persia and the Black Sea in the west to Korea and parts of China in the east. He left no permanent form of government but the Mongol Empire became the largest in history.

GENERAL AGREEMENT ON TARIFFS AND TRADE (1948)

GATT, part of the United Nations, was formed in 1948 to reduce controls on trade between nations, such as tariffs and subsidies. In 1995 the World Trade Organization superseded it.

GENETIC ENGINEERING

Manipulation of genetic material, in particular the addition of new DNA to a living cell. The purposes of genetic engineering include giving new functions to cells to produce useful biological materials such as enzymes and hormones, and having immunity from or resistance to disease.

GENETICS

The study of inheritance, genes and their effects. Inherited characteristics are controlled by genes, which are sections of the DNA molecule which make particular proteins. Genes can have two or more variants, called alleles, which give rise to alternative characteristics, for example eye colour.

GENEVA CONVENTION (1864)

Agreement and subsequent revisions, between nations, designed to restrict the excesses of war through regulations on treatment of wounded, prisoners, and civilians.

➡ *Human Rights*

GENOCIDE

Deliberate programme of mass murder designed to exterminate a group defined by race, religion or ethnicity. Genocide is most frequently applied to the 'Final Solution' instigated against the Jewish communities, and other groups considered undesirable, such as gypsies, during Germany's Third Reich. Communities were rounded up and systematically despatched to camps where those suitable for work were set to one side, and the remainder murdered in gas chambers. In more recent years genocide has returned, this time to the mass murder of Muslims in the Yugoslav civil war, and in Rwanda in Africa, showing that time and place are no guard against it.

➡ *Adolf Hitler, Nazism*

GEOLOGICAL TIME

Sequence of time applied to the Earth since its origin, possibly 4.65 billion years ago. Unlike most other scientists, geologists operate with a timescale that is usually measured in thousands and even millions of years. The major division of geological time is between Precambrian and Cambrian Time. The dividing line is drawn at around 530–570 million years ago, from when the earliest fossils are found. The time since the Precambrian is divided into three eras: Palaeozoic, Mesozoic and Cenozoic.

➡ *Earth, Fossils*

GEOLOGY

Study of the Earth, how it formed and the processes which continue to affect it. Geologists are concerned primarily with the study of rocks, their composition and the processes that act upon them. Geology has many uses including civil engineering, the location of valuable mineral resources and the prediction of catastrophic events such as earthquakes and landslides.

➡ *Earthquakes, Fossils*

GEOMETRY

Branch of mathematics concerned with the properties of space, usually in two dimensions (plane geometry) or three (solid geometry). In coordinate geometry, problems are solved using algebra.

GERMANY

North European country. **Capital**: Berlin. **Other principal cities**: Cologne, Munich, Essen, Frankfurt, Hamburg, Kiel. **Climate**: mild. **Geographical features**: Bavarian Alps in the south, dropping to central uplands and northern plains. **Main language**: German. **Main religions**: Lutheran, Roman Catholicism. **Rule**: liberal democratic federal republic. **Currency**: Deutschemark. **Primary industries**: mining, manufacturing of electrical, electronic, non-electrical, transport and chemical goods, agriculture (arable and pastoral). **Exports**: cars, electrical and electronic goods, metals, textiles.

In spite of eventual total defeat in 1945, Germany exhibited an astonishing capacity to manufacture war material, and devise radical new technologies in the war, anticipating post-war events. The reunification of Germany in 1990, after the 1945 division into West and East Germany, has created the largest and most populous state in Europe with a population of about 84 million.

Despite the ravages caused by aerial bombardment and land fighting during World War II, Germany has one of the world's strongest economies thanks to comprehensive industrial development, with a reputation for efficiency. The Ruhr Valley is the most important industrial area, though agriculture is still important farther south. German economic policy dominates the European Union.

➡ ***Berlin Wall, Cold War, Europe***

GEYSERS

Spurting of hot water and steam from underground sources in volcanic regions. Old Faithful, a geyser in Yellowstone National Park, spouts water up to 52 m (170 ft).

GHANA

West African coastal country (formerly Gold Coast). **Capital:** Accra. **Other principal towns:** Sekondi-Takoradi. **Climate:** tropical. **Geographical features:** interior tropical rainforest with coastal lowlands and northern savanna. **Main languages:** English and local languages. **Main religions:** Christianity, Islam. **Rule:** democratic republic. **Currency:** cedi. **Primary industries:** agriculture, mining, forestry. **Exports:** cocoa, coffee, gold, metal ores, diamonds, tuna.

➡ ***Africa***

GHOSTS

Spirits of dead people: shadowy in appearance and no physical body. Feared and often thought, by Roman Catholics, to be the result of a distressed soul trapped in Purgatory. Poltergeists are noisy ghosts, prone to making objects move. A priest, or specifically an exorcist, can be called in to expel a spirit from a place or person.

➡ ***Occult, Paranormal Phenomenon***

GIRAFFE

Grazing mammal of dry African lands south of the Sahara. Tallest of all animals, reaching 5.2 m (17 ft). Their long necks enable giraffes to reach acacia leaves, their main food.

GLACIERS

Rivers of slow-moving ice that form in conditions too cold for snow to melt. They begin in mountainous regions and move slowly down through valleys to warmer areas where they do melt. As they travel through the valley the huge weight of a glacier erodes the rock beneath it, transforming the landscape.

➡ ***Valleys***

GLASS

Transparent or translucent material which is strong but brittle, and which has many structural uses, for example for containers. The most common types of glass are made by melting sand with a variety of other materials. For example, soda glass is made using soda ash and limestone.

TOP: A glacier on the South Georgia Island, Antarctica.
ABOVE: Molten glass is blown into shapes which solidify on cooling.
LEFT: People dressed as ghosts at a festival in Malaga, Spain.

GLASTONBURY FESTIVAL

Rock music festival held in Glastonbury, Somerset in the UK. Usually occurring annually in June, the festival is one of the largest in Europe and attracts some of the top names in the music industry.

GLOBAL WARMING

General increase in the Earth's atmospheric temperature (estimated at between 0.3°C (0.5°F) and 0.8°C (1.4°F) during the twentieth century). The cause of global warming is a matter of speculation but increasing evidence suggests that human activity, especially the burning of fossil fuels and the production of methane by livestock, are important factors.

➡ ***Environment***

GLYNDEBOURNE FESTIVAL (1934)

Operatic festival begun by John Christie, named after his Sussex estate where the event is held in a specially built opera house. The festival concentrates on Mozart's operas.

➡ ***Wolfgang Amadeus Mozart, Opera***

GOETHE, JOHANN WOLFGANG VON (1749–1832)

German writer, poet and art theoretician, Goethe was a guiding influence in the spread of Romanticism (although he later rejected the movement's premises, returning instead to the ideals of Classicism, particularly those extolled by Raphael's work). His writing includes *The Sorrows of Young Werther* (1774) and his *Theory of Colours* (1810).

➡ ***Romantic***

GOGH, VINCENT VAN (1853–90)

Dutch painter, equally known for his tragic life as for his exemplary, ground-breaking art. In 1888 following an argument with the painter Paul Gauguin, van Gogh cut off his ear and spent most of his final years in an asylum before committing suicide. His work during this time shows the development of his unique style, with its heavy brushstrokes that create swirling, echoing patterns in intense, dramatic colours. While alive van Gogh sold only one painting; today his works sell for millions. He is now one of the most esteemed modern artists, whose enduring influence has been far-reaching.

➡ ***Post-impressionism***

GOLD

Shiny yellow metal with the chemical symbol Au. Valued because of its rarity and the ease with which it can be shaped and moulded into jewellery and coins.

➡ ***Silver***

GOLF

Popular sporting activity with global following. Well-developed professional courses attract enormous financial rewards. The game was invented in Scotland in the fourteenth century with the rules formulated in 1744. The two main disciplines are match play (least number of strokes for the round wins) and stroke play (least number of strokes wins the hole, winner of most holes in the round wins).

GONE WITH THE WIND (1939)

Epic film of Margaret Mitchell's novel, following the story of a Southern belle during the American Civil War. Directed by Victor Fleming and starring Vivian Leigh and Clark Gable.

➡ ***American Civil War, Clark Gable, Vivien Leigh***

GORGE

Any deep and narrow vertically sided valley, also known as a canyon. Gorges may be formed by the erosive action of a river or from the collapse of a cavern's roof.

➡ ***Erosion, Valleys***

FAR LEFT: The German writer Johann Wolfgang von Goethe.

GORILLA

The largest ape, living in west and central Africa. Gorillas live in extended family groups, are vegetarian and aggressive only when threatened. Males grow to 1.8 m (6 ft) and 200 kg (30 stones). Gorillas are a threatened species.

➠ ***Endangered Species***

GOTHIC ART, MUSIC AND LITERATURE

Gothic was initially a derogatory term that has been applied broadly to art, architecture and literature of medieval Europe, particularly that of the thirteenth to sixteenth centuries. The term comes from the word Goth – the people held responsible for the destruction of the Roman Empire. The description of art as Gothic began during the Renaissance (initially used by the art writer Vasari) to differentiate medieval art from the Classic style that was then the ideal. Artists such as Giotto, with their flat, ornamental style, are termed Gothic. Gothic architecture was elaborate, including flying buttresses and rib vaults.

➠ ***Medieval, Renaissance***

GOVERNMENTS

A system for exercising political and executive power. Aristotle, a Greek philosopher, defined a series of governments: monarchy (rule by one), oligarchy (rule by a few) and democracy (rule by many). However, these definitions need qualification, depending on the legal basis of any one government.

Rule by a single person ranges from hereditary monarchies ruling with absolute power or restrained by constitutions, to dictators ruling with unrestrained absolute power. Today, monarchy normally only survives as a component of a constitution, e.g. the British monarch is head of state, but the process of legislation and the exercise of power is through an elected parliament. Conversely, Saudi Arabia is ruled by an absolute monarch who is head of state and government.

Autocratic governments represent a variant, where the ruler, often a soldier or renegade politician who has seized power through a coup, operates a regime which uses force to stay in power for its own sake, rather than in pursuit of an ideology.

Presidential government substitutes an elected head of state and government, who is separate from the legislative body, as in the US. In parliamentary government, the government is taken from members of the elected legislature, as in the UK.

Government through party varies from the democratic system in which more than one political party vies for popular support through election, seeking dominance of the executive body which controls government. Such government is relatively open and differs from one-party totalitarianism.

Federal government devolves power to regions. In the US, the individual state legislatures are responsible for much local government, but all are answerable to the federal government for certain affairs such as national defence.

Totalitarian government often utilizes the process of election, but with only one party, choice is non-existent and opposition is excluded from the debate. Typically, government is closed and secretive.

➠ ***Dictatorship, Presidents***

GOYA Y LUCIENTES, FRANCISCO JOSÉ DE (1746–1828)

Spanish painter and graphic artist. Goya painted portraits at the Spanish court before losing favour when his work became increasingly burlesque (particularly in the *Caprichos* [1799]). An illness in 1792 left Goya deaf; his physical isolation is reflected by an increasingly bleak tone in his work. During the French occupation of Spain, Goya poignantly illustrated his horror of violence with works such as *The Third of May* (1814–15). Goya's later work shows a freedom of technique that was greatly admired by successive painters.

➠ ***Graphic Art***

GRAND CANYON

River gorge on the Colorado River in Arizona, US. Up to 1.7 km (1.1 mile) deep and 350 km (217 miles) long, the canyon is one of the world's most epic and colourful natural phenomena.

GRANT, CARY (1904–86)

English-born actor. Grant combined sophisticated charm with impeccable delivery to comic roles, playing romantic lead in films such as *Bringing up Baby* (1937). He later worked with Hitchcock in tense thrillers such as *Notorious* (1946).

➠ ***Alfred Hitchcock***

GRAPES OF WRATH (1940)

John Steinbeck novel turned into a highly praised film by John Ford (1940). The story follows the plight of Oklahoma farmers after the dust-bowl disaster of the 1930s.

GRAPHIC ART

Overall term applied to art, excluding painting, that is created through lines, symbols, characters or letters rather than through the use of colour. Types of graphic art are prints, engravings, woodcuts, lithography and typography. Graphic art can employ a variety of surfaces such as paper and silk for prints, wood or brass for engravings. Graphic arts were particularly important in pre-industrial society, as book illustration and print – many artists, such as Goya and Dalí, have explored graphic arts through these mediums.

➠ ***Salvador Dalí, Francisco de Goya, Typography***

GRAVITY

Force of attraction of every material object to every other object. The force between two objects depends on their total mass and their distance apart. The force that attracts an object towards the centre of the earth.

LEFT: Magnificent views over the Grand Canyon and surrounding area, Arizona, US.

RIGHT: Both the mainland of Greece and its islands continue to adhere to many age-old traditions in modern daily life; this man wears traditional Greek costume.

GREAT EXHIBITION (1851)

Exhibition held in 1851 in Hyde Park, London. The brainchild of Prince Albert, consort of Queen Victoria, it was the largest trade show of its time, with 100,000 exhibits in all, embracing raw materials, machinery and invention, manufacturing, and sculpture and plastic arts. The glass-walled exhibition hall, designed by the architect Joseph Paxton, became known as the 'Crystal Palace'. Over six million visitors attended the exhibition from May to October 1851, and the profits made were used to purchase land in Kensington, London, on which the Victoria and Albert Museum, Natural History Museum and Science Museum were later built.

➠ *British Empire, Crystal Palace*

GREAT LAKES

Five freshwater lakes, formed from ancient glacial valleys, along the US-Canada border: Superior, Michigan, Huron, Erie and Ontario. Their combined area is 245,000 sq km (94,600 sq miles). Canals connect them to the St Lawrence river and seaway. The Lakes are vital for commerce. Most of Canada's industrial production, and about half that of the US, takes place in lakeside cities.

➠ *Canada*

GREAT TREK (1828–36)

Name given to the mass migration of Boers (farmers of Dutch or Huguenot descent) from Cape Colony. Dissatisfied with living under British rule, the Boers headed north and crossed the Orange River in 1828, then crossed the Vaal eight years later, to create the South African Republic (Transvaal).

GREECE

South European Mediterranean country. **Capital**: Athens. **Other principal cities**: Piraeus, Thessaloniki, Patras. **Climate**: temperate with hot summers. **Geographical features**: mountainous and with numerous islands. **Main language**: Greek. **Main religions**: Greek Orthodox, Roman Catholics. **Rule**: democratic republic. **Currency**: drachma. **Primary industries**: food and wine, manufacturing, petroleum, textiles, tourism. **Exports**: fruit and vegetables, petroleum products, metals and alloys.

Greece's rocky and arid land limits agriculture. Its coastline and islands have fostered a great maritime tradition and a widely scattered population.

GREECE, ANCIENT

The cradle of western civilization, the city states of Greece began to emerge about 3,300 years ago, attaining their zenith in the fifth century BC. The Greek world extended far beyond the frontiers of the modern country, for the cities of the mainland established numerous colonies from Asia Minor and the Black Sea to North Africa, Sicily, Italy and Spain. The Greeks contributed more to democracy, drama, art and architecture than any other people up to that time. They founded the Olympic Games, perfected the alphabet and invented coinage, laid down the principles of western philosophy and created forms of government that endure to this day. They successfully resisted the Persians but fell to Philip of Macedon. Briefly the centre of the Alexandrine Empire, Greece was conquered by Rome in the second century BC but considerably influenced the development of Roman civilization.

➠ *Olympic Games, Ancient Rome*

GREEK GODS AND MYTHOLOGY

The Greek gods formed a pantheon and the related mythology was extensive. Although fictitious, the mythology contained fundamental human truths and it was later adopted by the Romans.

Zeus, the god of the sky, was supreme, and his two brothers ruled with him: Hades as god of the underworld and Poseidon as god of the sea. Mount Olympus was regarded as common territory of the gods and the earth was for mankind. Greek mythology contained extraordinary creatures, such as Pegasus, the Minotaur, Medusa, centaurs and sirens, and remarkable heroes such as Heracles (and his labours), Jason (and the Golden Fleece), Perseus, Odysseus (and the wooden horse), Oedipus (who killed his father and married his mother) and Achilles (and his vulnerable heel). Ancient Greeks believed that the gods should not be angered, for fear of retribution.

➠ *Roman Gods and Mythology*

GREENHOUSES

Buildings used in horticulture with transparent walls. Radiant heat from the Sun warms the air inside, increasing the growth rate of the plants.

GREENPEACE (1971)

International environmental pressure group founded in 1971. Greenpeace is a very active organization with a policy of aggressive, but non-violent protest. It has in turn attracted the attention of several national governments, the most famous example being the sinking of its ship, the *Rainbow Warrior*, by the French secret service in 1985.

➨ ***Animal Rights, Environment***

GREENWICH OBSERVATORY (1675)

Founded in 1675 by Charles I of England to determine the positions of stars to help in navigation. The work of the observatory moved to Herstmonceux, and later to Cambridge, under the name Royal Greenwich Observatory, and ceased in 1997. The Royal Observatory, Greenwich, is now part of the National Maritime Museum.

GREYHOUND RACING

Popular sport invented in its modern form in the US in 1919. Derived from earlier harecoursing and related 'sports', the hounds now chase a mechanical hare rather than a real one.

GROPIUS, WALTER (1883–1969)

German architect. Gropius created the Bauhaus school at Weimar in 1919. Taking his inspiration from William Morris, the Expressionists and the Arts and Crafts movement, Gropius believed that through architecture a powerful unity between artists and crafts people could be created. By 1923 Gropius turned his focus upon industrial design. Gropius left the Bauhaus in 1928.

➨ ***Architecture, Arts and Crafts Movement, Expressionism, William Morris***

GUATEMALA

Central American country. **Capital:** Guatemala City. **Other principal cities:** Quezaltenango, Puerto Barrios. **Climate:** tropical highlands, temperate lowlands. **Geographical features:** northern forests, mountains, fertile southern plain. **Main languages:** Spanish and Mayan dialects. **Main religion:** Roman Catholicism. **Rule:** democratic republic. **Currency:** quetzal. **Primary industry:** agriculture. **Exports:** coffee, bananas, sugar, beef, cardamoms, cotton.

GUGGENHEIM MUSEUM

The Guggenheim museum in New York houses Solomon R. Guggenheim's extensive collection of modern art. The building, designed by Frank Lloyd Wright, was completed in 1959. The architecture of the building reflects the modern art collection it houses in its dismissal of the traditional, with its twisting form and coils of white concrete.

➨ ***Museums, Frank Lloyd Wright***

GUINEA

West African coastal country. **Capital:** Conakry. **Other principal cities:** Labé, Nzérékoré, Kankan. **Climate:** tropical coastlands, hot and dry inland with cooler highlands. **Geographical features:** fertile, vast mineral reserves and an Atlantic coastline. **Main language:** French. **Main religion:** Islam. **Rule:** democratic republic. **Currency:** Guinean franc. **Primary industries:** mining, agriculture. **Exports:** alumina, bauxite, diamonds, gold, coffee, bananas, pineapples, rice.

➨ ***Africa***

LEFT: Thatched roofed buildings and an open meeting area are surrounded by tropical vegetation in a Maroni village, Guyana.

GUINNESS, SIR ALEC (1914–2000)

English actor. Guiness was a key figure in the Ealing Comedies of the 1940s and 50s. He was highly respected with an intensely reflective screen presence, noted in films such as *The Swan* (1956) and *Oliver Twist* (1948).

➤ *Films*

GULF OF MEXICO

Area of sea bounded on the west by Central America, to the north by the US, and to the east the islands of the Caribbean. The Gulf Stream current rises here warming the climate of north-western Europe. Reserves of gas and oil are drilled, and commercial fishing is of importance. Hurricanes form here in late summer and autumn.

GULF WAR (1991)

Conflict arising when a US-led alliance expelled the Iraqi occupiers of Kuwait, invaded in August 1990. Total Iraqi defeat followed a 100-hour ground war after aerial bombardment.

GUNPOWDER

The first explosive, a mixture of saltpetre (potassium nitrate), charcoal and sulphur in the proportions 15:3:2. It is uncertain who invented gunpowder, but it was in use by the Chinese in the tenth century for signal rockets and fireworks. Until the mid-nineteenth century, it was the only explosive available.

GUYANA

North-east South American country. **Capital:** Georgetown. **Other principal cities:** Linden, Rose Hall. **Climate:** tropical. **Geographical features:** coastal plain gives way to interior savanna and rainforest. **Main language:** English. **Main religions:** Hindu, Christianity. **Rule:** democratic republic. **Currency:** Guyana dollar. **Primary industries:** agriculture, mining. **Exports:** alumina, bauxite, diamonds, rice, rum, shrimps, sugar, timber.

GYMNASTICS

Ancient physical discipline that has become a global sport. Main types include floor exercises, parallel bars, asymmetric bars, pommel horse, vaulting horse, the beam and rings.

➤ *Olympic Games*

HADRIAN'S WALL (AD 121)

Wall extending across northern England from the Solway Firth to the North Sea, constructed in AD 121 by the Emperor Hadrian to protect the province of Britannia.

➡ *Ancient Rome*

HAIRSTYLES

Hair has been the subject of controversy just as much as fashion has over the ages. Styles range from the sublime to the ridiculous, indeed women's styles in the eighteenth century were so complicated that they could never be washed. Other milestones in hair fashion include the perms, crew cuts, the mohican and dreadlocks.

➡ *Fashion*

HAITI

Western part of Hispaniola island in the Caribbean. **Capital:** Port-au-Prince. **Other principal cities:** Cap-Haïtian, Gonaïves, Les Cayes. **Climate:** tropical. **Geographical features:** mountains limit agriculture, long coastline. **Main languages:** Creole, French. **Main religion:** Roman Catholicism. **Rule:** republic. **Currency:** gourde. **Primary industries:** agriculture, light manufacturing. **Exports:** bauxite, coffee, cotton, manufactured goods, sugar, sisal.

HALOPHYTES

Plants that are tolerant of high levels of salt in the soil or atmosphere and therefore usually found growing close to the sea e.g. marsh samphire.

HANDEL, GEORGE FRIDERIC (1685–1759)

German composer. Along with J. S. Bach, Handel was the leading Baroque composer. Although Handel devoted much of his career to opera, he gained his great reputation for his oratorios, choral music and instrumental works, such as the captivating *Water Music* (1717). Handel lived in England for many years, where he was given financial support to write operas – he was director of a Royal Academy of Music aiming to bring Italian opera to England. Handel incorporated the drama and exuberance of opera in his compositions, especially his superb oratorio arias. In 1742 Handel wrote the *Messiah* which remains one of the most popular and famous pieces of religious music.

➡ *Johann Sebastian Bach, Baroque, Opera*

HANOVERIANS (1714–1837)

Dynasty which ruled Britain and Ireland. It was founded by George Louis, Elector of Hanover (1660–1727), a great-grandson of James VI and I who succeeded to the British throne on the death of his cousin Queen Anne, last of the Stuart line. George I (the 'wee German lairdie') continued to live in Hanover and took little interest in his new kingdom. George II (1727–60) was the last British monarch to lead his troops into battle, at Dettingen (1742), during the War of the Austrian Succession. He was succeeded by his grandson, George III (1760–1820) during whose reign Britain lost her American colonies but began the development of Australia. The last years of his reign were marred by insanity, as a result of which his son became Prince Regent (1810). George IV was succeeded by his brother William IV in 1830 and, in turn, was followed by his niece Victoria in 1837. As Salic Law prevented a woman from inheriting the Hanoverian throne it passed to her cousin Ernest Augustus, Duke of Cumberland who became Ernst August (1837–51). Hanover, raised to the rank of kingdom in 1814, was annexed by Prussia in 1866 following the Austro-Prussian War.

HARE KRISHNA MOVEMENT

Hindu sect that worships Krishna, one of the avatars of the god Vishnu. They are recognizable by their shaven heads and yellow robes. Their holy book is the *Bhagavad Gita*. They believe in reincarnation through repeated mantra: 'Hare Krishna'.

➡ *Hinduism*

FAR LEFT: The leading Baroque composer George Frederic Handel.
LEFT: Author and scientist Stephen Hawking.
BELOW: A Hare Krishna temple in Bloomsbury, London.

HAWAII

Pacific, and most southerly, state of the US (joined 1959). Made up of 20 volcanic islands, the largest being Hawaii. **Capital:** Honolulu. Main industry: tourism.

➡ ***United States of America***

HAWKING, STEPHEN (b. 1942)

British theoretical physicist, and professor of gravitational physics at Cambridge University. Hawking is best known for showing that a black hole can lose mass by emitting particles and for his book *A Brief History of Time.*

HAYDN, JOSEPH (1732–1809)

Austrian composer. Haydn is chiefly remembered for his wealth of instrumental compositions: his symphonies, sonatas and especially his works for string quartets. Haydn superbly developed the string quartet (composing 68 of them) to become music for four equally important players rather than a solo piece for the first violin. In his later career his choral music was also greatly acclaimed, in particular the 1796 oratorio *The Creation*. Haydn's life spanned several changes in musical tastes, from Baroque to Classicism to Romanticism. Together with that of his friend Mozart and Beethoven (a one-time pupil of his), Haydn's music is seen as the definitive Classic style.

➡ ***Baroque, Ludwig van Beethoven, Classical, Wolfgang Amadeus Mozart, Romantic***

HEATING

Introduction of heat to the air and the water supply of a building. Main sources of power used are electricity, gas, oil and solid fuel (coke). Electric and gas-fired heating are most popular as they do not require road deliveries of fuel.

➡ ***Electricity, Gas, Oil***

HEBREWS

Hebrews, meaning 'wanderers', are Semites who lived in Palestine and are the descendants of Abraham. Hebrew is the Jewish liturgical language and the national language of Israel. Hebrew kings and prophets emerged *c.* 1000 BC and so did the concept linking religion with morality.

➧ ***Judaism***

HELICOPTERS

Aircraft which use a rotary wing, or rotor, to provide lift and motion. The helicopter can hover, or move by tilting the rotor in the direction of motion.

➧ ***Aircraft***

HEPBURN, AUDREY (1929–93)

Belgian-born actress. At the height of her career Hepburn appeared in the enduring films *Breakfast at Tiffany's* (1961), *Funny Face* (1957) and *Roman Holiday* (1953). Also remembered for her charity work for the United Nations.

HEPBURN, KATHARINE (b. 1907)

US actress. The only actress to earn four Oscars, Hepburn is perhaps best loved for her portrayal of feisty, intelligent women in films such as *Bringing up Baby* (1937) and *Adam's Rib* (1949).

➧ ***Cary Grant, Spencer Tracey***

HERALDRY

System of identifying individuals by hereditary insignia. In the Middle Ages heralds presided over tournaments and from this developed their role in recording pedigrees and armorial bearings. Richard III founded the College of Arms in England in 1484. Scotland has its own institution presided over by the Lord Lyon King of Arms.

RIGHT: Hieroglyphics are stylized pictures which represent words, syllables or sounds. Understanding Ancient Egyptian hieroglyphics has enable historians to gain a greater knowledge of this remarkable civilization.

FAR RIGHT: A Nepalese statue depicting a Hindu god.

HERBS

Seed-bearing, non-woody plants such as flowering plants and ferns. The term 'herb' is also used to refer specifically to plants with medicinal and culinary uses. Medicinal herbs have been used since ancient times and are commonly used in the practice of Chinese medicine. The recent growth in alternative medicine has resulted in herbal remedies and supplements becoming widely available. Culinary herbs, such as rosemary and basil, impart delicate flavours to cooking and have also been used since ancient times.

➧ ***Alternative Medicine, Spices***

HEROIN

Invented in the early twentieth century as a substitute for opium. The drug is very addictive and widely used, even though it is illegal in most countries. Its street names include 'scag', 'H', 'smack' and 'horse'.

➧ ***Drugs***

HIEROGLYPHICS

Greek word meaning 'sacred carving'. The term hieroglyphic was originally used to denote the script of the ancient Egyptians; the walls of their tombs and temples are covered with this symbolic form of writing. Today the term is used to cover any representation of a secret language where images replace words or syllables.

➧ ***Ancient Egypt***

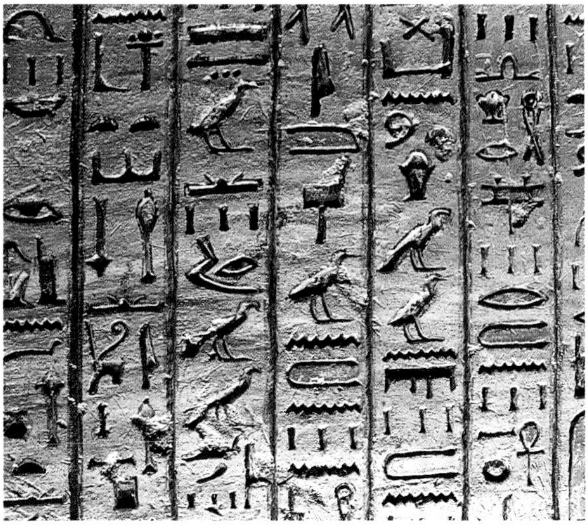

HILLARY, SIR EDMUND (b. 1919)

New Zealand mountaineer. In 1953, during the expedition led by John Hunt, Hillary and Tenzing Norgay, a Nepalese Sherpa, made the first recorded climb to the peak of Mount Everest. In January 1958 he reached the South Pole on foot, the first to do so since Robert Scott, during the Commonwealth Transantarctic Expedition of 1957–58.

➠ ***Mount Everest, Robert Falcon Scott***

HIMALAYAS

Central Asian mountain range, the highest in the world (highest are Everest and K2), running from Assam in the east to Kashmir in the west, covering southern Tibet, Nepal, Bhutan and Sikkim.

➠ ***Mount Everest***

HINDUISM

Religion originating in India *c.* 4000 BC. Its principal beliefs are in reincarnation and 'karma'. The oldest scriptures are the *Vedas*. The supreme spirit is Brahman, and the triad of Brahma (creator), Vishnu (preserver) and Siva (destroyer) are the key gods. There are 805 million Hindus worldwide today, organized in a caste system, and worship occurs in temples and is manifest in many festivals.

➠ ***Diwali***

HIPPOPOTAMUS

Large pig-like mammals that live in Africa. Hippopotami spend most of the day wallowing in rivers, coming out at night to graze on grass at the riverbank.

➠ ***Pigs***

HIROSHIMA (1945)

Industrial city in Honshu, Japan. On 6 August 1945 the world's first atomic bomb was dropped there by the Allies. It obliterated 10 sq km (4 sq miles), caused 137,000 casualties and 78,150 fatalities: many more died from fall-out later. A second bomb was dropped on Nagasaki.

HIRST, DAMIEN (b. 1965)

British artist, winner of the 1995 Turner Prize. His work is filled with images of death such as 1993's infamous *Mother and Child Divided,* (a bisected cow and calf).

HITCHCOCK, SIR ALFRED (1899–1980)

Bristish-born US film director. The undisputed master of the thriller genre in mid-twentieth century cinema, Hitchcock's catalogue shows enormous narrative skill, from the classic *The Thirty-Nine Steps* (1935) to the immense impact of 1960's *Psycho*.

➽ ***Film, Cary Grant***

HITLER, ADOLF (1889–1945)

German dictator. Austrian-born, Hitler was infuriated at Germany's defeat in World War I and her treatment by the victorious powers. Hitler founded the Nazi party, and exploited grievances through his anti-Semitic ideology as enshrined in his book, *Mein Kampf*. Much of Germany began to acquiesce in his extremism, entranced by his promises of restored German power. By 1934 Hitler had supreme power, leading Germany and her allies into World War II in a programme of conquest seeking to maximize territory and power for the German peoples. War broke out in 1939 but by 1942 the tide had turned. Total defeat and Hitler's suicide came on 28 April 1945.

➽ ***Dictatorship, Nazism, World War II***

HITTITES

Ancient people who dominated Syria and Asia Minor 2000–1200 BC. The Hittites rank after the Egyptians and Assyrians in importance among the civilizations of the Middle East. According to Genesis, they were the followers of Heth, son of Canaan. They are best remembered for their hieroglyphics and cuneiform script.

➽ ***Hieroglyphics***

ABOVE: The German dictator and founder of the Nazi party, Adolf Hitler. Hitler's suicide in 1945 led to the end of World War II.

HO CHI MINH (c. 1890–1969)

Vietnamese Communist leader. Following the division of Vietnam in 1954, Ho Chi Minh was made president of North Vietnam, and then sought to win the South, leading his country through the Vietnam War.

➽ ***Communism, Vietnam War***

HOCKEY

Game played between two teams of 11 players each, the aim being to hit a small ball into a goal with a hooked stick. It has been an Olympic sport since 1908.

➽ ***Olympic Games***

HOFFMAN, DUSTIN (b. 1937)

American actor. Hoffman shot to fame in the seminal film *The Graduate* (1967). He received the best actor Oscar for *Kramer vs Kramer* in 1979 and again for *Rain Man* (1988).

➽ ***Academy Awards, Anne Bancroft, Tom Cruise***

HOGARTH, WILLIAM (1697–1764)

British artist. Hogarth worked mainly in the Rococo style. He was initially trained as an engraver, a medium through which he gained much fame. Hogarth was also a skilled painter, specializing in narrative paintings such as *The Beggar's Opera*. From 1735 he directed an art academy that became the precedent of the Royal Academy, London.

➽ ***Rococo***

HOKUSAI, KATSUSHIKA (1760–1849)

Japanese painter and graphic artist. Hokusai's work had a great impact upon Western European art. His prints (in *Ukiyo-e* fashion), such as *The Wave* (*c.* 1820), influenced the Post-Impressionists.

➽ ***Graphic Art, Post-Impressionism,*** **Ukiyo-e**

HOLIDAYS

Rest days when people are generally not expected to work. The word is a contraction of 'holy day', the origins of most modern holidays. Most countries have a series of national holidays, based on religious, political or social events. Personal paid holidays were introduced in the UK in 1938. The Holidays with Pay Act initially stipulated one week per year.

➠ ***National Holidays, Tourism***

HOLOCAUST

Name given to the mass murder of approximately 15 million men, women and children by Hitler's Nazi Germany between 1933–45. The Nazi regime was founded on principles of Aryan 'purity', and a demand for more land for the German peoples. The Holocaust was instituted as a means of destroying as many 'undesirables' as possible to release land and resources for this purpose. The core group destroyed were the Jewish communities, but to them were added gypsies, homosexuals, prisoners-of-war, Slav peoples and the handicapped. A network of concentration camps was set up. On arrival, those capable of work were removed, while the remainder were mostly killed with poison gas and their bodies burned.

➠ ***Adolf Hitler, Nazism, World War II***

ABOVE: When a hologram catches the light in a certain way a 3-D image appears.
RIGHT: The Vatican, St Peter's Square in Rome, Italy.

HOLOGRAMS

Image produced using a laser beam split in two, which has three-dimensional information encoded in it. When viewed by laser light, an apparent 3-D image is seen.

HOLY PLACES

Places of religious significance, which have often subsequently become pilgrimage sites and shrines. Christian pilgrimage sites include Jerusalem, Rome and Lourdes, while for the Jews they include, again, Jerusalem, particularly the Western Wall. One of Islam's key expectations is that Muslims will make a pilgrimage to Mecca at least once in their lifetime. Hindus travel to the River Ganges to bathe, and Buddhists revere any place associated with an event in Buddha's life. Other sacred sites include the ancient Greek shrines of Delphi and Ephesus and the Aborigine shrine of Ayers Rock.

➠ ***Aboriginal People, Buddhism, Christianity, Greek Gods and Mythology, Hinduism, Judaism, Western Wall***

HOLY ROMAN EMPIRE

Loose federation of kingdoms, principalities, duchies and city states ruled by an emperor. It traced its origins from the western Roman Empire which collapsed in AD 476, re-emerged briefly under Charlemagne (AD 800–14) and was reconstituted in AD 962 when Otto I was crowned by Pope John XII. In theory the emperor was appointed by a group of prince electors but later it was ruled by Hohenstauffen and, from 1556, Habsburg monarchs. Although the various German states owed nominal allegiance, the Empire was weakened by the Reformation and the Thirty Years' War (1618–48), but it lingered on until 1806 when it was dissolved by Napoleon.

➨ ***Napoleon Bonaparte, Charlemagne***

HOME FRONT

Name given to the domestic war effort in Britain from 1939–45, defined by exhortations to willing sacrifices, saving of resources, and enforcement of precautions against aerial bombardment.

HOMER

There are few facts known about the ancient Greek poet Homer. His two major works the *Iliad,* (the siege of Troy) and *Odyssey* (Odysseus's 10-year journey) have inspired generations of poets and artists alike. Several English poets have translated Homer, including George Chapman (*c.* 1559–1634) whose translation suffers through the interjection of his own views.

➨ ***Classical***

HONDURAS

Central American country between Nicaragua and Guatemala. **Capital:** Tegucigalpa. **Other principal cities:** San Pedro Sula. **Climate:** tropical lowlands, temperate highlands. **Geographical features:** mainly mountainous with Pacific and Caribbean coasts. **Main language:** Spanish. **Main religion:** Roman Catholicism. **Rule:** democratic republic. **Currency:** lempira. **Primary industries:** agriculture, fishing, forestry. **Exports:** bananas, coffee, meat, sugar, timber, lobsters, shrimps.

HOOD, ROBIN

Mythical English hero first recorded in fourteenth-century ballads, who lived as a fugitive in Sherwood Forest, stealing from the rich to give to the poor.

HORSE RACING

Known as the 'Sport of Kings' and now a global sport with origins lost in the mists of time. Races can be over the flat, over hurdles (small jumps) or jumps and run on grass or sand. Betting is a large part of the sport's popularity, with many millions being wagered on some of the larger races.

➨ ***Red Rum***

HOUDINI, HARRY (1874–1926)

US escapologist, famous for his daring escapes, particularly when underwater. Born Erich Weiss in Budapest, Hungary, Houdini was keenly interested in spiritualism and exposed many frauds.

ABOVE: The Greek poet, Homer.

RIGHT: Escapologist Harry Houdini, aged 32.

HOUSE OF LORDS

Upper chamber of the UK parliament, debating and modifying legislation created by the House of Commons. The House of Lords is occupied by unelected peers. Hereditary peers are titles handed down through families, and include earls, marquesses and viscounts. Life peerages are awarded to individuals for services rendered, often in government, or law lords of the Court of Appeal and High Court of Justice. Spiritual peers are the archbishops of Canterbury and York, and 24 bishops. Since the Parliament Act of 1911, the House of Lords has been able only to modify and delay a bill for new legislation. Current reform is removing the right of hereditary peers to vote.

HOUSING

Provision of housing for its population is a basic need of any country. Styles of housing vary greatly across the globe and are dependent on such factors as climate, available resources and wealth. The provision of affordable housing for the less well off is usually the preserve of the government. In the UK this dates back to the Artisans Dwelling Act of 1875. The proportion of state and privately owned house varies greatly between different countries and is often more a reflection of political dogma than actual needs.

HOVERCRAFT

Vehicle which uses a cushion of high-pressure air to lift it free of the surface underneath. It can be used over water or relatively smooth land surfaces.

HUBBLE, EDWIN (1889–1953)

US astronomer. Among many other achievements, he demonstrated that the Universe is expanding, and formulated Hubble's law, relating the speed of recession to distance. The famous deep-space telescope is named after him.

HUMAN EVOLUTION

Origins and development of humans, resulting in modern *Homo sapiens sapiens* ('wise man'). The study of human evolution is dependent upon the fossil record; relatively few fossil traces have been discovered of humans and pre-humans so the story of how our species has developed is incomplete. Humans and apes are very similar so they probably shared a common ancestor – possibly an ape-like creature that lived in trees 22–10 million years ago (*dryopithecines*). The first hominids (human-like apes) lived around four million years ago but the first really human-like hominids (given the name 'homo') appeared 2.5–1.8 million years ago.

➡ ***Anthropology, Cro-Magnon Man, Charles Darwin, Fossils***

ABOVE: The Queen addresses the House of Lords during the State Opening of Parliament.

HUMAN RIGHTS

Basic set of rights that all human beings should have. Codified after the horrors of World War II, first in the United Nations Charter and later in the European Convention of 1956. Among these rights are the right to life, to religious freedom and to equal treatment regardless of sex or race. The European Convention became law in the UK in 2000.

➡ ***European Union, International Law, United Nations***

HUMAN WORLD RECORDS

Accumulated data recording the limits of human achievement, from the fastest runner to the longest lived. Human fascination with being the 'best' is as old as the species itself, and has its roots in primitive urges designed to ensure the survival of the species.

Sporting superlatives have been revered since the ancient Greeks, and in more modern times by the Olympic movement. In recent years record-breaking has become a far broader occupation, and judging by sales of the *Guinness Book of Records* a very popular one.

There are now categories of records in every conceivable form of human endeavour, including many that require great dedication, courage and even stupidity. The ultimate however must go to the Frenchman Monsieur 'Mangetout' Lotito, who, over a period of 15 days in 1977 ate a bicycle – tyres and all.

ABOVE: Strongman John Evans breaks the world record for milk crate balancing in April 2001 when he supports 96 crates on his head.
RIGHT: Trees litter Inverleith Park, Edinburgh, following a hurricane.

HUME, DAVID (1711–76)

British philosopher. Hume's greatest work *A Treatise of Human Nature* (1739), shaped and encouraged the views of the Enlightenment. By the 1760s Hume was enjoying fame and prestige as the foremost proponent of Enlightenment philosophy. Hume believed in the necessity to rationalize humanity's theories and ideologies and rejected the idea of a permanent *ego* or self.

➡ ***Enlightenment, Philosophy***

HUNDRED YEARS' WAR (1337–1453)

Series of conflicts between France and England. Family connections and marriages, and ancestral lands gave the English kings many interests in mainland France. The Hundred Years' War was thus only part of an even longer cycle of disputes.

The conflict broke out over disputed ownership of Gascony and control of trade with Flanders. Over the next 30 years, England enjoyed the upper hand with great victories at Crécy (1346) and at Poitiers (1356) when King John of France was captured. By 1360 France capitulated over England's control of Calais at the Treaty of Brétigny-Calais, and paid a vast ransom for John.

The next few decades were inconclusive with a variety of campaigns and truces. Henry V's campaigns of 1415–20 gave England control of northern France and a promise of the French crown through Henry's marriage. But French resistance followed, led initially by Joan of Arc. By 1453 England held only Calais.

HUNGARY

Land-locked central European country. **Capital:** Budapest. **Other principal cities:** Miskolc, Debrecen. **Geographical features:** flat plain. **Main language:** Hungarian. **Main religions:** Roman Catholicism, Calvinism. **Rule:** democratic republic. **Currency:** forint. **Primary industries:** food, engineering, steel, chemicals, petroleum, textiles. **Exports:** food, consumer goods, raw materials and manufactured goods, transport equipment.

Hungary was industrialized after World War II, though agriculture remains important. The post-Communist economy is being converted to a free market, though private ownership was permitted from 1968.

➡ ***Europe***

HUNS (AD 372–453)

Asiatic people from the steppes of the Caspian who ravaged and overran the eastern Roman Empire and reached their zenith under Attila.

Attila the Hun

HUNTING AND GATHERING

Ancient lifestyle requiring a nomadic way of life. Now only practised by a few remote peoples, notably the aboriginal people of Australia, native Papua Newguineans and the indigenous peoples of the Amazon Delta.

Aboriginal Peoples

HURRICANES

Powerful, tropical storms that are severe and often destructive. Also known as cyclones and typhoons. Hurricanes develop over warm seas then move westwards, attacking eastern coastlines with torrential rain and winds up to 350 kph (220 mph). A hurricane struck Bangladesh in 1970 and the floods it generated killed 266,000 people.

Tornadoes, Wind

HUSSEIN, SADDAM (b. 1937)

Iraqi president since 1979. A dictator in all but name, Saddam Hussein rules with absolute power and no effective opposition. Saddam led Iraq into the devastating Iran-Iraq war of 1980–88. In 1990 he invaded the oil-rich state of Kuwait to increase power over the oil trade in the Gulf but was expelled by an international US-led alliance in 1991.

Dictatorship, Iraq, Kuwait

HYDROLOGY

Study of water in all its forms and all the physical and chemical processes it is engaged in. Hydrologists also study the distribution of water on the planet and its relevance to life on Earth. The hydrological cycle (water cycle) examines the movement of water through living and non-living systems. Rainwater, for example, is drunk by an animal which breathes out water vapour which then returns to the atmosphere where it forms clouds.

Water

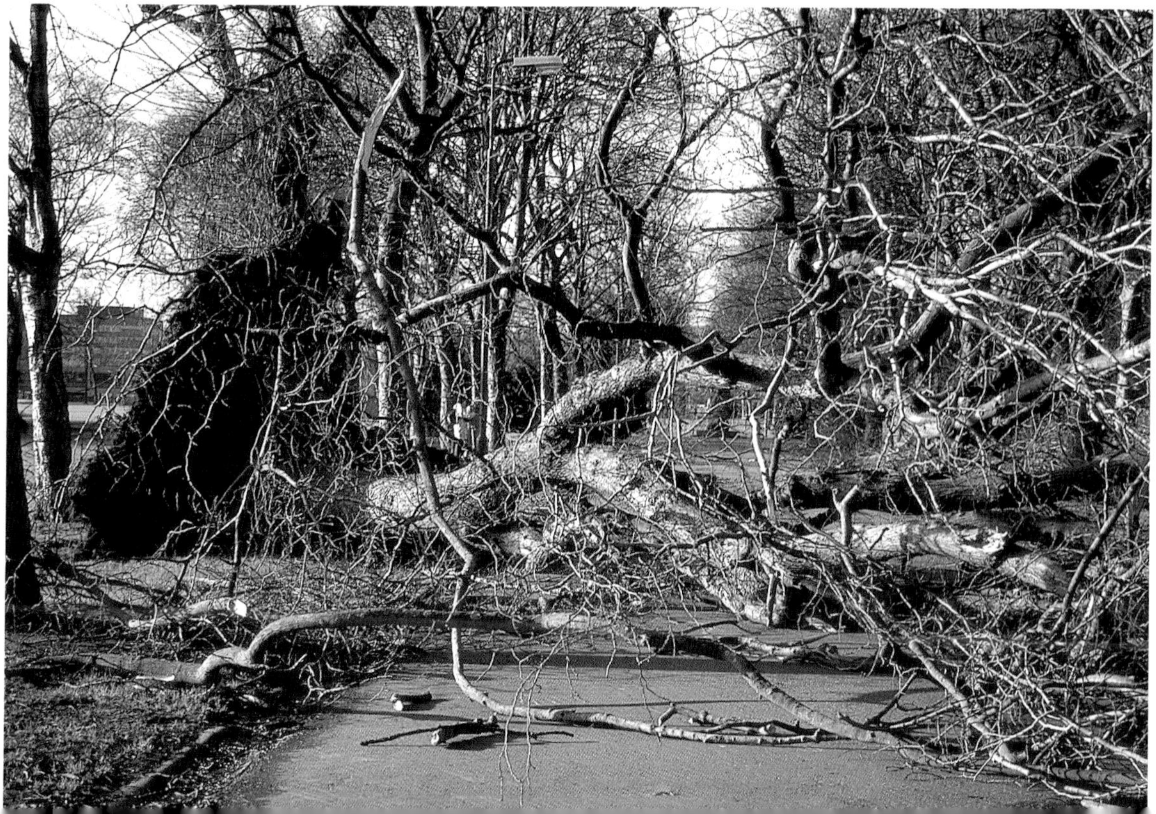

IBSEN, HENRIK (1828–1906)

Norwegian playwright. Ibsen greatly revived the art of the theatre with socially aware plays such as *Ghosts* (1881) and later innovative psychological drama such as *Hedda Gabler* (1890).

➡ ***Playwrights***

LEFT: The ice and snow-capped mountains of Nepal.

ICE

Solid state of water that melts at 0°C (32°F). Ice exists in a crystalline structure that takes up more space than the liquid form. Water therefore floats and expands upon freezing.

➡ ***Water***

ICE AGES

Periods of time, lasting millions of years, when the Earth, its oceans and atmosphere experience a significant drop in temperature causing the formation of large ice masses. The cause of ice ages is not known, although they may be owing to changes in the galaxy, the Milky Way, as it rotates in space. Ice ages tend to occur every 150 million years. The most recent ice age began about two million years ago and ice covered about 40% of the Earth's surface only 18,000 years ago.

➡ ***Glaciers***

BELOW: Now extinct, woolly mammoth herds existed during the last Ice Age.

ICE HOCKEY

Variation on hockey, played on ice. Players wear skates, extensive body armour and a small rubber disk, or puck is used instead of a ball.

ICELAND

North Atlantic island. **Capital:** Reykjavik. **Other principal cities:** Akureyri, Akranes. **Climate:** damp and mild. **Geographical features:** Arctic volcanic island with hot springs, lava flows and glaciers, warmed by the Gulf Stream. **Main language:** Icelandic. **Main religion:** Evangelical Lutheran. **Rule:** democratic republic. **Currency:** krona. **Primary industries:** mining, fish processing. **Exports:** fish, aluminium, ferrosilicon, diatomite, fertilizer.

Iceland's main resource is fish, now suffering from reduced catches. The landscape inhibits agriculture, but the active volcanic terrain attracts visitors and provides heating for homes.

ICONS

People or items that have become representative of a generation. Stars such as Elvis Presley, Marilyn Monroe and James Dean were all icons of their time and continue to be idolized even after their deaths. In much the same way, icons of design such as the Coca-Cola logo, the Sony Walkman, makes of cars or fashion labels can sum up a culture or lifestyle.

ILLUSTRATION

The art of book illustration became popular in medieval times, initially with hand-painted colour notations and ornamental calligraphy, but increasingly dominating the pages and also influencing the paintings of the time. With advanced techniques in printing such as lithography, illustrations became more widespread during the nineteenth century. Later artists, such as Aubrey Beardlsey, re-explored the art of illustration during the Art Nouveau era.

➡ ***Art Nouveau, Calligraphy, Lithography, Medieval***

IMMUNISATION

Use of artificial means to give immunity to infectious diseases. The most widely used technique is vaccination. The body has a natural protection against harmful micro-organisms like bacteria and viruses, in the form of white blood cells. These include macrophages, which can engulf and digest invaders.

Cells called lymphocytes produce antibodies, proteins which can destroy an invading organism. One method of immunisation is to make the lymphocytes produce antibodies in the body before infection occurs. By introducing a dead or weakened form of the micro-organism into the body, antibody production is stimulated, giving the body protection against the disease.

➡ ***Bacteria, Diseases, Viruses***

IMPORT AND EXPORT

Selling and buying goods by a state. Imports represent the items and raw materials purchased by the state, and exports the goods and resources it sells. Failure to keep these in equilibrium can lead to great problems. Many laws and rules exist in countries to ensure that their trade is protected. The interference in this by other countries has often led to wars.

IMPRESSIONISM (1860)

Art movement, mainly within painting, that both dominated the late nineteenth century and also impacted upon twentieth-century art. The first Impressionist exhibition was held in France in 1874, but the movement began in 1860. Although many artists have been associated with Impressionism, the key artists were Pierre-Auguste Renoir, Claude Monet and later Albert Sisley. The term Impressionism came from Monet's painting *Impression: Sunrise* and was originally widely criticized, but by the 1890s Impressionism was gaining in popularity and influence. Impressionism emphasizes colour and light; open-air painting was important, as were landscapes. Impressionism aimed to capture the essence of a scene rather than attempting a more exact representation.

➡ ***Claude Debussy, Edgar Degas, Claude Monet, Berthe Morisot, Pierre-Auguste Renoir***

IN VITRO FERTILIZATION

Carrying out the process of conception by bringing together egg and sperm outside the body, to form an embryo. The embryo can then be introduced into the mother's womb to develop. It is also possible to store embryos by freezing for later implantation. The technique has a fairly low success rate.

INCAS

Peruvian tribe speaking the Quechua language and originating in the highlands of the Alto Plano. According to tradition, the Inca were descended from

Manco, under whose leadership they spread westward. By the time of the Spanish conquest in 1533 they had become a ruling caste, presiding over an empire that stretched from Quito in Ecuador to the River Maule in Chile and extending inland to Lake Titicaca. They were renowned builders, as testified by the impressive ruins in and around Cuzco as well as Machu Picchu. Their empire was destroyed by the conquistadores under Francisco Pizarro.

➡ ***Machu Picchu***

ABOVE: The ruins of terraces, walls, a doorway and windows at the Inca fortress at Ollantaitambo, Cuzco, Peru.

INDIA

South-Asian sub-continent. **Capital:** Delhi. **Other principal cities:** Bangalore, Hyderabad, Ahmedabad, Calcutta, Bombay, Chennai. **Climate:** tropical monsoon to temperate. **Geographical features:** mountainous north, the fertile plain of the Ganges, and the Deccan plateau of the peninsula. **Main languages:** Hindi, English and other regional official languages, such as Bengali and Gujarati. **Main religions:** Hindu, Islam. **Rule:** liberal democratic federal republic. **Currency:** rupee. **Primary industries:** mining of metals, coal, and diamonds, manufacturing of ships, engineering goods, vehicles, sugar-refining and textiles, petroleum refining. **Exports:** tea (largest producer in the world), coffee, fish, iron and steel and engineering products, clothing, textiles, carpets, leather, gems.

The largest democracy in the world, India's population is approaching one billion. The majority live and work on the land, with agricultural techniques and equipment steadily improving since independence in 1947. Industry has expanded, attracting people to cities with an urban population now in excess of 25%. The country has vast natural mineral, coal, natural gas and oil resources, much of which remain to be exploited.

As a rapidly developing state, India is now experiencing problems of unprecedented urban growth and the consequences of a reduced death-rate. This is leading to unemployment and extreme urban poverty in some areas.

INDIAN INDEPENDENCE (1947)

In 1947 India became independent from British rule, ending a campaign lasting decades. British interests in India began in the seventeenth century through the East India Company. British influence continued to increase. In the early nineteenth century effective control throughout India followed a series of regional wars. In 1858, the Indian Mutiny was suppressed and India came under the British Crown.

In 1885 the Indian National Congress was founded. Concessions of provincial self-government followed but in the 1920s Gandhi led a campaign of non-co-operation in pursuit of national independence. The Government of India Act (1935) created autonomous provincial government. Under the independence settlement of 1947, the nation was split into Hindu India and Muslim Pakistan, leading to rioting and massacres.

British Empire, Mahatma Gandhi

INDONESIA

Far East archipelago. **Capital:** Jakarta. **Other principal cities:** Bandung, Yogyakarta, Medan, Tanjung Priok. **Climate:** tropical monsoon. **Geographical features:** more than 13,500 islands make up Indonesia (about 6,000 inhabited), straddling the sea route between Asia and Australia. **Main languages:** Bahasa Indonesia, and numerous regional languages. **Main religion:** Islam. **Rule:** nationalist republic. **Currency:** rupiah. **Primary industries:** oil refining, food processing, textiles, rubber, timber, cement, agriculture (rice). **Exports:** petroleum products, gas, timber, textiles, electrical goods, tea, coffee, copper, tin, coal.

Indonesia has the world's fourth largest population at about 210 million. Most people are Malay, living in small agricultural villages. The islands dominate a vital international trade route.

INDUS VALLEY CIVILIZATION

Ancient civilization of northern India, resulting from waves of migration (2400–1500 BC) by Aryan peoples who settled in the Indus Valley and created great cities. The magnificence of their remains suggests a high degree of culture. The petty kingdoms were eventually subjugated by the Persians under Darius.

➠ ***India***

INDUSTRIAL REVOLUTION (18TH CENTURY)

Time of change in Britain beginning in the late-eighteenth century which resulted in a change from an agricultural to an industrial economy.

Several inventions were developed which made possible the mechanical production of manufactured goods. The most important of these inventions was the improved version of the steam engine developed by James Watt, the cotton-spinning machine of Richard Arkwright, the 'spinning Jenny' of James Hargreaves and the spinning mule of Samuel Crompton. The revolution began with the mechanization of the cotton and woollen industries of Lancashire, Yorkshire and central Scotland. Among its effects were a large population increase. and urbanization.

➠ ***James Watt, Railways***

INDUSTRIALIZATION

The change from relatively low technology, unspecialized, labour-intensive society to a specialised, automated one. The industrialization process began with the Industrial Revolution in Britain, and has proceeded at varying speeds over many parts of the globe. A whole range of discoveries and inventions has made industrialization possible. The steam engine, and subsequently the internal combustion engine have provided not only the mechanical power for industry, but the economic means of transport. The development of chemistry in nineteenth-century Germany, petroleum production in the United States in the early twentieth century, and the development of electronics since World War II have all had a great impact in the conversion into an industrial society.

➠ ***Industrial Revolution***

FAR LEFT: The mountains of Bali, Indonesia.
LEFT: A miner from the city of Leeds, England, beside the enduring images of the industrial revolution: smoking chimneys and locomotives.
BELOW: Since the days of early industrialization huge technological advances have led to great leaps in the abilities of modern-day industry.

INDY CAR RACING

Type of motor racing popular in the US. The cars appear similar to Formula 1 vehicles but tend to be more powerful. Started in 1908, the Indy 500 is the sport's most prestigious event.

➠ ***Motor Racing***

INFANTRY

Foot soldiers. Always the staple component of ground forces, infantry are lightly armed but march alongside mechanized armour (e.g. tanks) seeking to take and hold ground. They are vulnerable to heavy fire. The Roman legionaries were one of the first and possibly best-organized infantry units in history.

➠ ***Armies, Cavalry***

INFLATION

The scourge of free market economies. Too much money chases too few goods and the price has to go up. Workers demand more money in wages to pay for them and a vicious circle is created.

INSECTS

Small organisms that have three pairs of legs and bodies divided into three sections: head, thorax and abdomen. Insects were the first animals to live on land and there are now over one million species.

Insect bodies are protected by external skeletons. They possess compound eyes, made up of many lenses, and they usually have excellent vision. Insects commonly have mouthparts that are modified to suit their method of feeding. Some insects have wings. Insects usually have a larval stage that is very different to the adult stage e.g. caterpillar/butterfly. The transformation from one stage to the other is called metamorphosis.

The earliest insect fossils date from 400 million years ago. Since that time insects have diversified into almost every available habitat on the planet. Insect species often show complex social behaviour e.g. bees and ants. Some insects, such as the Tsetse fly and mosquito, carry diseases injurious to humans.

➠ ***Invertebrates***

INTERNATIONAL LAW

Throughout the twentieth century a growing number of treaties have been signed to create pan-national laws. These range from agreements on shipping and trade through to the European Convention on Human Rights and the Geneva Convention. Enforcement of these laws is problematic, but Europe does have the Court of Human Rights in The Hague, the Netherlands.

➠ ***Human Rights, United Nations***

INTERNATIONAL MONETARY FUND (1947)

Agency of the United Nations and active since 1947. It seeks to ease balance of payments difficulties between nation states, and has the ability to loan money when necessary.

INTERNET

Global network of computers, which makes possible the exchange of information between individuals and organisations via electronic mail. The Internet originated in department of defence program in the US which was devised to provide a secure communications network.

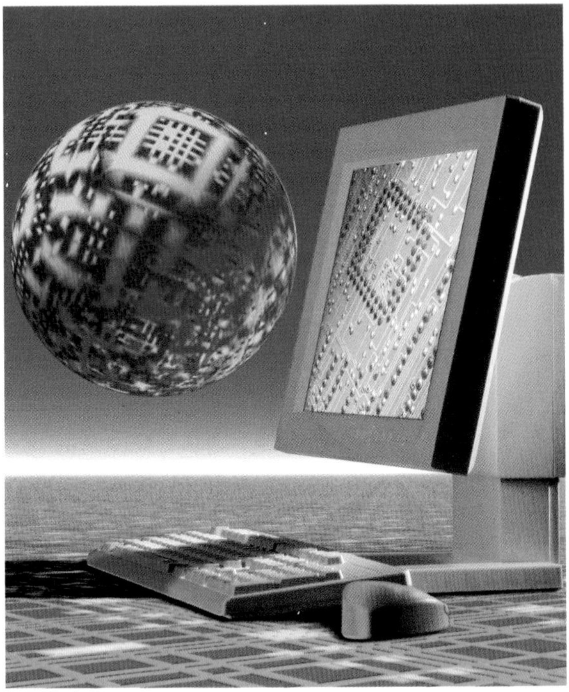

INTERREGNUM

Latin word signifying a period between reigns when the throne was vacant. It arose in Rome during the regal period when an interrex was appointed by the Senate to carry on the government between the death of one king and the election of his successor. The most famous interregnum occurred in Germany between the death of Conrad IV (1254) and the election of Rudolf of Habsburg (1273) as Holy Roman Emperor.

➠ ***English Civil War, Holy Roman Empire***

INVERTEBRATES

Animals that do not possess backbones. This group constitutes the huge majority of animals alive now and in the past. Invertebrates range in complexity from simple sponges to molluscs and insects.

Invertebrates tend to be limited in size because they lack the support of an internal skeleton, aquatic invertebrates, such as octopus and squid, can overcome this problem because of the buoyancy and support afforded by water. Brains of invertebrates are not as complex as those of vertebrates and these animals often lack the range of behaviour found in animals with spines. Nevertheless they are a diverse and successful group.

➧ ***Insects, Molluscs, Vertebrates***

IRAN

Middle Eastern country. **Capital:** Tehran. **Other principal cities:** Isfahan, Mashhad, Tabriz, Abadan. **Climate:** hot interior with sub-tropical Caspian Sea coast. **Geographical features:** dominated by vast arid central plain. **Main languages:** Farsi, Kurdish, Arabic. **Main religion:** Islam. **Rule:** Islamic republic. **Currency:** rial. **Primary industries:** agriculture, light-manufacture. **Exports:** petroleum, carpets, fruit, nuts, hides, steel.

Iran's modernization was slowed by the Islamic Revolution, and a devastating war with Iraq. Iran depends on oil exports to buy in food and military hardware.

➧ ***Oil***

FAR LEFT: The insect Pholidoptera griseoaptera, *the dark bush cricket.*
BELOW: England experienced a period without a monarch following the execution of Charles I. During the Interregnum years (1649–60), parliament, under Oliver Cromwell, effectively ruled. This painting shows Cromwellian and Royalist troops in battle.

IRANGATE (1987)

US political scandal. The Reagan administration had covertly sold arms to Iran, using the funds to free hostages in Lebanon, and sponsor rightwing guerrillas (Contras) in Nicaragua. This broke US federal law concerning dealing with 'terrorist' nations. US officials were convicted, and presidents Ronald Reagan and George Bush were shown to have known about the deals.

➧ ***Presidents***

IRAQ

Middle Eastern country. **Capital:** Baghdad. **Other principal cities:** Mosul, Basra, Kirkuk. **Climate:** hot and dry. **Geographical features:** mainly land-locked desert around the valleys of the Tigris and Euphrates. **Main language:** Arabic. **Main religion:** Islam. **Rule:** one-party socialist republic. **Currency:** Iraqi dinar. **Primary industries:** petroleum and some agriculture. **Exports:** oil, cotton, wool.

Iraq is completely dependent on its oil to purchase manufactured goods and food. The economy has been ravaged by the Iran-Iraq War, and later the Gulf War.

➧ ***Gulf War, Oil***

IRELAND (EIRE)

North-west European island (southern part), part of the British Isles. **Capital:** Dublin. **Other principal towns:** Cork, Dun Laoghaire, Limerick, Waterford. **Climate:** temperate maritime. **Geographical features:** fertile rolling landscape and a highland coastline, sharing the island with the United Kingdom's province of Northern Ireland. **Main languages:** English and Irish Gaelic. **Main religion:** Roman Catholicism. **Rule:** democratic republic. **Currency:** Irish pound (punt). **Primary industries:** textiles, machinery, electronics, vehicles, food, beer, tourism. **Agriculture:** cereals, sugar beet, cattle. **Exports:** beef and dairy products and livestock, electronics, computers, machinery.

Ireland's traditional agricultural economy gave way to a rapid process of industrialization in the 1950s, attracting foreign investment. Irish immigrants and sympathies in the USA were especially important for this. The economy has developed into one of the most diverse and active in the European Union, leaving memories of nineteenth-century poverty and potato famines long behind, though agriculture remains important, and the influence of the United Kingdom unavoidable. The armed struggle to reunify the island has now largely given way to political dialogue.

IRON AGE

Period during which iron became the most important metal for making tools and weapons, largely but not wholly replacing bronze.

Iron was available in prehistory in the form of iron meteorites but was little exploited because techniques of working it were lacking. The first known extraction of iron from its ores – smelting – occurred in Thailand around 1600 BC. This product was inferior to the bronze then available, and not until 1000 BC did techniques improve sufficiently. It was later discovered that by controlling the charcoal content of the furnace during smelting, the superior alloy steel could be made.

IRRIGATION

Aid to farming, undertaken by supplying land with water though the use of ditches or pipes. About 10% of total cultivated land depends on irrigation to succeed and the method allows crops to be grown where naturally they could not.

ISDN

Integrated Services Digital Network, a digital communications network in which data can be sent between computers at higher speeds than are available over normal telephone networks.

ISLAM

Monotheistic religion established by Muhammad in the early seventh century. The Angel Gabriel revealed the Qur'an, the holy book of Islam, to Muhammad on the subsequently named 'Night of Power'. The two main sects are the Sunni and the Shi'ite Muslims and Islamic law is called Shar'ia law. There is no priesthood, just holy men, Imams. Muslims worship in mosques and are called to prayer by a muezzin in a minaret (prayer tower). They must submit to the Five Pillars of Faith: recitation of the creed, prayer fives times daily facing Mecca, almsgiving, fasting (sunrise to sunset through Ramadan) and pilgrimage to Mecca. Islam is a major political and religious force in the Arab world.

➧ ***Qur'an, Ramadan, Religious Leaders***

ISLANDS

Pieces of land surrounded on all sides by water. The only difference between an island and a continent is size. Islands can be formed in many ways; they may be glacial, volcanic, fluvial or simply formed by the erosion of a land mass that previously joined the island to the mainland.

ISOZKI, ARATA (b. 1931)

Japanese architect, Isozki's early work in the 1960s perfected a blend of East-West traditions. He later developed his 'schizoid' style with the Tsukuba Building, Tsukuba Science City (1978–83).

➧ *Architecture*

ISRAEL

Middle-Eastern Mediterranean country. **Capital:** Tel Aviv. **Other principal cities:** Bat-Yam, Jerusalem, Haifa. **Climate:** temperate. **Geographical features:** coastal plains, mountains, Jordan Rift Valley and Negev Desert. **Main languages:** Hebrew, Arabic, English. **Main religion:** Judasim. **Rule:** democratic republic. **Currency:** shekel. **Primary industries:** food and drink, electrical goods, petroleum products, chemicals, transport equipment, tourism. **Exports:** machinery, cut diamonds, chemicals, clothing, textiles.

Israel depends on imported raw materials, tourism and injections of cash from other countries (principally the US) for economic growth, though it has remained subject to chronic inflation and has a trade deficit. Highly efficient agriculture has allowed it to approach self-sufficiency.

➧ *Jerusalem*

ITALY

South European Mediterranean country. **Capital:** Rome. **Other principal cities:** Milan, Turin, Genoa, Naples, Bologna. **Climate:** Mediterranean in the south, mild in the centre, cold in the Alpine north. **Geographical features:** peninsula characterized by a wide mountainous central strip and narrow coastal plains, the Italian Alps in the north, and islands, the largest being Sicily and Sardinia. **Main language:** Italian. **Main religion:** Roman Catholicism. **Rule:** democratic republic. **Currency:** lira. **Primary industries:** machinery, cars and motorcycles, clothing, footwear, leather, food, wine, tourism. **Exports:** vehicles, machinery, clothing, textiles, chemicals, wine, food.

Italy's commercial and industrial zone is mainly in the north around Turin and Milan, the richest part of the country. The Alps attract tourism. Further south, agriculture and tourism becomes more important to regional economies, but the mountainous interior restricts agriculture mainly to grazing. Italy remains an extremely regionalized nation socially and economically, reflected in politics and culture. Italy's archeological and artistic heritage is one of its most important resources.

➧ *Alps, Europe*

BOTTOM LEFT: Small Iron Age objects found at Colchester, Essex.
LEFT: Villagers in Bangladesh watch an irrigation system at work.
BELOW: A combination of a wealth of history and a thriving modern cultural scene make Italian cities some of the most sought-after tourist destinations.

JACKSON, MICHAEL (b. 1958)

US pop star. Jackson's career was launched as part of the Jackson 5 with his brothers. His 1979 album *Off the Wall* established him as a formidable solo artist, but it was *Thriller* that really put him on the map, with sales of over 20 million copies.

JACQUARD, JOSEPH MARIE (1752–1834)

French manufacturer and inventor. Jacquard invented a system of programming a carpet-weaving loom to produce particular patterns using punched cards.

JAINISM

Off-shoot of Hinduism, established by the all-knowing Mahavira (599–527 BC). His teachings became Jainism's sacred scriptures. Jainism aims not to harm any living creature and is a monastic religion that believes in karma. Its two main sects are the Digambaras and the Swetambaras (the latter originally went naked).

➠ ***Hinduism***

JAMAICA

Caribbean island country. **Capital:** Kingston. **Other principal cities:** Montego Bay, Spanish Town. **Climate:** tropical. **Geographical features:** coastal plains and beaches surround a mountainous interior. **Main languages:** English, Creole. **Main religion:** Protestant. **Rule:** constitutional monarchy. **Currency:** Jamaican dollar. **Primary industries:** agriculture, mining, tourism. **Exports:** bananas, alumina, bauxite, rum, sugar, cocoa, coconuts.

JAMES, HENRY (1843–1916)

American-born, British novelist whose work, such as *The Wings of a Dove* (1903), often explored differences between the two countries. James was also an important literary critic.

JAPAN

Far Eastern island country. **Capital:** Tokyo. **Other principal cities:** Fukuoka, Kitakyushu, Osaka, Nagoya, Yokohama. **Climate:** sub-tropical to temperate. **Geographical features:** about 1,000 mountainous volcanic islands, the two largest being Hokkaido and Honshu. **Main language:** Japanese. **Main religions:** Shinto, Buddhism. **Rule:** liberal democracy. **Currency:** yen. **Primary industries:** vehicle manufacture, electronic goods, heavy engineering, chemicals, textiles, fishing. **Exports:** vehicles, electronics, optical equipment, chemicals, iron and steel.

RIGHT: A traditional Yabusame archer at a Japanese festival.

FAR RIGHT: A lively, evocative painting entitled Jazz Horns *by Adolf Arthur Dehn (1895–1965).*

Despite lacking natural resources, Japan has used motivation, design, efficiency and technological innovation to make it one of the world's most successful post-World War II industrialized nations, in spite of the devastation caused by aerial bombardment. Fishing is important but manufacturing is the basis of the economy and raw materials and food almost all have to be purchased abroad. Society has experienced rapid westernization, but it retains a distinct cultural identity. In recent years the Japanese economy has suffered as demand for her products declined abroad.

JAZZ

Musical genre that combines elements from ragtime, blues, string and brass bands, producing a syncopated rhythm with a dominance of 'blue notes'. Beginning around 1900 in New Orleans, jazz was often improvized; the music was mostly unscored and the musicians were usually untrained. During the 1920s jazz grew in popularity as the desire for dance music increased, this led to the divergence of Jazz into genres like swing. Jazz's emphasis on solos led to fame for vocalists such as Billie Holiday (1915–59).

⟫➧ ***Blues***

JEHOVAH'S WITNESSES

Christian sect established in America in 1872 by Charles Taze Russell. Beliefs include Jesus' second coming, pacifism and denial of medical intervention.

⟫➧ ***Christianity***

JELLYFISH

Invertebrate marine organism that has a free-floating adult stage, often bell-shaped. Long tentacles, which bear numerous stings, may be suspended from the bell.

⟫➧ ***Invertebrates***

JENKINS, CHARLES FRANCIS (1867–1934)

Joint inventor of the Phantoscope; a projector that allowed films to be watched by groups of people. Jenkins's invention was later amalgamated into Thomas Edison's Vitascope in 1896.

⟫➧ ***Cinematography***

JENNER, EDWARD (1749–1823)

British physician who introduced the first vaccine – against smallpox. Having noticed that milkmaids who contracted cowpox never developed smallpox, he used material from cowpox sufferers and introduced it on to the roughened skin of a healthy boy. The boy proved to be immune from smallpox. Jenner coined the term vaccination.

⟫➧ ***Vaccination***

JERUSALEM

Chief city of Israel. Its history has been tumultuous: created the Jewish capital by David; destroyed by Nebuchadnezzar, 586 BC, and then by the Roman, Titus in AD 70; AD *c.* 29–30, Jesus was crucified there; and in AD 637 Islam first conquered the city. In 1967 Israel guaranteed freedom of access to the holy sites, for all religions. Some recognize Jerusalem as the capital city of Israel although this is not acknowledged by the UN.

➡ ***Israel, Western Wall***

JET PROPULSION

Means of propelling a vehicle, usually an aircraft, by a stream of fast-moving gases in the opposite direction to the direction of travel.

JEWISH DIASPORA

The dispersal of the Jews after the Babylonian conquest of Palestine by Nebuchadnezzar (586 BC) and after the Roman conquest by Titus (AD 70). The term is also used to decribe Jewish communities existing ouside Israel.

➡ ***Babylon, Jerusalem, Judaism***

JOHNSON, SAMUEL (1709–84)

English essayist and lexicographer. His most famous work was his *Dictionary of the English Language,* which was published in 1755 having taken over eight years to compile. Dr Johnson's biography was published by the lawyer James Boswell (1740–95) in 1791.

➡ ***Philosophy***

JORDAN

Middle East country. **Capital:** Amman. **Other principal cities:** Zarqa, Aqaba. **Climate:** Mediterranean to desert. **Geographical features:** deserts, plains, mountains and a small Red Sea coast. **Main language:** Arabic. **Main religion:** Islam. **Rule:** constitutional monarchy. **Currency:** Jordanian dinar. **Primary industries:** chemicals, fertilizers, agriculture, tourism. **Exports:** fertilizers, fruit and vegetables, textiles, soap, plastics.

JOYCE, JAMES (1882–1941)

Irish writer. Hugely influential and innovative, Joyce developed a stream-of-consciousness style of writing in his novel *Ulysses* (1922). Joyce's work was a great catalyst for change within twentieth century literature.

JUDAISM

Monotheistic religion of the Jews. Established after Abraham's covenant with God, *c.* 2000 BC, which was renewed by Moses and the Ten Commandments, *c.* 1200 BC. Judaism developed out of a Middle Eastern nomadic culture, and lack of a sustainable territory has been an enduring cause of conflict to the Jews.

Judaism has cultural and religious connotations and contains four sects that reflect this: Orthodox, Conservative, Reform and Liberal. The holy scriptures are the Old Testament, particularly the Torah (the first five books of the Bible that were kept in the Ark). Worship occurs in Hebrew in a synagogue and is led by a rabbi. Key holy days are Passover, Rosh Hashanah and Yom Kippur, and the Sabbath is observed weekly. The Kosher diet and circumcision are also Judaic laws.

Under David the Jews conquered Palestine, *c.* 1000 BC, then Solomon's reign engendered its gradual decline until its apogee in the eighth to thirteenth centuries AD. Christianity then became the dominant world religion and the Jews became segregated. Periodic persecution of the Jews continued in Europe, culminating in the Holocaust (six million fatalities). Zionism has campaigned for a Jewish homeland throughout the twentieth century, Israel, part of Palestine, gained independence in 1948.

Jerusalem, Jewish Diaspora

JUPITER

Largest of the major planets, over twice as massive as all the others combined, and fifth away from the Sun. Jupiter takes nearly 12 years to complete one orbit. It is composed mainly of gaseous and liquid hydrogen and helium. The Great Red Spot is a very long-lived storm in its atmosphere.

Planets, Solar System, Sun

LEFT: A man in traditional Jewish dress prays at the Western Wall, Jerusalem.
RIGHT: Jupiter, the largest planet in our solar system.

KAFKA, FRANZ (1883–1924)

Czech-born writer. Kafka's novel *Metamorphosis* (1912) explored the plights of modern human society, such as alienation and communication. *Metamorphosis* is Kafka's only completed work, he died of tuberculosis.

KANDINSKY, WASSILY (1866–1944)

Russian-born painter and art theoretician. Kandinsky founded the *Blaue Reiter* ('Blue Rider') group with Franz Marc in Berlin in 1911. Linked to Expressionism by his work with *Blaue Reiter*, Kandinsky is also reputed to have created the first truly abstract painting in 1910, although his work still retained elements of representation for another decade or so.

➧ ***Abstract Art, Expressionism***

KANT, IMMANUEL (1724–1804)

Considered by many to be the greatest theorist of the eighteenth century, the German Immanuel Kant was the inaugural critical philosopher. Kant originally studied astronomy, predicting Uranus's discovery over 100 years later. In his own words, Kant reflected upon 'the starry heavens above me and the moral law within me'.

➧ ***Philosophy, Uranus***

KEATS, JOHN (1795–1821)

English Romantic poet whose writings probe the meaning, beauty and impermanence of life. In his short career Keats explored a variety of poetic manners, such as narrative poetry in *Lamia* (1819). Following the death of his brother allusions to decay and the transience of life permeate his poems, such as *Ode to a Nightingale* (1819).

➧ ***Poetry, Romantic***

KENNEDY, JOHN F. (1917–63)

Thirty-fifth US president, from 1961. A Democrat, Roman Catholic and the youngest president ever elected, Kennedy was assassinated in Dallas, Texas on 22 November 1963. The assassination has remained a popular subject for conspiracy theorists.

➧ ***Presidents***

LEFT: In Einander *by Kandinsky. Kandinsky is one of the most influential artists of his era, with both his paintings and his writing have a far-reaching impact on his contemporaries.*
RIGHT: Married Samburu woman in traditional African dress, Kenya.
FAR RIGHT: Jungle vegetation chokes an Angkor ruin from the Khmer period.

KENYA

East African country on the Indian Ocean. **Capital:** Nairobi. **Other principal cities:** Kisumu, Mombasa. **Climate:** tropical coasts, temperate to arid interior. **Geographical features:** tropical beaches, scenic interior. **Main languages:** Kiswahili, English. **Main religions:** Roman Catholicism, Protestant, Islam. **Rule:** nationalist republic. **Currency:** Kenya shilling. **Primary industries:** food, petroleum, textiles, leather, chemicals, paper, tobacco, rubber, tourism. **Exports:** tea, coffee, horticulture, petroleum.

About 60% of Kenya is semi-desert, but agriculture is the prime activity, especially in the south-west tea and coffee plantation areas. Oil is imported for refining. The landscape attracts tourism, and large areas are set aside as national parks to conserve wildlife.

➧ ***Africa***

KHMERS

Civilization of south east Asia which attained its peak between the fifth and twelfth centuries and produced some remarkable art and architecture, reflected in the stupendous ruins of Angkor, the ancient capital. It declined in the thirteenth century when its territory was overrun by the Thais and Vietnamese.

KILIMANJARO, MOUNT

Extinct volcano in Tanzania, East Africa, the tallest in Africa at 5,900 m (19,364 ft). The main peak, Kibo, is permanently snow-covered. The smaller, Mawenzi, falls away to a ravine.

➧ ***Volcanoes***

KING, MARTIN LUTHER (1929–68)

US black civil rights leader. Born in Atlanta, Georgia, King's campaign for black rights was moderate and non-violent. In 1955 he led the Montgomery, Alabama, bus boycott. In 1963, he helped lead a march to Washington DC demanding black equality, winning the Nobel Peace Prize in 1964. He was assassinated in Memphis, Tennessee.

➧ ***Nobel Prize***

KINGS OF ENGLAND

Roman Britain collapsed in the fifth century but out of the Dark Ages emerged a number of Anglo-Saxon kingdoms by the end of the sixth century. By the middle of the eighth century Mercia and Wessex had become the leading powers. Beorhtric of Wessex married a daughter of Offa, King of Mercia and their son Ecgberht (AD 802–39) gradually amalgamated Wessex with Kent, Sussex, Essex and East Anglia and finally with Mercia itself by 830. Of the Anglo-Saxon rulers of all England the most notable was Alfred the Great (AD 871–99), much of whose reign was taken up in combating the menace of the Danes. Cnut of Denmark was king of England (1016–35), followed by his sons Harold and Harthacnut, but the last of the Anglo-Saxon rulers, Edward the Confessor, was restored to the throne in 1042. His death in 1066 was the pretext for the Norman invasion by William the Conqueror, Edward's cousin.

William I (1066–87) introduced the feudal system and instigated the national survey known as the *Domesday Book.* He was followed by his sons William II (1087–1100) and Henry I (1100–35). The throne was then contested by Stephen of Blois, Henry's nephew. First of the Plantagenet kings was Henry II (1154–89), followed by his sons, the crusading Richard I 'Lionheart' (1189–99) and John (1199–1216) during whose turbulent reign the revolt of the barons led to Magna Carta (1215). Henry III (1216–72) and his son Edward I (1272–1307) consolidated and re-organized government, the Westminster parliament being founded in 1295. Edward subjugated the Welsh (1284) and the Scots (1296) although the latter regained their independence under Robert the Bruce. Edward II (1307–27) was deposed and murdered. Edward III (1327–77) laid claim to the throne of France and embroiled England in the Hundred Years' War. His grandson Richard II (1377–99) suppressed the Peasants' Revolt (1381) but quarrelled with his powerful uncle, John of Gaunt and alienated his nobles who deposed him in favour of John's son Henry Bolingbroke.

Henry IV (1399–1413) was the first ruler of the House of Lancaster. His son Henry V revived the claim to the French throne and won a spectacular victory at Agincourt (1415). By the Treaty of Troyes (1420) he was recognized as heir to the French crown and sealed this by marrying Catherine of Valois, but died before he could claim his inheritance. Their only son, Henry VI, was crowned King of France in 1431. An ineffectual ruler, beset by bouts of insanity, he was opposed by Richard, Duke of York (a descendant of Edward III) who defeated the king's army at St Albans (1455) and triggered off the Wars of the Roses. Henry was deposed in 1461 but briefly restored in 1470–1 before he was murdered. Richard's son reigned as Edward IV (1461–70 and 1471–83). He was the father of the Princes in the Tower, the elder of whom was nominally Edward V. They were probably murdered at the instigation of their uncle, who seized the throne and reigned as Richard III. He was killed at the Battle of Bosworth in 1485.

His rival and successor, Henry VII (1485–1509), was the first of the Tudor monarchs. He was the grandson of Owen Tudor and Catherine of Valois, widow of Henry V. His accession brought the Wars of the Roses to an end and he laboured to restore the peace and prosperity of England. He built up a large treasury which his son Henry VIII (1509–47) dissipated in foreign ventures which helped to establish

ABOVE LEFT: Contemporaneous records tell us that James II was a good soldier, naval commander and public servant.
BELOW LEFT: Cnut (c. 995–1035) King of England from 1016–35.
ABOVE: George VI, England's king during World War II.

England as a world power. Best remembered for his six wives, he broke with the Papacy and seized the monasteries and other Church property. Ironically, however, he held on to the title Defender of the Faith, conferred on him by the Pope for writing a book condemning Martin Luther. His son, Edward VI (1547–53) died of tuberculosis at the age of 16. He was followed by his two half-sisters, Mary and Elizabeth, and it was not until 1603 that England had a king again. The throne then passed to James VI of Scotland, a great-grandson of Henry VII (through his daughter Margaret who married James V in 1503). Dubbed 'the wisest fool in Christendom', James authorized the version of the Bible that still bears his name. His son Charles I engaged in a long-running conflict with Parliament which led to the Civil War and his execution (1649).

The Restoration (1660) brought his son Charles II to the throne, followed by his brother James II in 1685. His Catholicism alienated his subjects and led to the Glorious Revolution (1688). He fled to France and was succeeded by William of Orange, his nephew and son-in-law, who reigned as William III jointly with his wife Mary II. The last of the Stuart dynasty was Queen Anne (1702–14) whose death without issue brought the Hanoverians to the throne.

The most recent kings were Edward VII (1901–10), George V (1910–36) and his two sons Edward VIII (1936) and George VI (1936–52).

➡ ***Queens of England***

KLEE, PAUL (1879–1940)

German painter. Klee is associated with the avant-garde *Blaue Reiter* art group and later with the Surrealists. His unique paintings often contained an hallucinatory quality. Klee was also a great art theoretician.

➡ ***Wassily Kandinksy, Surrealism***

KLINE, FRANZ JOSEF (1910–62)

American painter, chiefly remembered for his large black-and-white abstract paintings. With De Kooning and Pollock, Kline was a key figure in the post-war American Abstract Expressionism movement.

➡ ***Abstract Art, Willem de Kooning, Jackson Pollock***

KOALA

Australian tree-living mammal that carries its young in a pouch and eats eucalyptus leaves. Although bear-like in appearance koalas do not belong to the bear family.

Marsupials

KOREAN WAR (1950–53)

War between North and South Korea. At the close of World War II Korea was occupied by Japanese forces. Russian and US troops entered Korea and accepted the surrender of the Japanese. They then divided the country in two, at the '38th parallel' due to divided political interests. North Korea and South Korea were strictly isolated from one another in post-war years.

In 1950 North Korea invaded South Korea with a view to reuniting the two areas of territory under one Communist banner. The North Koreans were backed by China. South Korea quickly found defence support from the United Nations. Still holding on to a small area of territory in the south-east of the Korean peninsula, known as the Pusan perimeter, the South Koreans, with the support of US reinforcements, managed to begin pushing their way northward. By October 1950 the Chinese had become directly involved in the warfare and things reached a stalemate position. Negotiations for a truce began in 1951 but an armistice was not reached until 1953.

TOP RIGHT: Labour politician Gordon Brown and Prime Minister Tony Blair at a press conference before the election of the New Labour Government in 1997. RIGHT: Iraq's President, Sadam Hussein's invasion of Kuwait and his suppression of Kurds and Shi-is led to the Gulf War of 1990.

KOONING, WILLEM DE (1904–1997)

American painter. De Kooning gained repute for his series of paintings called *Women* (1952). His work was greatly emotive, utilising a violently energetic, seemingly chaotic style of painting.

Abstract Art

KREMLIN

Russian word for citadel. The present Kremlin in Moscow, with characteristic red walls and 20 towers, was built in the fifteenth century by Italians brought in by Ivan III. The sprawling complex contains cathedrals (of the Annunciation and of the Assumption) and the former royal residence of the Kremlin Great Palace, later used for meetings of the Supreme Soviet.

Russia

KUWAIT

Middle East state on Persian Gulf. **Capital:** Kuwait. **Other principal cities:** Jahra, Amadi. **Climate:** hot and dry. **Geographical features:** desert. **Main language:** Arabic. **Main religion:** Islam. **Rule:** constitutional monarchy. **Currency:** Kuwaiti dinar. **Primary industries:** oil. Agriculture: virtually nil. The economy is wholly dependent on oil, almost all goods being imported. **Exports:** petroleum, construction materials.

LABOUR PARTY

British political party, one of the two principal parties. It was founded to represent workers, was based on socialist ideals, it has strong links with trade unions. It forms part of the National Council of Labour, along with Co-operative organizations and the Trades Union Congress. Labour began in 1900 as the Labour

Foundation Committee, forming its first government in 1924. It came to power again in 1945, creating the National Health Service and nationalising industries. Governments of 1964–70 and 1974–79 saw Labour increasingly associated with militant trade unionism, and unilateral nuclear disarmament. A new charter in the mid-1990s, scrapping many traditional policies, led to a return to power in 1997.

➡ *Governments*

LACROSSE

Ball game played with netted sticks, derived from a Native American game. The first world championships were held in 1967. There are 10 players per team for men and 12 for women.

LAGOONS AND REEFS

Body of water that is cut off from the main body of water by a coral reef or sand bar. Lagoons commonly form close to land. They offer an environment that is different to both the open ocean or a river mouth as they are saline but are protected from the strongest effect of ocean tides and winds.

➡ *Coral Reefs*

LAKE BAIKAL

Siberian freshwater lake, the largest in Asia at 31,500 sq km (12,150 sq miles) and the world's deepest at 1,640 m (5,200ft), with many unique species.

➡ *Asia*

LAKE SUPERIOR

Second largest lake in the world, and largest and deepest of the North American Great Lakes system, at 83,300 sq km (32,300 sq miles).

➡ *Great Lakes*

LAKE TITICACA

Largest South American lake, in the Andes on the Bolivian-Peru border. Titicaca is the highest navigable area of water at 3,810 m (12,500 ft) above sea level, covering 8,300 sq km (3,200 sq miles). Locals manufacture reed boats. It has ports at Guaqui, Puno, and Huancane. Large edible frogs live here.

LALIQUE, RENÉ (1860-1945)

French designer of Art Deco jewellery and glassware. Lalique is particularly remembered for his exquisite glassware decorated with figures which became very fashionable and highly sought after.

➡ ***Art Deco, Decorative Art***

LANCASTRIANS

English royal house founded in 1399. It took its name from John of Gaunt, who married his cousin, the heiress Blanche of Lancaster, and was created Duke in 1362. His eldest son, Henry Bolingbroke, seized the throne from his cousin Richard II and reigned as Henry IV (1399–1413). He was succeeded by his son, the warrior king Henry V. The third and last of this dynasty was Henry VI.

➡ ***Kings of England, Queens of England***

LAND RECLAMATION

Process by which land that was previously unusable is restored to a state where it may be utilized for building, agriculture or general use. Low-lying land that is prone to sea flooding can be reclaimed by building sea walls and drainage systems. In the Netherlands large areas of land were reclaimed in this way.

LAND SPEED RECORDS

In 1997, a one-mile record of 1227.985 kph (763.055 mph) was set by Andy Green in the jet-powered car Thrust SSG, the fastest any land vehicle has travelled. A railway record was set by a Maglev (magnetic levitation) train locomotive which achieved 552 kph (343 mph) in Japan in 1999.

LANGUAGES

Use of sound, in the form of speech to communicate. There are approximately 6,000 languages spoken worldwide, although 90% of these are considered to be in danger of extinction. Just five languages: Chinese, English, Hindi, Russian and Spanish are spoken by more than half of the world's population. As well as distinct languages there are also different dialects of the same tongue, which can often be very different from each other.

LAOS

Land-locked country in south-east Asia. **Capital:** Vientiane. **Other principal cities:** Luang Prubang, Pakse. **Climate:** tropical monsoon. **Geographical features:** mountainous and fertile but still mostly rainforest, and mineral resources remain mostly unexploited. **Main languages:** Lao, French. **Main religion:** Buddhist. **Rule:** one-party Communist state. **Currency:** new kip. **Primary industry:** agriculture. **Exports:** hydroelectricity, timber, coffee.

LASERS

Devices which can produce a narrow, high-intensity beam of light of a single wavelength in which the waves are all in step. Laser stands for Light Amplification by Stimulated Emission of Radiation.

LATITUDE

On the Earth's surface, the angular distance of a place north or south of the equator, from 0 to 90°. Latitude affects the climate and thus the seasons.

LATVIA

North-east European country on the Baltic. **Capital:** Riga. **Other principal cities:** Daugavpils. **Climate:** temperate. **Geographical features:** forested plains. **Main language:** Latvian. **Main religions:** Lutheran, Roman Catholicism, Russian Orthodox. **Rule:** democratic republic. **Currency:** lat. **Primary industries:** manufacturing, forestry, meat and dairy products. **Exports:** electronic and communications equipment, railway equipment, timber, paper, textiles, meat and dairy products.

➡ *Europe*

LAUREL, STAN (1890–1965) AND OLIVER HARDY (1892–1957)

Comic film actors. Laurel and Hardy first began working together in the 1926 short film *Slipping Wives*. They made over 20 feature length films together.

➡ *Films*

LAW

The concept of Law is essential to any civilized society. Laws protect the people and mechanisms of a society and allow citizens to plan for the future. Laws should be made by the consent of the people. Often they are not, but there is a school of thought that maintains that even bad laws are better than no laws at all.

➡ *Anarchy, International Law*

LAWRENCE, THOMAS EDWARD (1888–1935)

British soldier and scholar, known as 'Lawrence of Arabia'. Based in Cairo with British military intelligence, he became guerrilla leader of the Arab revolt against Turkish rule during World War I. After writing a history of the revolt in *Seven Pillars of Wisdom*, he changed his name twice and withdrew to obscurity.

➡ *World War I*

LEAGUE OF NATIONS (1920)

Formed after World War I to provide a forum where international disputes could be settled without recourse to war. Although most of the world's nations were represented, the US did not participate and it was compromized by having no powers of enforcement. In 1946 the League was replaced by the United Nations.

➡ *Treaty of Versailles, United Nations, World War I*

FAR LEFT: Lake Superior, Canada, known as 'Moose Country' due to the high number of the animals that roam the beautiful shores.
LEFT: Language enables people to communicate. Telephones, computers and other such technological advances have aided global communication, breaking down language barriers.

LEBANON

Middle-Eastern Mediterranean country bordering Syria and Israel. **Capital:** Beirut. **Other principal cities:** Zahlé, Tripoli, Tyre, Sidon. **Climate:** Mediterranean. **Geographical features:** narrow coastal plain, central valley, inland mountains. **Main languages:** Arabic, French. **Main religions:** Islam, Christian denominations. **Rule:** democratic republic. **Currency:** Lebanese pound. **Primary industries:** agriculture, manufacturing. **Exports:** fruit, vegetables, metal goods, textiles, chemicals, jewellery.

Lebanon's affluence as a commercial and banking centre and popular tourist destination of the Middle East has been ruined by fighting since the mid-1970s, starting with civil war and then assaults by Israel on refugee Palestinian fighters. Most of the population works on the land.

➜ ***Israel***

LEGUMINOUS PLANTS

Members of the pea family. These plants bear fruits that consist of pods containing one or more seed e.g. peas, laburnum and lupin. Leguminous plants generally have root nodules that can fix nitrogen from the air and can therefore be grown in poor quality soils with low nitrogen levels.

LEIGH, VIVIEN (1913–67)

English actress who won two Oscars for portrayals of Southern belles – as Scarlett O'Hara in *Gone with the Wind* (1939) and Blanche DuBois in *A Streetcar Named Desire* (1951). She was married to Lawrence Olivier.

➜ ***Academy Awards, Clark Gable,* Gone with the Wind, *Lawrence Olivier***

LENIN, VLADIMIR ILYICH (1870–1924)

Russian revolutionary leader and politician. A committed Marxist from 1889, and author of revolutionary propaganda, Lenin was exiled after the 1905 Revolution. Lenin returned after the February (March by the western calendar) 1917 Revolution to lead the October 1917 Bolshevik Revolution, and became the Soviet leader. Lenin adapted Marxism to Russian conditions, creating a political model for Communist government.

➜ ***Communism, Karl Marx, Russian Revolution***

LENNON, JOHN (1940–80)

English singer/songwriter and former member of The Beatles. Lennon's solo career included work with his wife Yoko Ono, producing definitive albums such as *John Lennon and the Plastic Ono Band* (1970) and *Imagine* (1971). During the late 1960s to early 1970s Lennon's work was often radical and extremely personal in content. Lennon was shot dead in New York in 1980 by an obsessive fan.

➜ ***The Beatles, Paul McCartney***

LEOPARD

Large tree-climbing member of the cat family (*Felidae*) found throughout Africa and Asia. Leopards have tan fur patterned with open black circles. They are night hunters.

➜ ***Cats***

LESOTHO

Land-locked country, enclosed by South Africa. **Capital:** Maseru. **Other principal cities:** Teyateyaneng, Mafeteng. **Climate:** temperate. **Geographical features:** high altitude and mountainous. **Main languages:** Sesotho, English. **Main religions:** Protestant, Roman Catholicism. **Rule:** constitutional monarchy. **Currency:** loti. **Primary industries:** agriculture (mainly subsistence), diamond mining. **Exports:** diamonds, wool, cattle, wheat, vegetables.

➜ ***South Africa***

LIBERAL PARTY

British political party, which grew out of the Whigs, one of the two principal parties of the eighteenth and nineteenth centuries. During the nineteenth century, the party supported industry and commerce. The rise of the Labour Party steadily eroded the Liberals until after 1945 they had only a few members in parliament. The Liberals benefited from Labour's unpopularity in the late 1970s and 80s, joining forces with the Social Democratic Party in an alliance and eventually combining as the Liberal Democrats, campaigning for proportional representation.

➡ ***Labour Party***

LIBERIA

West African coastal country. **Capital**: Monrovia. **Other principal cities:** Buchanan, Greenville. **Climate:** hot and humid. **Geographical features:** coastal plain, plateaus, forest. **Main language:** English. **Main religions:** animist, Islam, Christian. **Rule:** democratic republic. **Currency:** Liberian dollar. **Primary industries:** mining, forestry, agriculture. Benefits from merchant fleets registered here. **Exports:** iron ore, rubber, timber, coffee.

➡ ***Africa***

LIBRARIES

Collection of books, films, manuscripts etc., that are available for public use. The first recorded library was that of Rameses II in Egypt (r. 1304–1237 BC). In Europe the spread of the largely text-based Christian religion led to collections of study and religious books becoming more common and by the Renaissance, with printing and the impetus to learn, libraries proliferated.

➡ ***Christianity, Renaissance***

LIBYA

North African Mediterranean country. **Capital:** Tripoli. **Other principal cities:** Benghazi, Misurata, Tobruk. **Climate:** warm coastal, desert inland. **Geographical features:** mostly desert with oil reserves. **Main language:** Arabic. **Main religion:** Islam. **Rule:** socialist republic. **Currency:** Libyan dinar. **Primary industries:** petroleum. **Exports:** petroleum products, natural gas.

LEFT: Painting showing Vladimir Lenin in Red Square.
BELOW: Lichen-covered rocks on the Isle of Muck, Scotland.

Libya's desert regions have restricted agriculture, worsened by population movements to the cities. Most people live on the coast, though some nomadic groups still live farther south. The nation's wealth almost entirely dates from discovery of oil in 1959. Almost all manufactured goods and food are imported. The country has been subjected to UN sanctions for its support of terrorism.

➡ ***Africa***

LICHENS

Plant-like life forms that are made up of two different organisms; fungi and green algae. The fungus and alga exist in symbiosis (a relationship in which both parties benefit). Lichens grow on trees and rocks in unpolluted areas. 15,000 species of lichen have been identified throughout the world.

➡ ***Fungi***

LIGHT

Electromagnetic waves which are visible to the eye. Different wavelengths give rise to different colours; the shortest visible waves give violet light, the longest ones red. White light contains all visible wavelengths. Like other electromagnetic waves, light travels at 300,000 km/s (190,000 m/s) in a vacuum.

LION

Most sociable member of the cat family, found in Africa and Asia. Lions live and hunt in groups (prides). Lions are threatened by hunting and a loss of habitat.

➡ ***Cats***

LITERACY

The ability to read and write. A key skill in the development of a complex civilization as it allows the ideas of one generation to be passed down to those of the next in great detail. There are still over a billion people in the world who are illiterate. Africa is the worst with just over 50% of its population unable to read or write.

➡ ***Education***

LITERARY GENRES

Literary genres, since the mass availability of literature, have sub-divided and increased substantially. The genre of the novel can now be separated into many classifications, such as detective fiction, science fiction, horror, magic realism, historical etc. Poetry and drama have become similarly divisive. Artistic movements have created new genres of fiction, such as Romanticism leading to the emergence of the Gothic and historical novels. The Victorian era's emphasis on reasoning can be seen to have affected the development of the detective novel. In the twentieth century the genre of science fiction became incredibly popular, crossing into other art forms, such as film and television, art and design.

RIGHT: Dusk on Loch Ness, the Highlands, Scotland, allegedly the home of a large underwater monster.
FAR RIGHT: Poster advertising the National Lottery in the UK

➡ ***Drama Forms, Poetry***

LITERARY PRIZES

Emerging and proliferating in the twentieth century, literary prizes are intended to both honour individual achievement and encourage growth within different literary genres and nationalities. Britain's best known prize is the Booker which began in 1969. Americas' is the Pulitzer (from 1917) and internationally the Nobel Prize (from 1901) is revered.

➡ ***Nobel Prize***

LITHOGRAPHY

Invented by Alois Senefelder in 1796, lithography was widely used in print-making and the technique was also explored by many artists, including Eugene Delacroix and Goya. The technique involved drawing on to stone using a chalk (greasy), then wetting the stone so that the applied ink sticks only to the stone. Colour lithography was mastered by French painter Toulous-Lautrec.

➡ ***Eugene Delacroix, Graphic Art, Francisco de Goya***

LITHUANIA

North-east European country. **Capital:** Vilnius. **Other principal cities:** Kaunas, Klaipeda, Siauliai. **Climate:** temperate. **Geographical features:** mainly flat, with forest and lakes. **Main language:** Lithuanian. **Main religion:** Roman Catholicism. **Rule:** democracy. **Currency:** litas. **Primary industries:** engineering, manufacturing, food production, agriculture. **Exports:** electronic goods, heavy manufactured goods, petroleum products, meat dairy products, vegetables, chemicals.

➡ ***Europe***

LOCH NESS

Scottish lake, 36 km (22.5 miles) long, 229 m (754 ft) deep. The lake forms part of the Scottish canal system between Inverness and Fort William. For centuries, rumours have abounded of a 'Loch Ness monster', manifested only in unconfirmed sightings and blurred photographs. Nonetheless, 'Nessie' is invaluable to Scottish tourism.

LOGIC

Analysis of the reasoning used to lead from a set of statements, called premises, to a conclusion. In deductive logic, if the premises are true, the conclusion must be true. Inductive logic studies the ways in which premises support a conclusion without it being an inevitable consequence.

LONGITUDE

On the Earth's surface, the angular distance between the meridian of a place and the meridian of Greenwich, measured east or west, from 0 to 180°.

LORD OF THE RINGS

Trilogy by English writer J. R. R.Tolkein, first published in 1954–55. The books are fantasy, following the adventures of dwarf-like creatures called Hobbits, in a tale of good-versus-evil.

➠ ***Literary Genres***

LOTTERIES

Games of chance in which tickets are sold. The proceeds are pooled and prizes allotted out of it. They are often state run with much money going to good causes.

➠ ***Charities, Gambling***

LOUVRE (1793)

The Louvre houses perhaps the world's most extensive art collection and an impressive museum. Francis I began the building and collections in 1546 and successive monarchs expanded them. Opened to the public in 1793, the building is now vastly complex. During remodelling in the 1980s American architect I. M. Pei added a distinctive glass and steel pyramid.

➠ ***Art Galleries, Museums***

LUTHER, MARTIN (1483–1546)

Founder of Protestantism and German Church reformer, renowned for pinning his '95 Theses' on the door of Wittenberg Cathedral. Luther opposed the pope's sale of indulgences to finance the refurbishment of St Peter's Basilica. The Lutheran World Federation headquarters is in Geneva.

➠ ***Protestantism***

LUXEMBOURG

Land-locked European grand-duchy between Germany, Belgium and France. **Capital:** Luxembourg. **Other principal cities:** Esch-Alzette, Dudelange. **Climate:** temperate. **Geographical features:** mountainous north, wooded south. **Main languages:** French, German, Letzeburgish. **Main religion:** Roman Catholicism. **Rule:** liberal democracy. **Currency:** Luxembourg franc. **Primary industries:** steel manufacturing, chemicals, paper, rubber and plastic, food processing, agriculture. **Exports:** aluminium, manufactured engineering and electronic goods, plastics, textiles, glass.

➠ ***Europe***

MACHU PICCHU

Hidden city of the Incas in the Andes near Cuzco. Machu Picchu is the most remarkable relic of that ancient civilization. It was discovered by the American explorer Hiram Bingham in 1911 and is now a World Heritage Site.

Incas

MACKINTOSH, CHARLES RENNIE (1868–1928)

Scottish architect and designer. Mackintosh, together with his future wife Margaret MacDonald, was a leader of the Glasgow Group. The group produced both architectural plans and interior designs, such as furniture and metalwork. Mackintosh combined beliefs taken from the Arts and Crafts Movement with elements of the Pre-Raphaelites and Japanese art into his own unique blend of Art Nouveau. Both in Britain and Europe, Mackintosh's designs brought him much acclaim and in 1897 he won the competition to design the new Glasgow School of Art. The building was one of the highlights of his career, beautifully combining a complex rationale with widespread influences, such as Scottish castles.

Architecture, Art Nouveau, Arts and Crafts Movement, Eastern Art, Pre-Raphaelites

MACLAINE, SHIRLEY (b. 1934)

US actress. MacLaine's early career is highlighted by her performance in *The Apartment* (1960). She won an Oscar for *Terms of Endearment* (1983) starring alongside Jack Nicholson, and is also an author.

Academy Awards, Jack Nicholson

MADAGASCAR

Indian Ocean island country off Mozambique. **Capital:** Antananarivo. **Other principal cities:** Fianarantsoa, Toamasina. **Climate:** tropical coasts, moderate inland. **Geographical features:** central highland zone. **Main languages:** Malagasy, French. **Main religion:** Christian denominations and local cults. **Rule:** democratic republic. **Currency:** Malagasy franc. **Primary industries:** agriculture. **Exports:** coffee, cloves, sugar, chromite, petroleum, vanilla.

MADONNA (LOUISE CICCONE) (b. 1958)

US singer/songwriter and actress. Madonna is a master of reinvention and is still producing best-selling, critically praised music, such as her album *Music* (2000).

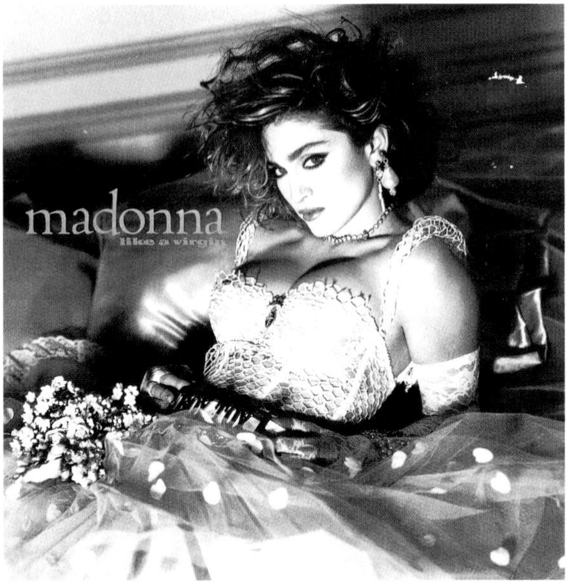

MAGNETISM

Effect by which certain materials can be attracted or repelled. Some materials such as iron can be made to acquire a permanent magnetic field, and an electric current produces a magnetic field.

Electricity

MAGYARS

Finno-Ugric people of Alpo-Carpathian stock. The Magyars migrated from the Caucasus under the leadership of Arpad, invaded the Danubian plain in AD 896 and settled in what is now Hungary at the end of the ninth century. Their conversion to Christianity by King Stephen in AD 998 marked the beginning of the Hungarian kingdom.

Hungary

MALAWI

Land-locked south-east African country. **Capital:** Lilongwe. **Other principal cities:** Blantyre, Mzuzu. **Climate:** sub-tropical. **Geographical features:** narrow territory along the African Rift Valley. **Main languages:** English, Chichewa. **Main religions:** Christianity, Islam. **Rule:** democratic republic. **Currency:** kwacha. **Primary industries:** agriculture. Poor harvests and vast population growth have impoverished Malawai. **Exports:** tobacco, tea, sugar, coffee, peanuts.

Africa

MALAYSIA

South-east Asian country in the Malay peninsula and part of Borneo. **Capital:** Kuala Lumpur. **Other principal cities:** Johor Baharu, Penang, Port Kelang. **Climate:** tropical. **Geographical features:** swamps, mountains and rainforests. Main language: Malay. **Main religion:** Islam. **Rule:** elective monarchy. **Currency:** ringgit. **Primary industries:** electronics, vehicles, food processing, rubber, chemicals, paper. **Exports:** machinery, electronics, petroleum, paper, rubber, timber.

Asia

MALDIVES

Island country off south-west India between the Indian Ocean and Arabian Sea. **Capital:** Malé. **Other principal cities:** Seenu. **Climate:** tropical monsoon. **Geographical features:** 1,100 islands with limited agricultural potential. **Main languages:** Divehi, English. **Main religion:** Islam. **Rule:** nationalist republic. **Currency:** rufiya. **Primary industries:** tourism, textiles, fishing. **Exports:** coconuts, fish, clothing.

India

MALTA

Mediterranean island. **Capital:** Valletta. **Other principal cities:** Rabat, Marsaxlokk. **Climate:** sub-tropical summers, temperate winters. **Geographical features:** Malta includes the smaller islands of Gozo and Comino. **Main languages:** Maltese, English. **Main religion:** Roman Catholicism. **Rule:** democracy. **Currency:** Maltese lira. **Primary industries:** tourism, shipbuilding, construction, light manufacturing. **Exports:** vegetables, lace, knitwear, plastic goods, electronics.

Malta's location south of Sicily made it historically a vital strategic possession. Modern development has seen it become more industrialized, and develop as a tourist destination. It now has one of the world's highest population densities. The soil is too poor for much agriculture. In spite of its coastline, fishing is not important.

MAMMALS

Animals that feed their young from mammary glands. Most mammals also have hair (although reduced in some species e.g. pig), three small bones in the middle ear (ossicles) and seven vertebrae in the neck. Considered to be a very successful group with a highly developed nervous system. Mammals are divided into three smaller groups: monotremes, marsupials and placentals.

Monotremes lay eggs outside their body (oviparous). When the young hatch they are nourished with milk from their mothers' bodies. There are few surviving monotremes e.g. platypus and echidna. Marsupials are mammals that give birth to live young (viviparous) which proceed to develop within a pouch e.g. kangaroo. Placentals are the largest mammalian group. The young develop inside the mother's uterus where they receive nourishment via the placenta; a specialized organ that passes oxygen and nutrients from mother to offspring.

Placentals, unlike monotremes and maruspials, are found throughout the world and mammals have adapted to many different habitats and lifestyles. There are mammals that walk on four legs (cats), two legs (humans), can fly (bats), and swim (seals). They range in size from a tiny shrew of two centimetres in length to the largest animal alive, the blue whale (30 m/100 ft).

Marsupials

LEFT: Small traditional boats in the idyllic setting of a Maltese harbour.
ABOVE: Whitecoat Harp Seal pup, one of the many mammals to be found on earth.

MAN ON THE MOON

The Apollo project of the 1960s and early 1970s resulted in six Moon landings. The first came when Neil Armstrong stepped on to the Moon in July 1969. Twelve astronauts eventually visited the lunar surface between 1969 and 1972. The missions carried out experiments on the surface and brought back rock samples from all the landing sites.

Moon, Space Exploration

MANDELA, NELSON (b. 1918)

South African politician and president. In 1964 Mandela was imprisoned on charges of sabotage and treason, in connection with his organization of the African National Congress; his incarceration became a symbol for anti-apartheid movements. Released in 1990, he negotiated reform in South Africa, and was elected president in 1994, serving until 1999.

Apartheid, South Africa

MANUFACTURING

The production of goods from raw materials, using machinery. Examples of manufacturing industries are the textile industry, food processing, the motor vehicle industry and computer manufacture.

MANUSCRIPTS

Until the invention of printing, books or documents were subject to the lengthy process of copying by hand. Books were rare and learning was limited to the few with access to them. Manuscripts were created largely for religious purposes by monks during the Middle Ages and their beautiful illustrations both promoted and influenced the development of European art.

Calligraphy, Illustration, Medieval, Publishing

ABOVE: The South African politician, anti-apartheid campaigner and twentieth century icon, Nelson Mandela at a press conference in London in 1993.

MAO ZEDONG (1893–1976)

Chinese political leader and prolific writer on Communist ideology and philosophy (also Mao Tse-tung). Founder of the Chinese Communist Party, Mao fought a civil war against the nationalists before and after World War II. After victory in 1949 he established the People's Republic, serving as both Chairman of the party and President of the republic.

China, Communism

MAORI

Polynesian inhabitants of New Zealand, whose cultural tribal tradition was largely destroyed with the arrival of British settlers after 1815. The settlers supplied the Maori with guns, with which they fought one another, then turned on the settlers (1845–47 and 1860–72) to reclaim their territory.

Aboriginal People, Native American Peoples

MARATHON

Longest-running race in the Olympics. It takes its name from the Battle of Marathon, fought between the Greeks and Persians in 490 BC. Pheidippedes ran the 42.16 km (26.2 miles) to Athens to bring news of the Greek victory. On relaying his message he died of exhaustion.

Olympic Games

MARCOS, FERDINAND (1917–89)

President of the Philippines (1965–86). Marcos' US-backed rule relied increasingly on repression of opposition, and was associated with corruption and theft. He was overthrown in 1986.

Philippines

MARLEY, BOB (1945–1981)

Jamaican singer. Born near Kingston, Jamaica, Marley has become the most commercially successful reggae artist of all time. He wrote, recorded and produced most of his music, whilst working with his band The Wailers.

➠ *Rastafari*

MARRIAGE

Traditional and formalized pairing of man and woman recognized across most religious, cultural and political systems. With the growing recognition of gay and lesbian rights the concept of same sex marriages is now gaining acceptance as well. Paradoxically this coincides with a general decline in heterosexual marriages in many developed nations.

MARS

Fourth of the major planets. During Mars' 687-day orbit its distance from the Sun varies considerably. Mars has just over half the diameter of the Earth, and surface conditions more Earth-like than those of any other planet. Visiting space probes have looked for evidence that the planet has harboured life, but so far none has been found.

➠ *Planets, Solar System, Sun*

MARSUPIALS

Mammals with pouches in which the young are nurtured. The pouch contains the mammary glands that provide the developing young with milk. Once born the immature young clamber to the pouch and remain there, feeding until old enough to forage for food. Members of the group include kangaroos, wombats (Australasia) and opossums (South America).

➠ *Kangaroos, Mammals*

MARTIAL ARTS

Strictly speaking any physical discipline associated with fighting. Generally used to refer to those originating in the Far East. These can be both armed (kendo, bushido) or unarmed (kung fu, karate). Now universally popular as sports across the globe, emphasis is placed on mental training as well as physical skills.

MARX, KARL (1918–83)

German philosopher, known for his theories on historical and economic change through conflict. In 1848 with Friedrich Engels, he produced *The Communist Manifesto,* leading to his expulsion from Prussia. Working thereafter from London, Marx began *Das Kapital* which expounded his theories on resisting exploitation of the working classes (the proletariat). Unfinished at his death, Engels completed it by 1893.

➧ ***Communism, Philosophy***

MASTROIANNI, MARCELLO (b. 1923)

Italian actor, made famous by the seminal film by Fellini *La Dolce Vita* (1959). He again worked for Fellini in 8½ (1963) and alongside Sophia Loren in *Marriage, Italian Style* (1963).

➧ ***Films***

MATHEMATICS

The study of number, quantity and space and their relationships. Mathematics is broadly divided into two branches – pure mathematics and applied mathematics. The applied branches are those which have been devised to meet practical needs, for example mechanics, statistics and thermodynamics. Branches of pure mathematics include algebra, geometry, calculus and trigonometry.

➧ ***Geometry***

MATISSE, HENRI (1869–1954)

French artist. Originally a law student, the French artist Matisse had relatively little formal training and this is reflected in the naiveté of his work. Taking on board influences of the Post-Impressionists, Paul Cézanne and Vincent van Gogh, Matisse was the instigator of Fauvism (*fauve* meaning 'wild beast'). His exploration of colour parallels the Cubists' exploration of form. Matisse's palette is vivid and extreme, colour dominates his paintings. Sometimes criticized for his exclusion of negative subjects, Matisse once wrote that he wanted his art to be like a 'good armchair'. His subjects were mostly figures and landscapes. One of his most popular paintings was *Joi de Vivre* (1905–06).

➧ ***Paul Cézanne, Cubism, Vincent van Gogh, Post-Impressionism***

MAUNA KEA AND MAUNA LOA

Pair of volcanoes in Hawaii, USA. Mauna Kea is 4,200 m (13,784 ft) high, and dormant. An astronomical observatory has been built here to take advantage of the altitude and clear air, including infrared devices. Mauna Loa is an active volcano at 4,169 m (13,678 ft), featuring numerous craters.

➧ ***Hawaii, Volcanoes***

MAURITIUS

Indian Ocean island east of Madagascar. **Capital:** Port Louis. **Other principal towns:** Beau Bassin-Rose Hill, Curepipe. **Climate:** tropical. **Geographical features:** tiny land area at 2,040 sq km (788 sq miles). **Main languages:** English, French. **Main religions:** Hindu, Christianity. **Rule:** democratic republic. **Currency:** Mauritian rupee. **Primary industries:** sugar, tourism, finance, light manufacturing. **Exports:** textiles, sugar, financial services.

MAURYA

Indian dynasty which flourished in the third century BC, attaining its zenith under its last king, Asoka (*c.* 264–238 BC). It was noted for the magnificence and range of its stone carving and architecture, much of it devoted to Buddhism to which Asoka converted. After his death, the kingdom declined rapidly.

Buddhism, India

MAYA

Tribe of Yucatán which became the dominant power in Mexico, Guatemala, Honduras and Salvador until they were overthrown by the Spaniards in the sixteenth century. They spread from northern Mexico at the beginning of the Christian era and created an empire renowned for its ornate sculptures.

Aztecs, Incas

MCCARTNEY, PAUL (b. 1942)

Singer/songwriter and bass guitarist of The Beatles. McCartney released his eponymous solo album just weeks before the final Beatles album was released in

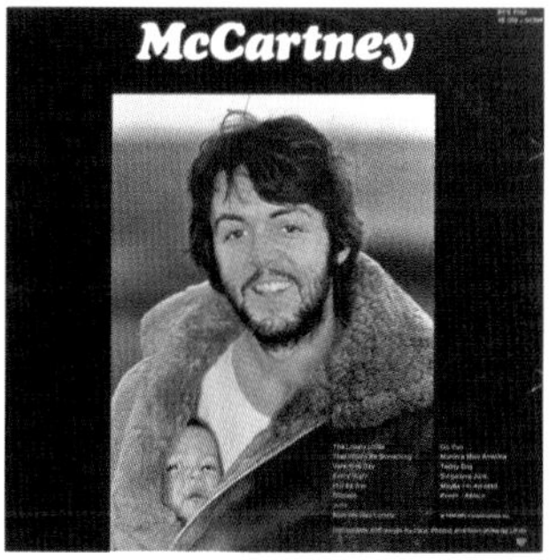

1970. He later formed his band Wings with whom he enjoyed some success, particularly with the 1973 album *Band on the Run.* McCartney married the photographer Linda McCartney in 1969.

Beatles, John Lennon

MEASUREMENT

Quantity found by comparing with a standard unit. The most commonly used measurements are length, mass and time, and combinations of these. For example, speed is measured as length divided by time. In SI, the modern scientific system, the units of length, mass and time are the metre, kilogramme and second, respectively.

LEFT: Goldfish and Sculpture *(1911) by Henri Matisse.*
RIGHT: The media – newspapers, television and radio – enable news to be circulated around the globe almost as it happens.

MEDIA

Blanket term used to describe vehicles of public communication and information, such as magazines and newspapers, radio and, most effectively, television. The immediacy of modern media, such as radio and television, allows almost instant worldwide broadcasting of events and has led to a massive upsurge of globalized knowledge.

Publishing, Radio, Television

MEDIEVAL ART, MUSIC AND LITERATURE

Medieval was a term applied by art critics and historians to a period of European culture prior to the Renaissance (around the ninth to fourteenth century). Medieval art has been revived in successive generations, such as the Gothic movement, Romanticism and the Pre-Raphaelites.

All areas of medieval art were dominated by the Christian religion that had swept across Europe. Art was largely reserved for religious themes, primarily because of the financial and social dominance of the Church but also because the artists, writers and musicians were often monks. However, the nobility also affected the arts – the ideas of chivalry were cultivated in the songs, literature and art of the courts.

Christianity, Gothic, Pre-Raphaelites, Romantic

MERCURY

Nearest planet to the Sun, orbiting once every 88 days. Mercury rotates on its axis three times for every two orbits of the Sun. Mercury's diameter is just over one-third that of the Earth, but has almost the same density. The planet has virtually no atmosphere.

Earth, Planets, Solar System, Sun

MERIDIAN

On the Earth's surface, the plane which passes through a place, the overhead point, and the north and south points on the horizon.

MESOPOTAMIA

Name derived from the Greek, meaning 'the land between the rivers' (Tigris and Euphrates) and approximating to modern Iraq. This fertile land was the cradle of several ancient civilizations, Sumerian, Hittite and Aramaean, before it fell under the sway of Assyria, then Persia and finally Alexander the Great.

Alexander the Great, Assyria, Hittites

METEOROLOGY

Study of the Earth's atmosphere, with the aim of predicting the weather. At weather stations, regular measurements are made of the temperature, air pressure, humidity, wind speed, cloud cover and precipitation (rain, snow, etc.). This information is combined with data collected by satellites to draw weather maps and make predictions.

Earth, Weather

MEXICO

Central American country bordering the USA. **Capital:** Mexico City. **Other principal cities:** Guadalajara, Monterrey, Puebla de Zaragoza, Tampico, Veracruz. **Climate:** tropical, desert and temperate. **Geographical features:** varied landscape, including tropical jungles, deserts, temperate coastal plains. **Main language:** Spanish. **Main religion:** Roman Catholicism. **Rule:** federal democratic republic. **Currency:** Mexican peso. **Primary industries:** manufacturing of motor vehicles, metal and electronic goods, food and drink, chemicals, petroleum refining, tourism, agriculture (arable and pastoral). **Exports:** vehicles and parts, electronic goods, petroleum products, vegetables, coffee, silver, cotton.

Mexico's economy is based on the production of petroleum, silver, vehicles, iron, and steel, coffee and other food products, with a vast market in the US due to the lower prices possible because of low wages. Some US companies have relocated production to Mexico for this purpose. But inflation and a trade deficit have led to high unemployment and the need for more economic controls and foreign aid.

Aztecs

LEFT: A handicraft stall on the street of Chiapas, Mexico.

FAR RIGHT: London's Millennium Eye, a Ferris wheel of massive proportions, is one of the most enduring images associated with the 2000 millennium.

MI5

Abbreviation for Military Intelligence, Section Five. MI5 is the counter-intelligence part of British intelligence services, dealing with internal affairs. Scotland Yard's Special Branch is the executive arm.

MI6

Abbreviation for Military Intelligence, Section Six, the secret intelligence part of British intelligence services, dealing with covert foreign affairs under Foreign Office direction.

MICROCHIPS

Devices in which electronic circuits containing thousands of components have been produced on small crystals of silicon or another semiconductor.

➧ ***Computers, Electronics***

MICROSCOPES

Instruments which produce magnified images of small objects. The main types are the optical microscope, using visible light to produce an image, and the electron microscope, which uses a beam of electrons. The finest detail that can be seen in an optical microscope is limited by the wavelength of light.

➧ ***Light***

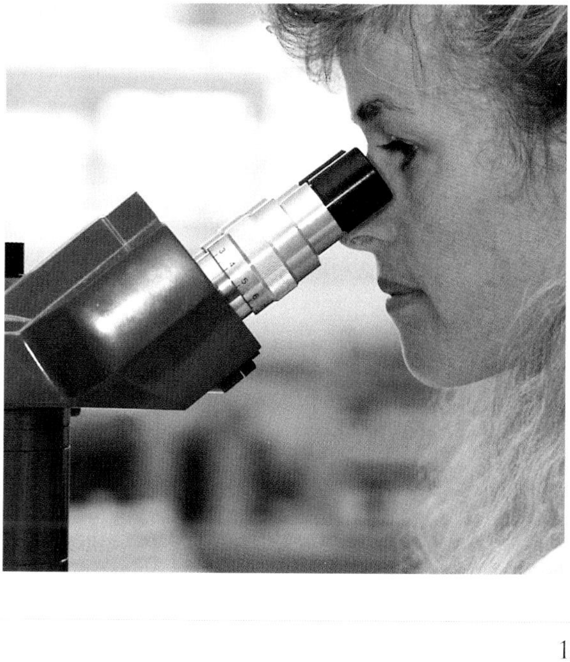

MICROWAVES

Electromagnetic waves with wavelengths ranging between 3–300 mm (0.12–1.18 in). They find applications in radio communications and radar. Because of their ability to heat materials which contain water, their most familiar use is in microwave ovens used to heat food.

MIES VAN DER ROHE, LUDWIG (1886–1969)

German architect. One-time director of the Bauhaus, Rohe emigrated to America in 1938. His style was distinctive and influential and among his best work is the Seagram Building in New York.

➧ ***Architecture***

MIGRATION

Movement of some animals to distant feeding or breeding grounds. Migrations may occur seasonally or only once in a lifecycle, but migrating animals usually return to the place from which they began their journey. Migration has been observed in species of mammals, birds and fish but the precise methods animals use to follow a migratory path remain a mystery.

➧ ***Birds, Wildebeest***

MILLENNIUM

Literally a period of 1,000 years, it has been applied specifically to the periods since the birth of Christ. It was believed that at the end of the First Millennium Christ would return to earth and rule in person. The Book of Revelation hinted that at the end of the Second Millennium Satan would briefly triumph before the Last Judgment.

MILLS

The original mills were machines used for grinding corn into flour, often powered by wind-driven sails. With the introduction of the steam engine, the term was extended to factories using powered machinery, such as cotton mills and woollen mills, and can now encompass other manufacturing plants such as steel mills.

➧ ***Industrial Revolution***

MINIMALISM

Minimalism was not a movement but a general coagulation of ideas that affected art, music, design, literature and architecture. Starting in America in the 1960s (but in architecture not until the 1980s), Minimalism, as the name suggests, was a stripping down to the fundamental elements. It focused upon the interpretation and possibilities within pure form. Minimalist art explored colour and light, space and solidity. It was prevalent in sculpture with artists such as Robert Morris (b. 1931).

MINING

Extraction from deposits of solid or liquid minerals from the land or beneath the sea bed. Some deposits can be extracted by removing the top surface: this is open-cast mining or quarrying. In other cases it is necessary to dig tunnels, or in some cases, drill holes to reach the deposit.

MISSILES

Weapons which are rocket-propelled. They can be launched from a fixed site, from ground vehicles, seacraft or aircraft. Most missiles have a computer-controlled guidance system to lead them to the target, and a warhead containing chemical or, in the case of long-range missiles, nuclear explosive.

➧ ***Nuclear Power, Weapons***

MOLIÈRE (1622–73)

Pseudonym of French dramatist (Jean Baptiste Poquelin), who gained popularity at Louis XIV's court with his unmatched skill in the writing of comedies. Molière influenced the spread of the dramatic genre of comedy to other countries, notably England. Producing some 30 plays, Molière concentrated upon the élite of Parisian society with plays such as *Le Misanthrope* (1666).

➧ ***Drama forms, Playwrights, Theatre***

MOLLUSCS

Invertebrate animals with three distinct body parts: head, 'foot' and visceral mass. Most molluscs are marine animals but some inhabit fresh water and others land. The group includes snails, shellfish, octopuses, squids and slugs. Molluscs have soft, limbless bodies and lack an internal skeleton, although some species have an external shell. Bivalves are molluscs with two shells, such as oysters, clams and scallops. Bivalves feed by filtering food out of the water through a tube called a siphon.

➧ ***Invertebrates***

MONDRIAN, PIET (1872–1944)

Dutch painter. Mondrian expounded the theory that motifs disrupt an artist's ability to portray raw emotion and so he began creating abstract art. His *Compositions* (1914–17) are solely boxes of colour; their harshness is heightened by the restrictive palette of primary and non colours only. Mondrian co-founded De Stijl and was one of the first truly abstract artists.

➧ ***Abstract Art, De Stijl***

MONET, CLAUDE (1840–1926)

French artist. Amongst the Impressionist painters, Monet appears to exemplify the ideals of the movement best. Eugène Boudin (1824–98) convinced Monet to paint in the open air and by 1864 he had begun to work on landscapes with an eye to the atmosphere that they evoked. Monet's life's work was the study of nature and the effect of light upon it. Famed for his many series of paintings, such as *Haystacks* (1890–92), Monet revisited the same scene or subject at different times of day and in different seasons to capture light fluctuations. Monet's final works were impacted by his encroaching blindness and with their vagueness they were both a great influence upon, and a pre-emption of, Abstract Art. The title of the Impressionist movement was taken from his *Impression: Sunrise.*

➧ ***Abstract Art, Impressionism***

LEFT: The Mansfield Colliery, Nottinghamshire, England. In modern mines machines have largely replaced people.
BELOW: Le Pont Japonais, Bassin aux Nympheas, *one of the many works of art which Monet painted in his garden at Giverny.*

MONGOLIA

Land-locked East Asian country between China and Russia. **Capital:** Ulaanbaatar (also Ulan Bator). **Other principal cities:** Darhan, Choybalsan. **Climate:** extremes of hot and cold with minimal rainfall. **Geographical features:** northern mountains, western steppes, southern desert. **Main languages:** Khalkha Mongolian. Religion is officially suppressed. **Rule:** republic. **Currency:** tugrik. **Primary industries:** agriculture. **Exports:** meat, hides, wool, minerals, grain, timber.

Mongolia's economy depends on livestock, supported by vast tracts of grazing land. The economy has suffered a downturn since the collapse of what were formerly guaranteed Soviet bloc markets.

➤ ***Asia***

MONGOLS

Warlike people of central Asia which, under the leadership of Genghis Khan, conquered the territory between the Black Sea and the Pacific, overthrowing the empires of northern China, Kara-Chitai and Kharezm by the time of his death in 1227.

➤ ***Genghis Khan***

MONKEY

Tree-living animals which, like humans and apes, belong to the primate group. Monkeys have five digits on each limb with nails rather than claws. The thumb and first finger are well developed and opposable to the other digits. Old World monkeys, of tropical Africa and Asia, have close-set nostrils and frequently have bare rumps covered with hardened skin e.g. baboons. New World monkeys of Central and South America often have prehensile tails that are adapted for grasping e.g. spider monkeys.

➤ ***Gorilla***

MONORAIL

Railway with trains which run on a single rail, either suspended from the rail or resting on it. Most monorails are electrically driven and operate over short distances, for example to transfer passengers and luggage within an airport. They can be fully automated driverless systems.

➤ ***Railways***

MONROE, MARILYN (1926–62)

US actress. Following her suicide in 1962, Monroe became a lasting icon of the twentieth century. Held by some to be the epitome of Hollywood exploitation, Monroe's most notable film successes were with *Some Like it Hot* (1959) and *Gentlemen Prefer Blondes* (1953). Monroe's face, as painted by Andy Warhol, became an enduring image of the last century.

➤ ***Films, Icons***

MONTEVERDI, CLAUDIO (1567–1643)

Italian Renaissance composer. Monteverdi's imaginatively innovative compositions helped shape future music. He developed monody (one voice or melody supported by the accompaniment), which meant his music could dramatically reflect the text of the piece through the solo refrains. His operatic works were particularly influential – his opera *L'Orfeo* (1607) was the first to use a full orchestra and to contain arias. Monteverdi became musical director at St Marks, Venice, there producing greatly admired church music, such as *Vespers* (1610), which brought him fame throughout Europe.

➤ ***Opera, Renaissance***

MOON

Earth's only natural satellite, diameter 3,476 km (2,160 miles). The Moon takes 29.5 days to go through its cycle of phases from one New Moon to the next, always keeping the same side facing Earth. The Moon has no atmosphere. and the surface experiences extremes of temperature each month.

➧ ***Man on the Moon, Space Exploration***

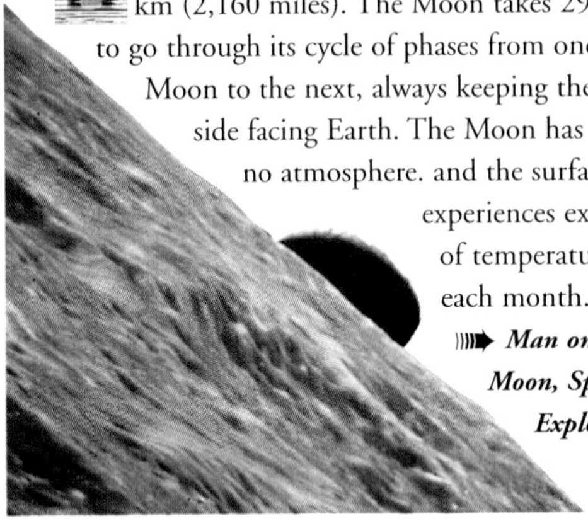

MOORS

Large areas of land that are usually covered with heather, bracken, coarse grass and moss e.g. Dartmoor and Exmoor. Moors are often poorly drained and quite boggy. They are frequently at a higher level than surrounding land, leaving them exposed to wind, thus restricting the growth of trees.

MOREAU, JEANNE (b. 1928)

French actress. Moreau was acclaimed for her parts in New Wave films and is best remembered for her role the classic *Jules et Jim* (1962), Moreau also directed with *Lumière* (1975).

➧ ***Film***

MORISOT, BERTHE (1841–95)

French painter. Morisot studied with Camille Corot (1796–1875) and Barbizon painters before becoming involved with the Impressionist group; her work was included in all but one Impressionist exhibitions and throughout her career Morisot remained faithful to the Impressionist ideals. Many of her paintings are skilled portrayals of domesticity. She was also equally accomplished in portraiture.

➧ ***Barbizon, Impressionism***

ABOVE: Earthrise showing the far side of the moon.
RIGHT: William Morris (front right) with fellow artist and member of the Pre-Raphaelite Movement, Sir Edward Coley Burne-Jones.

MORMONS

Christian sect, full name the Church of Jesus Christ of the Latter-Day Saints. The sect was established in 1830 by Joseph Smith who had the *Book of Mormon* revealed to him. A fellow Mormon, Brigham Young, propounded polygamy, but this was later rejected by the majority of Mormons. Membership: six million.

➧ ***Christianity***

MOROCCO

North-west African country. **Capital:** Rabat. **Other principal cities:** Marrakesh, Fez. **Climate:** semi-tropical coasts, desert inland. **Geographical features:** mountains, deserts, forests. **Main languages:** Arabic, Berber. **Main religion:** Islam. **Rule:** constitutional monarchy. **Currency:** dirham. **Primary industries:** phosphate mining, fertilizers, petroleum, food, clothing, leather, paper, tourism, agriculture. **Exports:** cereals, citrus, sugar beet, potatoes, fishing.

Phosphate mining and exporting is Morocco's main earner, though most of the workforce works on the land. Economic stability has been affected by drought, reliance on imported oil and a war with Mauritania over the disputed territory of Western Sahara. However, wider Arab investment in Morocco, and a growing tourism industry provide reason for optimism.

➧ ***Africa***

MORRIS, WILLIAM (1834–96)

British artist, poet, political theorist and designer. Morris's influence upon nineteenth-century art and interior design was far-reaching. A confirmed socialist, Morris's theories were the basis for the Arts and Crafts

Movement. He was also associated with the work of Pre-Raphaelites, collaborating with Dante Gabriel Rossetti. Morris founded a successful business in 1861, primarily to design wallpaper (believing that painting should literally be on walls), furniture and stained glass. Morris's distinctive paper and textile designs are still in use today.

➡ *Arts and Crafts Movement, Pre-Raphaelites, Socialism*

MORSE, SAMUEL (1791–1872)

US inventor who produced the first practical telegraph, and invented the Morse Code in which letters and numerals are represented by combinations of long and short signals.

MORTGAGES

Type of loan used to finance the buying of property, usually the home. The debt uses the property as security and may be forfeited if payments are not kept up. Repayment is usually over an extended period, typically 25 years. Varying the interest rate payable on mortgages is a key tool in the control of the economy.

➡ *Economy*

MOSAICS

Mosaics are produced by placing small multi-coloured shapes of stone, glass and sometimes wood together to create an overall picture or pattern. Mosaics date back to the Roman Empire and many of their fine examples have been preserved, showing the sturdiness of the artform. The craft was carried on to medieval times and reached a peak during the Byzantine Empire.

➡ *Medieval, Ancient Rome*

MOSQUE

Islamic place of worship. Originally based on the plan of Christian basilicas, mosques vary architecturally depending on their geographical location. Key elements are: the dome, the minaret (to call the faithful to prayer), the mihrab (prayer niche in one of walls, facing Mecca) and an open coutyard.

➡ *Islam*

MOTHER TERESA (1910–97)

Roman Catholic nun, born in Albania, who entered a convent in Calcutta, aged 18. In 1948 she received Indian citizenship and established the Missionaries of Charity, a unisex order to help abandoned children and dying people. She was awarded the Nobel Peace Prize in 1979.

➡ *Catholicism, Charities, Nobel Prize*

MOTOR RACING

Sport involving high-speed cars. Motor racing has many different classes, the most famous of which is Formula 1 Grand Prix, first formulated in 1906. There are also touring, rallying and endurance classes. Famous races include the Le Mans (1923), Indy 500 (1911), and the Lombard-RAC rally (1927). Specialist race car manufacturers include Bugati, Ferrari, Williams, Lotus and McLaren.

➡ *Motorcycle Racing, Indy Car Racing, NASCAR*

MOTORCYCLE RACING

Sport involving high-speed motobikes. The different classes include grand prix, motorcross, speedway and endurance. Major events include the annual grand prix circuit and the Isle of Man TT race (established in 1907). The first recorded motorcycle race in the UK took place in Surrey in 1897. There is even a variation on speedway where the bikes race on ice and have spiked tyres.

➧ ***Motor Racing***

MOTORCYCLES

Two-wheeled vehicles propelled by a petrol engine which is positioned low down between the wheels and drives the rear wheel. Motorcycles have a high power-to-weight ratio and can accelerate very rapidly. Air-cooled, single-cylinder engines are normally used, either two-stroke or four-stroke.

➧ ***Motorcycle Racing***

MOULDS

Common name for fungi that grow on food and other organic matter. Unlike plants moulds cannot photosynthesize; instead they gain their nutrients by dissolving organic matter which is then absorbed into its tissues. The development of penicillin from a mould has been responsible for important medical advances in the treatment of disease.

➧ ***Fungi, Penicillin***

MOUNTAINS

Elevated ground that is over 307 m (1,007 ft) in height. Mountains are formed from solid rock that has been pushed upwards by huge forces over millions of years. Many mountain ranges are still growing as the plates of the Earth's crust converge, forcing more rock upwards. The Himalayan mountains, which are 25 million years old, grow several centimetres every year.

➧ ***Mount Everest, Himalayas***

MOZAMBIQUE

South-east African coastal country. **Capital:** Maputo. **Other principal cities:** Beira, Nacala, Quelimane. **Climate:** tropical coast, milder inland. **Geographical features:** large coastal plain, interior plateaux and highlands. **Main language:** Portuguese. **Main religions:** animist, Roman Catholicism, Islam. **Rule:** democratic republic. **Currency:** metical. **Primary industries:** agriculture, fishing, petroleum. **Exports:** shrimp, cotton, sugar, cashew, copra, fruit.

Mozambique's colonial past on the trade route to the Far East has left it undeveloped, while southern African instability and the division of adjacent countries have lost it trade.

➧ ***Africa***

MOZART, WOLFGANG AMADEUS (1756–91)

Austrian composer. Mozart mastered, developed and influenced every sphere of music; from operas such as *Don Giovanni* (1787) to his magnificent symphonies, Mozart displayed an innate musical brilliance. Born into a musical family, Mozart was a child prodigy and with his family toured Europe giving concerts from the age of six and by nine he was already writing symphonies. He worked intermittently for the archbishop of Salzburg (1771–81) before moving to Vienna. Mozart did not receive respect or financial reward for his virtuosity at composing and was forced to teach and perform for money. Dying a pauper, Mozart was buried in an unmarked grave.

➧ ***Ludwig van Beethoven, George Frideric Handel, Opera***

MUGHALS

The preferred modern spelling for a name (formerly Mogul or Moghal) derived from Mongol and applied to the Muslim empire of India founded by the Kirghiz leader Babar (1483–1530) in 1526. It flourished for two centuries but in decline its possessions were taken over by the British.

RIGHT: Mughal warriors in the eighteenth century, at the beginning of the decline of this Muslim empire.

TOP RIGHT: An archaeologist next to the elaborately decorated coffins used to help preserve the mummified bodies of ancient Egyptians.

MULTINATIONAL CORPORATIONS

Some commercial organizations have grown so large that they span national borders and carry a considerable amount of influence and power. This effect is felt particularly in smaller and poorer countries, where the multinational may well be richer than the state itself. Multinationals have been accused of purusing their own interests to the detriment of the countries in which they operate. An example of this is the catastrophe that occurred at the chemical plant in Bhopal, India.

MUMMIES

Dead bodies preserved by the ancient Egyptians. The word mummy comes from the Persian for wax or pitch, substances used in the embalming process which developed out of the natural phenomenon whereby corpses were desiccated by the hot dry sand. Later bodies were wrapped in intricate bandages and placed in elaborate coffins to preserve their identity.

➧ ***Ancient Egypt***

MUSEUMS

Collection of historical, scientific or cultural objects of interest. Stemming from many private collections of antiquities and oddities, museums, such as the Louvre, began to open to the public in the nineteenth century with the upsurge of liberal ideas on public education and equality.

Museums have reflected and influenced societies over the years; Lord Elgin took sculpture from the Parthenon which were bought by the British Museum. Museums worldwide have paid for animals to be killed for their scientific displays, thereby impacting upon the decline of certain species. Today, museums have moved away from the nineteenth century values of simply conserving objects towards an emphasis on education and entertainment.

➧ ***Guggenheim Museum, Louvre***

MUSICAL NOTATION

Notation instructs musicians on the performance of a particular piece of music, giving the notes, key, speed and even mood of the music. Notation emerged in the Middle Ages when music was still mainly memorized. The necessity for musical instruction grew as more complex music styles were developed during the Renaissance.

➧ ***Renaissance***

MUSSOLINI, BENITO (1883–1945)

Italian Fascist dictator, 'Il Duce' (the Leader) from 1925. Mussolini founded the Italian Fascists in 1919, becoming prime minister in 1922. Wars of expansion in Ethiopia (1935–36) and Albania (1939) and support for Francisco Franco in Spain (1936–39) followed. In 1940, Italy joined Germany in World War II, but defeats forced Mussolini's resignation. He was captured by partisans and executed, his corpse being publicaly degraded in Milan.

➧ ***Dictatorship, World War II***

NAMIBIA

South-west African coastal country. **Capital:** Windhoek. **Other principal cities:** Swakopmund, Rehoboth. **Climate:** sub-tropical. **Geographical features:** high plateau with the Namib and Kalahair Deserts. **Main language:** English. **Main religion:** Christian denominations. **Rule:** democratic republic. **Currency:** Namibian dollar. **Primary industries:** mining, agriculture. **Exports:** copper, diamonds, lead, uranium, zinc, cattle, hides, fish.

➧ ***Africa***

NAPOLEONIC WARS (1803–15)

Name given to European wars of the period 1803–15, forming part of longer term conflict between Britain and France and their allies. The Battle of Trafalgar on 21 October 1805 ended Napoleon's hopes of invading Britain. British influence led to Russia, Austria and Prussia all going to war against Napoleon, but he inflicted major defeats at Austerlitz (1805), and Jena/Auerstadt (1806). The tide turned as the Spanish campaign of 1808 dragged on. An invasion of Russia finally ended in defeat at Leipzig (1813) by Russia, Austria and Prussia, and also in Spain. Forced to abdicate, Napoleon returned in 1815 only to face total defeat at Waterloo.

➧ ***Napoleon Bonaparte***

LEFT: French cavalry during the Napoleonic Wars (1803–15).

NASA

National Aeronautics and Space Administration. A US government agency which oversees space-flight and related matters. NASA's main facility is the Kennedy Space Center. Cape Canaveral, Florida.

➧ ***Man on the Moon, Space Exploration***

NASCAR

National Association for Stock Car Auto Racing. Popular motor sport in the US where production cars are adapted for racing. It is said to have originated from gangsters supercharging ordinary cars to evade the police.

➧ ***Indy Car Racing, Motor Racing***

NATIONAL DEBT

Cumulative deficit caused by too many imports and not enough exports. It is like an 'overdraft' on a national scale.

➧ ***Imports and Exports***

NATIONAL HOLIDAYS

Holidays decreed by a nation's government. They may be religious (Easter, Diwali), cultural (May Day) or political (Bastille Day) in nature. Often referred to as Bank Holidays in the UK.

➧ ***Diwali, Easter, Holidays***

NATIONAL PARKS

Tracts of land, often of particular beauty, set by for public enjoyment. The first national park, Yellowstone, was established in the US in 1872. Since then countries all over the world have adopted the idea of preserving areas of particular importance for conservation, historical or recreational reasons.

NATIVE AMERICAN PEOPLES

Also known as American Indians or Red Indians, because Christopher Columbus thought he had reached India when he first landed in the Americas. Native American Peoples have inhabited America since

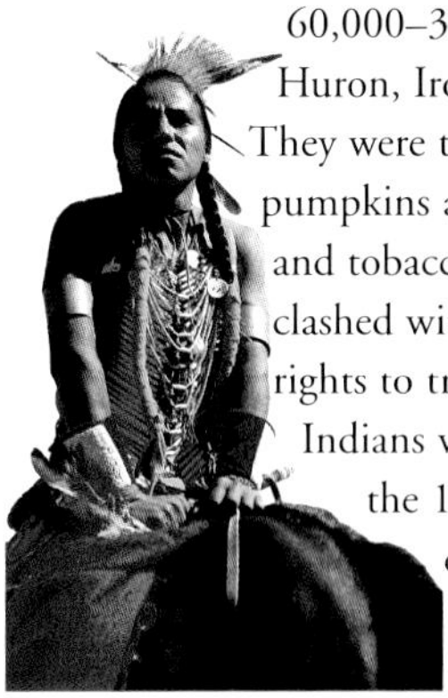

60,000–35,000 BC. Tribes include the Huron, Iroquois, Cherokee and Sioux. They were the first people to use potatoes, pumpkins and peanuts, cocaine, quinine and tobacco. The Native Americans clashed with European colonists over rights to traditional hunting-grounds: Indians were evicted and killed and by the 1890s the colonists had fully conquered America.

➧ ***Aboriginal People, Christopher Columbus, Maori***

NATO (1949)

North Atlantic Treaty Organization. Organization set up by countries in western Europe and North America in 1949 for mutual defence. The military headquarters is in Belgium.

➧ ***World War II***

NATIONALISM

Pride in, and a sense of belonging to, a nation. In extreme forms nationalism can lead to hatred of other nations and peoples, such as in Nazi Germany.

➧ ***Nazism, Racism***

NATURAL SELECTION

Process where certain characteristics that facilitate an organism's survival are passed on to the next generation. Over time, natural selection results in adaptations that enable an organism to succeed in its environment and may eventually contribute to the development of a new species. Natural selection was the mechanism used by Charles Darwin to explain his evolutionary theory.

➧ ***Charles Darwin, Evolution, Genetics***

NAVIES

Military organizations; the maritime part of a nation's armed forces. The earliest exponents were the Phoenicians and Athenians. The UK's first navy was instituted by Henry VIII, whose flagship *Mary Rose* famously sank on its maiden voyage. The UK was the dominant naval power from 1805 until World War II.

BELOW: Hitler and his followers exchange the Nazi salute at Nuremberg in the early 1930s.

The US Navy is now the most powerful, centred on the nuclear powered super aircraft carrier.

➧ ***Armies, Air Forces***

NAVIGATION

Technique of finding the position, direction and distance travelled of a vehicle, in particular seacraft and aircraft. Traditional methods using a magnetic compass and the positions of Sun and stars in the sky have been largely superseded by the Global Positioning System, which uses signals from satellites to fix positions.

➧ ***Longitude***

NAZISM

Derived from the name of the National Socialist German Workers' Party, Nazism was an ideology dedicated to nationalism, racism and subordination of the individual to the state. The German party was led by Adolf Hitler from 1921 to 1945, and was supported by Nazi parties in Austria and Hungary. Although widely banned, groups with Nazi sympathies still exist around the world.

➧ ***Adolf Hitler, World War II***

NEOCLASSICISM (18TH–19TH CENTURIES)

Art and architectural movement that spread through Europe and the USA during the eighteenth to nineteenth century. Neoclassicism was in part brought on by the eighteenth-century archeological finds at Herculaneum and Pompeii, which gave a greater knowledge and revived interest in Classical antiquity. As the name suggests, Neoclassicism aimed to revive Classicism but it differed from the Renaissance revival in its stricter application of the Classical model rather than interpretation. Neoclassicism pushed away from the ornamentation of the Baroque, returning to a simpler, more graciously disciplined and reasoned style.

➨ ***Baroque, Classical Era, Pompeii, Renaissance***

NEPAL

Central Asian country between India and China. **Capital:** Katmandu. **Other principal cities:** Pátan, Moráng. **Climate:** sub-tropical south, temperate north. **Geographical features:** the Himalayas. **Main language:** Nepali. **Main religion:** Hindu. **Rule:** constitutional monarchy. **Currency:** Nepalese rupee. The economy is one of the world's most undeveloped. **Primary industries:** agriculture. **Exports:** cattle, hides, jute, rice, timber, clothing, carpets.

➨ ***Asia***

NEPTUNE

Eighth of the major planets, almost a twin of Uranus in terms of diameter and mass, but twice as far from the Sun. Its blue-green colour is due to the presence of methane. Neptune was discovered after its existence and position had been predicted.

➨ ***Planets, Solar System, Sun***

RIGHT: Auckland, North Island, New Zealand.

NERNST, W. HERMANN (1864–1941)

German physical chemist. Nernst formulated the third law of thermodynamics, or Nernst heat theorem, and was awarded the Nobel Prize for Chemistry in 1920.

➨ ***Chemistry, Nobel Prize***

NETHERLANDS

North-west European country. **Capital:** The Hague. **Other principal cities:** Amsterdam, Utrecht, Eindhoven, Rotterdam. **Climate:** mild and damp. **Geographical features:** flat, requiring drainage. **Main languages:** Dutch, English. **Main religions:** Roman Catholicism, Dutch Reformed Church. **Rule:** constitutional monarchy. **Currency:** guilder (gulden). **Primary industries:** manufacture of metal, electronic, and electrical goods, food, chemicals, rubber and plastics, horticulture, diamond cutting. **Exports:** machinery, food, livestock, tobacco, natural gas, flowers and plants.

➨ ***Europe***

NEW ZEALAND

South Pacific island country. **Capital:** Wellington. **Other principal cities:** Hamilton, Auckland, Christchurch, Dunedin. **Climate:** temperate. **Geographical features:** two large islands, the North Island

and the South Island, and many smaller islands, with varied terrain including mountains, fjords and volcanic plateaux. **Main language:** English. **Main religion:** Christianity. **Rule:** constitutional monarchy. **Currency:** New Zealand dollar. **Primary industries:** agriculture (mainly cattle and sheep), manufacturing of paper and food-processing, tourism. **Exports:** wool, lamb, mutton, beef, cheese, fruit, fish, paper, chemicals.

NEWPORT JAZZ FESTIVAL (1954)

Started in 1954, the festival is a key event in jazz music. Named after the town in Rhode Island where the festival began, it is now held in New York.

➤ *Jazz*

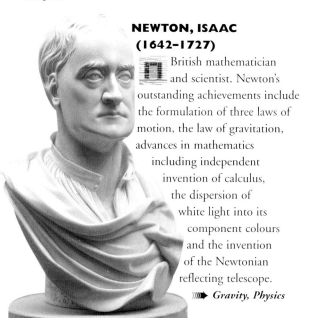

LEFT: *An ivory bust of Sir Isaac Newton, carved from life by David Le Marchand in 1718.*

NEWTON, ISAAC (1642–1727)

British mathematician and scientist. Newton's outstanding achievements include the formulation of three laws of motion, the law of gravitation, advances in mathematics including independent invention of calculus, the dispersion of white light into its component colours and the invention of the Newtonian reflecting telescope.

➤ *Gravity, Physics*

NICARAGUA

Central American country. **Capital:** Managua. **Other principal cities:** León. **Climate:** tropical. **Geographical features:** low-lying Caribbean and Pacific coastal areas with central mountains. **Main language:** Spanish. **Main religion:** Roman Catholicism. **Rule:** democracy. **Currency:** cordoba. The economy is hindered by foreign debt and political instability. **Primary industries:** agriculture: **Exports:** coffee, cotton, sugar, bananas, seafood, gold.

NICHOLSON, JACK (b. 1937)

US stage and screen actor. Nicholson plays the villain superbly; from zany (*Batman* 1989) to psychotic (*The Shining* 1980). He also won acclaim for his anti-hero McMurphy in *One Flew Over the Cuckoo's Nest* (1975).

➤ *Films*

NIETZSCHE, FRIEDRICH (1844–1900)

German existentialist philosopher. Nietzsche wrote *Thus Spake Zarathustra* in 1883 (considered to be his masterpiece). In 1889 Nietzsche collapsed and was declared insane. In his exploration of the unconscious, Nietzsche is considered a forerunner of Sigmund Freud but equally his ideas on the assertion of a new superior race of men have been condemned because of their misinterpretation by the Nazis in the 1930s.

➤ *Sigmund Freud, Nazism*

NIGER

Land-locked western Central African country. **Capital:** Niamey. **Other principal cities:** Zinder, Maradi, Tahoua. **Climate:** hot, dry. **Geographical features:** northern mountains and Sahara, southern savanna. **Main languages:** French, Hausa. **Main religion:** Islam. **Rule:** provisional military. **Currency:** franc CFA. **Primary industries:** uranium mining, agriculture. **Exports:** uranium, livestock, cowpeas, gum Arabic, peanuts, onions.

➤ *Africa*

NIGERIA

Coastal Central African country. **Capital:** Abuja. **Other principal cities:** Lagos, Port Harcourt, Ibadan. **Climate:** tropical. **Geographical features:** forest, savanna, semi-desert. **Main language:** English. **Main religions:** Islam, Christianity. **Rule:** military republic. **Currency:** naira. **Primary industries:** food, petroleum, vehicle assembly, iron and steel, chemicals, paper, textiles, cigarettes, agriculture. **Exports:** petroleum, cocoa, rubber, urea and ammonia, fish.

➤ *Africa*

NIGHTINGALE, FLORENCE (1820–1910)

British nurse, regarded as the founder of the modern nursing profession. During the Crimean War she went with a team of nurses to Turkey and dramatically reduced the death rate among the wounded by improving hospital hygiene standards. She founded the Nightingale School and Home for Nurses in London.

➡ ***Crimean War***

NILE, RIVER

North-flowing African river, the world's longest at 6,695 km (4,160 miles). The White Nile rises in Lake Victoria in Uganda, the Blue Nile at Lake Tama in Ethiopia. They join at Khartoum, Sudan, flowing northwards through Egypt to the Mediterranean. The flow through Egypt is regulated by the Aswan High Dam.

➡ ***Africa, Aswan Dam, Egypt***

NOBEL PRIZE

Annual international prize, founded by the Swedish inventor of dynamite, Alfred Nobel. The original categories were Physics, Chemistry, Physiology or Medicine, Literature and Peace, with Economics added in 1969. The prizes have a large cash value and can be awarded to organizations as well as individuals. Winners are decided by an academic committee based in Sweden, except for Peace, which is decided by members of the Norwegian Parliament. Famous winners include Albert Einstein, The United Nations and Mother Teresa.

➡ ***Albert Einstein, Mother Teresa***

NORMANS

People descended from Norse raiders who settled in north-western France in the early tenth century. Under Duke William they invaded England in 1066. Conquest was supported by the feudal system of land-holding based on military service which gradually extended over the whole country and later spread to Scotland and Ireland as Norman mercenaries were rewarded for their services with grants of land. The Normans revolutionized England in language, laws, customs and class structure. Although Normandy was eventually assimilated into France, the Channel Islands are the last remnant of the ducal dominions of the British Crown.

➡ ***Feudalism***

NORSE GODS AND MYTHOLOGY

Violent, elemental mythology that came to be dominated by the Vikings' mythology, reflecting the society in which it developed. Their creation myth held that the Earth emerged for the corpse of the slain giant, Ymir, whose bones became mountains and blood became lakes.

The oldest and pre-eminent Norse god, Odin, was the counterpart of Woden of the Anglo-Saxons. He was god of battle, inspiration and the dead, and increased in popularity under the Vikings. Valhalla was the mythological hall where his attendants, the Valkyries, sent the heroic victims of battle. Thor, the god of thunder (eponymous Thursday) had his chariot drawn across the sky by two goats and reclaimed the hammer that the gods used in self-defence against the giants. Freyr was the third principal Germanic god: god of fertility, sunlight and rain.

➡ ***Egyptian Gods and Mythology, Greek Gods and Mythology, Roman Gods and Mythology***

NORTH AMERICAN FREE TRADE AGREEMENT

NAFTA began moves towards free trade between Canada, the US and Mexico, from January 1994, an area responsible for 30% of the world's gross domestic product.

NORTH KOREA

South-east Asian country. **Capital:** Pyongyang. **Other principal cities:** Chongjin, Nampo. **Climate:** temperate. **Geographical features:** western coastal plain, mountainous interior. **Main language:** Korean. **Main religions:** Chondoist, Christianity, Buddhist. **Rule:** communist. **Currency:** won. Industry is nearly all government-owned, and agriculture collectivized, but people have suffered increasing food shortages. **Primary industries:** mining, agriculture: **Exports:** minerals, metal and agricultural products.

Asia, Korean War, South Korea

NORWAY

North-west Scandinavian country. **Capital:** Oslo. **Other principal cities:** Bergen, Trondheim, Stavanger. **Climate:** mild. **Geographical features:** mountainous plateau, and fjord-dotted coastline. **Main language:** Norwegian. **Main religion:** Evangelical Lutheran. **Rule:** constitutional monarchy. **Currency:** krone. **Primary industries:** mining, machinery manufacture, fishing, paper, shipbuilding, chemicals. **Exports:** aluminium, petroleum, natural gas, fish, ships, paper and pulp.

Europe

NOTRE-DAME (1200–50)

Notre Dame cathedral in Paris evinces High Gothic style with its twin tower facade and effusive decoration. It was made famous by Hugo's novel *The Hunchback of Notre Dame.*

Gothic

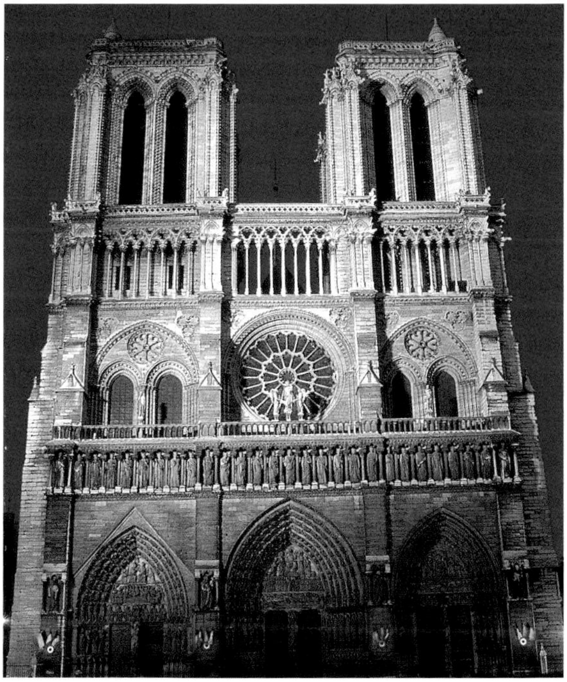

NUCLEAR POWER

Generation of power using processes involving changes in the nuclei of atoms. At present, all nuclear power stations use uranium or plutonium isotopes which release heat energy when the atoms split. The heat is used to produce steam which in turn is used to power electrical generators.

Hiroshima, Weapons

NUREMBERG TRIBUNAL (1945–46)

Set up to try the principal Nazi war criminals responsible for atrocities committed during World War II. Sitting between November 1945 and October 1946, the tribunal had a judge and prosecutor each from the UK, US, USSR and France. A subsidiary component dealt with accusations of criminal behaviour by members of the German government, the Gestapo and the SS.

Nazism, World War II

NUTRITION

Science of food and its effects on health. All animals require certain nutrients in their food in order to survive. The main types of nutrient are proteins, carbohydrates, fats, vitamins and minerals (including water). A healthy diet requires all these to be present in the right amounts.

Diet

NUTS

Dry, single-seeded fruit with a hard, woody wall e.g. acorn and hazelnut. The kernals of nuts are usually highly nutritious with high levels of fat and protein.

Fruit

ABOVE: A science has developed around foods – what we eat, when and how much. Failure to understand and fulfil basic dietary requirements leads to malnutrition and disorders ranging from obesity to starvation.

OASES

Areas of fertile land, often vegetated, in otherwise arid desert regions. Oases occur when the water table reaches or approaches the surface of the land.

Deserts

OCCULT

Magical, astrological and supernatural arts. A notorious occult religion is Voodooism which includes witchcraft, animalistic deities and communication with ancestors. The Ouija board also communicates with the past and is often regarded as dangerous, as are Tarot cards, which are used for fortune-telling. A shaman is a medicine man indigenous to Asia, Africa and the Americas. He mediates between Earth and the supernatural world to control good and evil spirits.

Witches

OCEANIA

Collective term for Australasia (Australia, New Zealand, and islands) together with all the scattered islands of Melanesia (including New Britain, Solomon Islands, Fiji) in the western south Pacific, Micronesia (Guam, Mariana Islands, Caroline Island and Marshall Islands) north of Melanesia, and Polynesia (Tahiti and the Society Islands, Samoa, Cook Islands, Marquesas Islands) in the central south Pacific.

Australasia, Australia, New Zealand

OCEANOGRAPHY

Science of the oceans, including the study of water movements, composition and temperature, the ocean beds, and the living organisms which depend on the oceans.

OCEANS

Vast bodies of salty water. Four oceans are usually recognized: Pacific, Atlantic, Indian and Southern. The Arctic is sometimes added to this list. The Pacific is the world's largest ocean, covering 181 million sq km (112 million sq miles) and with an average depth of 4,200 m (13,780 ft). Approximately 70% of the Earth's surface is covered by oceans, which are growing all the time owing to the divergence of tectonic plates at the centre of the ocean floor (mid-oceanic ridges). Life on Earth probably began in the oceans and today they support a huge array of life from the fertile continental shelves to the dark abyssal depths.

Oceanography, Plate Tectonics, Seas

OIL

Fossil fuel composed of carbon and hydrogen. Found mainly in certain formations of layered rock. Even the most ancient civilizations used crude oil. Saudi Arabia is one of the most oil-rich nations in the world today.

Gas, OPEC

OLIVIER, LORD LAWRENCE (1907–89)

English theatre actor. Olivier also made many films. Amongst his achievements are two Shakespeare plays, *Hamlet* (1948) and *Henry V* (1945), which Olivier also directed.

Vivien Leigh, Theatre

OLYMPIC GAMES (776 BC AND 1896)

Sporting event originally held in ancient Greece between 776 BC and AD 394. The modern games were revived in 1896 by the Frenchman Pierre de Fredi, Baron de Coubertin. The ancient games developed from a series of religious festivals and included many disciplines still in existence, including running races, javelin, discus and wrestling. They also included chariot racing and various military competitions. Artists and poets also exhibited their works.

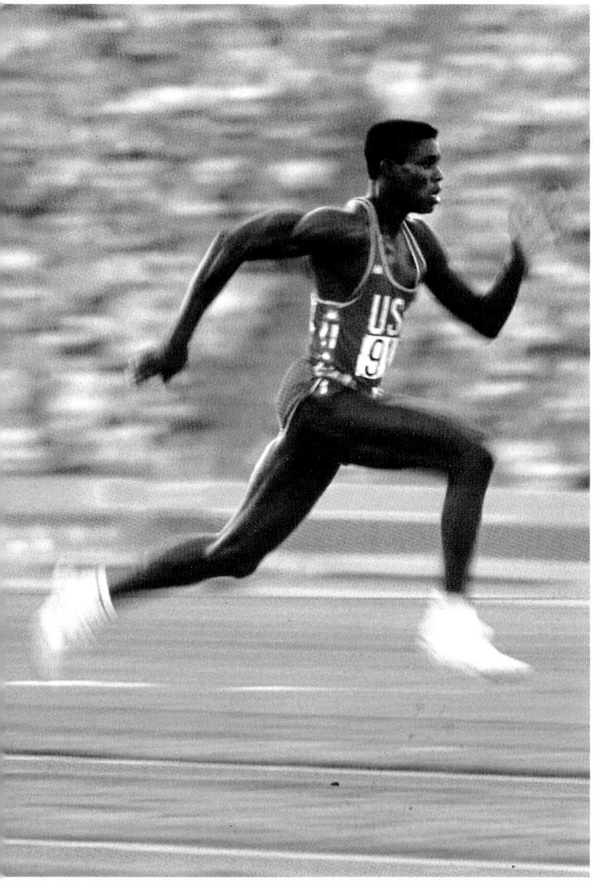

LEFT: America's Carl Lewis at the 1984 Olympic Games in Los Angeles, taking the gold in long-jump.

The modern games are now held every four years in a different location. The Winter Games were constituted in 1924. The Olympic flag of five rings represents the five continents of the world, and their coming together under the Olympic movement. This has unfortunately not stopped the game being used to make political points. The 1980 games held in Russia (the USSR) were boycotted by the USA and similarly the Russians boycotted the 1984 games held in the USA.

Athletics, Ancient Greece, Gymnastics, Running

OPEC (1960)

Organization of Oil Petroleum-Exporting Countries (mainly North Africa and the Middle East), founded in 1960 so that oil-producers could act in unity over supply and prices.

Oil

OPERA

Form of drama where text is sung not spoken. Opera was conceived in the 1590s in Florence by a group called the *Camerata* who tried to revive the Greek plays by setting them to music. Opera was skilfully developed by Claudio Monteverdi to use more complex vocals, the inclusions of arias (solo song) and to use a full orchestra. The first opera house was opened in Venice in 1637. As opera grew in popularity it continued to evolve and diverge. In the eighteenth century Mozart developed the idea of the comic opera with *Don Giovanni*. In the nineteenth century Richard Wagner (1813–83) explored Romanticism with his adherence to historical and German mythological themes and his expressive, intensely emotional music. Amongst the most popular and often performed operas are those by the Italians Giacomo Puccini (1858–1924), such as *Madame Butterfly* (1904), and Giuseppe Verdi (1813–1901), such as *La Traviata* (1853).

Claudio Monteverdi, Wolfgang Amadeus Mozart, Sydney Opera House

OPERA HOUSE, SYDNEY

The Danish architect Jørn Utzon (b. 1918) won the competition to design Sydney's most famous building in 1957. Under much controversy, the building was completed in 1973 after Utzon's resignation.

Architecture, Opera

OPIUM

Narcotic drug extracted from the seeds of the poppy, *Papaver somniferum*, a native of the Far East. It is addictive and is the basis for several other highly dangerous drugs, notably morphine and heroin. Its use became exceptionally pernicious in nineteenth-century China, and was used as a political tool by the British Empire to gain trading concessions on the Chinese mainland.

➧ ***British Empire, Drugs***

ORANG-UTAN

Member of the ape family native to Sumatra and Borneo. Orang-utans are covered in long red hair, live mainly in trees and eat fruit. They are now an endangered species.

➧ ***Endangered Species***

ORCHESTRAS

An orchestra comprises four sections: strings, wind, brass and percussion. The structure of orchestras still follows the nineteenth century example. A symphony orchestra has from 40 to 100 musicians, each reading their own score and led by a conductor. Orchestras are used to produce accompanying music (e.g. ballet).

➧ ***Brass Instruments, Percussion Instruments, String Instruments, Woodwind Instruments***

ORGANIC FARMING

Livestock or agricultural farming that does not use any factory-made chemicals in any part of the production process. This includes a ban on the use of any artificial fertilizers, pesticides, herbicides, drugs or feeds.

➧ ***Agriculture, Farming***

ORGANIZATION OF AFRICAN UNITY (1963)

Founded in 1963 to provide a unified African voice, dedicated to ending colonial rule, promoting national liberation and mediating in African disputes and wars. Based in Addis Ababa, Ethiopia.

➧ ***Africa***

BELOW: An organic chicken farm. The animals are allowed to roam with relative freedom, their feed will not be chemically treated and the birds will be free from any growth-promoting drugs.

ORGANOPHOSPHATES

Synthetic insecticides, used on both animals and plants. They are very toxic, and breathing the vapour can be fatal. Malathion and parathion are examples of organophosphates.

ORIENTEERING

Sport based on cross-country running and map reading. Competitors race against the clock between a series of checkpoints. The World Championships started in 1966.

➧ ***Running***

ORNITHOLOGY

Study of birds, their lifestyles, habitats, structure, scientific classification and distribution. Ornithology is not just a science but a popular pastime for millions of people.

➧ ***Birds***

ORTHODOX CHURCH

Principal branch of Christianity in eastern Europe and Asia. Notably the Eucharist is celebrated with much ceremony and belief in the Immaculate Conception is rejected. The Orthodox Church's roots are in

Constantinople and branches include the Greek and Russian Orthodox Churches. Total membership worldwide: 130 million.

⟫ ***Catholicism, Christianity, Protestantism***

OTTER

Aquatic, carnivorous member of the weasel family. Otters have streamlined bodies, thick fur, short limbs and webbed toes. They are found throughout the world except Australia.

OTTOMAN EMPIRE (13TH TO 20TH CENTURIES)

Empire founded by the Osmanli Turks, a tribe of Central Asia which began expanding in the thirteenth century. By 1600 they had established an empire which stretched from Hungary and Poland to the Caspian Sea and from Algeria to the Persian Gulf. It declined in the nineteenth century and ended in 1922.

⟫ ***Turkey***

OUIJA BOARD

Board marked out with the alphabet, used to communicate with spirits, who spell out their answers by moving an upturned glass, which the participants are touching.

⟫ ***Occult, Witches***

OWEN, ROBERT (1771–1858)

Pioneering English socialist. Owen was manager of a textile mill at New Lanark. He made many improvements to the workers conditions and founded an early trade union. He was a driving force behind the creation of co-operative societies.

⟫ ***Industrial Revolution, Mills***

OXYGEN

Tasteless, odourless invisible gas with the chemical symbol O. Oxygen is the most common element in the Earth's crust and also represents 21% of the atmosphere. It combines with hydrogen to form water (H_2O). Oxygen is a product of photosynthesis and is the basis of respiration. Ozone is a form (allotrope) of oxygen.

⟫ ***Atmosphere, Ozone Layer, Photosynthesis***

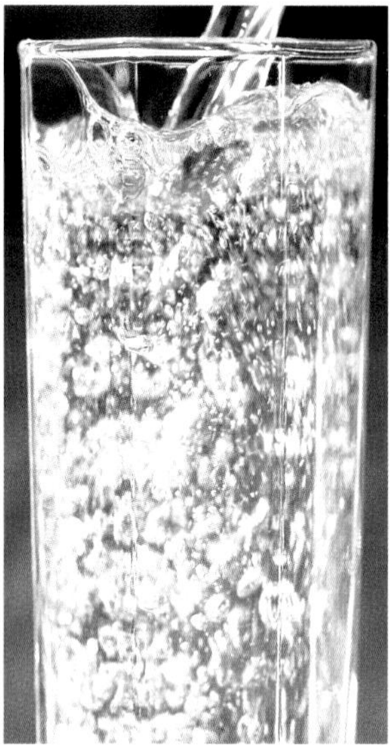

OZONE LAYER

Layer of the gas ozone found in the stratosphere where it shields the Earth from the Sun's ultraviolet rays. Holes in the ozone layer have been causing widespread concern. They are thought to be caused by pollutants such as chlorofluorocarbons (CFCs) which were banned in 1996. Ozone holes, however, continue to grow.

⟫ ***Oxygen, Pollution***

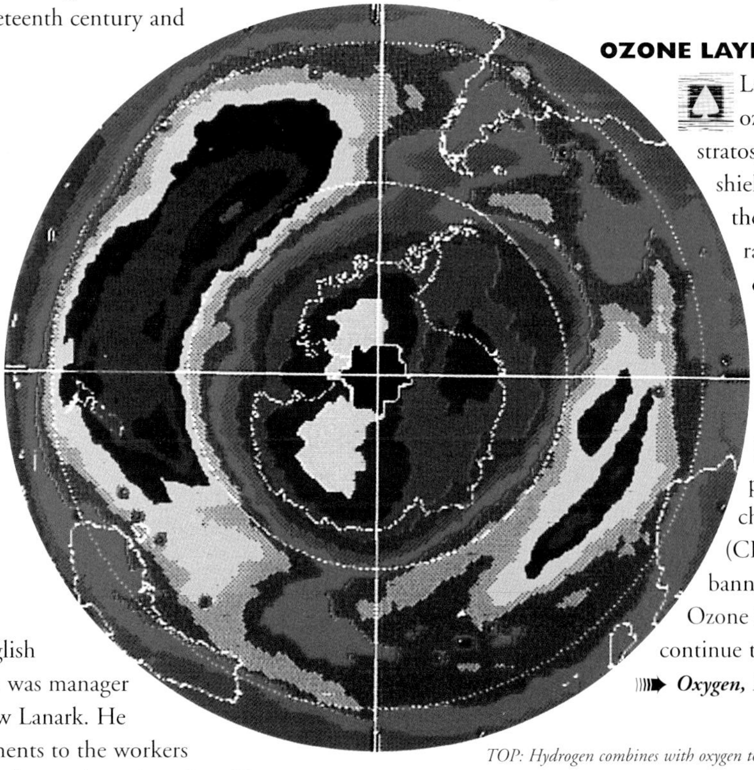

TOP: Hydrogen combines with oxygen to form water. We rely on both oxygen in the atmosphere, which we breathe, and water for survival. ABOVE: A satellite picture showing the distribution of ozone in Earth's atmosphere in the southern hemisphere in 1987.

PACINO, AL (b. 1940)

US actor. The darling of American films, Pacino is also equally at home on stage. His most remarkable roles have been in *The Godfather* trilogy and *Scarface* (1983).

Films

PAKISTAN

Central Asian country between Afghanistan and India. **Capital:** Islamabad. **Other principal cities:** Lahore, Rawalpindi, Karachi. **Climate:** continental with extreme hot and cold. **Geographical features:** mountains, desert, fertile plains and the Indus Valley. **Main languages:** Urdu, English, and numerous others. **Main religion:** Islam. **Rule:** democracy. **Currency:** Pakistan rupee. **Primary industries:** textiles and leather, cotton, petroleum refining, bicycles, agriculture. **Exports:** cotton, textiles, petroleum products, leather, carpets. Pakistan suffers from over-population, natural disasters, and refugees from Afghanistan.

Asia, Indus Valley Civilization

PALAEONTOLOGY

Study of fossils, traces of ancient life-forms preserved in rocks. Most fossils are mineral replacements of bones, teeth or shells, but impressions such as footprints on an ancient beach are also found. Palaeontologists use evidence from fossils to classify extinct organisms and draw conclusions about their life styles and evolution.

Dinosaurs, Fossils

PALAU GÜELL

Built by Antoni Gaudi in 1886–89, Palau Güell, Barcelona (Güell Palace) is one of Gaudi's and the world's most famous buildings. The palace is classified as a World Heritage site.

Architecture, Antoni Gaudi

RIGHT: The Panama Canal connects the Pacific and Atlantic oceans. The Cut on the canal, seen here, is the deepest in the world at 82 m (270 ft) deep.

PANAMA

Central American country between Colombia and Costa Rica. **Capital:** Panamá. **Other principal cities:** Colón, Cristóbal. **Climate:** tropical. **Geographical features:** mountainous interior and the Panama Canal connecting the Caribbean and Pacific. **Main languages:** Spanish, English. **Main religion:** Roman Catholic. **Rule:** democratic republic. **Currency:** balboa. **Primary industries:** agriculture, mining, petroleum. **Exports:** bananas, sugar, coffee, clothing.

PANDA

Bear-like mammal native to Asia. Although similar to bears, the panda is more closely related to raccoons. The Giant Panda is an endangered species; less than 1,000 survive in the wild.

Endangered Species

PANKHURST, EMMELINE (1858–1928)

English suffragette and founder of the Women's Social and Political Union in 1903. She launched the women's suffrage campaign in 1905, assisted by her daughters Sylvia and Christabel. Once women had been given the vote she joined the Conservative Party and was at one time a prospective MP.

Suffrage, Women's Emancipation

PAPUA NEW GUINEA

South Pacific island country. **Capital:** Port Moresby. **Other principal cities:** Lae, Madang. **Climate:** tropical. **Geographical features:** eastern half of New Guinea Island plus about 600 other Melanesian islands, with mountains, volcanoes, swamps. **Main language:** English. **Main religion:** Christianity. **Rule:** democracy. **Currency:** kina. **Primary industries:** agriculture, mining, timber. **Exports:** copper, gold, coffee, timber, coconut, palm oil.

PARAGUAY

Land-locked central South American country. **Capital:** Asunción. **Other principal cities:** Ciudad del Este. **Climate:** arid west, temperate east. **Geographical features:** marshy plain, divided by the Paraguay River. **Main languages:** Guarani, Spanish. **Main religion:** Roman Catholicism. **Rule:** democratic republic. **Currency:** guarani. **Primary industries:** agriculture: **Exports:** cotton, soya beans, timber, vegetable oil, coffee, meat, hides.

PARANORMAL PHENOMENA

Generally anything relating to things that are not normal. There is enormous popular interest in this field that encompasses everything from ghosts to the Loch Ness monster. So far, despite huge efforts, no concrete proof seems to have been produced for any paranormal phenomena. Things have either been proved to be normal phenomena, or remained unproved.

➧ ***Ghosts, Loch Ness, Occult, Ouija Board***

PARIS PEACE TREATY (1782–83)

Treaty ending the American Revolution. Several treaties signed at Paris between November 1782 and September 1783 between Britain on one side, and the United States, France and Spain on the other. The agreement guaranteed US borders up to the Mississippi, left Canada to Britain, and provided for mutual debt collection and protection for loyalist Americans.

➧ ***American Revolution, British Empire***

RIGHT: A view of Britain's Houses of Parliament across Westminster Bridge.

PARLIAMENT

Legislative body, deriving from the French for 'speaking', *parlant*, made up of a body of representatives meeting to debate and pass legislation, impose taxation and control the judiciary. The British parliament has two chambers: the House of Commons and House of Lords.

Britain's parliament is regarded as beginning in 1265, when Simon de Montfort called representatives from boroughs and shires to a meeting during the Barons' War. By the mid-fourteenth century the non-baron (commoners) representatives began to meet on their own, forming the basis of the House of Commons.

Thereafter, parliament's power fluctuated though precedents were being set over control of legislation, supervision of royal ministers, and voting financial resources to the crown through taxation. The Civil War of 1642–45 and the Glorious Revolution of 1688 made parliamentary consent for taxation essential, and gave parliament executive and judicial control.

Parliamentary reform has since involved extending the right to vote for members of the Commons to all adults, and restricting the rights of hereditary peers in the House of Lords.

➧ ***English Civil War, House of Lords***

PASSOVER

Jewish spring festival commemorating the Jews' exodus from Egypt. Lamb was traditionally sacrificed and, interestingly, the crucifixion of Jesus (the Lamb of God) occurred at the Passover.

➧ ***Judaism, Christianity***

PASTEURIZATION

Heat treatment of foodstuffs such as milk, to reduce the bacterial content. Milk is kept at 72°C (162°F) for 15 seconds, then rapidly cooled to 10°C (50°F). Named after Louis Pasteur (1822–95), pioneer of microbiology.

PENGUINS

Marine flightless birds that live mainly in the Antarctic. Penguins' streamlined bodies are covered with tightly packed feathers and fat, enabling them to maintain their body heat even in extreme cold. Their wings have been reduced to flippers which are used to propel the birds through water or along ice and rocks.

→ ***Birds, Polar Life***

PENICILLIN

Group of antibiotics derived from Penicillium moulds, effective against a wide range of bacteria. Penicillin was the first type of antibiotic to be discovered.

→ ***Antibiotics, Bacteria, Alexander Fleming***

PENINSULA

Narrow strip of land that projects into the sea or lake from the mainland. Surrounded on three sides by water. e.g. Florida.

PEPYS, SAMUEL (1633–1703)

Admiralty official who through the publication of his diary (1825) provided a unique portrayal of Restoration England, particularly pertinent with his literary and court contacts.

PERCUSSION INSTRUMENTS

The two streams of percussion instruments are idiophones which produce a sound from the vibration of their own material (e.g. bells) and membranos, that produce a sound from their stretched membrane being struck (e.g. drums). They can be further categorized as either untuned, such as drums, or tuned instruments that can produce melodies, such as xylophones.

→ ***Brass Instruments, Orchestras, String Instruments, Woodwind Instruments***

PERSIA

Ancient kingdom of western Asia, centred on modern Iran. By 490 BC, under Darius I, Persia controlled all of the Middle East, Turkey and Egypt and extended eastwards as far as India. The Greeks ended Persian expansion, with a final defeat by Alexander the Great in 330 BC.

→ ***Alexander the Great***

PERU

Western South American coastal country. **Capital:** Lima. **Other principal cities:** Arequipa, Iquitos, Chiclayo. **Climate:** mild coast, cool highlands, tropical interior. **Geographical features:** mountainous terrain, and substantial mineral resources. **Main languages:** Spanish, Quechua. **Main religion:** Roman Catholicism. **Rule:** democratic republic. **Currency:** nuevo sol. **Primary industries:** mining, agriculture, fishing. **Exports:** copper, lead, zinc, silver, petroleum, fish products, coffee, cotton, wool.

PETRONAS TOWERS

Situated in Kuala Lumpur, Malaysia these 452-m (1,483-ft) high, twin towers are amongst the world's tallest buildings. Designed by Cesar Pelli, the towers are linked by a sky bridge.

➧ ***Architecture, Malaysia***

PETS

Domesticated animals kept for the pleasure of their owners. Dogs were probably the first animals to be tamed and brought into the home as companions. Wild cats in Egypt are believed to have been the first felines to be domesticated. Selective breeding has led to modern pets that are relatively easy to care for and enjoyable to live with.

➧ ***Cats, Dogs, Ancient Egypt***

PFEIFFER, MICHELLE (b. 1957)

US actress. An ex-beauty queen, Pfeiffer first gained repute in *Scarface* (1983). Also acclaimed for her roles in *The Fabulous Baker Boys* (1989) and *The Age of Innocence* (1993).

➧ ***Films***

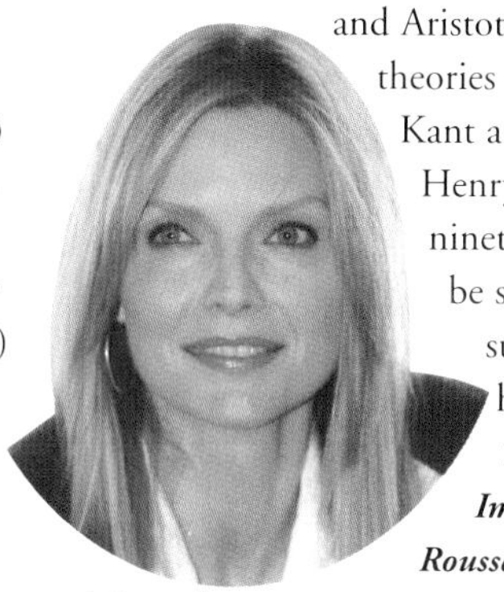

PHILATELY

Hobby of collecting postage stamps originated in Belgium in 1852. Philately is a very popular pastime most countries now generating extra revenue by producing sets of stamps especially for the collector.

➧ ***Crazes, Stamps***

PHILIPPINES

South-east Asian archipelago. **Capital:** Manila. **Other principal cities:** Quezon City, Cebu, Davao. **Climate:** tropical with typhoons. **Geographical features:** more than 7,000 islands, featuring volcanoes, mountains and extensive forest. **Main languages:** Tagalog, English, Spanish. **Main religions:** Christianity, Islam. **Rule:** democracy. **Currency:** peso. **Primary industries:** petroleum, refining, manufacturing, food, agriculture, textiles, chemicals, tourism. **Exports:** electronics, clothing, fruit, seafood, minerals, textiles.

➧ ***Asia***

PHILOSOPHY

Philosophy is an ancient Greek term meaning the love of knowledge or wisdom. The word describes the use of reasoning and argument in the pursuit of truth and knowledge, particularly in the questioning of ultimate realities or causes and principles. Philosophy looks at and challenges the concepts and perceptions of humanity.

The formation of new philosophical theories or trends, such as Jean-Jacques Rousseau's Romantic beliefs, can spread throughout the arts. Equally they can become the basis of political movements and thereby powerful agents of societal change.

Modern philosophies have their basis in those of the ancient Greek scholars, principally in the works of Plato and Aristotle, and have been shaped by subsequent theories by eminent philosophers such as Immanuel Kant and David Hume in the eighteenth century, or Henry David Thoreau and Friedrich Nietzche in the nineteenth century. As with all arts, philosophy can be seen as an evolution of thoughts through successive generations and societies; it reflects humanities' constant striving for definition.

➧ ***Aristotle, Ancient Greece, David Hume, Immanuel Kant, Friedrich Nietzsche, Jean-Jacques Rousseau, Henry David Thoreau***

PHOENICIANS

Semitic people who settled on the coast of Syria and Lebanon. Subject to Egypt, Assyria, Babylon, Persia, Alexander the Great and Rome, the Phoenicians only briefly enjoyed independence, but founded colonies in Cyprus and North Africa and traded extensively from Cairo to Cornwall.

PHOENIX

Mythical bird of resplendent plumage, always male, which lived to a great age, then died on a fiery nest. From the ashes arose a new bird, perfectly formed.

ABOVE: Michelle Pfeiffer

TOP LEFT: The diarist and social commentator Samuel Pepys.

FAR LEFT: Falklands Islands penguins.

PHOTOGRAPHY

Recording of images by focusing light on to surfaces coated with sensitive material. In most cases the process involves conversion of silver compounds to metallic silver, although silver does not necessarily form part of the final image. Both black and white and colour images can be made in this way.

PHOTOSYNTHESIS

Process by which green plants transform water and carbon dioxide into carbon compounds and oxygen. The absorption of sunlight by chlorophyll, present in green plants, provides energy for this process. Photosynthetic bacteria are unable to use water in the process and produce sulphur instead of oxygen as a by-product.

Plants

PHYSICS

Science of the laws governing the structure of the Universe and the matter and energy within it. The aim of physics is to use experiment and observation to find mathematical laws which describe the behaviour of matter as accurately as possible. These laws can be used to make predictions, which can be tested. An ultimate aim is to produce an all-embracing Theory of Everything, but this aim has not yet been realized. Physics has a large number of areas of study, including mechanics, optics, heat, electricity and magnetism, nuclear physics and particle physics.

Isaac Newton

PHYSIOLOGY

Study of the human or animal body in terms of the functions and processes and which occur. This may include interactions between cells, tissues or organs.

Biology

PIAF, EDITH (1915–63)

French singer. Piaf (her nickname, meaning sparrow), is forever linked with her signature tune *Non, Je ne regrette rien.* Piaf performed on stage, film, television and radio.

PICASSO, PABLO (1879–1953)

Spanish painter regarded as a genius of form and as the most influential and dominating twentieth-century artist. Throughout his long and prolific career, Picasso innovatively explored perceptions within art, working in a variety of mediums and styles. Picasso's influences are diverse; he learnt from the masters such as Paul Cézanne and Vincent van Gogh, but was equally stimulated by primitive art, such as African sculpture. He was largely responsible for the emergence of Cubism following his ground-breaking painting of 1907, *Les Demoiselles d'Avignon.* Although Picasso was later associated with Dadaism and Surrealism, he retained his own inimitable style that is beyond categorization.

Paul Cézanne, Cubism, Dadaism, Vincent van Gogh, Surrealism

PIGS

Hoofed animals with even toes, thick skin and moveable snout. Pigs do not have horns but some species are tusked e.g. warthog. Pigs are omnivorous (eat plants and animals).

PIPER ALPHA DISASTER (1988)

Series of explosions aboard the north sea oil rig of the same name. Caused by leaking gas, the accident claimed a total of 167 lives.

Oil

PLAGUE

Bubonic plague is caused by a bacterium, *Pasteurella pestis,* which can be transmitted by fleas borne by the black rat. It causes rapid and often fatal blood poisoning. In the fourteenth century bubonic plague reached Europe from Asia and up to half the population perished. The Great Plague which occurred in London in 1665 killed a quarter of the inhabitants. Although a vaccine is now available, bubonic plague is still endemic in some countries.

Diseases

PLANET X

Hypothetical planet, formerly supposed to lie in the outer Solar System to explain anomalies in the motions of Uranus and Neptune. Planet X probably does not exist.

Neptune, Planets, Uranus

PLANETS

Large bodies in orbit around a star, which do not emit visible light of their own, but reflect light from the star. In the Solar System there are nine planets in orbit round the Sun.

The innermost four, Mercury, Venus, Earth and Mars, are relatively small, primarily made of rocky and metallic material, and are called the terrestrial planets. They have only three satellites between them; Earth has one (the Moon), Mars two.

The next four, Jupiter (by far the biggest), Saturn, Uranus and Neptune are mainly composed of gaseous or liquid hydrogen and helium, and are called gas giants. Each of these has many satellites. Pluto, the outermost and much the smallest planet, is an icy world.

The planets are thought to have been formed from the same gas cloud as the Sun, some time after the Sun began to shine about 5,000 million years ago.

Earth, Jupiter, Mars, Mercury, Neptune, Pluto, Saturn, Solar System, Sun, Uranus, Venus

BOTTOM: The citizens of London flee the terrors of the plague. The highest numbers of deaths from the plague occurred in the towns and the cities.

PLANTAGENETS

English dynasty founded by Geoffrey of Anjou and the Empress Matilda (daughter of Henry I). The name was derived from the sprig of broom (*Planta genista*) which Geoffrey wore in his cap. The Plantagenet kings who reigned from 1154 to 1399 were Henry II, Henry III, Richard I, John, the first three Edwards and Richard II. The entire male issue of Geoffrey Plantagenet had died out by 1499, but later dynasties were created by indirect descent. The younger son of Henry III was created Earl of Lancaster. His great-grand-daughter Blanche married John of Gaunt, founder of the Lancastrian line. John's younger brother, Edmund of Langley, founded the rival Yorkist line. Although later used by historians, the name Plantagenet was seldom used contemporaneously and appears to have been confined to Richard, Duke of York, the father of Edward IV.

Kings of England

PLANTATIONS

Large agricultural estate, or farm, maintained for the commercial growth of one crop. Plantations were commonly established in colonial countries to produce crops such as sugar, cotton, tea, rubber and cocoa.

Coffee, Tea

PLANTS

Large group of organisms that are immobile, have rigid cells walls and photosynthesize. Plants are a diverse and complex group, ranging from a strand of cells (e.g. spirogyra) to a flowering tree. The study of plants is called botany.

The cell walls of plants contain a carbohydrate called cellulose. Cellulose gives the cell walls strength and rigidity and is the most common organic compound on Earth. The presence of chlorophyll inside plant cells enables the organism to turn carbon dioxide and water into carbohydrates. Plants are a primary source of food for other organisms and are therefore essential to all food chains.

There are many levels of complexity in the plant kingdom. Algae (e.g. seaweed) and mosses have simple, multicellular bodies. Ferns have spore-producing reproductive regions. The seed-bearing plants are typically separated into root, stem and leaves and have a vascular system (xylem) which transports water and salts around the plant body.

Botany, Chlorophyll, Food Chains, Photosynthesis

PLASTICS

Synthetic materials which can be shaped on heating and whose shape stays relatively fixed when cooled. All modern plastics are organic (carbon-based) polymers, whose molecules are made from long chains of simpler molecules. Thermoplastics can be re-shaped on heating, whereas thermosets can only be shaped once by heat.

ABOVE: A selection of herbs, including sage and tarragon.

RIGHT: Actors in a performance of the play Don't Dress for Dinner *at London's Apollo Theatre.*

FAR RIGHT: The Museum of Genocide in Cambodia displays skulls and other human remains as a gruesome reminder of Pol Pot's atrocities.

PLATE TECTONICS

Term used to describe the changes to the Earth's dynamic crust (previously known as 'continental drift'). The Earth's crust is a series of interconnecting plates. Each plate typically contains a continental shelf, sea and oceanic areas. The movement of one plate against another gives rise to various geological features and processes e.g. earthquakes, volcanoes, mountain ranges and mid-oceanic ridges.

Earthquakes, Mountains, Oceans, Volcanoes

PLATEAUX

Areas of elevated land. Plateaux are usually quite flat and may be surrounded by mountains (intermontane) or between a mountain and low-lying land (piedmont).

PLATYPUS

Indigenous Australian species of mammalian monotreme. The platypus lays eggs but feeds its young on milk. It lives in burrows at a river's edge and feeds on worms and insects.

Mammals

PLAYS

Dramatic work written with the intention of performance by actors, either on stage or recorded for film, radio or television. The first documented plays date from sixth-century Greece and were either tragedy or comedy. During the Middle Ages the genre of religious plays evolved but by the sixteenth century these had largely been banned. The Italian *Commedia dell'arte*

troupes, also dating from the sixteenth century, performed secular plays, usually romantic comedies; they greatly developed and popularized the production of plays, paving the way for the later playwrights and theatres.

➡ *Drama Forms, Ancient Greece, Playwrights, Theatre*

PLAYWRIGHTS

Among the earliest recorded playwrights are Sophocles (495–406 BC) and Euripides (484–406 BC), whose plays *Oedipus the King* and *Medea* are still popular in theatres today. Shakespeare remains the most internationally recognized playwright.

The role of the playwright has changed over the centuries; ostensibly to entertain, playwright such as Henrik Ibsen and Anton Chekov have used plays to explore socio-logical and psychological problems. Modern playwrights Harold Pinter and Samuel Beckett use the dramatic form to explore dialogue and to challenge perceptions.

➡ *Henrik Ibsen, Plays, William Shakespeare, Theatre*

PLUTO

Outermost planet of the Solar System (although it was closer to the Sun than Neptune from 1979 to 1999), and much the smallest with a diameter of 2,445 km (1,520 miles). It has one satellite, Charon. Mainly an icy body, Pluto is considered not to be a planet by some astronomers.

➡ *Planets, Solar System, Sun*

POETRY

Literary form that concentrates upon producing images, concepts or emotions in the reader. Poetry is rhythmical and has an emphasis on the sound of the words. Thought to be one of the oldest art forms, poetry pre-dates writing – its earliest uses were in the formal storytelling of ancient cultures or in ritual chants.

➡ *Literary Genres*

POL POT (b. c. 1925)

Cambodian politician and revolutionary leader. In 1975, the Cambodian government was toppled by the Khmer Rouge communist rebellion. Pol Pot's leadership of the new 'Democratic Kampuchea' plunged Cambodia into an orgy of civilian massacres until a Vietnamese invasion officially ended his rule in 1979. In 1997 Pol Pot was tried and imprisoned.

POLAND

North European Baltic country. **Capital:** Warsaw. **Other principal cities:** Lódz, Kraków, Gdansk, Szczecin. **Climate:** temperate. **Geographical features:** Baltic coastline, land mostly flat but southerly mountains. **Main language:** Polish. **Main religion:** Roman Catholicism. **Rule:** democratic republic. **Currency:** zloty. **Primary industries:** mining, manufacturing of machinery, forestry, footwear. **Exports:** coal, copper, transport equipment, vehicles, ships, sulphur, shoes.

Post-World War II policies saw Poland converted to an important industrial nation in the Eastern bloc. The collapse of Communism in 1989 was accompanied by strikes and rioting as a result of rising food prices. Since then, after a rapid restructuring programme, Poland has moved steadily towards privatization, but is affected by inflation and unemployment.

➡ *Europe*

POLAR LIFE

Unique conditions found at the Earth's extremes of the North and South Poles which affect the life-forms found there. The polar regions have reduced levels of solar radiation and typical temperatures of -30°C (-86 °F). Winter nights can last for 24 hours. The landscape is bleak; snow and ice predominate. Organisms that exist here have developed methods to either maintain heat (e.g blubber in whales and thick fur in polar bears) or prevent freezing (e.g. natural 'antifreeze' in polar fish).

➡ *Fish, Penguins*

POLICE

Executive arm of the tri-partite law making system, the other two being parliament and the courts. The police are responsible for enforcing law and order and presenting suspects and evidence to the courts. The UK's police can be traced back to the Bow Street Runners, founded by Henry Fielding in 1749.

POLITICIANS, BRITISH

Men and women who have pursued a career in politics as members of the mainstream British political parties, independent parties, or who have stood as individuals. Normally associating themselves with a cause, ideology or general principles, British politicians can serve as members of parliament, or members of county and city councils, often rising from jobs as aides or as 'behind the scenes' staff in political parties. They may be paid or unpaid, full-time or part-time, commoners or peers (elected or hereditary members of the House of Lords).

Individual politicians came to the fore during the reign of Charles I, when royal resistance to parliamentary control led to the emergence of prominent individuals in the House of Commons, such as John Pym.

Today, British politicians (including members of the European parliament) range from party or individual activists up to senior MPs, appointed as ministers in the government of the day. At the apex is the prime minister. Normally leader of his or her political party, most prime ministers of the last century have belonged to the Labour or Conservative parties. Although loyalty to the party is normally considered essential for rise to this position, some have changed sides on more than occasion, Winston Churchill being the most notable example.

Other senior and favoured members of the party in government are appointed to ministerial posts concerned with the nation's finances (chancellor of the Exchequer), defence, education, industry, home affairs, and foreign policy being among the most important.

The prime minister faces the leader of the second party in parliament, called the Leader of Her Majesty's Opposition, across the floor of the House of Commons. The two confront one another in Prime Minister's Question Time and the opportunity is frequently taken to trade abuse of party policy, individual performances and the government's standing. The opposition also fields senior members to 'shadow' government ministers and comment on their actions.

Much of this sparring is carried on in parliament but in recent decades politicians are continually called on to explain and defend government policy, or the opposition's viewpoint, on television and in the press. A poor performance can damage a politician's reputation, and even that of the government so politicians are now increasingly trained to field awkward questions and court popularity. However successful in public life, a private misdemeanour can quickly destroy a political career.

A slip in either area, or challenges to leadership, can prove Harold Wilson's maxim that 'a week is a long time in politics'. In the most notorious case of modern times, John Profumo, secretary of state for war 1960–63, resigned after his affair with Christine Keeler was exposed. More recently, Margaret Thatcher's career as first woman prime minister of Britain was abruptly ended after a damaging leadership contest in 1990.

Retired politicians often take up lucrative careers as company directors, broadcasters or lecturers. Some continue their political careers if offered peerages and a seat in the House of Lords.

➤ ***Governments, House of Lords***

POLLOCK, JACKSON (1912–56)

Most celebrated and controversial of American abstract artists, Pollock abandoned representational art to explore automatic techniques. His work included random elements and a physical awareness of the act of painting.

➤ ***Abstract Art***

ABOVE: Former Conservative prime pinisters of Britain, John Major and Baroness Thatcher.

RIGHT: A waste landfill site in Cardiff, Wales, is only partly biodegradable.

POLLUTION

Damaging environmental effect of human activity or natural geological processes such as volcanic eruptions. Various forms of pollution are recognized: noise, smoke, chemical, radioactive, sewage, car emissions and household rubbish. The effects may be noted in the air, soil and aquatic environments. Primary contributors of pollution are industrial and agricultural processes. Pollution is believed to be contributing to global warming, acid rain and environmental disturbance and destruction. Reducing pollution is in the long term interest of the entire planet and all its occupants but is expensive and therefore not in the immediate interests of the corporations and government bodies who could instigate change.

➡ ***Environment, Global Warming, Greenpeace, Worldwide Fund for Nature***

POLO

Game played on horseback with a ball and long-handled mallet. There are two teams of four. Believed to originate from Iran and first played in the UK in 1869. The rules were codified by the UK's Hurlingham Club in 1875.

POLO, MARCO (c. 1254–1324)

Venetian explorer. In 1271, Polo accompanied his uncles on an overland expedition from Europe to China. Polo became of a favourite of the ruler, Kublai Khan, learning Mongolian and not returning until 1295. Imprisoned during a war against Genoa, Polo wrote a book about his adventures in 1298.

➡ ***Exploration, Mongols***

POLYNESIA

South Pacific islands lying in a triangle formed by Hawaii, Easter Island and New Zealand. They include French Polynesia, containing the Society Islands of which the largest is the fertile and beautiful Tahiti. Other groups include Samoa and the Cook Islands. The islanders are mostly descended from South Asian settlers who arrived *c.* 2000 BC.

➡ ***Hawaii, New Zealand***

POMPEII

Ancient Roman town near Naples in southern Italy, on the southern slopes of the volcano, Mount Vesuvius. In August AD 79, Pompeii was totally destroyed by the eruption of Vesuvius which buried the town under a hail of pumice and rock. The town remained lost until excavations of the eighteenth and nineteenth centuries.

➡ ***Mount Vesuvius, Volcanoes***

POP ART

Pop Art rose to prominence in the 1960s in both America and Britain. Pop Art takes its subjects from contemporary society, such as advertizements, products and celebrities. The style is often detailed and hard edged. Prominent Pop artists are Andy Warhol (1928–87) with his acclaimed Monroe images, and Roy Lichtenstein (b. 1923) with his painting of comic strips.

➡ ***Comics, Graphic Art, Marilyn Monroe***

POP MUSIC

Broad term that covers commercially successful music (popular music) that does not fit into specific categories, such as Country and Western or Rock. Pop music originated in the 1950s with mainstream musicians whose musical appeal was combined with physical appeal. Pop music is normally marketed to a young audience.

➡ ***Albums, Singles***

ABOVE: The Villa of the Mysteries, one of the buildings that miraculously partly survived the eruption of the volcano which engulfed Pompeii.

POPES

Bishop of Rome and head of the Catholic Church. The spiritual descendant of St Peter, a pope is elected by the Sacred College of Cardinals and then crowned in St Peter's Basilica. The papacy's greatest temporal influence was in the Middle Ages under Gregory VII and Innocent III. The Reformation, however, curtailed its political power. The pope ruled the papal states from AD 756, but the headquarters were moved to Avignon (1309–78). Then the Great Schism occurred with rival popes (1378–1417). In 1929 the pope's territory was limited to Vatican City. Adrian IV (1154–59), was the only English pope and John Paul II, elected in 1978, was the first non-Italian pope since 1542.

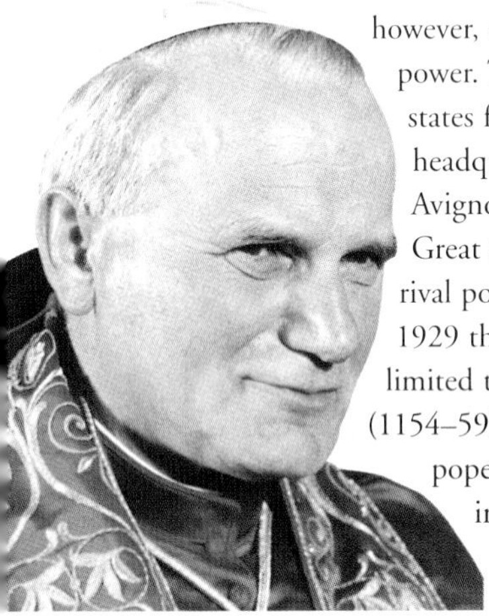

➠ ***Catholicism***

POPULATION GROWTH

The way in which the population of the globe has grown from around 2.5 billion in 1959 to over 6 billion in 2001. Most growth is taking place in less-developed countries and is a source of great concern. Some countries have adopted very draconian measures to stop it. China has legislated heavy disincentives to those having more than one child.

➠ ***China***

PORCELAIN

Ceramic substance used for making domestic articles and ornaments, originating in China. It is hard, shiny and translucent, and makes a ringing sound when struck.

PORTS

Harbours with facilities for seacraft to dock and load and unload, usually sited near to population centres. There are normally customs facilities within a port.

➠ ***Ships***

PORTUGAL

South-west Europe. **Capital:** Lisbon. **Other principal cities:** Coimbra, Pôrto, Setúbal. **Climate:** mild and sunny. **Geographical features:** Iberian peninsula, mostly plains and lowlands. **Main language:** Portuguese. **Main religion:** Roman Catholicism. **Rule:** democratic republic. **Currency:** escudo. **Primary industries:** textiles and footwear, paper, cork products, chemicals, petroleum, fishing, tourism. **Exports:** clothing, shoes, machinery, cork, papers, hides.

➠ ***Europe***

POST-IMPRESSIONISM (c. 1880 – c. 1905)

Art critic Roger Fry coined the term Post-Impressionism to define the loose grouping of artists that had rejected the Impressionist movement of the nineteenth century. Post-Impressionist style cannot be defined as each of the artists thus categorized worked in their own style and manner, with their own unique themes. Post-Impressionists include Paul Cézanne and Vincent van Gogh.

➠ ***Paul Cézanne, Vincent van Gogh, Impressionism***

POTATOES

Perennial plants producing edible tubers that are rich in starch. Potatoes are native to South America and were cultivated by the Andean Indians for over 2,000 years. Potatoes were brought to Europe by the conquering Spanish in the sixteenth century. Walter Raleigh reputedly introduced them to England.

➠ ***Sir Walter Raleigh***

POTTERY

Made from clay and hardened by heat, pottery is the oldest and most endemic decorative art. Primitive pottery was made through traditional techniques and local materials. Decoration was added by carving or glazes. Among antique pottery, China was by far the most sophisticated with its use of porcelain as far back as the ninth century.

⇛ ***Decorative Arts, Eastern Art, Porcelain***

POUSSIN, NICHOLAS (1594–1665)

Leading French Classicist painter-philosopher. Poussin hugely affected French art through his paintings and also his artistic theories. Working mainly in Rome, Poussin studied the Renaissance and Classical art that greatly shaped his own work. Initially Baroque in style, Poussin concentrated upon mythological themes from his mid-thirties, later moving to sombre biblical scenes, such as *The Baptism* (1642).

⇛ ***Baroque, Classical, Renaissance***

PRAGUE

Capital of the Czech Republic on the River Vltava (below), and former capital of Czechoslovakia. An industrial city producing vehicles, machinery, paper, clothing, food and brewing, Prague is also noted for its cathedral of St Vitus, and seventeenth- and eighteenth-century streets commonly used in historical dramas and films. Population: about 1.2 million.

⇛ ***Czech Republic***

PRAIRIES

Extensive grasslands of North America. Grassland plains typically develop where there is enough rainfall to support grass but not enough for trees to grow. The animals which live in prairies lack cover to hide themselves in and therefore tend to be fast runners with excellent sight and hearing as well as possessing the ability to burrow e.g. prairie dogs.

PRE-RAPHAELITES (1848)

Name taken by a short-lived British group of painters and sculptors whose aim was to revive the style of art before that of the immensely influential Renaissance painter Raphael (1483–1520). The group was formed in 1848 and among the members were Dante Gabriel Rossetti (1828–82), Sir John Everett Millais (1829–96) and William Holman Hunt (1827–1910). Their paintings took subjects from myths (such as King Arthur), poetry (Keats) and drama (Shakespeare), rejecting the more Classical themes from the Bible or antiquity. Although as a group the Pre-Raphaelites worked together only until the early 1850s their impact on art was great and Pre-Raphaelite paintings were – and remain –immensely popular.

⇛ ***John Keats, Medieval, Renaissance, William Shakespeare***

PRESIDENTS

Head of state in a republic, a president may enjoy powers extending from being head of the government (e.g. the US) to a more honorific role similar to a monarch (e.g. the Republic of Ireland). Powers are normally specified in the constitution. The word 'president' comes from the Latin *praseidens*, meaning 'one who presides'.

US Presidents are the most prominent holders of the office and for most of the last century have been the most powerful individuals in the world, even more so since the break-up of the Soviet Union.

ABOVE: President of Russia 1985–91, Mikhail Gorbachev.
RIGHT: US President 1989–92 George Bush.

George Washington's role in the American Revolution resulted in his becoming the first president of the United States and he is considered to be the father of the nation.

Washington DC, the US capital, contains many monuments to the presidents regarded as the most influential in US history. These include: Thomas Jefferson (served 1801–09), who was a signatory to the Declaration of Independence; Franklin D. Roosevelt (served 1933–45), who saw the country through the worst years of World War II and the Depression; and Abraham Lincoln (1861–65). Lincoln in particular, for his role in leading the Union through the bitter American Civil War, slave emancipation, and subsequent assassination, has been elevated to unparalleled mythic status.

In other countries, presidents have gained reputations for a variety of reasons. In South Africa, Nelson Mandela (served 1994–99) led his country to reform of apartheid legislation after a 27-year incarceration. Uganda's Idi Amin (served 1971–79) ruled through terror and has become notorious through his regime. Russian president Mikhail Gorbachev (served 1985–91) presided over the collapse of Soviet power in Eastern Europe. In Libya, General Moamer al Khaddafi (or Gaddafi) has only a nominal presidential role, but in practice has wielded colossal influence over his country since 1969 and is regarded as synonymous with his nation by most of the rest of the world.

➠ ***American Revolution, Nelson Mandela***

PRESIDENTS OF THE UNITED STATES OF AMERICA

TIMELINE

1789	George Washington
1797	John Adams
1801	Thomas Jefferson
1809	James Madison
1817	James Monroe
1825	John Quincy Adams
1829	Andrew Jackson
1837	Martin van Buren
1841	William Henry Harrison
1841	John Tyler
1845	James Polk
1849	Zachary Taylor
1850	Millard Fillmore
1853	Franklin Pierce
1857	James Buchanan
1861	Abraham Lincoln
1865	Andrew Johnson
1869	Ulysses S. Grant
1877	Rutherford B. Hayes
1881	James Garfield
1881	Chester A. Arthur
1885	Grover Cleveland
1889	Benjamin Harrison
1897	William McKinley
1901	Theodore Roosevelt
1909	William Howard Taft
1912	Woodrow Wilson
1921	Warren Harding
1923	Calvin Coolidge
1929	Herbert Hoover
1933	Franklin D. Roosevelt
1945	Harry S. Truman
1953	Dwight D. Eisenhower
1961	John F. Kennedy
1963	Lyndon B. Johnson
1969	Richard M. Nixon
1974	Gerald R. Ford
1977	Jimmy Carter
1981	Ronald Reagan
1989	George Bush
1993	Bill Clinton
2001	George W. Bush

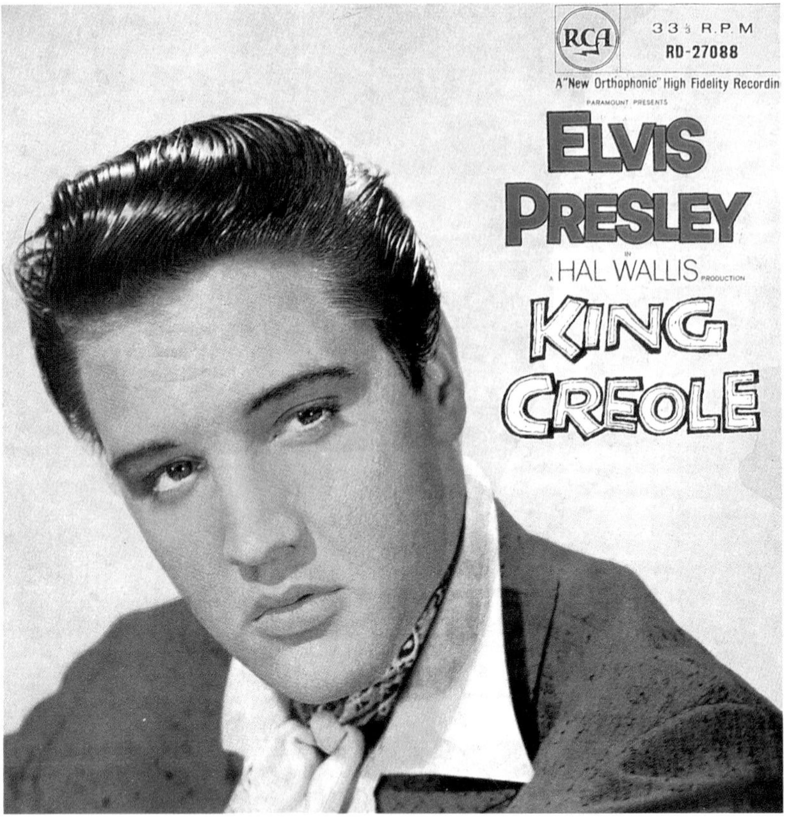

PRESLEY, ELVIS (1935–77)

US singer. Elvis began his career as a Country and Western singer but it was with his unique blend of Rock 'n' Roll music that he found fame. His first single *Heartbreak Hotel* (1955) went to number one across the world and thereafter his success was immense. Elvis also starred in many films during the 1950s and 60s.

Country and Western, Icons, Rock 'n' Roll

PRINCES

Title derived from the Latin *princeps* (literally 'one who takes first place'), it signified a sovereign ruler or a nobleman of very high rank, above a duke but below a king. It came to apply generally to the male members of a royal family and specifically to the ruler of a principality. In England, the title of Prince of Wales was created in 1301 and conferred on the future Edward II. Since then it has been conferred on the eldest son of the monarch, most recently on Prince Charles (1969). In other countries special titles have been applied to the heir-apparent, such as Dauphin (France) or Infante (Spain), although the title Crown Prince is also used. Albert of Saxe-Coburg-Gotha, husband of Queen Victoria, was granted the title of Prince Consort, whereas Lieutenant Philip Mountbatten who married Princess Elizabeth, though styled Prince Philip, was given the title of Duke of Edinburgh.

Kings of England, Princesses

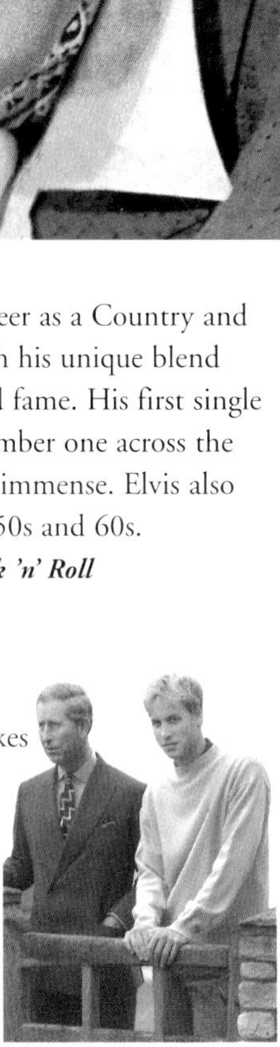

LEFT: Prince William with his father, Prince Charles, at Charles's home, Highgrove, Gloucestershire.

PRINCESSES

Female counterpart of princes. The word is applied not only to female members of the royal bloodline but also generally to the wives and daughters of princes. There are subtle distinctions, expressed in the manner in which these names are used. Thus the wives of princes who hold specific titles are known by the feminine form, e.g. Sarah, Duchess of York or Sophie, Countess of Wessex. On the death of her husband, however, the Duchess of Kent became known as Princess Marina, rather than the Dowager Duchess. After her divorce Princess Diana was styled Diana, Princess of Wales and lost the prefix of Her Royal Highness. In the Netherlands, both Queen Wilhelmina and her daughter Queen Juliana assumed the title of Princess when they abdicated, in 1948 and 1980 respectively. Princess Royal is an honorific title conferred on the eldest daughter of the monarch, the current holder being Princess Anne.

Princes, Queens of England

PRINTING

Process of reproducing text or images on paper or other surfaces, so that multiple copies can be made. Important methods are letterpress, in which the type is inked and then pressed on to paper; offset printing, where the paper picks up ink from a flat surface; and gravure or intaglio, using an inked recessed plate.

➨ ***Publishing***

PROTESTANTISM

One of the three pre-eminent branches of Christianity. Membership: 320 million worldwide. Denominations include: Anglicans, Baptists, Lutherans, Methodists, Pentecostalists and Presbyterians. The name 'Protestant' comes from their 'protest' against the sale of indulgences, the exclusivity of the Latin language and the widespread corruption of the Roman Catholic Church in the sixteenth century. Key founders include: Luther, Calvin, Zwingli and Knox.

All Protestants reject papal infallibility and the doctrine of transubstantiation. They vary considerably in doctrine and organization. Anglicans and Lutherans retain bishops, vestments and ceremony; the other denominations meanwhile are more minimalist (little or no liturgy and vestments).

➨ ***Catholicism, Christianity, Martin Luther, John Calvin***

PROTOCISTA

Also known as Protista. Unicellular organisms. In some instances this group is expanded to include all organisms of simple biological organization. e.g. diatoms, algae, bacteria and amoebae.

➨ ***Bacteria***

PROUST, MARCEL (1871–1922)

French writer. Proust won the *Prix Goncourt* in 1919 with his first book, *A la Recherche du temps perdu* (1913) – a psychoanalytical autobiography in several volumes.

➨ ***Literary Genres***

PSYCHIATRY

Branch of medicine which deals with the causes, diagnosis and treatment of mental disorders. Psychiatrists are trained medical doctors and can therefore prescribe drugs. Several approaches to treatment are used, such as psychotherapy in which the patient is encouraged to talk with the psychiatrist, or physical treatment such as electroconvulsive therapy.

➨ ***Psychology***

PSYCHOLOGY

Science of human and animal behaviour and experience. For convenience, psychology is divided into areas of study, including developmental psychology, inherited behaviour, educational psychology and occupational psychology, There is some overlap between clinical psychology and psychiatry, although clinical psychologists are not medical doctors.

➨ ***Psychiatry***

PUBLIC TRANSPORT

Methods of land transport taking fare-paying passengers, including buses, coaches and railway trains, available mostly within and between large population centres. Public transport has advantages over private transport: traffic congestion is reduced and less energy is needed for the same journey. It is however relatively inflexible and often more expensive.

➨ ***Railways, Underground Rail System***

ABOVE: Printing and publishing encompasses all forms of newspapers, magazines, books and leaflets.

PUBLISHING

Although ancient societies such as China and Hellenistic Greece had forms of publishing, it was not until the invention of printing by Johannes Gutenberg (*c.* 1440–50) that publishing really accelerated. With the introduction of cheaper paper in the nineteenth century publishing firms flourished and with twentieth century techniques like computerized typesetting, publishing today is a vast market.

➡ ***Typography***

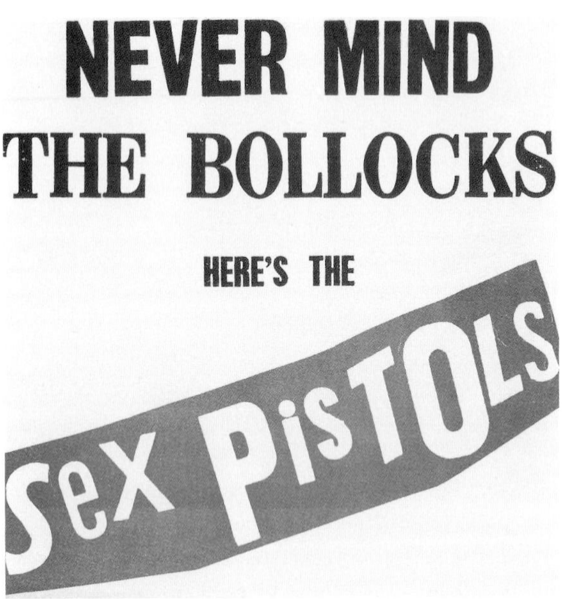

PUNK MUSIC

Form of rock music that emerged in the late 1970s. Punk was primarily British in origin and was a reaction to what was seen as the staid and confined music and society of the time. The punks' dresscode, as well as their anti-social stance, was aimed to shock and disrupt. The guitar and drum led music was abrasive, fast and energetic.

➡ ***Pop Music***

PURCELL, HENRY (1659–95)

English composer. Despite his short life Purcell left a lasting legacy of work that has been revisited by musicians such as Benjamin Britten (1913–76). Although Purcell was particularly admired for his instrumental music, his volume of work covers a great diversity from opera to choral. His opera *Dido and Aeneas* is thought of as the first great English opera.

➡ ***Opera***

PYRAMIDS

Ancient structures with a square ground plan and tapering sides rising to a point. The greatest of these were constructed in Egypt between the IV and XII Dynasties (before 3000 BC), the sides being perfectly smooth. The pyramids of Central America were of undressed stone raised in steps or tiers.

➡ ***Ancient Egypt***

PYRENEES

South-west Europe mountain range forming the border between France and Spain, and enclosing the tiny land-locked republic of Andorra. The range is about 435 km (270 miles) long with a highest point at Aneto (3,404 m/11,168 ft). Vineyards grow on southern slopes, winter sports are popular, and hydroelectric power is harnessed.

ABOVE LEFT: The Sex Pistols were key players in the 1970s Punk scene.
RIGHT: Her Majesty Queen Elizabeth II of England, photographed in Greenwich in July 2000.

QATAR

Persian Gulf state. **Capital:** Doha. **Other principal cities:** Dukhan, Halul. **Climate:** hot and arid. **Geographical features:** stony desert peninsula. **Main languages:** Arabic, English. **Main religion:** Islam. **Rule:** absolute monarchy. **Currency:** Qatari riyal. **Primary industries:** petroleum, fertilizer, cement, iron. **Agriculture:** being developed. **Exports:** oil, natural gas, petroleum products, fertilizer, iron, steel.

QUANTUM MECHANICS

Science of subatomic particles. Quantum theory began with the discoveries of Max Planck on radiated energy, and it was Planck who first expounded the theory of a unit of enrgy that was indivisible; this became known as the quanta.

➧ ***Physics***

QUEENS OF ENGLAND

Most of the queens of England held their position by virtue of their marriage to the reigning sovereign, but several were queens regnant, rulers in their own right as the heiress of kings in default of a male heir. One of the first and most famous was Boudicca (Boadicea), wife of Prasutagus, King of the Iceni. On his death in AD 60 the Romans seized his kingdom, but Boudicca raised an army, destroyed Camulodunum (Colchester) and captured Londinium and Verulamium (St Albans) before she was defeated by Suetonius. Matilda or Maud, heiress of Henry I, contested the throne which had been seized by Henry's nephew Stephen. After capturing her rival she styled herself 'Lady of the English' but was never crowned. The first queens regnant emerged in Tudor times. Following the death of Edward VI (1553) his cousin Lady Jane Grey was 'nine-days queen' but was forced to abdicate in favour of the elder daughter of Henry VIII who reigned as Queen Mary. On her death in 1558 she was succeeded by her half-sister Elizabeth. Popularly known as Good Queen Bess or the Virgin Queen, she reigned till 1603. Mary II was Queen of Great Britain and Ireland from 1689 till her death in 1694, reigning jointly with her husband William of Orange. On his death in 1702 he was succeeded by his sister-in-law Anne. Queen Victoria (1837–1901) and Queen Elizabeth II (since 1952) have had two of the longest reigns in British history.

➧ ***Kings of England***

QUR'AN

Also spelt 'Quran' and 'Koran', it is the sacred book of Islam. The Qur'an was revealed to Muhammad *c.* AD 616. It is written in pure Arabic and contains 114 suras (chapters).

➧ ***Islam***

RACETRACKS

Sporting venue designed for racing, specifically with horses or cars. Notable UK venues include Ascot, Goodwood and Aintree (Horses) and Brands Hatch and Siverstone (Motorcar). Other famous Grand Prix tracks include Monte Carlo.

Horse Racing, Motor Racing

RACISM

Belief that one particular race is superior to others (e.g. Nazi Germany and the Aryan race) or that a particular race is inferior to others (Nazi Germany and the Jews). Racism is a source of great concern in many countries, where friction between the indigenous population and migrants often occurs. A series of laws makes most aspects of racism illegal in the UK and many other countries.

Apartheid, Nazism

RADIATION

Term used in physics to describe radiant energy that exists in particles or waves. Heat and light are both forms of radiation. Only a tiny part of the Sun's radiation (insolation) reaches the Earth's surface. The emission of radiation also occurs when the nuclei of radioactive atoms are spontaneously altered.

RADIO

Transmission and reception of radio waves, electromagnetic waves with wavelengths in the range of 1 mm (0.4 in) to 10,000 m (32,810 ft). In transmission, an oscillating voltage is fed an aerial, which causes a radio wave of the same frequency to be emitted. In reception, minute voltages developed in an aerial are isolated and amplified.

ABOVE: Horse racing at Royal Ascot.

FAR RIGHT: One of Elizabeth I's favourite's, the explorer Sir Walter Raleigh attempted to establish settlements in the newly discovered Americas.

RAILWAYS

Method of transport whereby trains with flanged wheels move along a fixed track with two steel rails. Railways are used for the movement of both passengers and freight, and are relatively safe and efficient in use of energy, but lack the versatility of road transport.

Underground Rail Systems

RAIN

Water that falls to the Earth's surface in the form of liquid droplets. The term 'precipitation' includes rain, sleet, hail and snow. Water vapour collects in clouds and then condenses to its liquid form, falling as rain. The occurrence of the condensation depends upon movement and cooling of air.

Water, Weather

RAINFORESTS

Dense forests in equatorial regions characterized by a wet and warm climate. Located mainly in South and Central America, Africa and south-east Asia. Tropical rainforests accommodate up to 40% of the world's species, produce most of the planet's oxygen and are the site of many complex ecosystems. They once occupied 14% of the Earth's surface but are being rapidly destroyed; rainforests are an important source of timber and agricultural land for developing countries. The loss of the rainforests is likely to lead to localized soil erosion and flooding, the extinction of many species, global warming and climate change.

Ecology, Environment, Global Warming

RALEIGH, SIR WALTER (c. 1552–1618)

English adventurer. A favourite courtier of Elizabeth I, Raleigh received gifts of trading monopolies and estates. He financed unsuccessful colonizing schemes in America, but popularized potatoes and tobacco. James I was suspicious of his loyalty but allowed him a gold-hunting trip to Guyana in 1616. James executed him to appease the infuriated Spaniards, making Raleigh a popular hero.

➨ *Exploration*

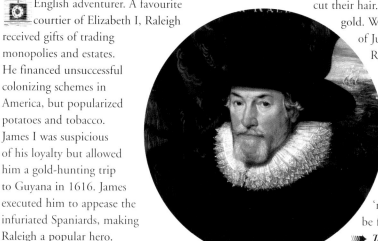

RAMADAN

Ninth month in the Muslim calendar, during which Muslims fast, sunrise to sunset, and are encouraged to read the entire Qur'an.

➨ *Islam, Qur'an*

RANKIN, JEANETTE (1880–1973)

American politician, militant feminist and social reformer. Rankin was the first woman member of the US Congress in 1917. She opposed America's involvement in World Wars I and II.

RASPUTIN, GRIGORI EFIMOVICH (1871–1916)

Russian religious charlatan. His teaching that salvation was only possible by physical union with him led to orgies (Rasputin means 'debauchee'). The fashion for mysticism led to his invitation to court where he gained influence over the credulous tsarina, desperate for a cure for her son's haemophilia, and her circle. In 1916 a group of noblemen murdered him.

➨ *Russian Revolution*

RASTAFARI

West Indian religion of Christian origins. Rastafarians have no churches, but have meetings, the major one being Nyabingi. They use marijuana as a sacrament, prefer natural food and medicines and do not cut their hair. Rastafarian colours are red, green and gold. When Haile Selassie (Ras Tafari, the Lion of Judah) was crowned emperor of Ethiopia Rastafarians thought he was the Messiah.

➨ *Bob Marley*

REAL TENNIS

Racket and ball game originating in twelfth-century France. An indoor game sharing many rules with lawn tennis. The 'real' in the title is a corruption of 'royal'. The oldest surviving court can be found at Hampton Court.

➨ *Tennis*

REALISM (19TH CENTURY)

Nineteenth-century art and literary movement aiming to represent only the real, discarding allusions to fantasy and myth. In art, Realism was pioneered by the French painter Gustave Courbet (1819–77) who attempted as naturalistic and true-to-life representation as possible. In literature, the great Realists were Leo Tolstoy and, in a more conventional manner, Charles Dickens.

➨ *Charles Dickens, Leo Tolstoy*

RECYCLING

Collection and processing of waste materials so that they can be re-used. The most readily recycled materials are paper products, glass, plastics and metals. The advantages of recycling include reducing the amount of waste entering landfill sites, reducing the rate at which sources of nonrenewable materials are depleted, and reducing energy use and pollution.

➨ *Environment, Pollution*

RED RUM

Legendary race horse, the only one ever to win the Grand National three times. He was 12 years old when he won the last time in 1977, and from there went into well-earned retirement.

➨ *Horse Racing*

RED SEA

Two thousand-km (1,200-mile) long sea separating East Africa (Egypt, Sudan, Ethiopia) from Western Asia (Saudi Arabia), and forming part of the African Rift Valley system.

➡ ***Seas***

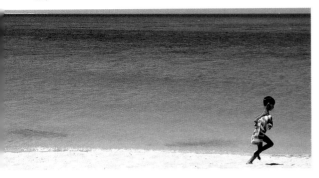

REDGRAVE, SIR MICHAEL (1908–85)

British actor. Redgrave starred in films such as *The Lady Vanishes* (1938) but his main love was for the theatre. He was the father of Corin, Vanessa and Lynn Redgrave.

➡ ***Vanessa Redgrave, Theatre***

REDGRAVE, VANESSA (b. 1937)

English actress. Redgrave became famous for her acclaimed roles in films such as *Howard's End* (1992) and for her substantial volume of theatre work. She is the mother of Natasha and Joely Richardson.

➡ ***Michael Redgrave, Theatre***

REFINING

Conversion or purification of a raw material into a more useful form, in particular the purification of metals after extraction from their ores, and the distillation of crude oil to produce more useful fractions.

➡ ***Oil***

REFRIGERATION

Process whereby heat is continuously removed from a body so that it stays colder than its surroundings. A refrigerant is passed around a circuit of tubing, evaporating and absorbing heat in one part, and condensing and evolving heat in another.

REGGAE

Jamaican dance music of the late 1960s, Reggae (meaning 'raggedy') is often socially aware and radical in lyrics. The music is beat-orientated, being bass driven and brings together themes from Latin American music and Rhythm and Blues. Reggae spread to Britain and later America and Europe. Many original reggae artists were of the Rastafari religion, including Bob Marley.

➡ ***Bob Marley, Rastafari***

RELATIVITY

Theory based on the relative, rather than absolute, nature of motion. The theory was developed in two stages by Albert Einstein. In special relativity, the laws of nature are the same for all unaccelerated observers, and the speed of light is constant for all observers. In general relativity, the effects of acceleration and a gravitational field are equivalent.

➡ ***Albert Einstein***

RELIGIOUS LEADERS

Each religion has its own leaders to illuminate and guide the followers. Social and cultural influences shape the nature of this role, for example, from prophets who receive revelation direct from God, to European kings and Chinese emperors who by custom received their authority direct from God.

A rabbi is the Jewish spiritual leader of a synagogue congregation and also a scholar of Jewish law. An imam is the Muslim prayer leader in a mosque and the term can also be applied to any important Islamic leader. A priest leads Christians in their worship in a church, while a bishop and an archbishop are also priests who do so in a cathedral. The religious leader with the greatest temporal and spiritual authority worldwide is the pope, who is specifically head of the Catholic Church.

➡ ***Popes***

REMBRANDT, HARMENSZ VAN RIJN (1606–69)

Dutch painter. Rembrandt is considered a virtuoso of painting. One of Rembrandt's many exceptional artistic skills was his ability to capture his subject's emotions, while equally able to bare his own soul in his numerous self-portraits. His narrative paintings, such as *The Night Watch* (1642), are expressive and emotionally literate. In subject, Rembrandt moved away from the Classical towards more realistic depiction; he inclined towards nature rather than adherence to artistic ideals. Rembrandt's life was marred by personal tragedies: his wife and four children died. While Rembrandt has since been acknowledged as a master of painting, during his lifetime his work was less popular and in 1656 he was declared bankrupt.

➧ ***Classical***

RENAISSANCE ART, MUSIC AND LITERATURE

The term Renaissance ('rebirth') broadly covers the period fourteenth to sixteenth centuries. The rebirth of learning in western Europe dates from the fall of Constantinople in 1453 and the influx of scholars and technicians among the refugees who fled from

Ottoman rule. Emerging in Italy, the Renaissance was a reflection of vast societal changes. There was an upsurge in trade that led to increased wealth which was reflected in patronage of the arts. Renaissance arts (with the exception of music) liberally referred back to the ancient Graeco-Roman cultures (many antiquities were being rediscovered at the time).

Two key Renaissance artists were Leonardo Da Vinci (1452–1519) and Michelangelo (1475–1564). The latter studied anatomy and in both his sculpture and painting explored the male form. Da Vinci was the idealized Renaissance man, skilled and learned in many areas, both scientific and artistic.

Key developments in art were the use of oil painting and perspective. There were many developments in musical techniques, one of the major being that of polyphony (the harmonious combining of melodies). Within literature, the invention of printing meant the increased availability of texts. Plato's work was rediscovered and the spread of the ideals of Humanists began.

➧ ***Ancient Greece, Ancient Rome***

RENOIR, PIERRE-AUGUSTE (1841–1919)

French artist. Renoir was a leading figure of the Impressionist movement. He founded the movement with Claude Monet, based upon their developing style of painting that attempted to capture the spirit of the subject by using a less precise and more evident brush stroke. Unlike Monet, Renoir was at his best in the portrayal of figures, as can be seen in the *Bathers* (1887). Renoir particularly enjoyed scenes of middle-class French society and females, either nude or in movement. Renoir's palette was characteristically light, his technique almost gentle in its application, which gives his genre paintings an almost welcoming air, drawing the viewer into the scene.

➧ ***Impressionism, Claude Monet***

REPRODUCTION

Mechanism by which organisms give rise to others of the same kind. A characteristic of all living things. There are two types of reproduction; asexual and sexual. Asexual reproduction produces genetically identical offspring – clones. Sexual reproduction involves the genetic input of two individuals and is common in higher animals and flowering plants.

➧ ***Genetic Engineering***

TOP LEFT: A child enjoys the freedom of the Red Sea and its beaches, Egypt.
FAR LEFT: Iran's Spiritual Leader Ayatollah Khamenei seen here below an image of Ayatollah Khomeini who led the country's Islamic revolution in 1979.

REPTILES

Vertebrate animals that have a dry scaly skin and lay eggs on land (unlike amphibians). The reptile group includes snakes, lizards, alligators and crocodiles and it has existed for about 300 million years. There are many extinct reptiles e.g. dinosaurs. Reptiles have slow metabolisms, cannot maintain their own body temperature (are exothermic) and rely on ambient heat. Some lizards and snakes keep their eggs inside their bodies and give birth to live young.

➡ ***Amphibians, Dinosaurs, Vertebrates***

REPUBLICAN PARTY (1854)

One of the two principal US political parties. Founded in 1854, the party is identified with big business and capitalism, and promoting the rights of states and individuals over the federal government. In recent years, Republican presidents like Ronald Reagan, George Bush, and George W. Bush, have been associated with more strident US defence policy.

➡ ***Presidents***

REYNOLDS, SIR JOSHUA (1723–92)

English portrait painter. Considered one of the finest portrait painters in England, Reynold's aim was to elevate art to the level seen in the Italian Renaissance. He believed only the elite of society made suitable portrait subjects and that art should be refined and regal in both style and content. Reynolds was also an accomplished art lecturer.

➡ ***Neoclassicism, Renaissance***

RIGHT: What began as a demonstration on the streets of Rangoon, Burma has become a riot, with civilians clashing with the military and police groups and their followers.

RHINOCEROS

Large, hoofed, grazing mammals found in Africa and southern Asia. Indian and Javan rhinos have one horn in the middle of their heads; white and black African rhinos have two horns.

➡ ***Endangered Species***

RICHTER SCALE

Scale used to measure the magnitude of an earthquake or earth tremor. An increase of one on the Richter scale represents a tenfold increase in energy released.

➡ ***Earthquakes***

RIOTS

Violent gatherings of people running amok in public places ostensibly in pursuit of political or social causes. Often beginning with peaceable intentions, mis-management by security authorities or malicious intent by a minority can lead to destructive behaviour. In the most extreme form, members of security forces can be murdered, shops and houses looted, and property set on fire.

RIVERS

Large and natural streams of fresh water that follow a definite path, usually into the sea. Rivers are fed by tributary streams along their courses.

➡ ***Amazon River***

ROADS

Routes built for the passage of wheeled vehicles. Many roads are reinforcements of pre-existing paths and tracks, and often do not match modern needs, so there is an incentive to build new routes, rather than improve existing ones. Both bituminous surfacing and concrete are widely used in road construction.

ROBERT THE BRUCE (1274–1329)

Robert I of Scotland from 1306. National leader and hero of Scotland, opposing the ambitions of the English kings in William Wallace's rebellion. Following Wallace's execution (1305) he was crowned and extended his control over Scotland with a decisive defeat of Edward II's army at Bannockburn (1314). His position was confirmed by the Treaty of Northampton (1328).

➧ ***Scotland***

ROBERTS, JULIA (b.1967)

US film actress. Roberts shot to fame playing the 'hooker with a heart' in the box office smash *Pretty Woman* (1990). She won the best actress Oscar for *Erin Brockovich* (2000).

➧ ***Academy Awards, Films***

ROBOTICS

Use of computer-controlled, programmable machines to carry out physical tasks. Examples include the use of 'robot arms' which reproduce the actions of a skilled assembly worker in a factory, the use of computer-controlled vehicles, and computer-guided missiles.

➧ ***Computers, Electronics***

ROCK MUSIC

Rock music can be seen as the natural progression of Rock 'n' Roll into a harder edged style in the 1960s. Rock music has been influenced and progressed through changes in society – rock music, with folk, was used in protest songs. Rock has become divergent and there are many different kinds of rock, including thrash, metal and country.

➧ ***Rock 'n' Roll***

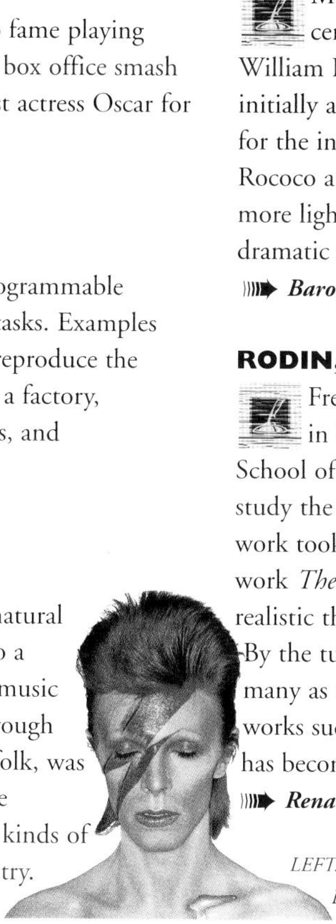

LEFT: The term 'Rock music' encompasses a broad range of music. David Bowie has tried most of them, here in his Aladdin Sane guise.

ROCK 'N' ROLL

Genre of music that mainly derives from the guitar-and-vocal based rhythm and blues music of African-Americans (which in turn combines blues and jazz) but also took strands from country and western music. Rock 'n' Roll emerged in the 1950s, firstly in America but quickly spreading to Europe and dominated radio and charts sales.

➧ ***Pop Music, Rock Music***

ROCKY MOUNTAINS

Largest North American mountain range, running south from Alaska through Canada and the Western USA to Mexico. The highest peak is Mount Elbert (4,400 m/14,433 ft).

➧ ***Canada. Mountains***

ROCOCO (18TH CENTURY)

Mainly French artistic style of the eighteenth century, although echoes of Rococo appear in William Hogarth's work, among others. Rococo was initially a derogatory term and the style was often used for the interior design of aristocratic women's boudoirs. Rococo art employed gentle colours and was generally more light-hearted than Baroque, while still keeping its dramatic tendencies.

➧ ***Baroque, William Hogarth***

RODIN, AUGUSTE (1840–1917)

French sculptor. Rodin struggled for acceptance in his earlier career and was rejected by the Paris School of Arts several times. Following a visit to Italy to study the sculpture of his hero Michelangelo, Rodin's work took on a Classical, monumental appeal with his work *The Age of Bronze* (1877). The sculpture was so realistic that Rodin was accused of working from a cast. By the turn of the century Rodin was proclaimed by many as the greatest sculptor of the time. With renowned works such as *The Thinker* and *The Kiss*, the name Rodin has become inseparable from the medium of sculpture.

➧ ***Renaissance***

ROGERS, GINGER (1911–95)

Dance partner to Fred Astaire. American actress/dancer Rogers found some success with her film career after the duo split, most notably for her Oscar-winning role in *Kitty Foyle* (1940).

➧ ***Academy Awards, Fred Astaire***

ROGERS, RICHARD (b. 1933)

English architect. Rogers worked alongside Norman Foster until 1967, developing their 'High Tech' approach. Perhaps his most prestigious work was the Centre Pompidou, Paris (1971–77).

➧ ***Architecture, Norman Foster***

ROLLING STONES, THE (1962)

London rock group. The Rolling Stones were marketed as the opposition to The Beatles. Remarkably, despite several band member changes (and deaths), the Stones are still recording and playing music together. Mick Jagger and Keith Richards are the key writers of their predominantly rhythm-and-blues orientated rock music.

➧ ***Beatles, Rock Music, Rock 'n' Roll***

ROMAN GODS AND MYTHOLOGY

The Roman pantheon and mythology is derivative of the Greeks. As self-validation they identified many of their own gods with the corresponding Greek ones. They also created two key myths to provide a historical background, that of Romulus and Remus, and of Aeneas.

Romulus and Remus, the sons of Mars and founders of Rome, were suckled by his sacred she-wolf. By 239 BC this story became the official version of the origins of Rome. Aeneas, in turn, allegedly provided the arriviste Roman nobility with Trojan origins: apparently he fled from Troy to Rome after the Greek infiltration of the city. Key Roman gods are Jupiter (the supreme god) and Juno (queen of the gods, cosort of Jupiter), Mercury (the messenger god), Minerva (goddess of wisdom), Neptune (god of the sea) and Janus (Roman god associated with beginnings, hence January). Also important are the Furies, the Fates and the Giants.

➧ ***Greek Gods and Mythology***

ROMANIA

East European country between Bulgaria and Ukraine. **Capital:** Bucharest. **Other principal cities:** Braslov, Timisoara, Galati, Constanta. **Climate:** warm summers, cold winters. **Geographical features:** mountainous, plateaus, and Black Sea shore. **Main language:** Romanian. **Main religion:** Romanian Orthodox. **Rule:** democratic republic. **Currency:** leu. **Primary industries:** manufacture of machinery, mining, smelting. **Exports:** machinery, transport equipment, electrical goods, iron, steel, petroleum.

➧ ***Europe***

RIGHT: One of the most enduring bands of all time, the Rolling Stones were a 1960s and 70s phenomenon.

ROMANTIC ART, MUSIC AND LITERATURE

The Romantic era began around 1790 (coinciding with the French Revolution) and declined about 1840. Romanticism was mainly European, particularly important in Germany, Britain and France. Romanticism eschewed the artistic restraint that Neoclassicism had enforced and aimed instead for a freer, more emotive self-expression. The imagination of the individual was valued; the interpretation of an artists' personal view was seen as preferable to a skilful regurgitation of some classic work.

In art, painters such as Eugène Delacroix and Goya came to prominence. Also landscapes were again popular – the wildness of nature was admired, often employed to reflect emotions and spirituality.

In literature writers such as Scott and Goethe revived the genre of Medieval romance and there was a general renewal of interest in history and in the exotic.

Romanticism within music lasted longer than the other arts and was still prevalent at the end of the nineteenth century. Composers such as Beethoven and Strauss have ensured Romanticism's longevity.

➧ ***Ludwig van Beethoven, Eugène Delacroix, French Revolution, Francisco Goya, Neoclassicism***

ROME, ANCIENT

The Eternal City dates its foundation by Romulus to 763 BC, but its expansion to control the surrounding territory began in the fourth century and after the defeat of Hannibal and the Carthaginians in 202 BC Rome emerged as a major power. In the course of the ensuing centuries it extended its conquests to the entire Mediterranean, and the Empire stretched from Scotland to the Black Sea, as well as the whole of North Africa and the Near East. The Empire gradually evolved out of the Republic under Octavian (27 BC). The western Roman Empire collapsed in AD 476, but the Byzantine Empire, based on Constantinople, survived until 1453.

➧ ***Roman Gods and Mythology***

ROOSEVELT, ELEANOR (1884–1962)

Wife of Franklin D. Roosevelt, four times president of the USA. Eleanor greatly influenced the New Deal policies of his administration. She was chair of the UN commission on Human Rights 1946–51 and a major contributor to the Declaration of Human Rights.

➧ ***Human Rights, Presidents, United Nations***

ROTHKO, MARK (1903–70)

American abstract artist. Rothko is remembered chiefly for his large canvases dominated by blocks of fusing colour. Rothko has an inimitable mastery of colour. He committed suicide in 1970.

➧ ***Abstract Art***

ROUSSEAU, JEAN JACQUES (1712–78)

Swiss Romantic philosopher, who argued that humanity had become alienated from the natural world and that human maladies were caused by the constructions and restrictions of society.

➧ ***Philosophy***

ROWING

Ancient means of water transport, now mostly a sport. It has two sub-divisions: rowing (one oar per person) and sculling (two oars per person). It is an Olympic sport.

➧ ***Olympic Games***

ROWLING, J. K. (b. 1965)

British writer of the phenomenally successful series of children's books that follow the character Harry Potter, a young boy who attends a school for wizards.

LEFT: A statue outside St Peter's Rome. The modern city continues to pay homage to the ancient philosophers, artists, academics and saints for which it has gained world renown.

RUBENS, PETER PAUL (1577–1640)

Flemish painter. Rubens was classically educated and travels to Italy furthered his interest in the Renaissance masters. His subjects varied from the religious and the mythological to hunting scenes and portraits. Typically for the Baroque period, his work shows a high sense of drama suffused with an energetic movement but given a naturalistic light and glowing colours that captivate the viewer.

➧ *Baroque, Renaissance*

RUGBY

Form of football first played at Rugby school in 1823, when a pupil called William Webb Ellis first picked up the ball and ran with it. There are two major variants: Union, with 15 players and League with 13. There are minor rule differences, with League popular in the North of the UK and Union in the South. Until recently Union was a strictly amateur sport.

➧ *Football*

RUHLMANN, JACQUES EMILE (1879–1933)

Paris-born designer. Ruhlmann was the leading figure of the French Art Deco style. He ran the successful workshop called Ruhlmann et Laurent that designed silks, carpets, textiles and lighting.

➧ *Art Deco, Decorative Arts*

RUNNING

Generally used to mean the act of running as a recreational activity. The growing awareness of our own health has lead to an explosion in its popularity, with the phrase jogging now in common use. It has also lead indirectly to one of the great fashion phenomena of the twentieth century – the training shoe.

➧ *Fashion, Orienteering*

RUSHDIE, SALMAN (b.1947).

Writer of *The Satanic Verses* (1988) which, in part, portrayed the life of Muhammad. The book was condemned by sections of the Muslim community, banned in India and Rushdie received death threats.

➧ *Literary Genres*

RUSSIA

Country of eastern Europe and northern Asia, now the Russian Federation. **Capital:** Moscow. **Other principal cities:** St Petersburg, Nizhni-Novgorod, Rostov-on-Don. **Climate:** hot summers, long cold winters. **Geographical features:** fertile plains, mountains and Arctic tundra. **Main language:** Russian. **Main religion:** Russian Orthodox. **Rule:** democracy. **Currency:** rouble. **Primary industries:** steel, heavy engineering, manufacturing, chemicals, building materials, food processing. **Agriculture:** cereals, potatoes, vegetables, livestock. **Exports:** fuels, chemicals, metals and alloys, machinery, weapons, timber, paper.

The largest country in the world, Russia's communist economy was controlled but subjected to endemic shortages, low productivity and a lack of innovation. The transition to a free market has improved some aspects, but Russia is dependent on foreign aid for economic reform.

➧ *Russian Revolution, Soviet Leaders*

RUSSIAN EMPIRE

The imperial expansion of Russia began under Peter the Great who assumed the title of Emperor in 1721. Defeating Sweden, he gained a foothold on the Baltic and built St Petersburg as his 'window on the west'. In campaigns against Persia and the Ottoman Empire, he extended his dominions to the south and east. His policies were continued by his successors and by 1881 the empire extended from Poland to the Pacific, from Siberia to the Caucasus and the khanates of Central Asia.

RUSSIAN REVOLUTION

A 12-year sequence of disruption involving three revolutions, culminating in the overthrow of the Russian monarchy and the establishment of a communist government founded on Marxist ideology.

On Sunday, 22 January 1905, unarmed workers marched on the royal palace at St Petersburg, calling for reform. Soldiers shot many demonstraters. A general strike in October forced reform of parliamentary control of legislation.

In February 1917 continuing repression, and the privations of World War I, led to a revolution and the tsar's abdication. A series of provisional governments failed to solve Russia's problems. In October 1917 the Bolsheviks seized power and established Lenin as leader, but a four-year civil war (1918–22) followed before the communist government had secured control.

➡ ***World War I***

RUSSIAN ROYALTY

The first Russian dynasty was established by Rurik the Viking at Novgorod in AD 862. Under Yaroslav the Wise (1019–54) the Kievan principalities were consolidated, but then fell under Mongol domination from which they were liberated by Ivan III who assumed the title of 'sovereign of all the Russias'. Ivan IV, grand prince of Moscow took the title of Tsar (Caesar), but Peter I was the first to style himself Imperator (Emperor). The last dynasty was founded in 1613 by Michael Romanov, notable sovereigns including Catherine I (widow of Peter I) and Catherine II 'the Great'. Last of the line was Nicholas II, murdered by the Bolsheviks in 1918.

➡ ***European Sovereigns***

RWANDA

Land-locked central African country. **Capital:** Kigali. **Other principal cities:** Butare, Ruhengeri. **Climate:** mild. **Geographical features:** hilly, with volcanic uplands. **Main languages:** Kinyarwanda, French. **Main religions:** Roman Catholicism, animist. **Rule:** republic. **Currency:** Rwanda franc. **Primary industries:** agriculture, mining. **Exports:** coffee, tea, cassiterite, wolframite, pyrethrum.

➡ ***Africa, Genocide***

TOP LEFT: Soviet leader Mikhail Gorbachev (left) introduced reforms in Russia and instigated increased levels of communication with the West. He was ousted, however, by Boris Yeltsin (right) in 1991.

ABOVE: A banner in Moscow bears the famous faces of Russian leaders, with Vladimir Ilyich Lenin (left) and Karl Marx (right) flanking Friedrich Engles.

SAINTS

Exceptionally pious people who are posthumously canonized, especially by the Roman Catholic and Eastern Orthodox Churches. The Bollandists (Belgian Jesuits) collated the lives of thousands of saints. In 1970, however, the revised calendar of saints recognized only 58 saints of worldwide significance. Saints can be appointed patrons of nations, parishes or special interest groups. Buddhism also has a limited number of saints.

➧ ***Buddhism, Catholicism, Francis of Assisi***

SALADIN (1137–93)

Sultan of Egypt and Syria (1174–93) and leader of the Muslims against the Crusaders in the Holy Land. Saladin defeated the Christians at Tiberias (1187) but they counter-attacked in the Third Crusade and destroyed his power at Acre (1191).

➧ ***Jerusalem***

SALZBURG FESTIVAL (1877)

Salzburg, the town of Mozart's birth, is home to the largest and most influential classical music festival. The festival began in 1877 and was initially confined to the music of Mozart. Distinguished composers have conducted at the festival, such as Gustav Mahler (1860–1911) and Richard Strauss (1864–1949) and the festival now includes music from Beethoven to Richard Wagner (1813–83).

➧ ***Wolfgang Amadeus Mozart***

ABOVE: King Richard II, kneeling, with his patron saints.

SAMURAI WARRIORS (12TH–19TH CENTURIES)

Japanese feudal class of armed retainers serving landowners from the twelfth to nineteenth centuries. Enjoying special privileges of carrying arms, samurai lived by strict codes of honour and behaviour.

SARACENS

Originally the term used by the Greeks and Romans to describe the nomadic tribes of Arabia who harried the frontier outposts of the Empire, it was revived by the Crusaders to denote their Muslim opponents in the Holy Land and the Balkans.

SARTRE, JEAN PAUL (1905–80)

French philosopher and writer. Sartre studied at the Sorbonne, where he met Simone de Beauvoir (his partner) there. His first novel *Nausea* (1938) was well received, as was his 1943 work *Being and Nothingness* in which Sartre gave full expression to his Existentialist philosophies. He was awarded (but declined) the Nobel Prize for his autobiography in 1963.

➧ ***Nobel Prize, Philosophy***

SATELLITES

Bodies which are in orbit around a larger one. Natural satellites of planets are also called moons. Artificial satellites have been launched since 1957 and many thousands are in Earth orbit at any time, although most eventually re-enter the atmosphere. Their main applications are communications surveillance, mapping, meteorology, navigation and scientific research.

➧ ***Moon, Planets, Space Exploration***

SATURN

Sixth of the major planets from the Sun, and the second largest. Its low density and rapid rotation cause the diameter at the equator to be 10% greater than the polar diameter. Saturn has a distinctive system of rings. made of tiny moonlets less than a few metres across.

➧ ***Planets, Solar System, Sun***

SAUDI ARABIA

Middle East country. **Capital:** Riyadh. **Other principal cities:** Mecca, Medina, Jiddah. **Climate:** desert, with some coastal rainfall. **Geographical features:** mostly desert, with Red Sea and Persian Gulf coasts. **Main language:** Arabic. **Main religion:** Islam. **Rule:** absolute monarchy. **Currency:** rial. **Primary industries:** petroleum, steel, fertilizers, plastics, cement. **Agriculture:** being encouraged. **Exports:** petroleum products, wheat.

Huge deserts restrict settlement and agriculture. The nation's wealth lies almost entirely in vast oil and gas reserves (the world's largest), found in the 1930s and systematically exploited after 1945. The government is encouraging diversification by improving communications and assisting agricultural development, and uses oil revenues to develop facilities, services and education.

SAVANNAHS

Large expanses of open grasslands in tropical areas. Savannahs are located in Africa, North and South America and Northern Australia. Savannahs are relatively arid regions; there is enough water to support the extensive growth of grass but only scattered trees and shrubs. The acidic soil of a savannah is another restriction on the growth of many plant species. Animals that thrive in savannahs tend to be grazing animals, such as antelope, that live in herds for protection from predators.

SAXONS

Strictly speaking, the inhabitants of the German state of Saxony, but applied loosely to one of the great tribal groups (with the Angles and Jutes) who invaded Britain in the fifth and sixth centuries. The kingdoms of the West, South and East Saxons gave rise to the territorial divisions or counties of Wessex, Sussex and Essex.

SCHINDLER, OSKAR (1908–74)

Former member of the Nazi Party who spent the immense wealth he made through his factory in occupied Poland to save the lives of more than 1,200 Jews. Steven Spielberg's film *Schindler's List* told his story.

➧ ***Nazism, Steven Spielberg, World War II***

SCHOOLS

Places of learning where children are taught skills on a rising scale as they grow older. Attending school is often required by a state's laws. Much debate exists on the best way to educate young people, generally polarized into those favouring that all be taught together (comprehensive) and those that feel brighter children should be taught separately (selective).

➧ ***Education, Universities***

SCHUBERT, FRANZ (1797–1828)

Austrian composer. Schubert taught music until 1818 when he began to concentrate solely on composing. Although working in a variety of genres it is for his songs that Schubert is best remembered: he was a highly accomplished composer of melodies. His music takes elements of Classicism and, through its emotive melodies, equally relates to the Romanticism. Schubert often set music to poetry, such as Goethe's *Gretchen am Spinnrade*. Despite his early death, Schubert was hugely prolific, writing over 600 songs and eight symphonies.

➧ ***Johann Wolfgang von Goethe, Romanticism***

LEFT: The wealth of the Saudi Arabian elite has been earned from the rich reserves of oil and gas to be found in this Middle Eastern country.

SCIENTOLOGY

The Church of Scientology is an organization which promotes a form of psychotherapy called dianetics by its founder L. Ron Hubbard, which claims to cure mental illnesses.

SCOTLAND

Northern part of the United Kingdom. **Capital:** Edinburgh. **Other principal cities:** Glasgow, Dundee, Aberdeen. **Climate:** mild and wet, with severe winters. **Geographical features:** rocky coastline, numerous islands, mountainous terrains characterized by deep valleys, crags, and lochs (lakes). **Main languages:** English, Gaelic. **Main religion:** Church of Scotland. **Rule:** constitutional monarchy, with its own parliament in Edinburgh subordinate to parliament in London. **Currency:** pound sterling. **Primary industries:** mining, offshore oil drilling, manufacturing of heavy engineering, electrical and consumer goods, chemicals, textiles, paper, printing, coal, tourism, agriculture (mainly livestock), fishing. **Exports:** manufactured goods, oil, gas, meat and dairy products, seafood, wool, jute.

Scotland and its islands are entirely surrounded by sea except for the southern border with England. The area is equivalent to about 25% of the British Isles. In addition to its considerable natural resources and booming local economy, Scotland has contributed large numbers of settlers to other parts of the world, e.g. North America and Australasia.

SCOTT, ROBERT FALCON (1868–1912)

English Antarctic explorer. As a naval captain, Scott led two expeditions to the Antarctic. In 1901–04 he explored the Ross Sea. His 1910–12 expedition in the *Terra Nova* included a sledge journey to be the first to reach the South Pole. Beaten by Roald Amundsen, Scott and his colleagues perished on the return trip.

➧ ***Exploration***

ABOVE: The children of King George V and Queen Mary wear traditional Scottish tartan at Balmoral in 1911. Different clans have different colours and weaves of tartan.

SCOTT, SIR WALTER (1771–1832)

Scottish poet and the first historical novelist. Scott was decidedly Romantic in style. With novels such as *Waverley* (1814) and *Rob Roy* (1817) Scott focused upon the history and myths of the Anglo-Scot border. For commercial reasons he later explored English medieval legends. Among his most famous poems is *The Lady of the Lake* (1810).

➧ ***Literary Genres, Romanticism***

SCOTTISH CLANS

Social grouping based on the extended family, theoretically descended from a common ancestor. The word clan is from Gaelic and means 'children', each clan being identified by a unique tartan. The clan system has contributed to the fragmented nature of much of Scottish history. Inter-clan rivalries were always fierce and often developed into violence and sometimes war.

➧ ***Costumes***

SEAS

Term used to describe an expanse of salt water on the Earth's surface. A sea may represent a section of an ocean e.g. Irish Sea or a large region of inland water e.g. Black Sea. Seas are smaller and shallower than oceans and have no major currents running through them.

➡ *Oceans*

SEISMOLOGY

Study of earthquakes, mainly by detecting the shock waves they transmit through the Earth, which provide information about the interior of the Earth as well as the earthquake.

➡ *Earth, Earthquakes*

SELLERS, PETER (1925–80)

English comedian/ actor. Sellers began his career in radio as a member of *The Goon Show*. On film, he is best remembered as Inspector Clouseau in the numerous *Pink Panther* films.

➡ *Films*

SENECA, LUCIUS ANNAEUS (c. 4 BC–AD 65)

Roman statesman and philosopher of Stoicism (the acceptance of one's fate), as evinced in his major writing *Moral Letters*. Seneca died through enforced suicide.

➡ *Philosophy, Ancient Rome*

SENEGAL

West African coastal country. **Capital:** Dakar. **Other principal cities:** Thiès, Kaolack. **Climate:** dry and rainy seasons. **Geographical features:** plateaux, massifs, swamps. **Main language:** French. **Main religion:** Islam. **Rule:** socialist democratic republic. **Currency:** franc CFA. **Primary industries:** agriculture, fishing, petroleum, tourism. **Exports:** fish, petroleum products, manufactured goods, peanuts, cotton, phosphates, livestock.

➡ *Africa*

SEQUOIA

Redwood conifer, found in the western US. Largest varieties can reach a base circumference of 30 m (100 ft) and live in excess of 3,000 years.

➡ *Trees*

SEVEN YEARS' WAR (1756–63)

War fought as part of a long-term European struggle. War broke out over Austria's attempt to recover Silesia from Prussia. Their allies, France and Britain, used the war to pursue colonial conflict over North America and India. The end of the war confirmed Britain's control of those territories but left unfinished business in Europe pursued in subsequent wars.

SEX

Biologically, the coupling of male and female in order to reproduce, but in a social context very much more. Issues surrounding the subject are at the core of many social and religious systems, from the strict abstinence of Catholic priests through to the use of erotic images to sell products.

SEYCHELLES

Indian Ocean islands off East Africa. **Capital:** Victoria. **Other principal cities:** Cascade, Port Glaud. **Climate:** tropical. **Geographical features:** about 100 mountainous granite and flat coral islands. **Main languages:** Creole, English, French. **Main religion:** Catholicism. **Rule:** democracy. **Currency:** Seychelles rupee. **Primary industries:** tourism, cinnamon, seafood. **Exports:** copra, cinnamon, fish (tuna), shark.

➡ *Africa*

SHAKESPEARE, WILLIAM (1564–1616)

Influential playwright and poet. Shakespeare was born in Stratford-upon-Avon, the son of a merchant. He married Anne Hathaway in 1582, moving to London thereafter. In London Shakespeare began working as a dramatist and by 1598 his many successful plays had gained much repute. Shakespeare became a part owner of the Globe theatre in 1598 and this brought him royal support through King James's subsequent patronage. Besides his dramatic writings, Shakespeare is equally regarded for his poetry, particularly his enduring sonnets which he published in 1609. However, it is through his plays (many are in constant production), that Shakespeare's immense influence upon the arts continues.

➡ *Playwrights, Poetry, Theatre*

SHEEP

Hoofed, ruminant and grazing mammals found throughout the world. Sheep are widely domesticated and kept in flocks as a source of meat, wool and milk.

➡ ***Mammals***

SHELLEY, PERCY BYSSHE (1792–1822)

Romantic English poet. Shelley did not gain great acclaim or popularity during his lifetime. Due to his radical beliefs his movements were followed by government spies. His poems such as *Prometheus Unbound,* were often political and evinced his idealism. Shelley left his wife Harriet (later marrying Mary Shelley, author of *Frankenstein*) and fled England for Italy, where he drowned.

➡ ***Romantic***

SHERLOCK HOLMES

Fictional character of novels by Arthur Conan Doyle. The discerning detective, together with the simpler Dr Watson, first appeared in the 1887 novel *A Study in Scarlet.* Based on Dr Joseph Bell, under whom Doyle studied medicine.

SHINTO

Indigenous religion of Japan that emphasizes oneness with natural forces (the Sun goddess, Amaterasu-Omikami is worshipped) and loyalty to the emperor: Hirohito finally denied his own divinity in 1946. Sectarian Shinto has 130 sects.

➡ ***Japan***

SHIPS

Large seagoing forms of transport, both civil and naval. Ships are now used mainly for bulk movement of raw materials and goods, passenger ships having become largely supplanted by aircraft. Most ships are powered by oil-fired steam turbine driving propellers, although older propulsion methods including sail still exist.

➡ ***Navies, Ports***

SHOPPING MALLS

Large complexes of shops first popularized in the US but now spread to all developed countries. Ever-more complex, they are sometimes called temples to consumerism. The UK government has passed legislation to prevent new ones destroying existing town centre shopping area.

SIEGES

Campaigns conducted against strongholds or towns inside which defenders have locked themselves. The length of a siege is dictated by the quantity of stores within; the maintenance of covert supplies; and the endurance of defenders; against the ability of attackers to destroy defences and break in, or enter through subterfuge or by treachery. Famous sieges include the Siege of Leningrad during World War II and the Siege of Mafeking during the Boer Wars between Britain and South Africa.

➡ ***World War II***

SIERRA LEONE

West African coastal country. **Capital:** Freetown. **Other principal cities:** Koidu, Bo. **Climate:** tropical and wet. **Geographical features:** coastal swamps and plains with inland mountains. **Main language:** English. **Main religions:** animist, Islam. **Rule:** military government. **Currency:** leone. **Primary industries:** mining, agriculture (poor yields due to lack of modernization). **Exports:** rutile, bauxite, diamonds, coffee, cocoa.

TOP RIGHT: The mosque at Makeni, Sierra Leone.

FAR RIGHT: The Seine at Suresnes, *1877 by Alfred Sisley (1839–99).*

SIKHISM

Monotheistic religion, established by Guru Nanak (1469– *c.* 1539). Membership: 16 million. Sikhs believe in the equality of all humans, an imortal creator, reincarnation, God's grace, daily prayer and meditation. The Sikh holy book is called *Guru Granth Sahib*. They adopt the day of rest of the host country. The faithful are called the *Khalsa* ('pure') and have five symbols: long hair, a comb, a sword, short trousers and a steel bracelet.

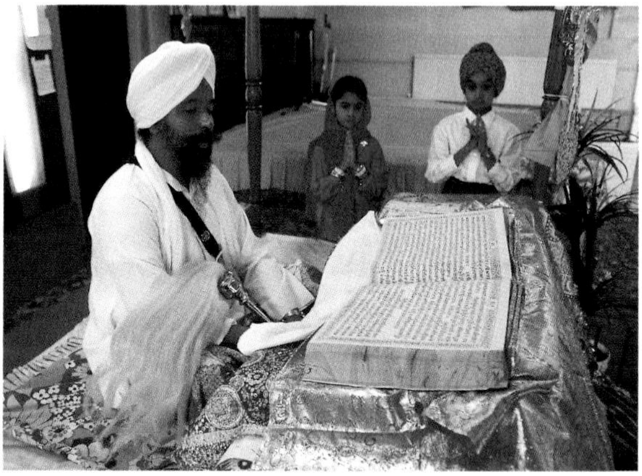

In 1966 Sikh fundamentalists began fighting for an independent Sikh state, the Punjab. They succeeded, gaining government in the Punjab with representatives from India.

SILVER

Shiny lustrous metal with the atomic symbol Ag. Silver is very malleable and ductile (can be drawn into a wire) and is therefore used extensively in the manufacture of jewellery. It conducts both heat and electricity. Silver forms compounds that darken upon exposure to light; these are the basis of photographic emulsions.

➡ ***Chemical Elements, Gold***

SINGAPORE

South-east Asian island city-state at the end of the Malay peninsula. **Capital:** Singapore. **Climate:** tropical. **Geographical features:** Singapore Island and 57 lesser islands. **Main languages:** Malay, Chinese, English. **Main religion:** Buddhism. **Rule:** democracy with repressive tendencies. **Currency:** Singapore dollar. **Primary industries:** manufacturing, especially electrical goods, petroleum, food, financial services, tourism. **Exports:** manufactured goods (electrical, clothing, machinery), chemicals, petroleum, rubber.

SINGLES

Term originally coined to mean an analogue plastic disc spinning at 45 revolutions per minute. This format revolutionized the marketing of music and enabled the creation of pop music. The format is continued in the present day by short-play compact discs that usually last about 20 minutes.

➡ ***Albums, Pop Music***

SISLEY, ALFRED (1839–99)

Anglo-French artist. Sisley was sent to London in 1857 to become a businessman but soon found his interests lay in the arts. His main love was landscapes (he painted near Barbizon with other artists), and while in England he studied Constable and Turner. Back in Paris, Sisley trained at the studio of the Swiss artist Charles Gleyre from 1863. It was there that he met Monet and Renoir and with them he contributed to the Impressionist Exhibitions from 1874.

Sisley's style remained the same throughout his career, full of light and expression, and with works such as *The Flood* (1876), he seemed to encapsulate the essence of Impressionism.

➡ ***Barbizon, John Constable, Impressionism, Claude Monet, Pierre Renoir, Joseph Turner***

SKATING

Originally the use of blades fitted to shoes for use on ice, it now also encompasses both roller-skating and roller-blading which use wheels instead and can be used on any flat surface. Roller skates were invented by James Plympton in 1866. Ice skating is an Olympic sport, with additional world championships starting in 1896.

➡ ***Winter Sports***

SKIING

Skis were known over 3,000 years ago, but only developed enough to allow sporting use at the end of the nineteenth century. There are several major disciplines including slalom, downhill, cross country and ski jump. The sport is governed internationally by the Fédération Internationale des Skieurs, founded in 1924. As well as a competitive sport, skiing is a popular holiday activity which has led to the development of resorts throughout the European Alps and US Rockies.

➡ *Winter Sports*

SLAVERY

Any system in which human beings are held in bondage as the possessions of others, to work without payment, rights or civil liberties. It dates from the earliest history of humanity, when prisoners taken in war were sold by their captors, a practice common in biblical and classical times. Britain took the lead in abolishing the slave trade (1807), but slavery itself was not abolished in the British Empire until 1826–33 and was a major cause of friction leading to the American Civil War. Although outlawed by UN conventions, slavery persists in Africa and Asia to this day.

➡ *American Civil War*

SLOVAKIA

Land-locked central European country, formerly part of Czechoslovakia. **Capital:** Bratislava. **Other principal cities:** Košice, Nitra, Prešov. **Climate:** temperate. **Geographical features:** Carpathian mountains bound a central plain. **Main language:** Slovak. **Main religions:** Roman Catholicism, Lutheran. **Rule:** democracy. **Currency:** Slovak koruna. **Primary industries:** agriculture, mining, manufacturing. **Exports:** metals and ores, machinery, armaments, chemicals, textiles.

➡ *Europe*

SLOVENIA

North-east Adriatic country, formerly part of Yugoslavia. **Capital:** Ljubljana. **Other principal cities:** Maribor, Koper. **Climate:** mild. **Geographical features:** mountainous. **Main language:** Slovene. **Main religion:** Catholicism. **Rule:** democracy. **Currency:** tolar. **Primary industries:** agriculture, mining, forestry, manufacturing. **Exports:** machinery (including vehicles), fuels (coal), chemicals, coal, grain, sugar, livestock, cotton, wool.

SMALLPOX

Highly contagious disease which was once widespread but has been eradicated due to vaccination programmes led by the World Health Organization. In the eighteenth century this disfiguring and sometimes fatal disease caused by the Variola virus was brought under control in Europe, following the development of a vaccine by Edward Jenner.

➡ *Edward Jenner, Vaccination*

SMOG

Fog that has been polluted by impurities, such as those contained in smoke. Produced most commonly in highly industrial areas. Smog can cause severe breathing difficulties, even death.

➡ *Fog*

SNOOKER

Indoor game played on a large flat table with six pockets. There are 22 balls which are propelled with a cue, the object being to get the balls into the pockets. The game was developed in India in 1875 by members of the Devonshire Regiment. The word snooker is derogatory slang for a junior officer.

SNOW

Precipitation, from clouds, of water that has been frozen into ice crystals. It occurs when ambient temperatures are too low for the ice crystals to melt into rain.

➡ *Ice*

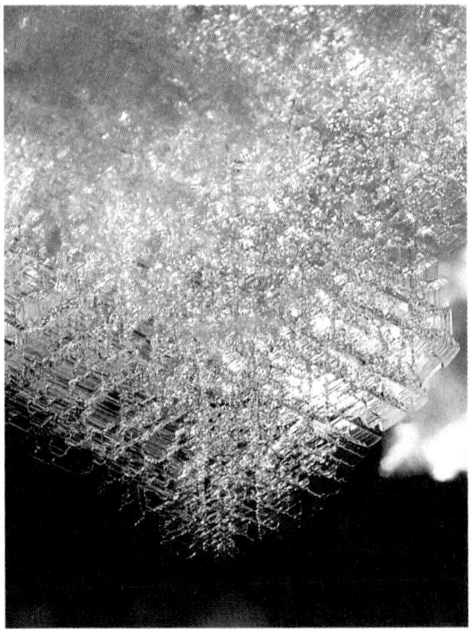

BELOW: In Botswana, in the Okavango Delta, some fortunate camps benefit from experimental solar-powered showers.

SOCIAL CLASSES

In one sense a system for categorizing people according to income and occupation, a useful, if problematic tool for social scientists. In another sense it refers to series of prejudices around a person's place in society. It is particularly marked in Hindu society where even the shadow of an untouchable class (caste) member is regarded as unclean.

➧ ***Hinduism, Socialism***

SOCIALISM

Political ideal that opposes the theory of class and private ownership. Such ideas can be traced back to Ancient Greece and beyond, but became popular only with the industrial revolution and large urban populations.

Many modern socialist principles were set down by the German Karl Marx in the nineteenth century and these formed the basis for the Communist system. However many forms of socialism were not so extreme, notably the various democratic socialist parties and the UK's own Labour Party, which was founded in the late-nineteenth century.

Extreme socialism now appears to be a spent force, with only a few states, notably North Korea and Vietnam, still adhering to its principles. Moderate socialism on the other hand continues to flourish.

➧ ***Communism, Karl Marx***

SOCRATES (c. 469–399 BC)

Greek philosopher who lived and taught in Athens. Socrates believed that true knowledge could be attained through a constant process of questioning and debate. Socrates wrote nothing himself, but his teachings were recorded by his pupil Plato. Condemning what he regarded as contemporary tyranny, he was obliged to commit suicide.

➧ ***Ancient Greece, Philosophy***

SOLAR POWER

Harnessing of the Sun's radiation to provide power, either by absorbing heat, for example in water, or by using silicon panels which generate electricity.

➧ ***Electricity, Sun***

SOLAR SYSTEM

The Sun and all the bodies in orbit around it, including the major planets and their satellites, asteroids, comets, and interplanetary gas and dust. The Sun comprizes 99.86% of the total mass of the Universe. There is considerable evidence that there was a common origin for these bodies.

➧ ***Earth, Moon, Planets, Sun, Universe***

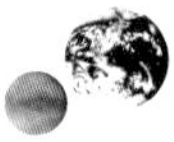

SOLOMON ISLANDS

South-west Pacific islands of Melanesia. **Capital:** Honiara. **Other principal cities:** Yandina. **Climate:** warm, moist. **Geographical features:** forested mountains, and low-lying atolls. **Main languages:** English and numerous local dialects. **Main religion:** Christianity. **Rule:** constitutional monarchy. **Currency:** Solomon Islands dollar. **Primary industries:** agriculture, fishing, tourism. **Exports:** fish, wood, copra, palm oil, cocoa.

SOMALIA

Coastal country in the Horn of Africa. **Capital:** Mogadishu. **Other principal cities:** Hargeisa, Berbera. **Climate:** hot and prone to drought. **Geographical features:** northern hills, southern lowlands, agricultural land restricted to river valleys. **Main languages:** Somali, Arabic. **Main religion:** Islam. **Rule:** changeable. **Currency:** Somali shilling. **Primary industries:** agriculture. **Exports:** bananas, livestock, hides, fish.

➧ ***Africa***

SOUL MUSIC

Originating in America during the 1960s, soul music is a form of popular music that amalgamates rhythm and blues with gospel music. The music is vocally based and as such the genre of music has attracted some of the finest singers of our time, such as Aretha Franklyn and Otis Redding, and continues to enjoy success today.

SOULAGES, PIERRE (b. 1919)

Self-taught French painter, known for his abstract art which often comprizes of black slabs painted against a white background (a style referred to as *Tachisme*).

➜ ***Abstract Art***

SOUND

Compression waves which move through the air or another medium and can be detected by the ear. The frequencies of sound detectable to the human ear range from 20 to 15,000 Hz (cycles per second). The velocity of sound at standard temperatre and pressure in dry air is about 331 mps (741 mph).

SOUTH AFRICA

Southern Africa. **Capitals:** Cape Town (legislative), Pretoria (administrative), Bloemfontein (judiciary). **Other principal cities:** Durban, Johannesburg, Port Elizabeth, East London. **Climate:** temperate. **Geographical features:** coastal beaches, plateaux, mountains, valleys and vast mineral resources. **Main languages:** English, Afrikaans. **Main religions:** Dutch Reformed Church and other Christian denominations. **Rule:** democracy. **Currency:** rand. **Primary industries:** mining, petroleum, manufacturing of heavy engineering and metal goods, fertilizers, textiles, paper, timber. **Agriculture:** cereals, sugar, fruit, vegetables, livestock. **Exports:** metals, precious metals (e.g. gold), precious stones (diamonds), pearls, machinery, fruit, sugar.

One of the richest and most industrialized nations in Africa. Most of the population is indigenous black but development began white colonial exploitation of gold and diamond reserves in the late nineteenth century. Mining promoted industry, and agriculture was developed to feed a growing urban population. Former exclusion from much world trade for its apartheid policies encouraged self-sufficiency. However, residual effects of apartheid (repealed 1991) mean that economic benefits are still inequitably distributed.

➜ ***Apartheid, Nelson Mandela***

SOUTH KOREA

East Asian peninsula country. **Capital:** Seoul. **Other principal cities:** Taegu, Pusan. **Climate:** temperate. **Geographical features:** southern and western plains, northern mountains. **Main language:** Korean. **Main religions:** Shamanism, Buddhism, Confucianism, Christianity. **Rule:** democracy. **Currency:** won. **Primary industries:** manufacturing of ships, vehicles, electrical, consumer goods, and textiles, chemicals, food-processing.. **Exports:** manufactured goods (vehicles, ships, machinery, telecommunications), food, clothing.

➜ ***Korean War, North Korea***

SOVIET LEADERS

Vladimir Ilyich Lenin led the Bolshevik Revolution (1917) and became the first Soviet leader. His successor, Joseph Stalin, wielded supreme power as General Secretary to the Party Central Committee (1922–53), responsible for the deaths of millions of peasants (1932–33) and the death or imprisonment of many others during the purges of 1934–38. He was briefly followed by Gyorgy Malenkov, prime minister in 1953–55, who ended his career as manager of a hydro-electric plant in Kazakhstan. His successor was Nikolai Bulganin (dismissed 1958), though the real power was in the hands of Nikita Khruschev. Alexei Kosygin succeeded Khruschev in 1964, resigning in 1980. Leonid Brezhnev gradually emerged as the most powerful figure after Khruschev, holding the posts of General Secretary and President simultaneously. After his death in 1982 power passed to Yuri Andropov (1982–84), Konstantin Chernenko (1984–85) and latterly Mikhail Gorbachev (1985–91).

TOP LEFT: One of the fathers of modern Soul Music, Stevie Wonder.
ABOVE RIGHT: The lift-off of the space shuttle Discovery *in September 1988. This was the first manned space flight since the* Challenger *disaster of February 1986.*

SPACE EXPLORATION

One motivation for launching spacecraft is to travel to other bodies of the Solar System. All the major planets except Pluto have been examined at close hand by unmanned spacecraft, but only the Moon has been visited by Man. Manned missions to Mars are in the planning stage.

Man on the Moon, Moon, Solar System

SPACECRAFT

Vehicle designed to move in space, beyond the Earth's atmosphere. There may be a means of propulsion, but not necessarily. Spacecraft may be manned or unmanned. Unmanned spacecraft in Earth orbit are usually called satellites, whereas those which are designed to visit other Solar System bodies are space probes.

Satellites, Space Exploration

SPAIN

South-west Europe. **Capital:** Madrid. **Other principal cities:** Zaragoza, Seville, Barcelona, Valencia. **Climate:** Mediterranean south, milder north. **Geographical features:** Iberian peninsula, northern mountains, dry central plateau. **Main language:** Spanish. **Main religion:** Catholicism. **Rule:** constitutional monarchy. **Currency:** peseta. **Primary industries:** manufacturing of machinery, vehicles, and electrical appliances, textiles, wine, olive oil, fishing, tourism. **Exports:** vehicles, machines, electrical goods, food, wine.

Spain's industry has been steadily developed since the 1950s, reducing the traditional dependence on agriculture, and now accounting for 30% of the population. Tourism has also increased national revenue, with visitors from across Europe. Government has become more democratic since Francisco Franco's death in 1975.

Europe, Francisco Franco

SPANISH SUCCESSION, WAR OF (1700-14)

War fought by the principal European powers over the Spanish Crown, and forming part of a century of European conflict.

In 1700 Charles II of Spain died, willing the crown to Philip of Anjou, grandson of the French king Louis XIV. But the Partition Treaty of 1700 had allocated it to Charles, archduke of Austria, later the emperor Charles VI. This pitted France and Spain against Britain, Austria, the Netherlands, Portugal and Denmark. Britain and her allies defeated France on four occasions (Blenheim 1704, Ramillies 1706, Oudenaarde 1708 and Malplaquet 1709), preventing French plans to march into Austria. But an invasion of Spain in 1705 was inconclusive. The war was ended by treaties in 1713 (Utrecht) and 1714 (Rastatst). Philip was accepted as king of Spain, but Britain and Austria received territory in compensation (Britain was awarded Gibraltar, Minorca and Nova Scotia).

Spain

SPICES

Plant substances that are used, in small amounts, to add flavour and sometimes colour to a dish. Spices frequently come from tropical plants, e.g. pepper, nutmeg, cumin.

Herbs

SPIDERS

Invertebrate group of small carnivorous animals with four pairs of legs and body divided into two segments; cephalothorax and abdomen. Related to scorpions and ticks.

Invertebrates

SPIELBERG, STEVEN (b. 1947)

Phenomenally successful film director, Spielberg's career took off following the hit *Jaws* (1975). He has since won admiration for his more serious films such *Schindler's List* (1993).

Films, Oskar Schindler

SPIRITS

Life-force of living things or alternatively the spirit of the dead. They also contribute to mythology and religion, from the Greek naiads and dryads to the Christian Holy Spirit.

➡ ***Ghosts, Greek Gods and Mythology, Occult, Roman Gods and Mythology,***

SPRINGS

Natural outflow of ground water, such as the source of a stream. Springs occur where the water table reaches the surface of the ground.

➡ ***Hydrology***

SPYING

Theft of state, industrial or private secrets through illegal and usually covert means. Secrets include plans for the declaration or prosecution of war, inventions, and information about private lives. Spying is as old as political and commercial rivalry. Most nations operate secret intelligence organizations charged with spying on enemies at home and abroad. Counter-intelligence involves spying on spies.

➡ ***FBI, MI5, MI6***

SRI LANKA

Indian Ocean island country. **Capital:** Colombo. **Other principal cities:** Kandy, Jaffna, Galle. **Climate:** tropical. **Geographical features:** coastal plain, mountainous and forested interior. **Main languages:** English, Sinhala, Tamil. **Main religions:** Buddhism, Hinduism. **Rule:** democratic republic. **Currency:** Sri Lankan rupee. **Primary industries:** mining, textiles, agriculture. **Exports:** textiles, tea, petroleum, gemstones, coconut, rubber.

ST PAUL'S CATHEDRAL

English cathedral situated in London. Designed by Christopher Wren. St Paul's is the largest place of Christian worship in Britain. The dome stands out on London skyline having remarkably survived the Blitz during World War II.

➡ ***Christopher Wren***

STADIUMS

Sporting arenas designed for sporting activities. Notable venues include the UK's Wembley, the Stade de France in Paris and the Olympic Stadium in Sydney, Australia.

➡ ***Olympic Games, Racetracks***

STAËL, NICHOLAS DE (1914–55)

Russian-French painter of aristocratic lineage. Staël specialized in apparently abstract works, with blocks of overlapping extravagant colours that were loosely representational, as in *Countryside* (1952).

➡ ***Abstract Art***

STALIN, JOSEPH (1879–1953)

Soviet leader and dictator from 1927. An early recruit to Bolshevism, Stalin won the contest for power against Leon Trotsky. Stalin imposed a ruthless ideological Communist rule on the Soviet Union, collectivizing industry and agriculture and exterminating opposition in the Great Purge of 1936–38. Hitler's invasion of Russia in World War II caused him to join Britain and America. After 1945 he turned Eastern Europe into a communist buffer zone.

➡ ***Communism, Dictatorship, World War II***

STAMPS (1840)

Adhesive labels or printed devices denoting the prepayment of postage. First used in the UK (1840), they spread to the rest of the world (1843–60).

➧ *Philately*

STAR WARS (1977)

Science fiction film by writer/director George Lucas, which was a worldwide commercial success, earning $46 million in its first week of release. The film has spawned three sequels.

➧ *Films*

STARS

Term used to describe any celestial body observable in the night sky as a point of light. More accurately the term 'star' refers to a hot gaseous mass, such as the Sun, which produces its own heat and light by nuclear reactions. Stars may shine for many billions of years but do change over time.

➧ *Astrology, Solar System, Sun*

STATUE OF LIBERTY (1886)

Copper and steel statue presented to the USA by the French in 1886. In the form of a woman holding aloft a torch, it was originally called Liberty Enlightening the World and is 92 m (302 ft) high.

LEFT: The imposing dome of St Paul's Cathedral continues to stand out in London's skyline, despite the growth of the city around it.

ABOVE: Steam trains, such as this Argentinean Patagonian Express, are an impressive sight. In the developed world, however, steam trains are limited to private enthusiasts' railways and railway museums.

STEAM POWER

Work obtained by the heating of water to evaporate it, and using the steam to drive a piston in a cyclinder, as in the steam engine, or a fan, as in the steam turbine. The steam engine is now virtually obsolete, but the steam turbine is widely used.

➧ *Industrial Revolution, Railways, Steam Trains*

STEAM TRAINS

Railway trains powered by steam locomotives, using coal or wood as fuel. Steam trains became practical with the first locomotives such as the *Rocket* which enabled a national rail network to be set up. In the 1960s the steam locomotive was phased out in Great Britain, although operating steam trains still exist.

➧ *Industrial Revolution, Railways*

STEPHENSON, GEORGE (1781–1848)

British engineer, pioneer of the steam locomotive. Stephenson was the engineer of the first passenger railway, the Stockton and Darlington Railway. His most successful locomotive was the *Rocket.*

➧ *Railways, Steam Power*

STEWART, JAMES (1908–97)

US actor, star of the 1946 quintessential Christmas film, *It's a Wonderful Life.* Stewart won an Oscar for his role in *The Philadelphia Story* (1940) and much praise in Hitchcock's *Vertigo* (1958).

➧ *Films, Alfred Hitchcock*

STILL, CLYFFORD (1904–80)

American abstract artist. Still became famous for his later works that are filled with blocks of strong colour seemingly disintegrating into each other.

➧ *Abstract Art*

STIRLING, JAMES (1926–92)

British architect, admired for his 'High Tech' concepts as illustrated in the New Art Gallery, Stuttgart, for which Stirling won the design competition in 1977 with partner Michael Wilford.

➧ *Architecture, Richard Rogers, Norman Foster*

STONEHENGE

Neolithic, megalithic monument, built *c.* 2000 BC on Salisbury Plain, UK. Possibly an observatory, definitely ritual, it includes an inner and outer circle of stones.

➡ ***Druids***

STOCKS AND SHARES

Means by which Public Limited Companies raise money. Investors buy shares in a company and then benefit from the company's profits in the form of dividends.

➡ ***Economics***

STONE AGES

Earliest period of prehistoric human culture, characterized by the use of stone implements and weapons. Archeologists have divided the Old Stone Age into the Upper, Middle and Lower Palaeolithic periods, each of which is represented by various cultures: Magdalenian, Solutrean, Aurignacian, Mousterian, Micoquean, Acheulean, Chellean and Prechellean, derived from important sites of artefacts characteristic of each. The Mesolithic period gave rise to the Azilian, Tardenoisean, Asturian, Maglemosean and Kitchen Midden cultures. By the New Stone Age (Neolithic period) man was domesticating animals, making pottery, grinding and polishing tools and building complex tombs. It was gradually superseded by the Bronze Age.

➡ ***Bronze Age***

STONE, LUCY (1818–93)

Pioneering feminist. Born in Massachusetts, US, Stone started giving lectures against slavery in 1847. She then became involved in women's rights and suffrage, marrying Henry Blackwell, a famous radical in 1855. She kept her own surname and created the term 'Lucy Stoner' in so doing; a vaguely insulting phrase used by men to describe strong-willed women.

➡ ***Slavery, Suffrage, Women's Emancipation***

STRAITS

Narrow channels of sea between two land masses which link two larger areas of sea e.g. Straits of Gibralter which links the Atlantic Ocean to the Mediterranean Sea.

STRASBERG, LEE (1901–82)

Influential American acting teacher. Strasberg led the Actor's Studio and founded his own acting school in 1969. Proponent of 'The Method' as used by De Niro, Strasberg has also taught Al Pacino.

➡ ***Robert de Niro, Al Pacino***

STRATIGRAPHY

Sequence of formation of layers of sedimentary rocks. The assumption is that upper layers are younger than lower ones, enabling relative dating of the layers and the fossils within them.

➡ ***Archeology, Fossils***

STRAVINSKY, IGOR (1882–1971)

Russian composer. One of the most distinguished composers of the twentieth century, Stravinsky came to eminence and international acclaim with his ballets *The Firebird* and *Petrushka.* By 1913 Stravinsky developed the challenging technique of polytonality (the use of numerous keys at the same time). In his later works, such as *Orpheus,* Stravinsky turned to a Neoclassical style.

➡ ***Neoclassicism***

ABOVE: Druids at the magical stone circle, Stonehenge. It is believed that the site has been a place of pagan worship since its creation.

STREEP, MERYL (b. 1949)

Distinguished American actress, whose first major film role was in *The Deer Hunter* (1978). Streep has won Oscars for *Kramer vs Kramer* (1979) and for *Sophie's Choice* (1982).

➤ ***Academy Awards, Films***

STRIKES

Period of withdrawal of labour. Strikes are normally called in disputes over working conditions or pay, normally by a trade union, representing workers' interests. Strikes have also played parts in national political disputes, e.g. the Russian Revolution of 1905, or in Poland's democratic reforms. Strikes may be banned or restricted by national laws.

STRING INSTRUMENTS

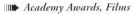

A string instrument's sound is produced by taut strings; the sound coming from a vibration in the string when struck, plucked or bowed. Usually referring to instruments such as the violin and guitar, the term can also be applied to the piano and harp. In orchestral terms, strings refers solely to violin, viola, cello and the double bass. String instruments have the ability to individually produce multiple sounds as two or more strings can be struck simultaneously. String instruments are essential to music creation – in popular music guitar, bass and piano dominate the genres and in classical music strings create structure for the orchestra.

➤ ***Brass Instruments, Orchestras, Percussion Instruments, Woodwind Instruments***

STUARTS

Dynasty which ruled Scotland and latterly England and Ireland as well. It began in the fourteenth century when Marjorie Bruce, daughter of Robert I, married Walter the Steward and produced a son Robert in 1316. During the exile and captivity of David II in England, Robert was regent, and succeeded to the throne in 1371. He was followed by his son Robert III (1390–1406). The throne passed to his younger son, James I (1406–37). James II (1437–60) was killed when a cannon exploded at the siege of Roxburgh. James III (1460–88) was put to death after he was defeated by rebels at Sauchieburn. James IV married the daughter of Henry VII but died with the flower of his army at Flodden (1513). James V died soon after his army was routed at Solway Moss (1542), the crown then passing to a newborn girl. Mary Queen of Scots was deposed and fled in 1567 to England where she was held captive by her cousin Elizabeth and beheaded in 1587. Her son, James VI, succeeded Elizabeth on the English throne in 1603. The last of the Stuarts was Queen Anne (1702–14).

➤ ***Kings of Engalnd, Queens of England***

SUBMARINES

Naval seacraft designed to operate underwater. Modern submarines are powered by a nuclear reactor driving a steam turbine, allowing them to stay submerged for extended periods.

➤ ***Navies***

SUDAN

East African country. **Capital:** Khartoum. **Other principal cities:** Omdurman, Port Sudan. **Climate:** desert north, tropical south. **Geographical features:** the Blue and White Niles join at Khartoum, southern forests and savanna, northern desert. **Main language:** Arabic. **Main religion:** Islam. **Rule:** military republic. **Currency:** Sudanese dinar. **Primary industries:** agriculture. **Exports:** cotton, livestock, meat, gum arabic.

➤ ***Africa***

SUEZ CANAL

Canal (160 km/100 miles long) joining the Mediterranean and the Red Sea between Egypt and Sinai, creating the shortest maritime route between Europe and the Far East. Completed in 1869, the canal was owned by multiple international interests, until Egypt nationalized it in 1956. This led to the Suez Crisis, an unsuccessful British and French military campaign to reverse nationalization.

SUFFRAGE

Term used to identify which citizens are eligible to vote in elections. The UK has universal adult suffrage (over 18 years old) with a few exceptions. For instance, convicted criminals serving a prison sentence at the time of the election are ineligible to vote. Universal suffrage is a key tenet of modern democracy.

➨ ***Democracy, Women's Emancipation***

SULEIMAN THE MAGNIFICENT (1494–1566)

Turkish sultan from 1520. Suleiman's wars took the Ottoman Empire to its greatest extent, seizing Rhodes, much of southern and central Europe, Persia and North Africa.

➨ ***Ottoman Empire***

SUN

Name given to the star at the centre of our Solar System. The Sun measures 1,392,000 km (864,972 miles) across and at its interior temperature reaches 15,000,000°C (27,000,000°F). Heat is generated by the fusion of hydrogen atoms in the sun's interior. This nuclear fusion produces billions of light photons that take 10 million years to reach the Sun's surface.

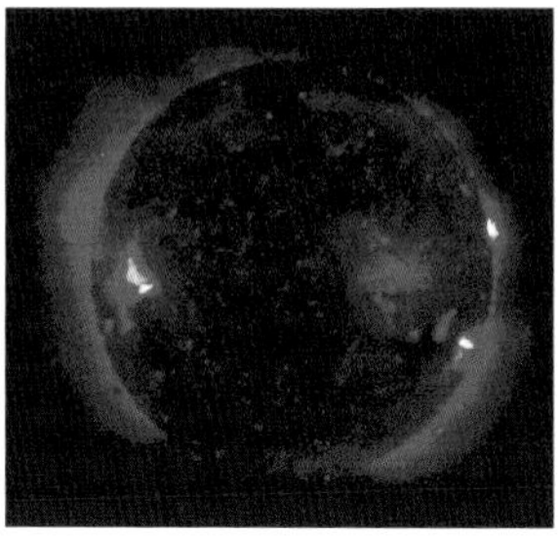

➨ ***Astrology, Solar System, Stars***

SUPERREALISM

Term used to describe art from the 1960s to present day that attempts an exact, naturalistic representation of its subject, sometimes based upon photographs and linked to Photorealism.

SUPPLY AND DEMAND

Way in which a free market economy matches peoples needs with available resources. This is achieved via price. Low supply and high demand means a high price and vice versa.

➨ ***Economics***

SURGERY

Branch of medicine concerned with physical repair of the body and removal of diseased parts or foreign bodies. Surgery is usually carried out using local or general anaesthetics, and under aseptic conditions. Less invasive techniques such as keyhole surgery which avoid many of the hazards of traditional procedures have been widely adopted.

➨ ***Diseases***

SURINAM

North-east South American country. **Capital:** Paramaribo. **Other principal cities:** Nieuw Nickerie, Brokopondo. **Climate:** tropical. **Geographical features:** coastal swamps, inland forests and jungle-covered hills. **Main languages:** Dutch, creole. **Main religions:** Christianity, Hinduism, Islam. **Rule:** democratic republic. **Currency:** Surinam guilder. **Primary industries:** mining, agriculture. **Exports:** alumina, bauxite, rice, seafood, bananas, timber.

SURREALISM (1924)

Originally a French movement led by the writer André Breton, Surrealism spread throughout Europe and, especially with the aid of European exiles, to America. Breton founded his primarily literary movement in 1924 taking influences from Dadaism and from Sigmund Freud. Breton believed the arts should attempt to access the subconscious, to tap hidden reserves of imagination and explore the arena of dreams and fantasy; the name Surrealism means 'surpassing the real'. Surrealist artists employed new techniques such as collage and automatism to access the subconscious. Many Surrealist artists, such as Salvador Dalí and Max Ernst, ensured the great impact and proliferation of Surrealism.

Dadaism, Salvador Dalí, Sigmund Freud

SWAMPS

Areas of land that are permanently waterlogged and usually overgrown. A swamp provides a unique ecological niche, supporting animal and plant life that may be dependent upon its unusual conditions.

SWANSON, GLORIA (1897–1983)

Star of the silent screen, especially under the direction of Cecil B. de Mille, Swanson's only truly successful talking role was in Billy Wilder's *Sunset Boulevard* (1950).

Films

SWEDEN

Central Scandinavian country. **Capital:** Stockholm. **Other principal cities:** Uppsala, Norrköping, Helsingborg, Malmö. **Climate:** temperate, with cold northern winters. **Geographical features:** mountains, forests, plains, long Baltic coastline. **Main language:** Swedish. **Main religion:** Evangelical Lutheran. **Rule:** constitutional monarchy. **Currency:** Swedish krona. **Primary industries:** manufacturing of vehicles, ships, precision instruments, and electrical goods, foodstuffs, forestry. **Exports:** cars, heavy machinery, iron, steel, ships, paper, pulp.

SWITZERLAND

Land-locked west European country. **Capital:** Bern. **Other principal cities:** Zürich, Geneva, Lausanne, Basel. **Climate:** temperate, varying with altitude. **Geographical features:** mountains, plateaux. **Main languages:** German, French, Italian. **Main religion:** Christianity. **Rule:** federal democratic republic. **Currency:** Swiss franc. **Primary industries:** engineering (heavy and precision), clothing, jewellery, chocolate,

LEFT: An Israeli bridge over the Suez Canal into Egypt.
BELOW: The spectacular Jewish synagogue in Berlin.

dairy, business services, tourism. **Exports:** machinery, clocks, watches, chemicals, metals, food.

Europe

SYDOW, MAX VON (b. 1929)

Swedish actor. Sydow is famous for his work in Ingmar Bergman's films, and is best known for his roles as Emperor Ming in *Flash Gordon* (1980) and Father Merrin in *The Exorcist* (1973).

Films

SYNAGOGUE

Jewish place of worship. After the final destruction of Solomon's rebuilt Temple in AD 70, synagogues gradually emerged. Synagogues comprize: the ark (containing the Torah), the bimah (the raised platform for leading the service from) and two tablets inscribed with the Ten Commandments. The word synagogue is derived from the Greek for 'coming together'.

Jerusalem, Judaism, Torah

SYNTHETIC FIBRES

Fibres for textile, made either from chemically modified natural products (such as rayon from cellulose), or synthetic plastics such as nylons, by drawing into fine filaments.

SYRIA

Middle East country. **Capital:** Damascus. **Other principal cities:** Aleppo, Homs, Latakia. **Climate:** hot and dry. **Geographical features:** mountains, arid plateau, Euphrates valley. **Main language:** Arabic. **Main religion:** Islam. **Rule:** socialist republic. **Currency:** Syrian pound. **Primary industries:** petroleum, rubber, plastics, clothing, leather, tobacco, agriculture. **Exports:** petroleum, clothing, industrial goods, cotton, fruit, vegetables.

TABLE MOUNTAIN

Flat-topped mountain overlooking Cape Town, South Africa, renowned for creating a spectacular backdrop. The highest point is Maclear's Beacon at 1,086 m (3,563 ft).

➤ *Mountains, South Africa*

TAIWAN

Western Pacific island off China. **Capital:** Taipei. **Other principal cities:** Kaohsiung, Keelung. **Climate:** maritime sub-tropical. **Geographical features:** fertile west rising to mountainous east. **Main language:** Mandarin Chinese. **Main religion:** atheism official. **Rule:** democracy. **Currency:** New Taiwan dollar. **Primary industries:** manufacturing (electronics, machinery, metal goods, plastic goods), clothing. **Exports:** electronics, machinery, toys, games, steel, clothing, footwear.

TAJ MAHAL

White marble mausoleum on River Jumma, India, featuring a central dome, four minarets and a facade inlaid with semi-precious stones. Built by Shah Jehan to commemorate his wife.

➤ *India*

TANGUY, YVES (1900–55)

French artist. Tanguy was inspired to paint by De Chirico, a precedent of the Surrealists whom Tanguy joined in 1925. His work echoes the dreamlike state that Surrealism aspired to.

➤ *Surrealism*

TANKS

Armoured vehicles powered and steered by tracks, and equipped with weapons systems which include a large long-range gun as well as weapons for short-range combat.

➤ *Armies, Weapons*

TANZANIA

East African coastal country. **Capital:** Dodoma. **Other principal cities:** Zanzibar Town, Dar es Salaam. **Climate:** equatorial monsoon. **Geographical features:** central plateau, lakes Victoria, Tanganyika, Mount Kilimanjaro. **Main languages:** Kiswahili, English. **Main religions:** Islam, Christianity. **Rule:** democracy. **Currency:** Tanzanian shilling. **Primary industries:** food, agriculture, mining, clothing, tobacco, paper, manufacture (electrical goods, vehicles). **Exports:** coffee, cotton, cashews, sisal, tea, tobacco, diamonds, gold.

➤ *Africa*

TAOISM (6TH CENTURY BC)

Chinese religious philosophy established by Lao Zi in the sixth century BC. Tao means 'the way' and harmony is the goal. The holy scriptures are called *Tao Te Ching*. By the fourth century AD Buddhists and Taoists conflicted in China, but later assimilated.

➤ *Buddhism, China*

TAPESTRY

Term applied to material with images, often figurative or narrative, woven into it. Most commonly made from wool or silk, tapestry is divided into two types – *basse klisse* and *haute lisse* (low and high warp). Associated with the Medieval and revived by the Romantics, the most famous styles of tapestry come from the French factories at Aubusson and Gobelin.

➤ *Medieval, Romantic*

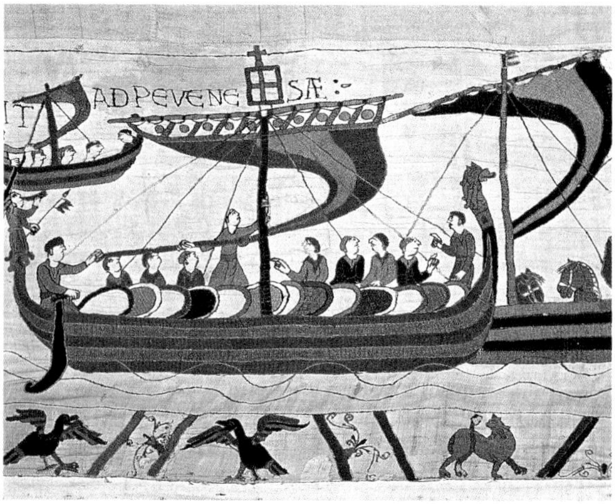

ABOVE: Perhaps the world's most famous tapestry, the Bayeux Tapestry *was made in* c. *1090. The 71-m (231-ft) long 51-cm (20-in) wide tapestry was commissioned by Odo of Bayeux to record the invasion of England in 1066 by his half brother, William the Conqueror.*

TAROT CARDS

Pack of special cards almost exclusively used to tell fortunes. There are four suits: Cups, Swords, Wands and Discs, and Court Cards, such as *Death,* the *Hyrophant* and the *Hanged Man.*

Occult

TATE MODERN

Opened in 2000, the Tate Modern is a converted power station in London, UK, that now displays modern art formally housed in the Tate Gallery, Pimlico, as well as collecting new works by prominent artists.

Art Galleries, Museums

TAXES

Way in which a government raises revenue and manipulates an economy. Income tax started in the UK at 6d (2.5 p) in the pound to finance the Napoleonic Wars.

Economics, Economy

TAXIS

Road vehicles which transport fare-paying passengers to a specified destination. An instrument called the taximeter records the distance travelled and calculates the fare.

Cars

TAXONOMY

Classification of living organisms. The basic unit is the species; one or several similar species form a *genus.* Each species is given a two-part name using the genus and species; e.g. Man is *Homo sapiens. Genera* (plural of *genus*) are grouped into families which in turn form orders, classes, phyla and kingdoms.

TAYLOR, ELIZABETH (b. 1932)

English-born actress. As a child star, Taylor received her highest praise during the 1950s and 60s for films such as *A Place in the Sun* (1951) and *Butterfield 8* (1960).

Films

TCHAIKOVSKY, PIOTR ILYICH (1840–93)

Russian composer. Tchaikovsky trained at the St Petersburg Conservatory before teaching at the Moscow Conservatory. Today Tchaikovsky is one of the most popular classical composers and works such as the ballet *Swan Lake,* his *Romeo and Juliet* or the *1812 Overture* are essential pieces for any classical music collection. Tchaikovsky's music is Romantic in style: emotionally charged, dramatically sweeping and often pervaded by a melancholic feel (achieved through a dominance of minor keys). This melancholy reflects Tchaikovsky's own personal emotions; plagued by depression (and allegedly a homosexual scandal) Tchaikovsky committed suicide.

Ballet, Romantic

TEA

Evergreen shrub grown commercially for its leaves, which are dried and infused to produce the beverage of the same name. Tea has been drunk in China for over four thousand years and arrived in Europe in the early seventeenth century. Tea is grown on plantations in Sri Lanka, India, South America and Indonesia.

India, Plantations

TELEGRAPHY

Means of communication which uses coded electrical signals. The signals can be sent using telegraph wires, by land-line, submarine cables or radio.

TELEPHONES

Instruments designed to allow two-way voice or data communication over a distance. The features common to all telephones are a microphone, an earpiece and a keypad or dial to enter numbers. Signals may be sent and received via some combination of copper wire, optical fibre cable, microwave transmitter and satellite link. The telephone was invented by Alexander Graham Bell in 1876.

Alexander Graham Bell

TELESCOPES

Instruments for collecting and focusing light to make an object appear closer. Objects which are otherwise too faint to see can be made visible. The first telescope was invented by a Dutchman named Hans Lippershay in 1608 and his design was developed by Galileo Galilei.

TELEVISION

Reproduction of visual images over a distance, via microwave transmitter and land-line. The camera produces an electrical signal which is encoded in a broadcast radio wave. The receiving aerial collects the radio wave from which the picture signal can be decoded and displayed using a beam of electrons moving across a screen. John Logie Baird (1888–1946) is credited with inventing the television, which he first demonstrated in 1926.

»» ***Media***

TEMPERATURE

Measure of the heat of an object and the degree to which it transfers or receives heat from other objects. Temperature scales ensure consistent measurement e.g. Kelvin, Fahrenheit and Celsius.

TEMPLE, SHIRLEY (b. 1928)

Child movie-star. Temple's many starring roles as a cute, ringletted child during the Depression of the 1930s inspired a multitude of copycats. Temple has since turned to politics.

»» ***Depression, Films***

TENNIS (1873)

Ball and racket game invented around 1873 by Major Walter Wingfield, and first played at Christmas in Nantclywyn, Wales. Correctly called lawn tennis, to differentiate it from real tennis, it was originally called *Sphairistike.* It is now a global sport for both amateurs and professionals. Major competitions include Wimbledon, the US Open and the Davis Cup.

»» ***Real Tennis***

TERRORISM

Action intended to produce political or diplomatic changes through violent acts against innocent non-combatants. Devised to create terror, terrorist acts are indiscriminate in location and victims, and usually involve explosive devices hidden in public places. Terrorism is operated by individuals, secret groups or sometimes by nations, and absorbs vast amounts of defensive security effort.

TEXTILES

Materials made by weaving. Natural fibres from animal sources such as wool, or plants, like cotton, are now supplemented by synthetics such as polyester.

»» ***Tapestry***

THAILAND

South-east Asian country. **Capital:** Bangkok. **Other principal cities:** Chiangmai, Nakhon Sawan. **Climate:** tropical monsoon. **Geographical features:** mountainous, heavily-forested. **Main languages:** Thai, Chinese. **Main religion:** Buddhist. **Rule:** constitutional monarchy. **Currency:** baht. **Primary industries:** manufacturing (electrical, electronics, furniture, vehicles), petroleum refining, agriculture, textiles, tobacco, plastics, tourism. **Exports:** clothing, food, electronic goods, sugar, fish, machinery.

»» ***Asia***

CENTRE LEFT: A young woman dressed in traditional costume for a Poi Sang Long novice ordination in Thailand.

THEATRE

Theatre originated in western civilization in sixth century Greece. Greek theatre evolved from ceremonial rituals (for the worship of Dionysus) gradually becoming more secular. Its 'actors' were masked choruses who performed in buildings specifically designed for the purpose; the first theatres. The first recorded actor was Thespis (hence the term Thespian), who developed dialogue within the plays, moving away from the dominance of the chorus.

During the flowering of theatres that occurred in the Renaissance, theatre as an art drew closer to the form we now know with actors performing from a stage, more elaborate sets and an increased use of music.

➠ ***Drama Forms, Ancient Greece, Plays, Playwrights, Renaissance***

THIRD WORLD

Blanket term for the developing world, distinguished from the West (Europe, North America, Australasia), and the developed Communist or former Communist countries. The unit of measurement is per capita income, calculated by dividing the gross national product by the population.

Most Third World countries are in Asia, Africa and South America, typically with subsistence economies, minimal industrial development, high death rates and high levels of disease, natural disasters, national debt. Political instability and war frequently worsen debt and disorder.

THIRTY YEARS' WAR (1618–48)

European war fought by Catholic and Protestant German states for control of Germany. Beginning with Bohemian resistance to Austrian Habsburg rule, Denmark and Sweden were drawn in to support Protestant states. France entered to attack Austria's Spanish allies. Protracted fighting and use of mercenaries caused widespread devastation of Germany. The Treaty of Westphalia (1648) allocated territory to France and Sweden, and left the emperor with nominal control.

THOREAU, HENRY DAVID (1817–62)

American writer, poet and transcendentalist (along with his friend Emerson), famous for his book *Walden* (1854). Thoreau also advocated passive resistance with his inspiring essay *Civil Disobedience* (1849).

➠ ***Ralph Waldo Emerson***

TIANANMEN SQUARE (1989)

'Square of Heavenly Peace' in Beijing, China, notorious for the 1989 suppression by troops of anti-government protests, killing hundreds of demonstrators. At 100 acres (40.5 hectares), the Square is the largest public space in the world, laid out in its present form in 1958, and is surrounded by national monuments and museums.

➠ ***China***

TIDES

Cyclical rise and fall of the sea level caused by the gravitational force of the Moon, and to a lesser extent the Sun, on the Earth.

➠ ***Moon, Oceans, Seas***

TIGER

Largest member of the big cat family, indigenous to south and central Asia. Maximum size is about 3.6 m (12 ft). Now under severe threat from destruction of its natural habitat.

➠ ***Cats, Endangered Species***

TIMBER

Wood prepared for use in construction. Hardwoods such as oak and ash are more valuable and used for more demanding situations: softwoods like pine generally have high-volume uses.

TIME

Continuous passage of existence in which events pass from the future, to the present and eventually to the past. Historically time has been measured using the movements of the Earth, Sun and Moon as main reference points. Radiation patterns of the element Caesium are used in a more accurate modern method.

➠ ***Calendars, Geological Time***

TITANIC (1912)

White Star liner which sank on her maiden voyage in April 1912 after colliding with an iceberg, with the loss of 1,490 passengers and crew.

TOBACCO

Plant, grown commercially for its large leaves. These are dried to produce a substance of the same name that is used in cigars and cigarettes. Tobacco is native to South America and grows in warm wet climates. It contains an addictive element, nicotine, and is a major cause of cancer.

Drugs

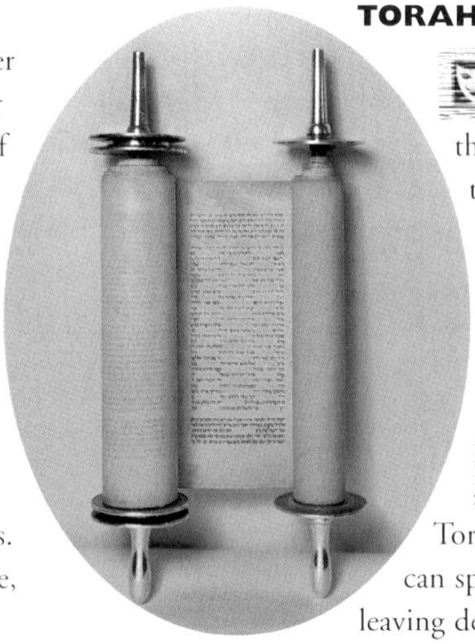

TORAH

The first five books of the Old Testament, the Pentateuch, are the holy scrolls of Judaism, ascribed to Moses. Each synagogue holds a handwritten Hebrew copy.

Bible, Judaism, Synagogues

TORNADOES

Tall funnels of violently spiralling wind, also known as 'twisters'. Tornadoes form below thunderstorms and can spiral at speeds of 400 kph (250 mph), leaving devastation in their path.

Hurricanes, Wind

TOLSTOY, COUNT LEO (1828–1910)

Russian novelist and philosopher. Tolstoy was one of the literary giants of our time and his two epic novels *War and Peace* (1865–69) and *Anna Karenina* (1875–77) have become hallmarks of literature. Tolstoy wrote during a turbulent time in Russian history which is reflected in his profound, brilliantly written, morally aware novels. Serving in the Russian army during the Crimean War, Tolstoy later became a pacifist and rejected the domineering religion of Russia.

Crimean War, Russian Empire

TOMBS

Graves and burial mounds are an important source of archeological and historical material, often yielding valuable evidence of art, customs and culture. One of the most famous tombs is that of the Egyptian pharaoh Tutankhamen, rediscovered in 1922 and supposedly holding a curse on those who disturb it.

TOOLS

Artificial means of making a task possible or easier. A tool can be a physical object like a sewing needle, or an abstract entity such as a piece of computer software. The design and use of tools is a feature of human behaviour which distinguishes us from nearly all other animals.

TOURISM

Term originally coined in the eighteenth century, referring to the Grand Tour of Europe undertaken by the wealthy. Now a multi-billion pound global industry. In many countries it is the biggest income-generating activity, and even in the UK accounts for around 4% of the gross domestic product.

Holidays

TOYS

Articles used for pure amusement, usually, though not always by children. They have been found buried in Egyptian tombs more than 3,000 years old. In earlier times toys were simple and often made of wood; today, in the electronic generation many toys are interactive.

TRACEY, SPENCER (1900–67)

US actor. Tracey was romantically linked with co-star Katharine Hepburn. Exemplified American ideals with his unpretentious sincerity in films such as *Woman of the Year* (1942) and *Inherit the Wind* (1960).

➜ ***Katharine Hepburn***

TRAINS

Method of transport consisting of a powered vehicle, the locomotive, pulling a number of undriven vehicles. Although there are road trains used in some parts of the world, trains normally have steel flanged wheels, which run on steel rails. There is sufficient friction between wheel and rail for traction provided the gradient is gentle. Train locomotives were originally powered by steam, but have lately been replaced by diesel-engined and electric locomotives.

➜ ***Railways, Steam Power, Steam Trains, George Stephenson***

TREATY OF VERSAILLES (1919)

Treaty signed 28 June 1919, between Germany and the Allies ending World War I and setting up the League of Nations. Germany handed over territory to western and eastern neighbours, and was ordered to pay reparations. Strict controls were placed on German rearmament. The terms provoked resentment in Germany and contributed to the rise of Nazism.

➜ ***Nazism, World War I***

TREES

Long-living plants with woody stems (trunk) and root systems. There are no obvious differences between a shrub and a tree except height. A tree, at full height, is usually defined as one over 6 m (20 ft). Flowering trees (*angiosperms*) are usually deciduous in temperate countries such as the United Kingdom. This means that they have a period of rest over the winter and lose their leaves e.g. oak, apple, beech. In tropical countries angiosperms are normally evergreen. Coniferous trees are non-flowering (*gymnosperms*), evergreen and are hardy enough to withstand tough weather conditions e.g. pine. Many trees contained in one area are collectively termed a forest.

➜ ***Forests, Plants, Rainforests, Sequoia***

ABOVE: The 'Hotel Strip' alongside Condesa Beach, Acapulco, Mexico. As incomes in the West have increased and travel times have been reduced, tourists seek increasingly exotic and luxurious resorts for holidays.

TREVITHICK, RICHARD (1771–1833)

British engineer. Trevithick built a new double-acting steam engine which was more powerful and efficient than that designed by James Watt. This engine was used in mines, mills and ironworks. Trevithick also produced the first steam-powered passenger vehicle, and the first steam-powered railway locomotive.

➜ ***Steam Power, Steam Trains, James Watt***

TRINIDAD AND TOBAGO

Caribbean islands off Venezuala. **Capital:** Port-of-Spain. **Other principal cities:** San Fernando, Scarborough. **Climate:** tropical. **Geographical features:** rainforests, coastal swamps. **Main language:** English. **Main religions:** Christianity, Hinduism, Islam. **Rule:** democratic republic. **Currency:** Trinidad and Tobago dollar. **Primary industries:** petroleum, agriculture. **Exports:** petroleum, asphalt, sugar, cocoa, coffee, fruit, chemicals, steel.

TROJAN HORSE

Hollow wooden horse. Devised by Odysseus of Ithaca to end the legendary ten-year siege of Troy, by concealing troops who would open the city gates at night and let the Greeks in.

➜ ***Ancient Greece, Greek Gods and Mythology***

TROTSKY, LEON (1879–1940)

Russian revolutionary politician. Trotsky's political activities led to two periods of exile in Siberia. During World War I he worked abroad. He returned to Russia after the February 1917 Revolution and joined the Bolsheviks, helping Lenin to organize the October Revolution. His belief that revolutions should be started in the west marginalized him, and he was expelled in 1929. He was assassinated in Mexico.

➜ ***Vladimir Ilyich Lenin, Russian Revolution, World War II***

TRUCKS

Vehicles mainly used for transport of raw materials, either open-topped railway wagons, or large motor vehicles.

➧ *Cars*

TSARS

Title (derived from Caesar) borne by Russian monarchs from 1547 in the reign of Ivan the Terrible. The queen consort was called the Tsarina and the heir to the throne the Tsarevich. The title was also adopted in Bulgaria by Ferdinand III in 1908 and retained by Boris III (1918–43) and Simeon II (1943–46).

➧ ***Russian Royalty***

TSUNAMI

Massive waves which are often destructive. Tsunamis are caused by a violent occurrence in the sea or ocean e.g. earthquake, landslide or volcanic eruption.

➧ ***Earthquakes, Volcanoes***

TUDORS

English dynasty which traced its descent from the Welsh nobleman, Owen Tudor who married Catherine of Valois, widow of Henry V, its founder was their grandson Henry Bolingbroke, born at Pembroke Castle in 1457. He supported the Lancastrian faction in the Wars of the Roses, defeating Richard III at Bosworth to become Henry VII. He cemented an alliance with Spain, marrying his elder son Arthur to Catherine of Aragon. Soon after his accession, his younger son, Henry VIII, married his brother's widow, by whom he had a daughter Mary (1553–58). By his second wife Anne Boleyn he had a daughter Elizabeth (1558–1603), but his third wife, Jane Seymour, presented him with a son, the future Edward VI (1547–53) who died young and was succeeded by his half sisters in turn. Mary married Philip II of Spain and sought to reverse the English Reformation but died childless. Elizabeth evaded the various foreign princes who sought her hand in marriage and allied herself with Protestant rulers against Spain. The dynasty ended when the crown passed to the son of her cousin and rival Mary Queen of Scots.

➧ *Stuarts*

TUNISIA

North African coastal country. **Capital:** Tunis. **Other principal cities:** Sfax, Sousse. **Climate:** Mediterranean, desert. **Geographical features:** fertile north and coastal plain to arid interior. **Main languages:** Arabic, French. **Main religion:** Islam. **Rule:** democratic republic. **Currency:** Tunisian dinar. **Primary industries:** petroleum, agriculture, light manufacturing, tourism. **Exports:** oil, phosphates, chemicals, fruit, clothing, shoes, olive oil, dates.

➧ ***Africa***

TUNNELS

Passage carrying roads or railways, to provide a link through a mountain, under rivers or other bodies of water, or underground. Tunnels are very costly to construct and require considerable time, so are only economically viable if there are great benefits to the transport system. The most famous tunnel built recently was the Channel Tunnel, linking England with France.

➧ ***Channel Tunnel***

TURIN SHROUD

Controversial piece of linen with an image of a body on it, allegedly Jesus. Independent tests dated the material to between 1260 and 1390. Presently kept in Turin Cathedral.

➧ ***Christianity***

TURKEY

Country of Asia Minor and south-east Europe. **Capital:** Ankara. **Other principal cities:** Adana, Istanbul, Izmir. **Climate:** Mediterranean temperate, interior more extreme. **Geographical features:** central plateau, mountains, islands, rocky west coast, Black Sea shores. **Main language:** Turkish. **Main religion:** Islam. **Rule:** democratic republic. **Currency:** Turkish lira. **Primary industries:** petroleum, coal, chemicals, steel, food-processing, agriculture, tourism. **Exports:** clothing, cereals, tea, figs, nuts, petroleum, tobacco, leather.

Turkey is primarily an agricultural country, with an extensive variety of terrain. Industrialization has increased since World War II, with the government controlling most larger concerns. Tourism has expanded at a substantial rate, particularly on the west and south coasts.

TURNER, JOSEPH MALLORD WILLIAM (1775–1851)

British painter, associated with Romanticism. Turner is popularly viewed as the greatest English landscape painter. He refused to hide his humble background and retained both his cockney accent and manners, despite his aristocratic friends and patronage. He exhibited at the Royal Academy at the precocious age of 15 before touring North Wales, Scotland and Switzerland, making numerous sketches and watercolours of landscapes. After 1819 he made several other such tours, visiting Italy repeatedly, particularly Venice which deeply inspired the artist. Turner's late paintings are blurred, with whirls of seeping colours and in this aspect they anticipate the Impressionist movement, especially Monet.

Claude Monet, Romantic

TUTANKHAMEN

Egyptian pharaoh of the XVIII Dynasty. Tutankhamen reigned 1361–52 BC. He came to the throne at the age of 12 and would have been completely forgotten but for the extraordinary richness of his tomb at Thebes, excavated by Lord Carnarvon and Howard Carter in 1922. The treasures, including his gold funerary mask, are now preserved in the Cairo Museum.

Ancient Egypt

TUTU, RT REV. DESMOND MPILO (b. 1931)

Archbishop of Cape Town 1981–96, and general secretary of the South African Council of Churches 1979–84. Awarded the Nobel Peace Prize (1984) for his struggle against apartheid.

Apartheid, Nobel Prize

TWENTIETH-CENTURY FOX

One of the major Hollywood film studios. Established in 1935 from the Fox Film Corporation which was founded by William Fox in 1915. Produced films such as *Star Wars.*

Films, **Star Wars**

TYPOGRAPHY

Term that covers both the design of printed texts (e.g. typeface such as *Cursive* or *Roman*) and printing as an art form, such as the lithographs of Goya.

Francisco Goya, Printing, Publishing

RIGHT: The spectacular gold inner funerary mask of the Egyptian child-king, Tutankhamen.

UFOs

Unidentified Flying Objects. Most reports of sightings in the sky prove to be hoaxes, aircraft or natural phenomena, others remain unidentified due to a lack of evidence.

UGANDA

Land-locked central African country. **Capital:** Kampala. **Other principal cities:** Jinja, Mbale, Entebbe. **Climate:** equatorial, moderated by altitude. **Geographical features:** plateau, and Lake Victoria shoreline. **Main language:** English. **Main religions:** Christianity, animist. **Rule:** democratic republic. **Currency:** Uganda new shilling. **Primary industries:** agriculture (largely self-sufficient), mining. **Exports:** coffee, cotton, tea, copper.

➜ ***Africa***

UKIYO-E

Meaning 'pictures of the floating world'. *Ukiyo-e* are Japanese colour prints made with woodblocks. Popular in the seventeeth to nineteenth century, *Ukiyo-e* showed scenes of Tokyo, of Geishas, legends and landscapes.

➜ ***Katsushika Hokusai***

UKRAINE

Eastern European country. **Capital:** Kiev. **Other principal cities:** Kharkov, Donetsk, Dnepropetrovsk. **Climate:** Mediterranean Black Sea coast, greater extremes inland. **Geographical features:** flat fertile plains, mineral resources. **Main language:** Ukrainian. **Main religion:** Ukrainian Orthodox. **Rule:** democracy. **Currency:** hryvna. **Primary industries:** agriculture, engineering, manufacturing, petroleum, chemicals. **Exports:** grain, energy, coal, oil, minerals, transport equipment.

➜ ***Europe***

RIGHT: Russian Cossacks in uniform. The mounted soldier is holding a knout, a whip used to inflict punishment in Imperial Russia at the beginning of the twentieth century.

UNDERGROUND RAIL SYSTEM

Many major cities have rail systems which run in tunnels underground, at least in part. Their main virtue is that they can operate independently of surface transport and reduce congestion. The underground system in London was the first to operate, and is still the largest in the world.

➜ ***Railways***

UNIFORMS

Style of dress deigned to show that the wearer is a member of a larger group. Usually associated with the military and other services. It is a criminal offence to wear a political uniform on the streets of the UK.

UNITED ARAB EMIRATES

Persian Gulf state. **Capital:** Abu Dhabi. **Other principal cities:** Sharjah, Dubai. **Climate:** hot and dry. **Geographical features:** desert. **Main language:** Arabic. **Main religion:** Islam. **Rule:** absolute monarchy. **Currency:** UAE dirham. **Primary industries:** petroleum, fishing, tourism. **Agriculture:** mostly prevented by terrain. **Exports:** oil, petroleum products, natural gas, dates, fish.

UNITED KINGDOM

North-west European island country, consisting of England, Wales, Scotland and Northern Ireland. **Capital:** London. **Other principal cities:** Birmingham, Manchester, Liverpool, Edinburgh, Glasgow, Belfast. **Climate:** mild with variable extremes. **Geographical features:** extremely varied with extensive coastline, southern rolling landscape, western and northern hills and mountains. Mostly extremely fertile, well-watered and drained. **Main language:** English. **Main religion:** Christian denominations. **Rule:** constitutional monarchy. **Currency:** pound sterling. **Primary industries:** engineering, manufacturing (vehicles, ships, electrical goods, electronics, aircraft), petroleum, telecommunications, chemicals, financial and service businesses, tourism, agriculture. **Exports:** machinery, computers, cars, lorries, communications equipment, chemicals, petroleum products, foods.

The United Kingdom exhibits its history in its geographical combination of several nations under one crown, and the origins if its peoples in waves of immigration from across Europe and latterly the nation's former possessions across the world. The United Kingdom now has significant ethnic groups drawn from central and eastern Europe, Africa, the Indian subcontinent, the Far East and the West Indies.

The United Kingdom's economy has traditionally depended on trading, with maritime transport of raw materials and finished products both in and out playing a vital role. The high population density and large number of industrialized towns and regions provides an extensive workforce.

However, there has been a significant decline in heavy industry in recent years, mainly at the expense of traditionally industrialized areas of the north and west. Service and financial industries in the south have expanded. Agriculture has experienced a severe decline in profitability, despite intensive farming methods and large areas of farmable land.

➡ ***British Empire, Kings of England, Queens of England***

UNITED NATIONS (1945)

Established 1945 with headquarters in New York as a replacement for the League of Nations. Most of the world's states are members, contributing manpower and funds to the enforcement of resolutions by the Security Council in peacekeeping, and to the various agencies of the UN such as the World Health Organisation (WHO) and the UN Educational, Scientific and Cultural Organisation (UNESCO).

➡ ***League of Nations***

UNITED STATES OF AMERICA

North American nation between Canada and Mexico. **Capital:** Washington DC. **Other principal cities:** Atlanta, Boston, Chicago, Dallas-Fort Worth, Denver, New York, Seattle, San Francisco, Los Angeles. **Climate:** extremes of cold and hot in western highlands, north and north-east; temperate and wet north-west, hot in the southern mid-west and south-west; tropical in the south.

Geographical features: the most varied national terrain in the world from mountains, gorges and volcanoes, vast grassy plains, desert, swamps and sandy beaches. **Main languages:** English, Spanish. **Main religion:** Christian denominations. **Rule:** federal democratic republic. **Currency:** US dollar. **Primary industries:** mining, manufacturing, financial services, agriculture, entertainment, tourism. **Exports:** machinery, vehicles, military equipment and weaponry, electronic goods, agricultural products.

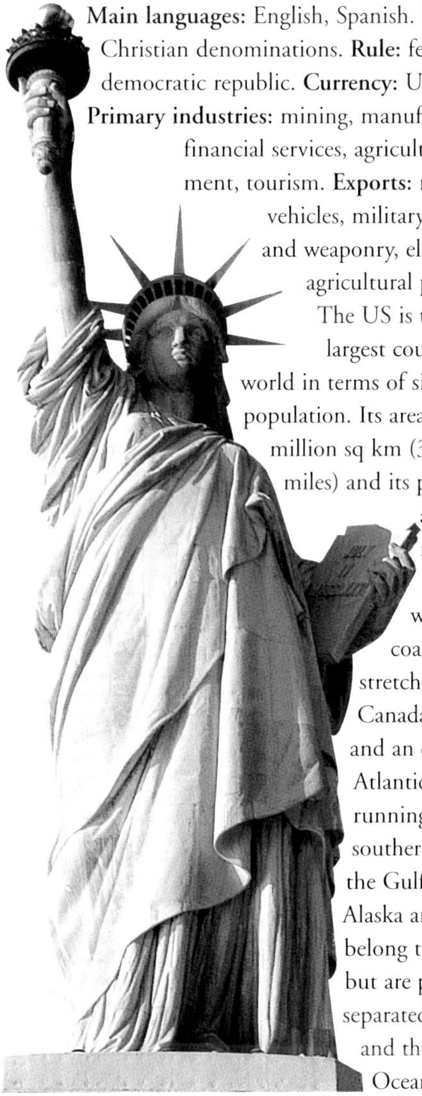

The US is the fourth largest country in the world in terms of size and population. Its area is 9.37 million sq km (3.62 million sq miles) and its population about 270 million. The nation has a western Pacific coastline stretching from Canada to Mexico, and an eastern Atlantic coastline running round to a southern coastline in the Gulf of Mexico. Alaska and Hawaii also belong to the USA, but are physically separated by Canada, and the Pacific Ocean respectively.

The US's vast natural resources, and a population drawn from all parts of the world, many of whom have been pioneers in every respect, make it the wealthiest nation in the world. Some of its individual states, e.g. California, are substantially wealthier than most other countries. Regional differences remain, however, and the South is still the poorest part of the US with real poverty a significant social and political issue.

No part of the economy has escaped development. Agriculture is among the most intensive in the world with yields outstripping those of comparable fertility, such as the Ukraine. Mineral and fuel resources are exploited wherever they are available, supporting the US's unparalleled level of industrial development and relative self-sufficiency.

However, US demands per capita of energy are so great that the nation is dependent on imported oil. US energy consumption is an increasing international issue. Manufacturing is widespread, with all types of goods being produced, but is particularly concentrated in the north around the Great Lakes and the east. Tourism is extremely popular, both with Americans themselves and an increasing number of foreign visitors.

The US population is exceptionally diverse. The largest proportion is white, descended mainly from European settlers arriving here from the seventeenth to mid-twentieth centuries, with a peak during the nineteenth and early twentieth. Black, or Afro-Americans, are descended largely from the black slave population brought to the US from the seventeenth century up to the Civil War period of 1861–65. In more recent years, peoples of Asian and Spanish origin have entered the US in large numbers, predominantly in the western and eastern seaboards.

However, the US population also contains significant numbers of other ethnic groups, of which the most important are the indigenous peoples of Hawaii, Alaska (the Inuit), and North America (Native Americans).

Ethnic diversity and identity is proudly proclaimed and sustained across the US, with many places preserving traditional customs and languages which have all but vanished in their places of origin. This is particularly true of Jewish communities representing places annihilated in the Holocaust. However, great uniformity has also been created. English and Spanish are the two main languages spoken and loyalty to the American flag is widespread.

Settlement of the USA area began with immigration across the Bering Strait land bridge several tens of thousands of years ago. European settlement began, falteringly, with the Viking settlement of Newfoundland (Canada) in *c.* AD 1000. The arrival of Christopher Columbus in 1492 began the opening up of North America but significant European immigration did not begin until the seventeenth century.

Settlement was largely confined to the thirteen colonies of the north-east (New England). The American Revolution (1775–83) resulted in the creation of the United States of America, then restricted to a very small part of the present area. Gradual admission of territories, organized into new states, encroached further and further west throughout the nineteenth century. Oklahoma, for example, was not admitted until 1907. Hawaii and Alaska were added in 1959.

The only serious threat to the physical integrity of the US was the Civil War, or 'War between the States', of 1861–65. The Southern States broke away from the Union, fearing that as slave states they would be in a minority in the US government system. Their consummate defeat ended secession and allowed the US to develop further as a cohesive whole. However, it was World War I which saw the arrival of the US as a major world power. Unlike that of the European nations, US industry benefited from the needs of war materiel. The nation's subsequent intervention in World War II was decisive in ending the territorial ambitions and totalitarianism of Germany, Italy and Japan.

US culture has proved the most pervasive social influence in world history and geography. US domination of world media and entertainment is now so unchallenged that its effects can be felt in every corner of the globe, helped by the popularity of US icons of entertainment or commercial products.

➧ ***American Revolution, American Civil War, Presidents***

UNIVERSE

The totality of everything that exists. There is compelling evidence that the Universe had a beginning, the 'Big Bang', that it is around 15 billion years old, and that it is expanding. What is not yet clear is whether or not it has an infinite future: that is, whether the expansion will continue, or whether it will eventually stop expanding and begin to contract down to a single point – the 'Big Crunch'.

The crucial factor deciding which scenario is correct depends on the density of the Universe. And the jury is still out on this question, although there are reasons to prefer an infinite Universe with an infinite future.

TOP RIGHT: The courtyard and fountain of one of England most prestigious academic establishments, Trinity College, Cambridge University.
RIGHT: Uranus was discovered in 1781 by William Herschel.

UNIVERSITIES

Places of further learning after secondary education has been completed. The first one was established in Salerno, Italy in the ninth century. The UK's oldest are Cambridge and Oxford, both dating from the twelfth century. Harvard in the USA was founded in 1636. The UK's Open University was established in 1969.

➧ ***Education, Schools***

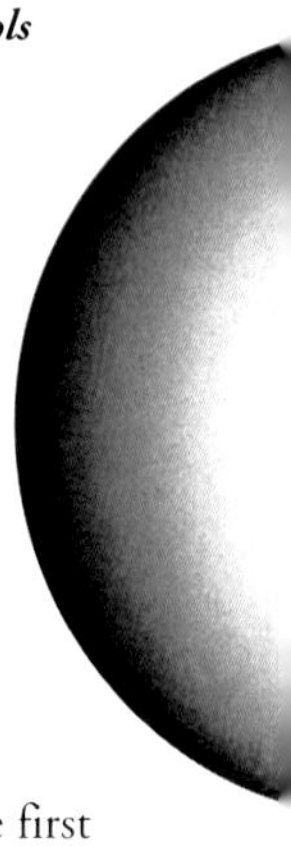

URANUS

Seventh major planet, discovered by William Herschel in 1781. It takes 84 years to complete one orbit. Its diameter is about four times the Earth's, and its green colour is due to methane in the atmosphere. The spin axis has an extreme tilt, almost in the plane of the orbit.

➧ ***Planets, Solar System, Sun***

URBANIZATION

Process of town and city development. The first great example of this was Rome, which in its heyday supported a population of over one million. However it is largely a modern phenomena, starting with the Industrial Revolution. At a stroke this provided both well-paid jobs in urban areas, and the technology to provide food and services to the people doing them.

➧ ***Cities, Industrial Revolution***

URUGUAY

South American Atlantic country. **Capital:** Montevideo. **Other principal cities:** Salto, Payasandú. **Climate:** temperate. **Geographical features:** fertile grassy plains suitable for extensive agriculture. **Main language:** Spanish. **Main religion:** Catholicism. **Rule:** democratic republic. **Currency:** Uruguayan peso. **Primary industries:** agriculture, petroleum refining. **Exports:** beef, hides, leather, wool, leather, textiles, rice.

VACCINATION

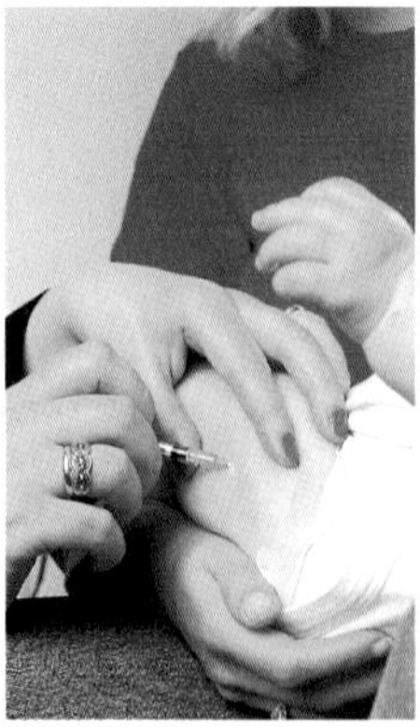

Method of giving immunity or resistance to a disease. A vaccine is prepared using dead or weakened bacteria or viruses, and injected or taken by mouth. Vaccination prepares the body's immune system to fight infection. The first vaccine was made from the cowpox virus, which gave immunity to smallpox.

➡ *Edward Jenner, Smallpox*

VACUUM CLEANER

Device for cleaning surfaces, mainly in the home. Dust and dirt are taken up by a fan-driven flow of air and collected, usually by a filter. Today the most famous vacuum cleaner is the Dyson, taking the fame from the Hoover, a brand name that came to be used as a generic term for the accessory.

VALENTINO, RUDOLPH (1895–1926)

US actor. Star of the silent screen, Valentino inspired a legion of adulating women in 1920s' America. His early death ensured his reputation as a film idol remained intact.

➡ *Films*

VALLEYS

Channels carved out of rock by the erosive force of a river as it flows. A youthful river or stream is likely to produce a v-shaped valley. An older stretch of river or one that is wide and slow-flowing (or a glacier) produces a u-shaped valley. The type of underlying rocks also affects a valley's structure.

➡ *Glaciers, Rivers*

VATICAN

Continuous papal residence since 1377. The Vatican Palace, Rome, includes the Sistine Chapel and St Peter's Basilica. Vatican Councils organize Roman Catholic Church policies. Since 1929 the Vatican City State has been a country in miniature.

➡ *Catholicism, Popes*

VENEZUELA

Most northerly country of South America. **Capital:** Caracas. **Other principal cities:** Barquisimeto, Maracaibo, Valencia. **Climate:** tropical, cooler at altitude. **Geographical features:** southern mountains, high plateaus and plains. **Main language:** Spanish. **Main religion:** Roman Catholicism. **Rule:** federal democratic republic. **Currency:** bolivar. **Primary industries:** mining, petroleum. **Exports:** petroleum, aluminium, bauxite, iron ore, coffee, timber, chemicals.

VENUS

Second major planet from the Sun and similar to Earth in size, but with a very high surface temperature and an atmosphere, mainly carbon dioxide, with nine times the pressure of Earth's. It rotates very slowly east to west once in 243 days – longer than it takes to orbit the Sun.

➡ *Planets, Solar System, Sun*

VERMEER, JAN (1632–75)

Dutch painter. It was not until the 1860s with the resurgence of artistic naturalism that Vermeer gained the acclaim that his prowess deserved. Vermeer created his remarkably realistic images using several techniques, such as *camera obscura* (based upon photographic principles). Vermeer is best known for scenes of everyday domestic life such as *Maidservant Pouring Milk* (*c.* 1658).

VERSAILLES (1669)

French palace. Louis XIV employed Baroque architect Louis Le Vau (1612–70) to design his palace at Versailles from 1669. With the immaculate gardens (by André Le Nôtre) and the sweeping magnificence of the building, Versailles epitomizes French aristocratic grace. However, its mass of gold inlay and staggering cost soon made it the epitome of the careless extravagance of royalty.

➡ *Baroque, French Royalty*

VERTEBRATES

Animals with a backbone, a skull that surrounds a well-developed brain and a skeleton of cartilage or bone. Sometimes referred to as the chordates. Includes fish, amphibians, reptiles, birds and mammals. There are 41,000 species of vertebrates and they mostly represent the larger animals. The group is tiny, however, when compared with the invertebrates.

➡ *Invertebrates*

VESUVIUS, MOUNT

Active volcano on the Bay of Naples, southern Italy. Height 1,277 m (4,190 ft). Vesuvius last erupted in 1943, but the most celebrated eruption was in AD 79 leading to the destruction of the Roman town, Pompeii.

➡ *Pompeii, Volcanoes*

VIDEO

Machine for recording images and sound on plastic tape coated with magnetic material and contained in a cassette. The most popular format is Matsushita's VHS.

VIETNAM

South-east Asian country. Capital: Hanoi. Other principal cities: Ho Chi Minh City (Saigon), Da Nang. Climate: tropical. Geographical features: tropical rainforest, Mekong Delta, mountains. Main language: Vietnamese. Main religions: Taoist, Buddhist, Roman Catholicism. Rule: Communism. Currency: dong. Primary industries: agriculture, mining, rubber. Exports: agricultural produce, livestock, rice, rubber, coal, iron, marine equipment.

➡ *Asia*

VIKINGS

Literally 'bay people' from Scandinavia. The Vikings raped and pillaged the British Isles and the coasts of western Europe from the eighth to the eleventh centuries. They were traders as well as raiders, penetrating the Aegean and Black Seas and even crossing the Atlantic to Greenland, Newfoundland and Maine about AD 1000.

VINES

Climbing plants, native to Asia Minor, grown commercially for their fruit (grapes). Grapes may be eaten fresh or dried (raisins and currants) or fermented to produce wine and vinegar.

➡ *Wine*

VIRUSES

Sub-microscopic agents that infect plants and animals. Viruses often cause disease but are unable to exist outside their host. Viruses have a simple structure; they contain a strand of genetic material (DNA or RNA) inside a protein shell. By releasing the genetic material into its host a virus can instruct the host to replicate it.

➡ *Diseases, Genetics*

VOLCANOES

Vents or fissures in the Earth's crust through which molten rock (magma), hot gases and other fluids escape to the surface of the land or the bottom of the sea. When the magma reaches the surface it is called lava. Volcanoes are commonly found at plate margins where two plates are converging.

➡ *Plate Tectonics*

VOLLEYBALL

Ball game played between two teams of six or two people (beach volleyball). Invented in 1895 by William Morgan in Massachusetts. It is an Olympic sport.

➡ *Olympic Games*

LEFT: The Vietnam War (1957–75) fought between the US and the Vietnamese killed and maimed soldiers and civilians alike. As the horrors of the war were realized around the world. protestors led demonstrations demanding peace.
ABOVE: The Vikings were a sea-faring race and their robust, fierce ships struck fear into the peoples of Europe as they were sighted from the shores.

WAR AND PEACE

Tolstoy's ambitious chronicle of the Napoleonic invasion of Russia and its effects upon one family. Although occasionally maligned for historical prejudice, the novel remains Tolstoy's epic masterpiece.

Napoleonic Wars, Russian Empire, Leo Tolstoy

WARNER BROTHERS

Now one of the dominant Hollywood studios, Warner Brothers Pictures was created by brothers Harry, Albert, Jack and Sam Warner in 1923 and has had phenomenal success ever since.

Films, Twentieth-Century Fox

WARSAW PACT (1955)

Military alliance formed between the USSR and its East European Communist allies, and devised as a response to NATO to enhance diplomatic and military muscle. Forces were to be combined under one command, and Soviet troops could be based in the other states. After the collapse of Communism in Eastern Europe it was disbanded in 1991.

NATO, World War II

WATER

Liquid formed of two hydrogen atoms and one oxygen atom (H_20) that boils at 100°C (212°F) and begins to freeze at 0°C (32°F). Water is colourless, odourless and tasteless. It covers 70% of the Earth's surface and is essential for the survival of every life form on the planet. The human body is 60–70% water.

RIGHT: The spectacular waterfalls, the Victoria Falls, on the Zambezi River, Zimbabwe, Africa.

FAR RIGHT: From humble – although lethal – beginnings where knives, swords and daggers were used in battle, through to the more powerful and accurate longbow, cannons and hand guns, weaponry has developed to include automatic guns, heat-seeking missiles as well as chemical and nuclear deterrents.

WATER POLO

Ball game played by two teams of seven, and played in a swimming pool. Invented in the UK in 1869 it was originally called soccer in water.

Olympic Games, Polo

WATER SKIING

Sport pioneered by Ralph Samuelson of the US in the early 1920s. First World Championships held in 1949, with disciplines for slalom, tricks and jumping.

WATER SPEED RECORDS

Speed records set on and in water. The highest speeds achieved are constantly improving, though are very much slower than comparable records set on land. Donald Campbell was the only man ever to hold both land and water speed records at the same time, in 1964. He was later killed atempting to break his own Water Speed Record at Coniston Water in the English Lake District.

WATERFALLS

Point in the course of a river where water descends vertically, cascading into the pool below (plunge pool). Caused by the erosion of a softer band of rocks below a harder band or the presence of a hard rock bed lying across the river. The world's highest waterfalls are the Angel Falls in Venezuela (978 m/3,209 ft).

WATERGATE (1972)

American political scandal. Agents of the Republican Party were caught breaking into the Watergate building, headquarters of the Democratic

National Committee during the 1972 election. It emerged that the Nixon administration was involved in corrupt use of government money and resources to pursue electoral gain. President Nixon eventually resigned to avoid impeachment.

Presidents

WATT, JAMES (1736–1819)

British engineer who made improvements to the steam engine first devised by Thomas Newcomen. In Watt's engine the used steam was condensed outside the cylinder, greatly increasing the efficiency. He also devised the double-acting engine and compound engine, a governor to control speed, and sun-and-planet gears.

Railways, Steam Power, Steam Trains, George Stephenson

WATTEAU, JEAN-ANTOINE (1684–1721)

French artist. The chief proponent of Rococo art, Watteau began his career as a theatrical costume and set designer in Paris and elements of drama and fantasy later filled his painting. He also made much use of themes from the Italian comedies, such as Pierrot and Harlequin. Greatly inspired by Rubens, Watteau was himself much admired, particularly by Hogarth.

Rococo, Peter Paul Rubens

WAYNE, JOHN (1907–79)

US actor. Best remembered for his roles as tough, macho cowboys, Wayne began his film career in the 1930s. Among his best work are the films *Rio Bravo* (1950) and *The Quiet Man* (1952).

Films

WEAPONS

Hardware of war and terrorism. Weapons range from the personal, e.g. handguns, to nuclear missiles, the tools of intercontinental destruction. In a constant process of technological development, weapons are cripplingly expensive but research also yields advantages for civilians. World War II produced staggering improvements in aviation and metallurgy from which the world population now benefits.

Nuclear Power, World War I, World War II

WEATHER

Prevailing short term meteorological conditions in a certain place. The weather is judged by measuring precipitation, humidity, temperature, visibility, wind and cloud cover. Climate is determined by monitoring weather over a long period of time. The prediction of weather (forecasting) is based on meteorological readings and information gathered from satellites.

Climate, Meteorology

WEAVING

Method of making textiles from fibres on a loom. A set of parallel threads, the warp, is interlaced with threads at right angles, the weft.

WELLES, ORSON (1915–85)

Welles' career was dominated by his legendary film *Citizen Kane* (1941). He co-wrote, directed and starred in the film that is held by some as the most formative film ever made.

➡ ***Films***

WEST, MAE (1892–1980)

US actess. Star of less than a dozen films, Mae West still left an indelible impression. Her roles, (reflections of her caricatured self), were all overtly sexual, sharp-witted women.

➡ ***Films***

WESTERN SAMOA

South Pacific island group in Polynesia. **Capital:** Apia. **Climate:** tropical. **Geographical features:** volcanic islands featuring mountains, forest, coral reefs. **Main languages:** English, Samoan. **Main religions:** Congregationalist, Roman Catholicism. **Rule:** democracy. **Currency:** tala, Samoan dollar. **Primary industries:** agriculture. **Exports:** coconut oil and cream, taro, copra, cocoa, fruit juice, timber, cigarettes.

WESTERN WALL

Also called the Wailing Wall, it is the remaining wall of Solomon's Temple. An on-site fax machine allows the distant faithful to send prayers to the pilgrimage site.

➡ ***Jerusalem, Judaism***

WHALES

Large ocean-living mammals with streamlined bodies and reduced limbs. Porpoises and dolphins belong to the same group (cetaceans). Whales have thick layers of fat, large brains and are capable of complex communication.

➡ ***Mammals***

ABOVE: Orthodox Jewish men leave the Western Wall, Jerusalem.

FAR RIGHT: The Prince of Wales, next in line to inherit the throne of England.

WHEELS

Wheeled transport has existed since 3000 BC, and the spoked wheel since around 2000 BC. Two developments led to the transport system now in existence: the pneumatic tyre, which is fitted to the vast majority of road vehicles, and the discovery that steel wheels could run satisfactorily on steel rails.

WHITEHALL

Taking its name from the former palace, Whitehall is the street that runs between Trafalgar square and Parliament and has become the term used to denote English government bureaucracy.

WHITE HOUSE

Personal residence of the US President in Washington DC, address No. 1 Pennsylvania Avenue. Built 1792–99, it was burnt by the British in 1814 and painted white to conceal the damage.

➡ ***Presidents***

WHITTINGTON, RICHARD 'DICK' (c. 1358–1423)

In legend Whittington came to London as a poor boy in search of his fortune. He rose to become a cloth merchant and held served terms as Lord Mayor of London.

WILDE, OSCAR (1856–1900)

Aesthetic writer and witticist, immortalized through his publicly traumatic personal life. Wilde wrote in a variety of genres: children's tales in the style of

Hans Christian Andersen (1888) and his novel *The Picture of Dorian Grey* (1891). Wilde is equally remembered for his poetry and drama, with comedies such as *The Importance of being Ernest* (1895).

➠ ***Literary Genres***

WILDEBEEST

Species of African antelope also known as gnu. Wildebeest are grazing animals that gather in herds. The wildebeest of the Serengeti migrate northwards to greener grasslands every summer.

➠ ***Migration***

WILLIAM THE CONQUEROR (1027–1089)

Duke of Normandy, and William I of England from 1066. William pursued his claim to the English throne by invading in 1066 defeating and killing Harold of England at the Battle of Hastings. This, and his subsequent conquest of England led to his title 'the Conqueror', and he remains the last successful invader of the British Isles.

➠ ***Normans***

WIND

Current of air, generally moving laterally and usually with some force. Wind usually moves from areas of high atmospheric pressure to areas of low pressure.

➠ ***Hurricanes, Tornadoes***

WIND POWER

Harnessing the force of the wind to drive a propellor and generate electricity. Installations have low maintenance and are nonpolluting in action, but expensive to set up.

➠ ***Mills***

WINDSOR CASTLE

One of the chief residences of the British royal family, it was built by William the Conqueror and enlarged by Edward III (1344) as headquarters of the Order of the Garter.

➠ ***William the Conqueror, Kings of England, Queens of England***

WINDSORS

The British royal family abandoned its German name of Saxe-Coburg-Gotha in 1917, when the First World War was at its height and raids by Gotha bombers on England caused intense embarrassment. George V decreed that all members of his family would take as their surname Windsor, seat of the castle associated with monarchs since 1066. George V, the first of this dynasty, reigned from 1910 to 1936. His eldest son David (1894–1972) took the regnal title of Edward VIII but his refusal to give up an American divorcee, Wallis Warfield Simpson, led to his abdication ten months later and the assumption of the title of Duke of Windsor. His brother Albert, Duke of York, became George VI (1936–52) and, assisted by his wife (now the Queen Mother) restored public confidence in the monarchy. His elder daughter Elizabeth married Philip Mountbatten, formerly Prince of Greece, and became queen in 1952. Their eldest son Charles became Prince of Wales in 1969. By his late wife Diana, Princess of Wales, he has two sons, Prince William of Wales (b. 1982) and Prince Harry (b. 1984).

➠ ***Kings of England, Queens of England***

WINE

Alcoholic beverage from the fermented juice of the grape, it was being produced in Egypt by 2400 BC and in China by 2000 BC. It is believed to stem from a single species from the shores of the Caspian, whence it spread throughout the world.

WINTER SPORTS

General term describing sports involving either snow or ice. These include skiing, skating, bob sleigh and so on. They are understandably far more popular in countries whose climates accommodate these activities. A separate Olympic Games was instituted for these sports in 1924, and is held every four years.

➡ ***Athletics, Curling, Olympic Games, Running, Skating, Skiing***

WITCHES

Witches and wizards can be white (beneficial) or black (occult) and are thought to have animal familiars. Despite utilizing their expert knowledge of herbal medicine, society has feared witches' supernatural powers. It has also persecuted them: tried them (most significantly the Salem Witch Trials) and executed them (last death sentence in Europe in 1782).

➡ ***Occult***

WOMBAT

Burrowing marsupials, up to 1 m (3.3 ft) long, native to Australia and Tasmania. Wombats are herbivorous (plant-eaters) with powerful bodies and large heads suited to burrowing underground dens.

➡ ***Marsupials***

WOMEN'S EMANCIPATION

Series of events which began to put women on an equal legal and social footing as men, typified by the Suffragette movement and the right to vote. This campaign was launched in 1905 and was lead by Emmeline Pankhurst and her two daughters. In 1918 women were finally granted limited suffrage and this was extended to all women over 21 in 1928.

➡ ***Suffrage, Emmeline Pankhurst***

WOODSTOCK FESTIVAL (1969)

American musical festival first held in 1969 with reportedly half a million people attending and legendary performances from 1960s' musicians, such as Jimi Hendrix and The Who.

WOODWIND INSTRUMENTS

Not a literal meaning, woodwind refers to a group of orchestral instruments and covers the families of flute, bassoon, clarinet and oboe. The sound is created by the player's outbreath into either a reed in the case of oboe, clarinet and bassoon or across a mouth hole in the case of flutes.

➡ ***Brass Instruments, Orchestra, Percussion Instruments, String Instruments***

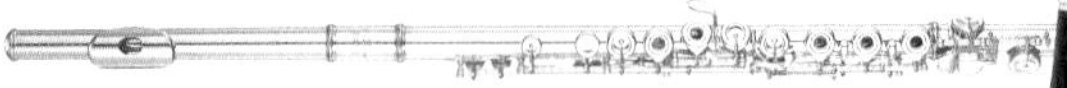

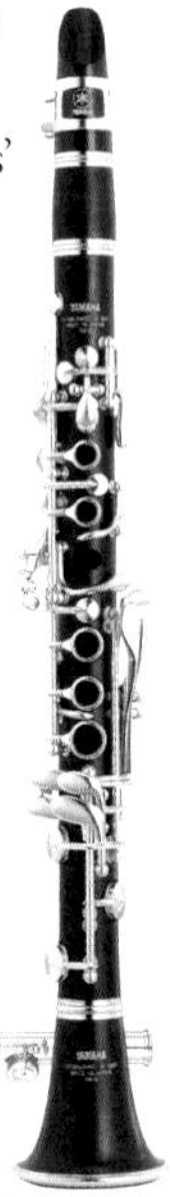

WORDSWORTH, WILLIAM (1770–1850)

The progenitor of Romantic poetry, Wordsworth produced *Lyrical Ballads* with his friend Coleridge in 1798. In later poems like *Resolution and Independence* (1807) Wordsworth explored a preoccupation with the discarded members of society: the mad and the poor. His works eloquently reflect upon emotions and the majesty of nature while employing a simpler language than his predecessors.

➡ ***Poetry***

WORLD BANK

Name for the International Bank for Reconstruction and Development, a UN agency providing loans for capital investment in reconstruction and development of member states.

ABOVE: The flute (left) and oboe (right)

RIGHT: World War I was one of the most horrific wars in living memory. The full horrors of the individual battles and life in the trenches, seen here in the front line at Verdun, were not fully realized until the few surviving soldiers returned home.

WORLD WAR I (1914–18)

War fought by Germany and Austria-Hungary against Britain, France, Russia and their allies. Fought mainly in Europe on either side of Germany (the western and eastern fronts), the Near and Middle East, and at sea.

The land war was characterized by stalemate interspersed with suicidal advances of infantry leading to unprecedented casualties from machine-gunning. The war also saw the beginning of aerial bombardment of civilians, aerial dogfights, and the torpedoing of passenger ships by submarines.

Nationalism grew in the late nineteenth century out of colonial and economic rivalry, destabilising international relations and among the nations making up Austria-Hungary. An arms race followed, along with fears of German expansionism. These fuelled expectations of war for which the catalyst was the assassination of archduke Franz Ferdinand of Austria-Hungary on 28 June 1914 by Serbian nationalists.

The assassination triggered mobilisation of forces as alliances promising military aid were activated. The Germans invaded France via the Low Countries to knock her out before engaging Russia, an ally of Serbia, in support of Austria-Hungary. Britain then entered to resist this threat to Belgian neutrality along with France. Britain also involved troops from her dominions (Australia, Canada, India and New Zealand among others), with the USA joining in 1917.

The consequences of the war were to ravage European economies, cost millions of lives, elevate the USA to the status of a world power, and cause the Russian Revolution. Tactics exposed the futility of battles like the Somme (1916), remaining vivid images of the colossal waste of human life expended on minimal territorial gains. Armaments underwent vast changes, e.g. tanks and the submarine, while aviation, a recent innovation, came to the fore.

Germany's defeat and the humiliating peace terms of the Treaty of Versailles created the conditions fostering the rise of Nazism and lead to World War II.

WORLD WAR II (1939–45)

War fought between the Axis Powers (Germany, Italy and Japan) and the Allies (Britain and her Commonwealth, USA, USSR, China and France), but involving many more countries indirectly or directly. Fighting occurred in most of Europe, Russia, North Africa, the Near East, the Far East and across the Atlantic and Pacific Oceans. The war also involved unprecedented levels of genocide, including the Holocaust.

The interwar years saw the rise of totalitarian dictatorships, and uncompromising ideologies of which German Nazism was the most prominent. Germany and Japan were committed to ruthless wars of territorial expansion.

Germany's invasion of Poland on 1 September 1939 opened the war through Britain and France's guarantee of military support for Poland. Germany's lightning advance west (Blitzkrieg) in May 1940 took the Allies by surprize, with France falling in days and the remains of the British Expeditionary Force being rescued from Dunkirk.

Britain remained in isolation, subjected to intense aerial bombardment and privations caused by submarine packs destroying merchant shipping, though American aid moderated the effects. The Japanese attack on Pearl Harbor, 7 December 1941, brought the US openly into the war and took the conflict to global proportions.

Defeat in Europe followed Germany's disastrous invasion of the USSR, a defeat of the German armies in North Africa, the invasion of Italy, and the invasion by Allied forces of France (June 1944). Continuous fighting and aerial bombardment followed until unconditional German surrender in May 1945.

The Battle of Midway (1943) ended Japanese advances. A protracted campaign across the Pacific finally ended with an onslaught on Japan herself, culminating in the two atomic bombs dropped on Hiroshima and Nagasaki in August 1945, bringing unconditional surrender.

The outcome was the division of Europe and the Cold War, the creation of agencies like the UN, and bringing of, for good or ill, the nuclear age.

WORLD WIDE WEB

Collection of pages of digital information available via the Internet. Originally developed for the use of Univsersities, the Web is now accessible to all Internet users.

Computers, Internet

WORLDWIDE FUND FOR NATURE

Independent organization established in 1961 to protect endangered species. Now operates in over 100 countries and aims to preserve the environment for people and nature.

Conservation, Endangered Species

WREN, CHRISTOPHER (1632–1723)

English architect, Wren began a career as an outstanding scientist but following the Great Fire of London (1666) his architectural career took off. Best known for St Pauls (1675–1709) which is largely Classical in style with touches of Baroque, Wren is also admired for St James, Piccadilly (1676-84) and for the Greenwich Hospital (from 1696).

Architecture, Baroque, Classical, St Paul's Cathedral

WRESTLING

Popular spectator sport. The professional side is now largely an entertainment rather than a sport, with bouts carefully stage-managed. Other forms include Greco-Roman (Olympic sport) and Japanese Sumo.

WRIGHT, FRANK LLOYD (1869–1959)

Proponent of 'organic architecture', Wright was perhaps the greatest American architect of the twentieth century. He did not follow any set style or movement but was compellingly innovative.

Alvar Aalto, Architecture, Walter Gropius

LEFT: One of the most horrific aspects of World War II were the Nazi concentration camps. The banner over the entrance of perhaps the most infamous of these, Auschwitz, Poland, translates as 'Work makes you free'.

XIZANG GAOYUAN PLATEAU

Xizang is the Chinese name for Tibet, an autonomous highland region of China. Gaoyuan is the plateau area of north central China averaging 1,000 m (3,300 ft) in height.

X-RAYS

Electromagnetic waves of very short wavelength which can pass through materials which are opaque to light. They are therefore used in medicine to examine the body internally, for security purposes and in industry. Prolonged or repeated exposure is a hazard to health, so strict safety measures are needed.

YACHTING

Sport using small sailing vessels. Currently seven recognized classes from soling (largest) to winglider (smallest). All are Olympic sports. The UK's yacht racing association was founded in 1875.

➧ ***Olympic Games***

YASUNARI, KAWABATA (1899–1972)

Distinguished Japanese writer. Yasunari wrote *The Izu Dancer* (1925) combining the literary impact of Surrealism and Dadaism while also retaining Japanese traditions. Yasunari won the Nobel Prize in 1968.

➧ ***Dadaism, Surrealism***

YEASTS

Unicellular fungi of economic importance in the bread-making and brewing industries. Yeast secretes chemicals (enzymes) that convert sugars into alcohol and carbon dioxide. It is the carbon dioxide that causes bread to rise.

➧ ***Beer, Fungi***

YELLOW RIVER

English name for the Huang He river in China. Named after its muddy water, it is 5,464 km (3,395 miles) long. Projects to control flooding are troubled by silting.

➧ ***China, Rivers***

YORKISTS

English faction in the Wars of the Roses which took its name from Richard, Duke of York, who claimed the throne through his descent from Edmund of York, the fifth son of Edward III. Following Richard's death at the battle of Wakefield (1460) his claim passed to his eldest son who became Edward IV on defeating the Lancastrians at Towton (1461). Following Edward's death his brother Richard III seized the throne (1483) but was overthrown by Henry Bolingbroke two years later.

➧ ***Kings of England***

YUGOSLAVIA

Southern European country. **Capital:** Belgrade. **Other principal cities:** Novi Sad, Nish, Kragujevac. **Climate:** Mediterranean to mild. **Geographical features:** mountainous and hilly, with river valleys. **Main language:** Serbo-Croat.

Main religions: Serbian and Montenegrin Orthodox. **Rule:** democracy. **Currency:** Yugoslav dinar. **Primary industries:** manufacturing (vehicles, electrical), agriculture. **Exports:** machinery, transport equipment, electrical goods, chemicals, clothing, tobacco, agricultural produce.

The break-up of the old, larger, Yugoslavia, left most industry in Croatia. Political instability, war prosecuted to restrain the collapse of the federation created in 1945, UN sanctions, and failed initiatives have left the economy foundering. Recent reform and Western aid is raising hopes for improvement.

➧ ***Europe***

ZAMBIA

Land-locked African country, formerly Northern Rhodesia. **Capital:** Lusaka. **Other principal cities:** Kitwe, Ndola, Mufulira. **Climate:** sub-tropical. **Geographical features:** high plateaux, Zambezi River, Victoria Falls. **Main languages:** English, Bantu languages.

Main religions: Christianity, animist, Hindu. **Rule:** democratic republic. **Currency:** Zambian kwacha. **Primary industries:** mining, agriculture being encouraged. **Exports:** copper, cobalt, lead, zomc, tobacco.

ZEBRA

African member of the horse family, characterized by its black and white stripes. Zebras live in family groups within herds. Their stripes create an effective camouflage when viewed as part of the herd.

ZIMBABWE

Land-locked African country, formerly (Southern) Rhodesia. **Capital:** Harare. **Other principal cities:** Bulawayo, Gweru, Kwekwe. **Climate:** subtropical. **Geographical features:** plateaus, Zambesi River, Victoria Falls. **Main language:** English. **Main religions:** Christianity, Islam, Hindu. **Rule:** socialist republic (opposition repressed). **Currency:** Zimbabwe dollar. **Primary industries:** manufacturing (metal and wooden goods), mining, chemicals, fertilizers, food, clothing, agriculture. **Exports:** tobacco, gold, ferrochrome, metal goods, furniture, clothing.

➠ *Africa*

ZOOLOGY

The science of animals. Animals are multi-celled living organisms which form one of the kingdom of biology. Studies include the classification of animals, extinct and present-day animals and their evolution, anatomy and physiology, behaviour and geographical distribution.

ZOROASTRIANISM

Pre-Islamic Persian religion established by the prophet Zoroaster (Zarathustra) (*c.* 628–551 BC). Holy scripture is Zendavesta. Strong good-evil morality, as manifest in Ahura Mazda (the good God) and Ahriman (the bad God). Return of Zoroaster was thought to lead to the resurrection of the dead.

ZULU WAR (1879)

War between Zululand and Britain. The Zulu kingdom expanded in Natal, South Africa, during the nineteenth century. Cetshwayo, Zulu king by the 1870s, built a highly trained army of approximately 50,000 men and refused demands to back down. The British army invaded but complacency enabled the Zulus, despite heavy losses, to wipe out a British column at Isandhlwana, on 22 January 1879, seizing their rifles and ammunition. The following day, a further Zulu army was held back in the celebrated engagement at Rorke's Drift. On March 28–29 1879, the Zulus were defeated at Kambula. By July the British had captured the Zulu capital at Ulundi. In 1887 Zululand was incorporated into Natal.

ZÜRICH

Largest city in Switzerland (population about 0.35 million), on the northern shore of Lake Zürich and the Limmat River, and capital of the Zürich canton. Zürich is now a major financial and industrial centre, with its own stock exchange, but is also renowned for its University and Federal Institute of Technology.

GAZETTEER

CONVERSIONS - METRIC TO IMPERIAL

	To convert multiply by:
centimetres to inches	0.3937
metres to feet	3.281
metres to yards	1.094
kilometres to miles	0.6214
square centimetres to square inches	0.155
square metres to square feet	10.76
square metres to square yards	1.196
square kilometres to square miles	0.3861
hectares to acres	2.471
square kilometres to acres	247.105
cubic centimetres to cubic inches	0.061
cubic metres to cubic feet	35.31
cubic metres to cubic yards	1.308
litres to cubic inches	61.03
litres to UK pints	1.7598
litres to gallons	0.22
grams to grains	15.43
grams to ounces	0.0352
grams to pounds	0.0022
kilograms to pounds	2.205
kilograms to tons	0.0009
tonnes to long tons	0.9842

TEMPERATURE		SPEED		TYRE PRESSURE	
°C	°F	km/h	mph	lb/sq in	kg/sq cm
0	32	32	20	1.41	20
5	40	48	30	1.55	22
10	50	64	40	1.69	24
15	60	80	50	1.83	26
20	70	96	60	1.97	28
25	75	112	70	2.11	30
30	85	128	80	2.25	32
35	95	144	90	2.39	34
40	105	160	100		
60	140				
80	175				
100	212				

THE HUMAN SKELETON

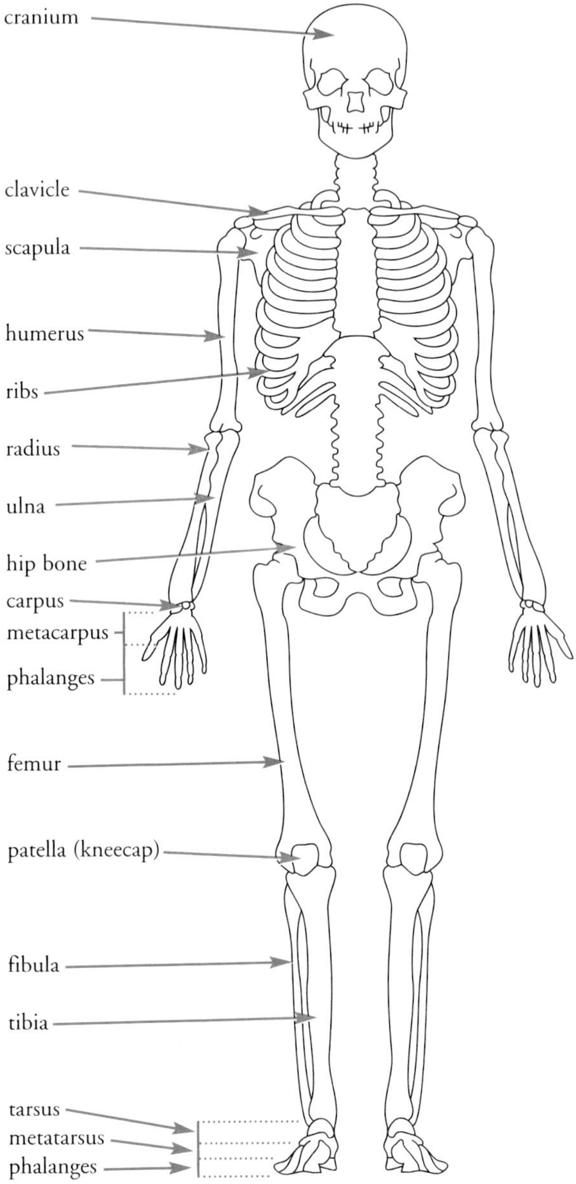

SECTION OF A TIME ZONE MAP

Time zones extend from -12 to +12 GMT. This map gives the meridian lines and angle of each meridian at the top with the bottom axis showing clocks measuring the time before and after GMT at noon and the number of hours to be added or subtracted to GMT.

Times in cities around the world compared with time at 12 noon GMT

Auckland	24.00	Kuala Lumpur	20.00
Athens	14.00	Montreal	07.00
Bangkok	19.00	Moscow	15.00
Barcelona	13.00	Munich	13.00
Beijing	20.00	New York	07.00
Berlin	13.00	Paris	13.00
Boston	07.00	Rio de Janeiro	09.00
Buenos Aires	09.00	Rome	13.00
Cairo	14.00	Sydney	22.00
Calcutta	17.30	Tel Aviv	14.00
Dubai	16.00	Tokyo	21.00
Hong Kong	20.00	Vancouver	04.00
Johannesburg	14.00	Washington DC	07.00

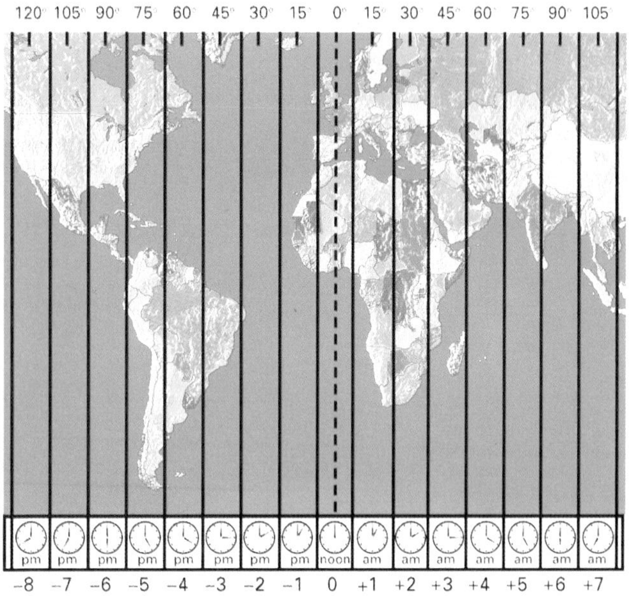

TOPOGRAPHICAL MAP OF THE WORLD

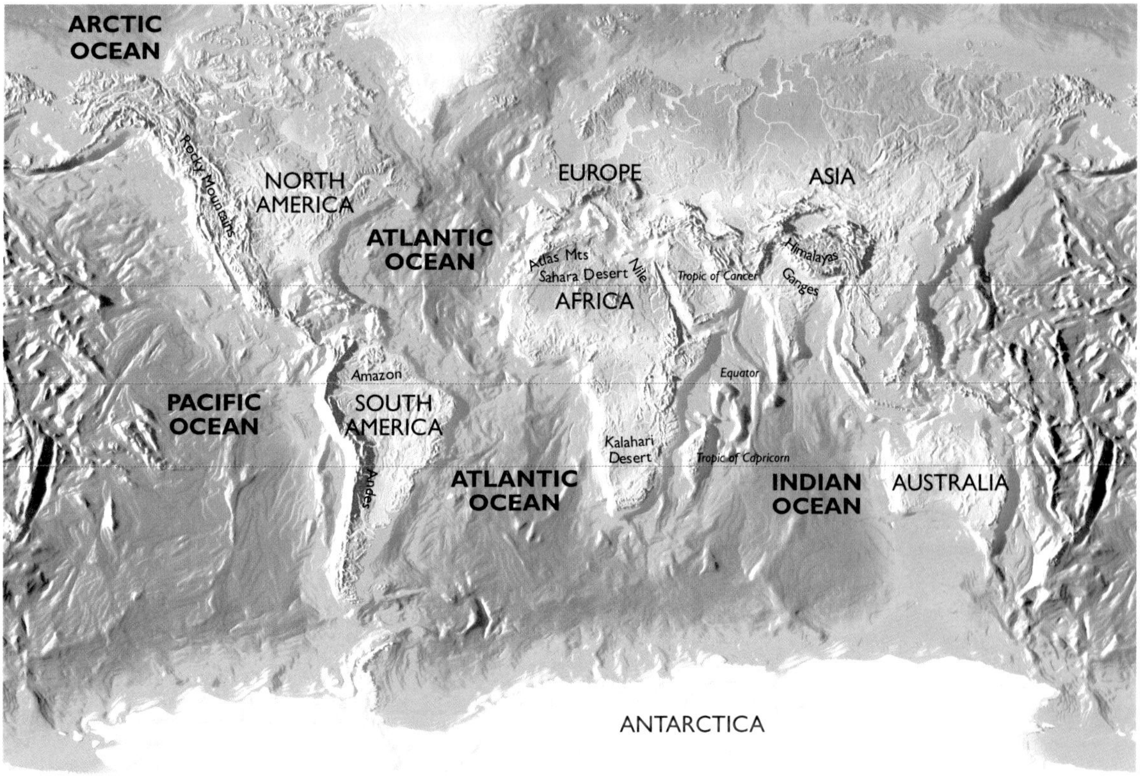

A SIMPLE HISTORY OF EARTH

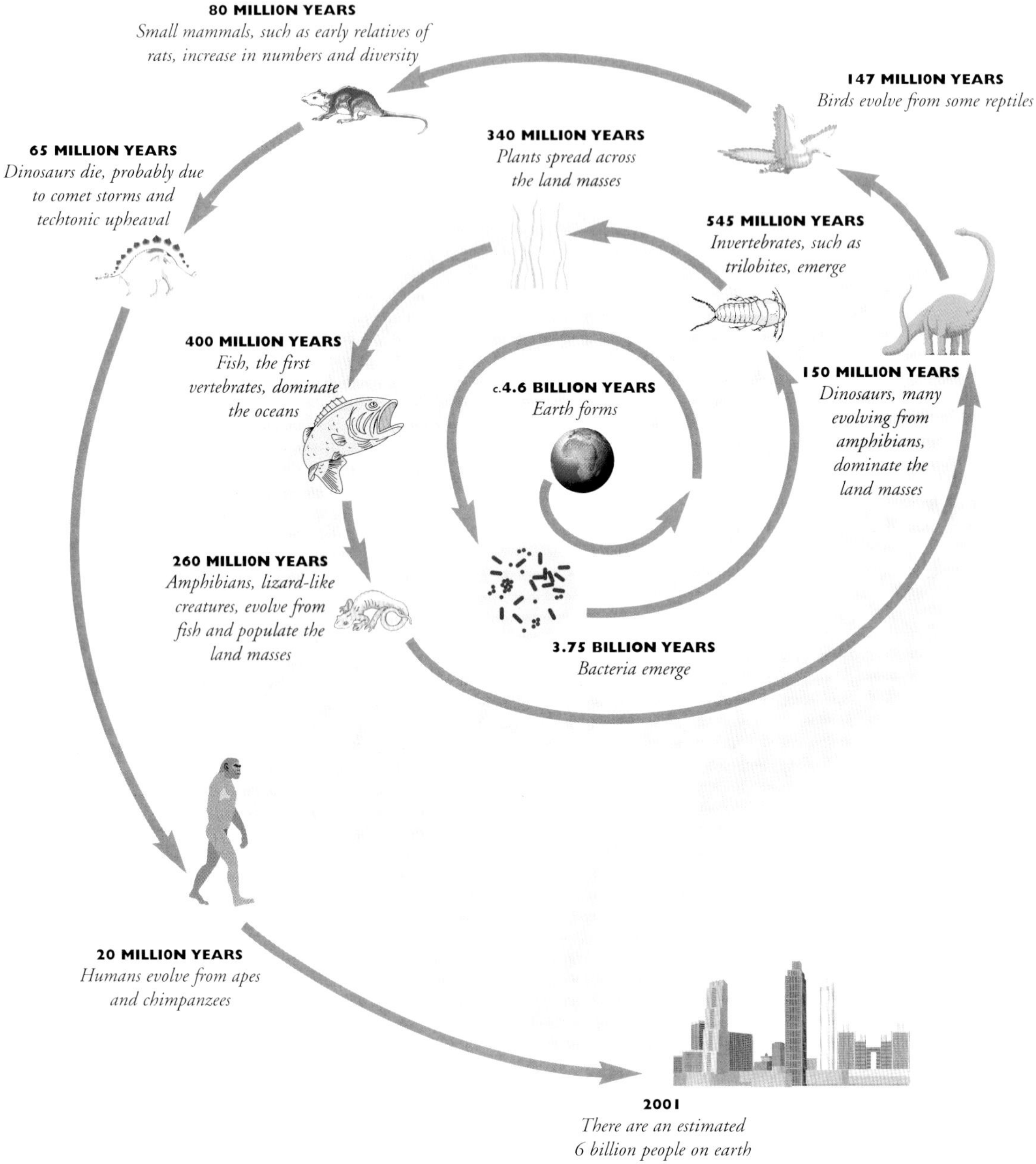
c.4.6 BILLION YEARS
Earth forms
3.75 BILLION YEARS
Bacteria emerge
545 MILLION YEARS
Invertebrates, such as trilobites, emerge
400 MILLION YEARS
Fish, the first vertebrates, dominate the oceans
340 MILLION YEARS
Plants spread across the land masses
260 MILLION YEARS
Amphibians, lizard-like creatures, evolve from fish and populate the land masses
150 MILLION YEARS
Dinosaurs, many evolving from amphibians, dominate the land masses
147 MILLION YEARS
Birds evolve from some reptiles
80 MILLION YEARS
Small mammals, such as early relatives of rats, increase in numbers and diversity
65 MILLION YEARS
Dinosaurs die, probably due to comet storms and techtonic upheaval
20 MILLION YEARS
Humans evolve from apes and chimpanzees
2001
There are an estimated 6 billion people on earth

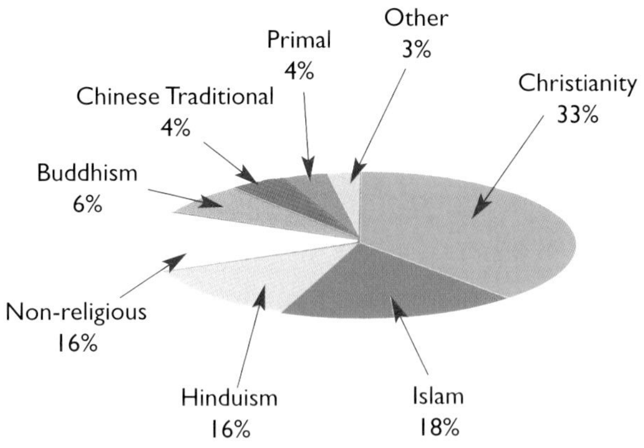

PROPORTIONS OF THE WORLD'S MAJOR RELIGIONS

MAJOR RELIGIONS

Christianity - 1500 million people includes Catholics, Protestant, Eastern Orthodox and other believers in Jesus Christ as the Son of God
Islam - 1000 million people
Hinduism - 720 people
Non-religious - 850 million inlcudes aethiests, humanists and agnostics
Buddhism - 330 million
Chinese Traditional - 225 million
Primal - 190 million
Sikhism - 23 million
Yoruba - 20 million
Juche - 19 million
Spiritism - 14 million
Judaism - 20 million
Baha'i - 7 million
Jainism - 7 million
Shinto - 4 million
Cao Dai - 3 million
Tenrikyo - 2.4 million
Neo Paganism - 1 million
Unitarian-Universalism - 800 thousand
Scientology - 750 thousand
Zoroastrianism - 200 thousand
Rastafarianism -100 thousand

WORLD'S LARGEST POPULATIONS

WORLD POPULATION IN MILLIONS

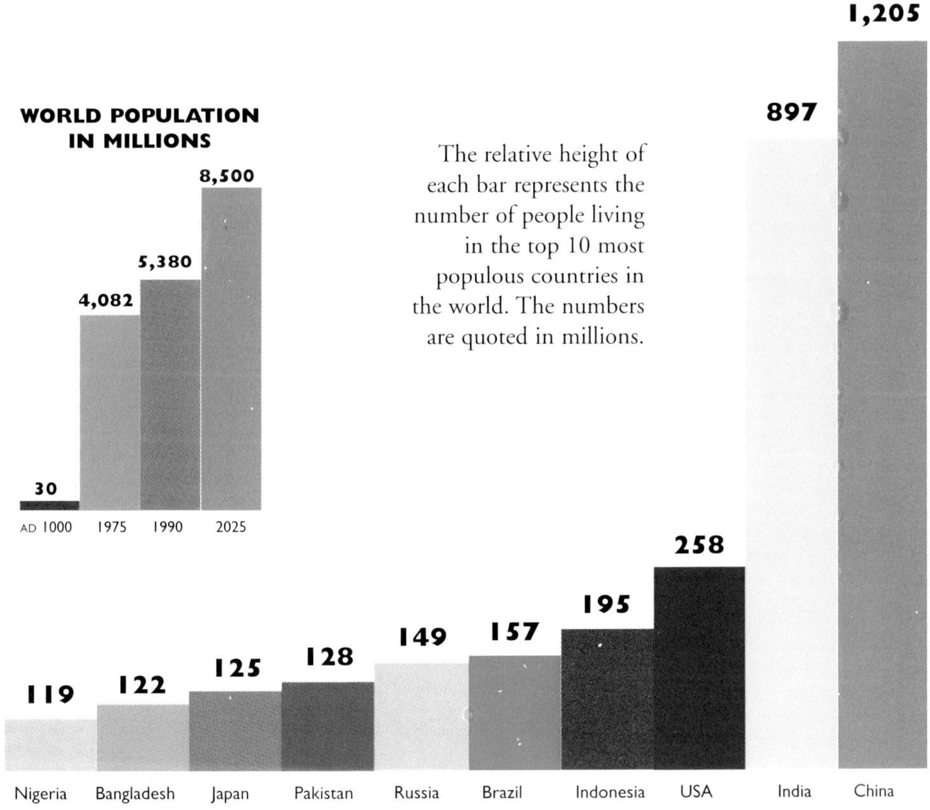

The relative height of each bar represents the number of people living in the top 10 most populous countries in the world. The numbers are quoted in millions.

BIBLIOGRAPHY

Baker, D., *Spaceflight and Rocketry*, A Chronology, Facts on File Inc, 1996

Black, Jeremy (ed.), *The Encyclopedia of World History*, Dempsey Parr, Bath, 1999

Blackburn, Simon, *Oxford Conise Dictionary of Philosophy*, Oxford University Press, Oxford, 1996

Blanning, T. C. W. (ed.), *The Oxford Illustrated History of Modern Europe*, Oxford University Press, Oxford, 1996

Borowski, E. J. and J. M. Borwein, *The Unwin Hyman Dictionary of Mathematics*, HarperCollins, London, 1989

Bruce, George, *Harbottles Dictionary of Battles*, Granada Publishing, London

Colvin, Leslie and Emma Speare, *The Usborne Living World Encyclopedia*, Usborne Publishing, 1992

Cotterell, Arthur, *The Encyclopedia of World Mythology*, Dempsey Parr, Bath, 1999

Cranfield, Ingrid, *100 Greatest Natural Wonders*, Dragon's World, 1996

Dixon, Dougal, *Earth Facts*, Apple Press, London, 1993

Downer, John, *Lifesense*, BBC Books, London, 1991

Duffy, Christopher, *Siege Warfare*, Routledge and Kegan Paul, London

Dyson, Peter, *PC Users Pocket Dictionary*, Sybex, 1995

Encyclopaedia Britannica, 14th Edition and Yearbooks, 1951 to 1998

Evans, Eric (ed.), *The Illustrated Guide to British History*, Dempsey Parr, Bath, 1999

Everyman's Factfinder, Dent, London, 1982

Falls, Cyril, *Great Military Battles*, Spring Books

Farry, Eithne et al, *Snapshots in Time*, Dempsey Parr, Bath, 1998

Featherstone, Donald, *Colonial Small Wars*, David and Charles Publishing, London

Fraser, Antonia (ed.), *The Lives of the Kings& Queens of England*, Weidenfeld and Nicholson, London, 1993

Gardiner, Judith, *The History Today Who's Who in British History*, Collins and Brown, London, 2000

Gatland, K., *Space Technology*, A Comprehensive History of Space Exploration, Salamander Books, London, 1980

Gilbert, Martin, *First World War*, HarperCollins, London, 1994

Grant, James, *British Battles on Land and Sea*, Cassells, London

Grimwade, Keith, *Discover Human Geography*, Hodder and Stoughton, London, 1988

Halliwell, Leslie, *Halliwell's Film Guide*, Grafton, London, 1987

Harrison, Percy and Gillian Waites, *The Cassell Dictionary of Science*, Cassell, London, 1997

Hartnoll, Phyllis, *The Theatre: A Concise History*, World of Art Publishing, 1995

Hinnells, John R. (ed.), *Who's Who of Religions*, Penguin, London, 1996

Holmes, George (ed.), *The Oxford Illustrated History of Medieval Europe*, Oxford University Press, Oxford, 1988

Holmes, Richard, *Battle Plans*, Helicon Press, London

Kay, Dennis, *Shakespeare: His Life, Work and Era*, Sidgwick and Jackson, London, 1992

Kennedy, Michael, *Oxford Concise Dictionary of Music*, Oxford University Press, Oxford, 1996

Kerrod, Robin, *Weather*, Lorenz Books, 1997

Langmuir, Erika and Norbert Lynton, *The Yale Dictionary of Art and Artists*, Yale University Press, 2000

Laque, Pierre, *Ancient Greece: Utopia and Reality*, Thames and Hudson, London, 1994

Mackay, James (ed.), *The Encyclopedia of World Facts*, Dempsey Parr, Bath, 1999

McBride, Angus, *The Zulu War*, Osprey Publishing, London

McEvedy, Colin, *The Century World History Factfinder*, Century Publishing, 1984

McHenry, Robert (ed.), *Webster's New Biographical Dictionary*, Miriam Webster, Inc., 1988

McNab, D. and J. Younger, *The Planets*, BBC Worldwide, London, 1999

Montgomery, Field Marshall Viscount of Alamein, *A History of Warfare*, HarperCollins, London

Moore, Patrick, *The Guinness Book of Astronomy*, Fifth Edition, Guiness, London, 1995

Norwich, John Julius (ed.), *The Oxford Illustrated Encyclopedia of the Arts*, Oxford University Press, Oxford, 1984

Ousby, Ian (ed.), *The Cambridge Guide to Literature in English*, Cambridge University Press, London, 1989

Penny, Malcolm, *Exploiting the Sea*, Wayland, 1993

Raw, Michael and Peter Atkins, *Agriculture and Food*, Collins Educational, London, 1995

Reed, Herbert (ed.), *Art and Artists*, Thames and Hudson, London, 1994

Revie, Alastair, *Land Battles*, Marshall Cavendish, London

Ridpath, Ian (ed.), *The Collins Encyclopedia of the Universe*, HarperCollins, London, 2001

Roberts, J. M., *The Penguin History of the World*, Penguin, London, 1997

Sadie, Stanley (ed.), *The Collins Classical Music Encyclopedia*, HarperCollins, London, 2000

Smith-Morris, Miles (ed.), *The Economist Book of Vital World Statistics: A Complete Guide to the World in Figures*, Hutchinson, London, 1990

Steinbrugge, Karl, *Earthquakes, Volcanoes and Tsunamis: An Anatomy of Hazards*, 1982

Stratton, Peter and Nicky Hayes, *A Student's Dictionary of Psychology*, Edward Arnold, 1992

Thomas, Keith, *Religion and the Decline of Magic*, Penguin, London 1991

Thomson, David, *A Biographical Dictionary of Film*, André Deutsch, London 1995

Walker, John, *Halliwell's Film and Video Guide 2000*, HarperCollins, London, 1999

Watkin, David, *English Architecture*, Thames and Hudson, London, 1979

Wynne-Davies, Marion (ed.), *The Bloomsbury Guide to English Literature*, Bloomsbury, London, 1989

AUTHOR BIOGRAPHIES

CAMILLA DE LA BÉDOYÈRE
Natural World

After leaving university with a degree in zoology, Camilla de la Bédoyère taught biology and chemistry O-levels in a Kenyan school. She has been writing educational material and books for children and adults for a number of years as well as contributing articles on health to newspapers and magazines.

GUY DE LA BÉDOYÈRE
Geography, War & Politics

Guy de la Bedoyère is an archeologist and historian with numerous books to his credit on the Roman world, seventeenth-century literature and World War II aviation amongst others. He has also written numerous travel articles on a variety of historical sites for *The Independent* and has made a number of appearances on television and radio history programmes.

KIRSTEN BRADBURY
Arts

Kirsten Bradbury was born in the West Country and now lives in London, where she combines her writing career with working in the music industry. She has an arts degree from the University of Surrey and has written books on Salvador Dalí and Michelangelo as well as contributing to volumes on art history.

ALAN DRUMMOND
Science, Technology & Industry

Formerly a lecturer in Chemistry at Brighton, Alan Drummond now works in nature conservation. He has a wide range of interests in science subjects, specializing in astronomy, chemistry and cosmology.

NIGEL GROSS
Society

Nigel Gross has been an author for some 15 years and is a keen collector of trivia. He has written over 30 books and contributed to numerous television shows and magazines. Surrounded by an ever-growing library, he now lives in Kent.

JAMES MACKAY
General Editor, History

Dr James Mackay is a journalist and broadcaster, biographer and historian. A former salesroom correspondent of the *Financial Times*, he has also written numerous books on stamps, coins and other collectibles. A history graduate of Glasgow University, he has written and contributed to many historical works.

HELEN TOVEY
Culture, Belief & Faith

Helen Tovey completed her degree in History from the University of Exeter. Since then she has been working as a writer and editor, specializing in British and European social history, religion, art and architecture.

PICTURE CREDITS

All Sport/David Cannon: 141 (t).

Arbiter Group Plc: 6 (t); 185 (b).

Foundry Arts: Corbis U.K. Ltd.; 22 (t); 26 (b); 29; Jennifer Bishop: 38 (bl); 43; 47 (b); Jennifer Bishop: 59 (r); 61 (b); 75 (t); Photodisk: 99 (b); Comstock: 100 (b);104 (t); Comstock: 115; 120; 123; 125 (l); 158 (t); 160 (l); 167 (b); 168; 180; 195; 198; Comstock: 209.

Graham Stride: 44 (l); 88 (r); 103; 109 (r); 136 (l); 153 (r); 165.

Impact: Impact/Frederick Baker: 1, 3, 5; Michael George: 12; Charles Milligan: 15 (b); Piers Cavendish: 18 (l); Christopher Bluntzer: 19; Tom Webster: 24 (b); Frederick Baker: 27; John Cole: 30; David Slimings: 31 (r); Piers Cavendish: 37; Petteri Kokkonen: 42 (l); Andy Johnstone: 57 (r); Mohamad Ansar: 59 (l); Steve Parry: 65; Piers Cavendish: 66 (t); Charles Coates: 68 (b); Jorn St Jerneklar: 70 (cl); Tony Page: 70 (b); James Barlow: 79 (bl); David Reed: 81; Eliza Armstrong: 84; Mohamed Ansar: 85 (l); Philip Gontier: 91 (t); Michael Good: 95 (b); David S Silverberg: 96 (t); Alain Evrard: 98; Piers Cavendish: 102 (t); Mohamed Ansar: 104 (b); Rachel Norton: 106; Jorn St Jerneklar: 109 (l); Steve Pahlke: 112; Simon Shepheard: 113 (t); Piers Cavendish: 113 (b); Michael Good: 117; Giles Barnard: 118; Ray Roberts: 119 (r); Neil Morrison: 119 (l); Tony Page: 121 (l); Neil Morrison: 121 (r); John Cole: 122 (l); Ben Edwards: 127 (l); Javed A Jafferji: 131; Martin Black: 139 (l); Charles Worthington: 142; Colin Jones: 144; Ben Edwards: 145; David Reed: 146 (l); Pamla Toler: 150 (l); Tom Webster: 151; Bruce Stephens: 153 (l); John Arthur: 156; Piers Cavendish: 157; Chris Moyse: 159; Brian Rybolt: 162 (l); Christophe Bluntzer: 164 (b); Mike McQueen: 164 (t); Alain Evrard: 166; Wendy Aldiss: 169 (l); Mark Cator: 169 (r); Julian Calder: 170 (b); Nikolai Khorounji: 170 (t); Alain Le Garsmeur: 171; Mohamed Ansar: 172 (r); Caroline Penn: 176; Christopher Cormack: 177 (l); Charles Coates: 179 (b); Aerial Portraits: 182; Robert Gibbs: 183; Brian Harris: 184; Stefan Boness/Ipon: 187; Mark Henley: 188 (t); David Reed: 189; Piers Cavendish: 190 (b); Alain Evrard: 190 (t); Peter Arkell: 192 (b); Rupert Conant: 197 (r); Piers Cavendish: 200 (b); Charles Milligan: 200 (t); John Arthur: 203; Mark Henley: 204 (l); Simon Shepheard: 208; Andy Johnstone: 210 (t); Alain Le Garsmeur: 210 (b); David Reed: 211.

Mary Evans Picture Library: 6; 14; 20; 21 (t, b); 28 (c); 28 (r); 36 (r); 40 (b); 42 (r); 56; 58; 67; 70 (t); 72 (r); 74 (b); 75 (b); 77 (l, r); 80 (l, r); 82 (t); 85 (b); 86; 88 (l); 90; 92 (l, r); 96 (b); 114; 133 (b); 134; 135 (b); 138; 172 (l); 196.

NASA: 7; 62; 179 (r); 186 (b); 199 (r).

Topham Picturepoint: 1; 3; 5; 8 (l, t); 9; 10 (t, b); 11; 13 (l, r); 15 (t); 16 (l, r); 17; 18 (r); 22 (b); 23; 25; 26 (t); 28 (l); 31 (l); 33; 34 (t, b); 35 (l, r); 36 (l); 38 (t, r); 39; 40 (t); 41; 43; 44 (r); 45; 46; 47 (t); 48; 49 (t, b); 50 (t, b); 51; 52 (l, r); 53; 54 (t, b); 55; 57 (l); 60; 61 (t); 62 (l); 63 (l, r); 66 (b); 68 (t); 69; 71; 72 (l); 73; 74 (t, b); 76; 79 (t, b); 82 (b); 83; 87 (t, b); 89; 91 (b); 93; 94; 95 (t); 97; 99 (l); 100 (l); 101 (b); 102 (b); 105; 107; 108; 110 (t, b); 111; 116 (t, b); 122 (r); 124; 125 (r); 126; 127 (r); 128; 129; 130 (t, b); 132; 133 (t); 135 (t); 136 (b); 137; 139 (r); 140; 141 (b); 143 (t, b); 146 (t); 147; 148; 149 (t, b); 150 (r); 152; 154 (t, b); 155; 156 (b); 158 (b); 160 (r); 161; 162 (r); 163; 166 (t); 173; 174 (t, b); 175; 177 (r); 178; 181 (l, r); 185 (t); 186 (t); 188 (b); 191; 192 (t); 193; 197 (l); 199 (t); 201 (t); 202 (l, r); 204 (b); 205; 206 (b); 207.

SUBJECT INDEX

Page references in **bold** refer to major articles, those in *italics* to illustrations.

INDEX OF NAMES

Page references in **bold** refer to major articles, those in *italics* to illustrations.